— Captures some of the human drama of the campaign, which must be buried somewhere in her <u>notes</u>

— certainly is a political campaign.

— has made China poorer

— is mistaken about the reason for agricultural shortages

→ Curiously bloodless account. I know she feels passionately about these issues – she got in arguments or places over it – but may somehow that it unacceptance to descent to the level of <u>anecdote</u>.
– two paras on coercion on p. 197. when audiences pull them punks, it means that they are or wary of the regime. Don't know if this is the are here.

CHINA'S LONGEST CAMPAIGN

CHINA'S LONGEST CAMPAIGN

Birth Planning in the
People's Republic,
1949–2005

TYRENE WHITE

CORNELL UNIVERSITY PRESS

ITHACA AND LONDON

First published 2006 by Cornell University Press

I acknowledge the following for permission to reprint selected materials.

Harvard University Press for permission to reprint from "The Origins of China's Birth Planning Policy," in Christina Gilmartin, Gail Hershatter, Lisa Rofel, and Tyrene White, eds., *Engendering China: Women, Culture, and the State* (Cambridge: Harvard University Press, 1994). Copyright © 1994 by the President and Fellows of Harvard College.

Thomson Publishing Services (UK) for permission to reprint from "Domination, Resistance, and Accommodation in China's One-Child Campaign," in Elizabeth Perry and Mark Selden, eds., *Chinese Society: Change, Conflict and Resistance,* 2nd ed. (Routledge, 2003), 183–203.

Portions of chapter 5 were previously published as "Post-Revolutionary Mobilization in China: The One-Child Policy Reconsidered," *World Politics* 43, no. 1 (October 1990): 53–76.

Printed in the United States of America

Library of Congress Cataloging-in-Publication Data

White, Tyrene.
 China's longest campaign : birth planning in the People's Republic, 1949–2005 / Tyrene White
  p. cm.
 Includes bibliographical references and index.
 ISBN-13: 978-0-8014-4405-0 (cloth : alk. paper)
 ISBN-10: 0-8014-4405-5 (cloth : alk. paper)
 1. Birth control—Government policy—China—History—20th century.
2. China—Population policy—History—20th century. I. Title.
 HQ766.5C6W485 2006
 363.9'60951—dc22   2006001676

Cornell University Press strives to use environmentally responsible suppliers and materials to the fullest extent possible in the publishing of its books. Such materials include vegetable-based, low-VOC inks and acid-free papers that are recycled, totally chlorine-free, or partly composed of nonwood fibers. For further information, visit our website at www.cornellpress.cornell.edu.

Cloth printing   10 9 8 7 6 5 4 3 2 1

For my mother

Anna S. White
(1924–1993)

and the Smithfield women who nurtured her—
Sabina, Ruth, Blanche, Frances, Helen, and Margaret

Contents

Tables

Preface

In the fall of 1979, in my first graduate seminar on Chinese politics, I learned that China had launched a "one-child-per-couple" birth control campaign. I can still remember vividly my reaction—astonishment and awe. Astonishment because, as a young woman of childbearing age, I could easily imagine the implications for Chinese women of being subject to a regime of state regulation of childbearing. Awe because, as a student, I was astounded by this latest and fearsome assertion of power by China's leaders, by their conviction that it was the right thing to do and that it could be done. I was also curious to know how the state expected to enforce such a policy in the face of what was sure to be massive resistance.

This book bears the imprint of that initial reaction and of the unique opportunity I have had over a quarter century to examine the implementation of a world-historic policy, one comparable to other grand state-initiated social engineering projects of the twentieth century. For all of the attention it has received, both in the U.S. political arena and in the population studies community, China's population control efforts have yet to receive the sustained scholarly attention they deserve. The rural reforms of the early and mid-1980s, along with the broader economic reform project, have generated innumerable and varied scholarly studies. The one-child policy, by contrast, though arguably just as important, has been neglected, despite its critical role in bridging the politics of the Maoist, Dengist, and post-Deng eras. As of 2005, only a handful of books have been written on the subject. My purpose here is to help remedy that problem by examining the political origins and evolution of the one-child policy and the vital role it has played in China's quest for modernization. Rather than approach the issue from a demographic, sociological, or anthropological perspective, I focus on why and how the Chinese Communist regime sought to enforce birth limits, and with what results.

The extension of state regulation to childbearing, and the imposition of a system of rationed childbirth, was seen by some observers as a harsh but unsurprising policy choice. This was a regime, after all, whose leaders had repeatedly shown themselves capable of launching radical programs of social transformation (e.g., the Great Leap Forward and the Cultural Revolution). Once leaders reached a consensus on the threat population growth posed to China's modernization program, there was every reason to expect them to launch a campaign to check the problem. Since the late 1960s, moreover, many Western population experts had urged the use of all necessary measures to halt the rapid growth of global population, and a few went so far as to advocate the use of coercive and punitive ones. Although China publicly condemned this pessimistic, Malthusian view, it arrived at the same place by a different analytical and ideological pathway. When it declared rapid population growth a major threat to its modernization goals, therefore, and began to set strict targets for local and national growth rates, many observers outside China applauded the move as a reasonable reaction to a grave and debilitating, even crippling, problem of "overpopulation."

Other observers condemned China's move to regulate childbirth and to penalize unauthorized births (unauthorized, that is, by the local authorities), just as they rejected the arguments of Western pessimists who advocated a similar approach. In the United States, China's birth control program became for conservatives in the 1980s and 1990s a galvanizing symbol of the need for pro-life legislation, and for liberals a prime example of the terrible consequences of state intrusion into a domain best left to personal and private decision making.

A divide also emerged in China during the 1980s. Because China's birth limitation program had begun in earnest in urban areas in the early 1970s, and because urban living had already begun to encourage lower levels of fertility, most urban couples of childbearing age either agreed with the state's arguments or acceded reluctantly. In the countryside, however, rural couples were far more skeptical. Experience had taught them that, while having too many children could deepen poverty and indebtedness, having too few could be catastrophic, resulting both in short-term and long-term poverty and in a decline in social status.

As these divided views were opening up in the United States and China in the early 1980s, I began my research. By the early 1990s, three rounds of fieldwork and research in China, plus sustained library research in the

United States and conversations with many friends and colleagues, had illuminated my understanding not only of China's birth planning program but also of the sensitivities around the issue. As more and more people in the United States learned about China's policy, conversations that meandered along a variety of trails always seemed to have one point in common. Sooner or later I was asked for my view of China's policy. Having heard of China's population challenge, but having also heard of the draconian measures used to enforce the policy, friends and colleagues, strangers and family members were all curious to know whether I thought the policy was justified. At times, the question came from harsh critics of China who were clearly hoping I would offer an unequivocal condemnation; at other times it was asked by those who were so worried about global population and the environment that they were willing to overlook the evidence of coercion in China's efforts to limit population growth. They, of course, hoped to hear a defense of the policy as a necessary part of China's struggle to lift its people out of poverty. My attempts to avoid these categoricals and offer a more nuanced view—one that acknowledged the gravity of China's demographic challenge while rejecting coercive means to tackle it—were usually heard politely, but most likely did little to alter previously held views.

It has sometimes been even more difficult to discuss this issue with Chinese acquaintances, friends, and strangers. Discussions about China's birth planning program almost always provoke the deployment of defensive armor in anticipation of being judged harshly by someone who doesn't understand China's situation. Perhaps my most striking encounter along these lines was with a stranger I encountered in the 1980s, a female graduate student who happened to be sitting in my row on a flight from San Francisco to Beijing. A middle-aged Chinese man sat between us in the three-seat row, and when he saw me working with my research materials, he struck up a conversation. Before long, he was expressing his regret that Mao Zedong had not supported birth control in the 1950s and 1960s, and I relayed some of my own findings on that topic. The woman in the window seat soon joined in and spoke in an agitated way about the necessity for strict birth control in China. A wiser person would have listened carefully and respectfully, and asked about her own experience. Instead, I engaged her on several points that challenged her view. Soon, the poor man between us was trying to will himself into another seat as we argued across his tray table.

Why recount this story? Because it is emblematic of the sensitivities that continue to surround China's population policy, sensitivities that persist after twenty-five years. These sensitivities make it easy to start an argument but hard to actually communicate. This book is my attempt to communicate, to interpret the one-child policy against its historical and political backdrop. It is also my attempt to show how an understanding of China's birth planning program is inseparable from an understanding of the political economy of development, from the efforts of China's leaders since 1949 to chart a course to modernization. Perhaps it is also my attempt to start another conversation with the woman on the airplane.

This project has benefited greatly from the help and hospitality of many people and institutions. The journey began at Ohio State University, where Mike Lampton tutored me in the intricacies of Chinese politics and encouraged my interest in China's population policy. His efforts to create an exchange program with Wuhan University were reciprocated by the late Gao Shangyin (then vice president of Wuhan University), who gave me the opportunity to conduct research in China during a pivotal period of reform in the early 1980s. Professor Chen Chung-min, with whom I conducted township and village interviews in the spring of 1982, gave me an invaluable short course on the art and discipline of fieldwork, preparing me well for solo work later that year. I was graciously received and assisted by Wuhan University officials and staff members during three extended stays between 1982 and 1990. Their efforts to arrange interviews and field visits made this work possible, as did the many officials and individuals who agreed to talk with me. I am particularly grateful to the township and village officials in Donghu (a pseudonym), whose hospitality and cooperation were essential to this project. The Office of Village Self-Governance of the Ministry of Civil Affairs arranged field visits and interviews in villages in Hebei, Shandong, Liaoning, and Hubei in the early 1990s, allowing me to continue exploring the links between rural political reform and birth planning. I am particularly indebted to Wang Zhenyao, along with the many other central, provincial, and local Civil Affairs officials who assisted with these arrangements and shared their insights with me.

Financial support for this project came from Ohio State University, the Committee on Scholarly Communication with China, the Swarthmore College Faculty Research Support Fund, and in 1989–90 a post-doctoral fellowship at the Fairbank Center for East Asian Research, Harvard University. For their support during the fellowship year and after, I am especially grateful to Rod MacFarquhar, James Watson, and Merle Goldman.

Colleagues have provided support and encouragement along the way, some giving generously of their time to comment on parts of this manuscript. I am particularly indebted to Jean Oi, Marc Blecher, Dorothy Solinger, Thomas Bernstein, Elizabeth Perry, and Mark Selden, all of whom read parts or all of this work at various stages of development. Special thanks also to Christina Gilmartin, Gail Hershatter, and Lisa Rofel. My work with them on a 1992 conference on women and gender in China, and on the conference volume we edited together, was a wonderful experience, not least because of their persistent efforts to shake up the intellectual categories and ways of seeing that came naturally to a political scientist. I am also indebted to Kay Johnson, who has generously shared some of her research findings, and from whom I have learned much.

Special thanks to Nancy Hearst, librarian at the Fairbank Center Library, for her help in finding research materials. I thank my students at Swarthmore College who have taught me so much. Special thanks to Susan Lin, Matthew Williams, and Rebecca Strauss, who served as research assistants.

My colleagues in Political Science and Asian Studies at Swarthmore College have been a constant source of support. I am particularly indebted to Lillian Li, who read and commented on a draft of this manuscript. I am also grateful to Roger Haydon for shepherding the project at Cornell University Press and to Candace Akins for her editorial assistance.

I have also had the good fortune to be supported by a large and loving family, to whom I owe a great debt of thanks and gratitude. They have encouraged and supported and, when necessary, simply put up with me, for as long as I can remember. My daughter, Mingming, is my inspiration and joy. I learn from her every day.

And last, a special thanks to Aunt Helen, to whom I made a promise.

TYRENE WHITE

Swarthmore, Pennsylvania

CHINA'S LONGEST CAMPAIGN

1

The Collectivization of Childbearing

When China adopted a one-child-per-couple birth limitation policy in 1979, the state claimed dominion over the most intimate personal behavior of its people, sovereignty over the production of life itself. The scope of this claim was breathtaking even by Maoist standards. With few exceptions, each childbearing-age couple was to bear only one child, state officials were to decide who had permission to conceive in a given year, and contraception after birth was required and state administered. This policy was to be enforced in a country of over one billion people, more than eight hundred million of them spread across the vast Chinese countryside. Modern nation-states are not known for their record of modesty or restraint, but the drive to enforce a one-child policy in an overwhelmingly agrarian society surely ranks among the most ambitious acts of social engineering ever attempted.

The official explanation for China's decision to launch a one-child policy was very quickly set forth in the Chinese media. China was forced drastically to curtail childbearing due to the immediate and future threat to economic development posed by rapid population growth. Intent on ending the revolutionary turmoil and stagnation of the Maoist era (1949–76) by leading a forced march to modernization, Mao Zedong's successors were convinced that the containment of population growth was a necessary prerequisite to achieving that goal. They were saddled with a population that was enormous, overwhelmingly rural, and preponderantly young and thus poised to reproduce itself on an even larger scale. By 1978, China's population was thought to be closing in on the one billion mark, with 65 percent estimated to be under age thirty. This demographic structure, which resulted from the baby boom of the 1950s and 1960s, meant that an extremely large cohort of young couples was or would be bearing children during the last two decades of the twentieth century. If these couples were allowed to have two or more children, it was argued, the ripple effects would last throughout the twenty-first century, pushing the population ever upward and fatally retarding the prospects for economic advancement. These concerns served to concentrate the minds of the leadership on the population problem as never before, and their attention was duly reflected in an intense propaganda barrage aimed at convincing young people to make the necessary sacrifices. The appeals were backed up by a series of new rules and regulations governing childbearing and by an aggressive and frequently brutal campaign to stop all unauthorized births.

There was great irony in the decision to launch a massive one-child campaign at this moment in China's history, when much of the Maoist legacy, including Mao's preference for mobilization campaigns, was being officially repudiated. Mass campaigns had been one of the most distinctive features of the Maoist era and were relied on heavily to bring about the socialist transformation of the economy and society. Organized by the party center and launched from Beijing, mass campaigns were the means by which the revolutionary, collectivist goals of the Chinese Communist Party (CCP) were achieved, but, even more, the campaign process was an end in itself. The mass campaign galvanized the entire party and society to focus on a particular goal or issue and to work collectively to achieve it; the education and transformation wrought by the act of mass participation and political struggle were equally important in instilling a revolutionary ethic deep within society. Although most Leninist regimes relied on campaign methods at key stages of their revolutions, the CCP's long history of revolutionary struggle, combined with Mao's relentless emphasis on political struggle led to an enduring preference for the mass campaign and a resistance to settled bureaucratic routine.

Mao's culminating effort at smashing the party-state during the Cultural Revolution had such destructive force that his successors, many of whom were victims of that process, formally repudiated the politics of mass mobilization and called for a return to normalcy in political life. By normalcy they meant a shift from populist, revolutionary methods of mass participation to stable political rule, an increased emphasis on the rule of law, and tolerance of a private realm beyond the state's scope of regulation. The post-Mao elite also was prepared to be far more pragmatic in its economic development strategy. Whereas all vestiges of a market economy had been ruthlessly suppressed during the Cultural Revolution, the collective economy would now be supplemented with private incentives and market forces. In short, the post-Mao elite fundamentally redefined its historical mission, abandoning the rapid achievement of revolutionary ends by means of class struggle in favor of the steady development of the "primary stage of socialism" and the construction of a "socialist spiritual civilization."

Against this background, the one-child campaign stood out in stark contrast. With its radical goal, its privileging of collective welfare over personal preferences, and its massive effort to mobilize for compliance, the one-child campaign bore all the characteristics of a classic mass mobilization campaign.[1] A massive propaganda campaign was launched, resources were reallocated to birth planning work, and activists were mobilized to enforce the policy. Telephone conferences and mobilization meetings were employed to energize cadres and to disseminate campaign targets. Special medical teams were sent to perform sterilizations and abortions and to insert intrauterine devices. Propagandists filled newspapers with model stories and educational editorials, and cadres who violated the new policy were used as negative models for public discussion. Normative and material incentives were used to encourage compliance, but coercion, or the threat of it, was often the key instrument of enforcement. Struggle sessions were held against targeted offenders who were recast as state enemies and subjected to public humiliation. Though the scope of the birth planning campaign did not quite rival the most radical campaigns of the Maoist era, it was a classic campaign of major proportions.

By the mid-1980s, the urban campaign had basically achieved its goal of limiting nearly all young childbearing-age couples to only one child. Despite encountering resistance, especially in provincial cities and towns where the three-child household was still common, the urban campaign succeeded because of the ability of the state to monitor childbearing closely, to offer meaningful incentives to comply, and to threaten heavy punishments against policy violators. Given the tight urban collective control net, having an unauthorized child could mean losing one's job, apartment, food ration tickets, and urban residency permit. What the state provided in social security, the state could also take away. Just as important, the tightly organized surveillance of all childbearing-age women both at home and in the workplace meant it was nearly impossible to escape detection of an unauthorized pregnancy. In addition, many young couples were willing to have only one child. Crowded urban conditions, low standards of living, and the high costs of child rearing made childbearing less appealing and the state's argu-

---

1. On the dynamics and mechanics of mass campaigns, see the classic studies by Gordon A. Bennett, *Yundong* (Berkeley, 1976), and by Charles P. Cell, *Revolution at Work* (New York, 1977).

ments persuasive. Some might grieve over not having a second or third child, but others were quite willing to stop at one.[2]

These sentiments did not transfer to the countryside, however. Peasants in widely differing circumstances saw the one-child limit as a profound threat to the integrity of family life and to their economic well-being. It threatened family traditions by ignoring the cultural imperative of having a son to carry on the family line. One daughter, or even two or three, could not substitute for a son. He alone could maintain the family lineage, and failure to produce a male descendent was a pitied and dreaded fate in the village. The policy also threatened the economic well-being of the rural family by reducing household labor power and leaving parents dependent in their old age on the survival and prosperity of a single child. With two or more sons, the family had a better chance of improving its economic status in the village, and the parents had two children on whom they could depend for support when they were old. With only one son their fate hinged on the good health, skill, and luck of only one child. With a single daughter, the situation was disastrous, since she would marry out of the family and be obliged to support her husband's parents, not her own. Rather than accept these threats to the patterns of rural life, millions of peasants dug in their heels, frustrating the state with a repertoire of tactics that were always inventive and often very effective.

These efforts at evasion were aided by important changes in the rural context in which the campaign was unfolding. In a climate where rural cadres were as likely to resist the one-child policy as their fellow villagers, from the beginning the collective control system worked less well in the countryside than in urban areas. Yet even that imperfect system was in disarray by the mid-1980s. Collectivized agriculture had been replaced by household farming, the people's commune had been abolished, and the revival of free markets had broken the party's grip on rural authority and income. Getting rich was the new path to virtue and glory, and costly regulatory programs such as population control took a backseat to local profit-making activities. These structural changes diminished the political and economic power of rural cadres and substantially reduced the dependency and vulnerability of the peasantry. At the same time, they encouraged many couples to have more children, not fewer, to increase the total labor

2. On the implementation of the one-child campaign in urban China, see Penny Kane, "The Single-Child Family Policy in the Cities," and Elisabeth Croll, "The Single-Child Family in Beijing: A First-hand Report," both in Elisabeth Croll, Delia Davin, and Penny Lane, eds., *China's One-Child Family Policy* (New York, 1985), 83–113 and 190–232; and Cecilia Milwertz, *Accepting Population Control: Urban Chinese Women and the One-Child Policy* (Richmond, Surrey, 1997).

power and income of the household. Maintaining the authority to enforce strict birth limits became increasingly difficult, and the 1984 decision to modify rural policy to allow sonless couples to have a second child did little to ameliorate the problem.

Given these rural realities, why did the Deng Xiaoping regime choose an approach to population control guaranteed to provoke a troubling confrontation with the peasantry? Why choose a method—the strict rationing of children through the use of blunt, universally imposed birth limits—that would necessarily engender a hostile reaction and create a tense climate for enforcement? How could such a policy be enforced, given the contradiction between deregulatory market-oriented reforms and the strict regulation of population growth? And why was the state impervious to the widespread and persistent display of resistance to its claim of authority over childbearing? These questions are the focus of this book, and the answers I will offer are previewed below.

Why Rationing?

The economic logic driving the new one-child policy was spelled out repeatedly by the Chinese in the late 1970s and 1980s, and it appeared to explain what many saw as a radical departure in China's ongoing family planning program. Appearances were deceptive, however. It was true that China's new, concrete modernization goals were the impetus for instituting a one-child birth limit, but the new limit, startling as it was, represented only an incremental tightening of a birth limitation program that had been in place for some time. The modernization goals explain the ratcheting upward of population control pressures, but they do not explain why China began the strict rationing of children through the use of blunt, universally imposed birth limits. The goals of population control may have been shaped by economic fears, but the method of enforcement was determined by politics.

The origins of the Chinese approach can be traced to the 1950s, when debates over development strategy dominated elite decision making. The CCP had come to power with one overriding goal—to transform China's backward agrarian society into a modern socialist one. Achieving that goal required two interrelated efforts—mobilizing human and material resources to fuel a rapid industrialization process, and restructuring the agricultural sector to solve the food-supply problem and place the surplus firmly in state hands. In the Soviet Union, the first country to face this challenge, Stalin used a swift and brutal process of collectivization and expropriation to transform rural life and assert absolute state control over the food supply. In the People's Republic of China, the challenge was the same but the context was radically different. Unlike the Soviet Union, China had a huge and rapidly growing population of nearly six hundred million people, including 525 million peasants. This population factor was unique to China and posed questions about development strategy that the Soviet Union had not had to address. Controlling the harvest in the USSR meant finding an effective mechanism for extracting and distributing the agricultural surplus. In China, there was a prior question: Would population growth leave any surplus to extract?

Initially, the official state answer to that question was yes. In the absence of capitalist exploitation, it was argued, human labor power could only be an asset; a mobilized and energized labor force could break through all obstacles to development. From the beginning, however, there were dissenting voices, both within the leadership and among intellectuals and advisers. These voices pointed out the economic burden posed by such a vast and growing population and raised questions about the economic implications of a pro-natalist policy. During this period, however, population policy stood on the periphery of a much more fundamental struggle over the broad direction and shape of China's development strategy. How to achieve socialist transformation, at what pace to move forward, and under allegiance to what conception of Marxism-Leninism were the paramount questions of the day.

Wherever China's leaders turned in these debates, the population question was there to confront them. Despite rapid gains in economic recovery and expansion in the 1950s, there was not enough food grain, not enough land, not enough housing or employment to meet the need. And given the rate of population growth, finding enough to meet basic needs in the future *and* to generate the necessary surplus to fuel rapid industrialization would be a formidable task. These concerns triggered a fierce debate over whether to promote birth control, and an even fiercer political struggle over the construction of a socialist theory of population that could be accepted as official orthodox thought. The debates were confounded when Chairman Mao began to define a theoretical position which, in itself, was neither pro-natalist nor anti-natalist. Though supremely optimistic that China's large population was its greatest resource, Mao embraced the Marxist conception of human reproduction as a corollary to material production, and thus, as a process that should properly fall within the scope of a fully planned socialist society. All parties, whether sanguine or alarmed about population growth, could agree on this principle of planning population in accordance with society's needs, even while they disagreed violently over the immediate issues of whether to promote birth control and fewer births.

As China moved to create a comprehensive planning apparatus in the

1950s, therefore, population control was included in principle as a part of that process. In practice, the pro-natalist impulses of the Great Leap Forward prevailed in the late 1950s. In the aftermath of that disaster, however, birth control supporters within the leadership used the theory of population planning to provide the ideological justification for an anti-natalist policy. From that departure point, the theory of birth planning began to be put into practice, and a distinctive revolutionary concept slowly began to take root: *that human reproduction, like economic production, could and should be organized rationally through state intervention and administration; that childbearing, like grain production, should and could be regulated according to state need and state plan.* When Chinese officials spoke of "birth planning" (*jihua shengyu*), therefore, it bore no relation to the liberal notion of family planning in which childbearing-age couples choose whether and when to have children. Rather, it implied the subjection of childbearing to the state's machinery of economic planning.

The full implications of this theory were not felt until the early 1970s, when population planning targets were inserted into economic plans for the first time and birth limits began to be vigorously enforced. The one-child policy, when it was launched by the Deng regime in 1979, merely built on the pattern that had already been established. It was the logical and radical outcome of the idea of *jihua shengyu*.

The Means of Enforcement

Inaugurating a one-child policy and enforcing it were two different things, and implementation of the one-child limit proved to be one of the most formidable challenges the Communist regime ever faced.

Apart from the state's provision of free contraceptives, which was a crucial prerequisite for imposing birth limits, the key to enforcement was the mobilization campaign, which had two distinct faces. One face—most often conjured up by the term and most often reflected in the scholarly literature on campaigns—was that of an extraordinary, revolutionary political technique designed to mobilize the entire political apparatus and galvanize mass participation to achieve a concrete policy objective. The other face, integral to the success of many campaigns but rarely acknowledged as a core characteristic of them, was one of organization, planning, and repetition. To have the greatest chance of success, both faces of campaign politics, the extraordinary and the ordinary, had to be deployed.

The classic, Mao-era mobilization campaigns generally began with the articulation by party leaders, usually in the form of a new party document or government directive, of a particular goal. This was followed by central-level planning meetings involving all relevant bureaus and organizations and similar meetings at lower levels of government to specify campaign goals and the time periods for meeting them. At the county level, cadres from lower levels—urban neighborhoods, rural people's communes, and large factories or other work units—were called in for propaganda, training, and dissemination of campaign targets, after which they would move in a concentrated and sometimes frenzied way to organize the local populace under their jurisdiction. Mass meetings were called to galvanize local participation, which could range from denouncing designated political enemies, laboring on large-scale irrigation projects, or building backyard steel furnaces. All such activities were carried out in a heightened political atmosphere of varying degrees of intensity, with newspapers, radios, and public speakers producing a constant barrage of propaganda linking the success of the current campaign to the success of the revolution.[3]

Although campaigns have always required effective planning, organization, and execution, their disruptive results and radical goals are the features that have come to be seen as synonymous with campaign politics. In his classic description of the campaigns that unfolded in Canton in the 1950s, Ezra Vogel wrote that they were characterized by "careful planning and groundwork at all levels" followed by "a sudden burst of all-out mobilization" and "waves of assault."[4] Nevertheless, it is the metaphor of the revolutionary "wave" or "high tide" and the language of domestic warfare (enemy targets, force deployments, and surprise attacks) that has come to dominate our conception of the campaign.[5]

However apt this metaphor may be for describing some campaigns, over time the entire campaign method lost some of its salt, its ability to induce shock and upheaval. As early as the 1960s, scholars began to point out how the constant "waves of assault" came to have a certain predictability and regularity, not necessarily in their timing but in the process by which they unfolded.[6] Cadres, intellectuals, workers, and peasants all adopted strategies of survival under campaign conditions. Commenting on this phenomenon, Michel Oksenberg has pointed out that learning to adapt to campaigns took some time but was essential for survival. People of all walks of life had

3. Bennett, *Yundong;* Cell, *Revolution at Work.*
4. Ezra F. Vogel, *Canton under Communism* (Cambridge, 1969), 167–68.
5. Bennett, *Yundong;* Cell, *Revolution at Work.* See also Lowell Dittmer, *China's Continuous Revolution* (Berkeley, 1987).
6. In 1967, A. Doak Barnett wrote that "repeated campaigns have tended to inure many cadres to them," making it "increasingly difficult" over time "to mobilize cadres and inject a high degree of tension into the system." See Barnett, *Cadres, Bureaucracy, and Political Power in Communist China* (New York, 1967), 70.

to "develop life plans" that assumed the repetition of the campaign cycle; they had to learn to weather the inevitable mobilizations and "the temporary reversals" they might bring. To do so they developed a series of stratagems for "getting ahead and along," stratagems designed to make life bearable at minimum and to advance one's career whenever possible.[7] With repetition, then, the campaign became less of a disruptive force and more of an institution.

This was especially true of routine production campaigns, that is, those devoted to the achievement of material production targets or concrete administrative targets. In the planned economy, all production units had annual and five-year plans for production with specific output quotas. Meeting those tasks was the basic assignment of the unit, and success or failure had political as well as economic consequences. Unlike political campaigns, which came and went at unpredictable intervals, the production campaign was ongoing. The technological and organizational requirements of production campaigns demanded a degree of consistency, predictability, and orderliness. At the same time, managers and cadres had to mobilize workers and peasants to complete their production assignments under conditions of scarcity, resulting in periodic "high tides" of production. In the annual plan, a big production push came in the final quarter of the year or at key points in the agricultural cycle. In the five-year planning cycle, efforts were redoubled in the fourth and especially the fifth year of the plan, by which time all revisions of the plan were generally complete, final production targets had been specified, and pressures to meet the targets had intensified. Sudden and irregular pressures to fulfill even higher production targets did occur, but with time and repetition even the "high tides" and the processes associated with them became routinized and predictable.[8]

The one-child campaign is best understood as one that involved both these faces of campaign politics. At certain times, it was a classic example of extraordinary, "high tide" mobilization, with intense pressure on meeting campaign targets within a short period of time. These "high tide" mobilizations were usually triggered by the need to meet plan targets, or by spikes in the anxiety level of central leaders when grain harvests were particularly disappointing. Like economic production campaigns, however, the goals of birth planning could not be achieved in a single mobilizational sweep. They required an organized, ongoing administrative process, one in which there

---

7. Michel Oksenberg, "Getting Ahead and Along in Communist China: The Ladder of Success on the Eve of the Cultural Revolution," in *Party Leadership and Revolutionary Power in China*, ed. John Wilson Lewis (Cambridge, 1970), 304–47.

8. In the countryside, in particular, the cycle of planting and harvesting lent itself to a predictable and repetitious campaign pattern.

was a regularized process for monitoring and inducing compliance. With that in mind, major efforts were made in the 1970s to develop a central- to local-level bureaucratic structure to oversee birth planning work. Further efforts were made to coordinate birth planning offices with public health and pharmaceutical agencies. At the grassroots, senior leaders were lectured about the importance of birth planning, and women's leaders were trained for the crucial work of monitoring local-level compliance. The birth planning target was added to other local economic targets to be accomplished during the annual production cycle. Bureaucratic routines were developed for assuring enforcement and reporting results. Pressures intensified at predictable moments in the annual and five-year planning cycles. In short, the birth limitation campaign came to resemble a methodical and perpetual economic production campaign, punctuated by particularly intense periods of mobilization.

This resemblance to production processes helps to explain the survival of the campaign method of implementation in the post-Mao era. Even in an era of reform, production processes followed predictable cycles of mobilization and demobilization. In addition, mobilization had become an entrenched political habit, and like all habits, it took time to change.[9] Party leaders at all levels were accustomed to relying on campaign tactics to achieve new policy goals. They were familiar practices and useful for pushing through reforms.

Campaigns also served to mobilize and discipline the cadre force; they helped to override inertia and resistance within the bureaucracy and promote new policies and programs. This explains the odd pattern by which a reform initiative such as strengthening China's legal system, whose goal was ultimately incompatible with campaign tactics, was nevertheless launched in a national campaign.[10] This function of campaigns was especially important in maintaining party control of the vast countryside, where elite demands regularly outstripped the routine bureaucratic capacity to meet them. It became even more important as the post-Mao reform process loosened organizational ties, multiplied opportunities for corruption, and highlighted the divergence of interests between central, intermediate, and local levels of state administration. Under these new conditions, campaign mobilization remained a crucial counterweight for preserving organizational discipline.

9. On campaigns as one of several administrative habits in Maoist China, see Lynn T. White III, *Policies of Chaos* (Princeton, 1989), 9.
10. See Barrett L. McCormick, *Political Reform in Post-Mao China* (Berkeley, 1990).

A fourth and final reason that campaigns persisted into the post-Mao era was that, despite their costs and limitations, they continued to work. As I will show, the sudden arrival of higher-level officials (sometimes backed by force and always backed by party authority), the house-to-house search for targets of "mobilization," and the threat of punishment for resistance remained very effective means of intimidating villagers into compliance, at least temporarily. The special challenge posed by the one-child policy, however, was its relentlessness. Today's act of reluctant compliance by a young childbearing age woman could become tomorrow's act of subversion and resistance. Compliance today did not guarantee compliance for the rest of her twenty-plus childbearing years, and for every woman who aged out of the childbearing cohort, even more young women were added. Success was always temporary, and vigilance was always necessary. This made the birth planning campaign China's longest-running campaign, and its most vexing to enforce.

State Power and Rural Resistance

Not even an ongoing campaign could defeat rural resistance to the one-child policy. By resistance, I mean any action intended to thwart, deflect, or defeat the state's claims over childbearing behavior, whether the claim be direct and material (efforts to prevent the birth of "unplanned" children and increase contraceptive use) or ideological and symbolic (attempts to reshape peasant beliefs about childbearing behavior through persistent and pervasive indoctrination). Following James C. Scott, I take a broad view of resistance, including within its scope not only overt, collective, and organized acts and behaviors but an entire world of covert, individual, and spontaneous gestures that may or may not succeed in their purpose or even appear to be resistance. An appearance of accommodation or compliance, for example, is insufficient to rule out the presence of resistance.[11]

Resistance to the one-child policy came in a startling variety of forms, but it could be measured most concretely in the tens of millions of "illegal" births that occurred after the policy's inception in 1979 and in the millions of pregnancies that were aborted under the pressure of state-imposed economic sanctions or more direct coercion. The case of birth planning in China thus confronts us with the apparent paradox of what appears to be a strong state, capable of mobilizing its resources to impose one of the most

11. On the notion of accommodation or conformity as resistance, see James C. Scott, *Weapons of the Weak* (New Haven, 1985), chap. 7.

extraordinary and invasive policies ever devised, and a strong society, capable of sustained and successful resistance in the face of intense pressures to comply.

This paradox is more apparent than real, however. It is premised on a simplistic model of state-society relations that assumes that the distribution of power between state and society is zero sum; as the state gains in power, society loses, and vice versa. Such a model predicts that state gains in compliance, and thus, social control, come at the expense of societal resistance, which is gradually defeated by the inexorable expansion of state power. This conception of state-society relations has been subjected to thorough criticism by scholars who see both the state and society, and the relationship between them, as far more complex than earlier models assumed.[12] Starting from this recognition of complexity, the critics generally reject the notion that states are organic, unified entities that operate over and against society. Instead, they emphasize the internal conflict and friction that inevitably exists between different levels and units of state administration, and the impact of that conflict, as well as societal cleavages, on state-society relations.

In China, where village cadres function as both agents of the state and defenders of local interests, confounding all attempts to draw clear boundaries between "state" and "society," it is the latter view of state-society relations that is persuasive.[13] At the lowest level of government administration, the village level, cadres serve as double agents, serving their superiors as they must and serving their villages as they are able. When village interests are in concert with those of the township, county, or higher-level authorities, village leaders may faithfully enforce central directives. Such perfect harmony is a rare thing, however. As a result, rural cadres have developed a variety of strategies designed for handling intrastate conflicts,

12. See Joel S. Migdal, *State in Society* (Cambridge, 2001); also by Migdal, *Strong Societies and Weak States* (Princeton, 1988), and Migdal, Atul Kohli, and Vivienne Shue, eds., *State Power and Social Forces* (Cambridge, 1994).

13. Vivienne Shue, *The Reach of the State* (Stanford, 1988); Jean C. Oi, *State and Peasant in Contemporary China* (Berkeley, 1989); Helen F. Siu, *Agents and Victims in South China* (New Haven, 1989). For discussion of scholarship on state-society relations in China, see Elizabeth J. Perry, "Trends in the Study of Chinese Politics: State-Society Relations," *China Quarterly* 139 (September 1994): 704–13; Kevin J. O'Brien, "Rightful Resistance," *World Politics* 49 (October 1996): 31–55; Elizabeth Perry and Mark Silden, eds. *Chinese Society: Change, Conflict, and Resistance*, 2nd ed. (New York, 2003); Kenneth G. Lieberthal and David M. Lampton, eds., *Bureaucracy, Politics, and Decision-Making in Post-Mao China* (Berkeley: University of California Press, 1992); also by Lieberthal, *Governing China: From Revolution to Reform* (New York: W. W. Norton, 1995).

all involving efforts to appease their superiors while protecting their villages, neighbors, or family.[14]

Although the divergence between central and local interests is a universal administrative problem, in this case it occurred in an uncommon context. Tight fertility control applied to all childbearing-age couples, whether they were senior officials in Beijing or poor peasants in a remote village. Moreover, party members, family planning officials, and rural cadres were asked to set an example by taking the lead in embracing the one-child limit. If they were past their childbearing years, they were pressed to see that their children and relatives complied. The significance of this—that no one was left untouched by the policy—cannot be overstated. It meant that the distinction between state and society was dissolved, not only because of state-society interpenetration and structural porousness but because those charged with policy enforcement were also policy targets. The party-state was at least as vulnerable to resistance from policy targets within its own ranks as it was to resistance from non-state targets. As with peasant targets, resistance from state and collective cadres might involve active, material resistance to the one-child limit, or ideological resistance, that is, rejection of the party line on population control and a continuing preference for multiple offspring. The long struggle over childbearing, then, was more than a struggle by the state to dominate the childbearing behavior of society. It was also a prolonged intrastate struggle to discipline and induce compliance from reluctant cadres charged with enforcing the policy.

The permeable boundaries between targets and implementers help to account for the state's inability wholly to defeat rural resistance. Given the scope and invasiveness of the one-child project, however, and the enduring rural incentives to have more than one child, this limit on state capacity should come as no surprise. What *is* surprising, and what must be explained here, is the degree to which the state succeeded in reshaping rural childbearing behavior, particularly in the face of reforms that progressively eroded state power in other arenas.

One explanation, noted above, is the effective use of campaign methods to enforce compliance by policy targets, but this element, although crucial, is insufficient to explain how the state sustained solid enforcement for more than a quarter century. Two additional factors must be considered. The first is the state's success in preventing the development of an urban-rural coali-

---

14. Understanding this reality at the grassroots, the central leadership routinely tolerated a small degree of policy slippage during implementation, even as it urged cadres to a better performance. Oi, *State and Peasant.*

tion of resistance. In part, this was accomplished indirectly, through social change and the provision of free birth control, both of which contributed to a shift in urban childbearing preferences and behavior. Just as important, however, was the state's intensive and prolonged effort to alter popular beliefs and consciousness about the relationship between population and development and the role of the state in childbearing decisions. The full weight of the state's formidable propaganda apparatus was used to associate the desire for a multichild family with backwardness and ignorance and to link the one-child family to patriotism and modernity. To help China become a modern nation by the year 2000, the argument went, couples had to exercise modern childbearing choices. This campaign was remarkably successful in urban China, reinforcing and exacerbating a deep division between urban and rural residents. Urbanites, who tended to blame the peasantry for excess population growth and resent them as they arrived in cities in migratory droves by the late 1980s, were more prepared to accept the state's arguments about the necessity of strict population control. This opened up a wide social cleavage that left resistant peasants in their traditional political position—weak, unorganized, and with limited resources. They could engage in isolated acts of resistance, or in small, localized, collective acts, but they could not pose a serious challenge to state power, even when they claimed the sympathies of rural elites, as they often did.

A second and more important reason for the state's persistent strength, however, was the unity and cohesion of the party leadership on the issue of population control. Writing of democratic states, Eric Nordlinger has argued that elite cohesion is a key determinant of state autonomy, that is, the ability to act according to its own preferences without regard for other influences. Elite cohesion enhances the array of resources states can muster in order to blunt societal pressures and preferences and pursue its own preferences. Elite division, in contrast, leaves the state vulnerable to social forces capable of capitalizing on the disagreement and on internal opposition and resistance.[15] Though China's neo-Leninist authoritarian regime severely limits the influence that social groups and intraparty dissenters can bring to bear, elite division nevertheless maximizes the opportunity to use the limited resources they do have to press for policy change. No such opportunity ever materialized in this case, however, because central leaders were united and immovable in their conviction that strict birth control was vital to the success of modernization. Unlike other policy areas, where the party was

15. On the complexities of rural administration in China, and the tension between vertical (*ti ao*) and horizontal or territorial (*kuai*) oversight, see Eric Nordlinger, "Taking the State Seriously," in *Understanding Political Development,* ed. Myron Weiner and Samuel P. Huntington (Boston, 1987), 353–90.

often divided and uncertain (at least temporarily), the signal from Beijing on population control was clear, consistent, and relentless. Even when conservatives and liberal reformers could agree on nothing else, they agreed on and believed in the premise on which their population control policy was based—that population growth constituted the single biggest threat to China's modernization. They disagreed over just how strict the one-child policy should be, about how many exceptions to grant, and how to enforce birth limits, but the necessity for state intervention was taken for granted. Faced with this impenetrable belief system, which justified even harsh "administrative measures" for the sake of the nation, neither the peasantry nor their local cadres could hope to bring about policy change through their scattered actions. What they could do, however, and what they did do, was to challenge the state's claims with a repertoire of resistance tactics that gave constant voice to their discontent. Only as the leadership was very gradually persuaded between 1995 and 2005 that the success of China's modernization program had rendered the birth planning regime all but obsolete and that China's new political economy and demographic profile required a more balanced and sophisticated approach to population control did they finally revisit the questions of how to achieve their demographic goals and what those goals should be.

The purpose of this book is to examine the course of China's longest-running campaign, a campaign premised on the radical idea of engineering fertility according to plan. It seeks to illuminate how the impulses and institutions of central planning transformed a voluntary birth control program into a mandatory program of state-regulated childbirth and to explain how an approach to birth control conceived in a climate of radical politics could survive and be intensified by a more moderate and pragmatic leadership. Beyond that is a story of tremendous historical portent. It is the story of how the imperative of economic growth and material power that was such a powerful idol of the twentieth century led one nation, facing extraordinary political, economic, and demographic challenges, to resort finally to rationing its children.

In treating the period from the early 1970s to 2005 as a single campaign, this analysis departs from other important contributions to the literature on this topic. Thomas Sharping tracks policy evolution over most of the same period covered here, but treats campaign mobilization as an enforcement practice used repeatedly to close the gap between goals and results. Implicitly, the campaign is a method of last resort, not because leaders are reluctant to wage them but because campaign mobilizations come and go in response to elite decisions regarding the urgency of enforcement. James Lee and Wang Feng frame China's birth control and birth planning campaigns as extensions of longstanding practices in China's historical fertility regime, with the state taking a much more aggressively interventionist role in the post-1949 period than in earlier periods. Susan Greenhalgh and Edwin Winckler focus on the progressive deepening of China's governance of population and childbirth, organizing the modes of state activity into three core categories: Maoist-style mobilization, Stalinist methods that rely on central planning and bureaucratization, and reformist neoliberal methods that emphasize rule of law, indirect regulation, and professional administrative oversight.[16]

Each of these works contributes greatly to our understanding of the history and dynamics of China's population control regime. An important area of difference, however, is my treatment of campaign mobilization. In contrast to other studies, I argue that, for rural China, mobilization campaigns were not simply a method to be chosen or a phase of China's political life. Rather, mobilization, through constant use after 1949, became an institutionalized method of reaching from Beijing to the countryside. In Beijing, mass mobilization competed with bureaucratization and marketization in debates over the goals and methods of advancing Chinese socialism, and the preeminence of one of these approaches signaled the (usually temporary) eclipse of the others. In rural China, however, these distinctions were less clear. To be sure, everyone knew a campaign when they saw one, especially a political campaign. But in the absence of the sort of complex bureaucracies that were found at the county and higher levels of government, and with heavy responsibilities for achieving production targets and other regime goals, township and village cadres came to rely on a basic set of routines to organize their work, routines that bridged all three leadership styles but tilted toward mobilization whenever the character of the work called for it. At the grassroots, mobilization functioned as an institutionalized and routinized method of enforcement, and as an institution, it persisted into the post-Mao era. Faced with the extraordinary demands of birth planning and entrenched, protracted resistance, campaign methods were very slow to fade.

This book draws on the extensive written record on the birth planning program in China (found in Chinese newspapers, academic journals, and other printed media) and on interviews with family planning officials, party

---

16. Thomas Sharping, *Birth Control in China, 1949–1999: Population Policy and Demographic Development* (Richmond: Curzon, 1999); Susan Greenhalgh and Edwin Winckler, *Governing China's Population: From Leninist to Neoliberal Biopolitics* (Stanford: Stanford University Press, 2005); James Z. Lee and Wang Feng, *One Quarter of Humanity: Malthusian Mythology and Chinese Realities, 1700–2000* (Cambridge: Harvard University Press, 1999).

secretaries, township and village leaders, and women's leaders at the grass-roots. I conducted many of these interviews in Hubei Province between 1982 and 1984, and again in 1990. In addition to interviews at the provincial level, I conducted interviews with municipal officials in Wuhan, district officials in Hongshan District, and township and village leaders in one township within the district. I have given this township the fictitious name of Donghu (East Lake). This series, which includes three rounds of interviews at the village level (1982, 1984, and 1990), was supplemented by interviews in 1990, 1991, and 1992 with numerous county, township and village officials, in Hebei, Shandong, and Liaoning provinces. This combination of sources is used to develop a broad national picture of the development and implementation of the birth limitation campaign. If such a study cannot capture the wide variety of conditions across the Chinese countryside at different times and places, it can perhaps provide a roadmap against which to compare local experience.

Finally, two technical notes. First, for those unfamiliar with China's governmental system, a basic organizational overview may be helpful. There are five main levels of organization below Beijing: provinces (and provincial-level municipalities, such as Beijing and Shanghai); prefectures; counties; towns and townships (distinguished by the size of the population and the degree of urbanization); and villages. Although villages are not designated as an official level of state organization, they function de facto as the most basic unit of government. In urban areas, there are also large municipalities, including the capital cities of most provinces (such as Wuhan, the capital of Hubei Province), which enjoy the same status as prefectural governments. Such municipalities are further divided into counties or districts (such as Hongshan District in Wuhan), which in turn are composed of smaller cities, towns, and townships. Please also keep in mind that today's townships are the successors to the Maoist-era rural people's communes and villages are the successors to the production brigades. Where they exist, today's village small groups are the successors to the production team, the lowest level of rural organization during the Maoist era.

Second, a note about terminology, and about what this book does and does not address. This book is not a study of China's entire family planning and reproductive health program or its population policy, nor is it a demographic analysis of China's population. This is a study in politics, a study of an ongoing struggle over childbearing sovereignty. The exclusive focus here is the Chinese state's effort to regulate childbearing through the adoption of explicit numerical birth limits. Because of that focus, I consistently refer to the policy as a "birth planning policy" or a "birth limitation campaign." As explained more fully in chapter 2, "birth planning" is the more precise translation of the Chinese phrase "jihua shengyu" (literally, "planned birth"). It captures far better than does "family planning" the true meaning of the Chinese phrase and the Chinese program. Although the official Chinese translation of jihua shengyu is "family planning," this translation obscures the origins of the program and its essential character. The concept of family planning, as used by the international community, is better captured by the phrase *jiating jihua* (literally, "family planning"). Chinese sources also use this phrase to distinguish between a voluntary family planning program and their own and to refer to international family planning activities and organizations.[17] In this volume, I use the language of birth planning to highlight the distinctive meaning and operation of the Chinese program. I use "family planning" only when referring to specific organizations whose names are routinely translated in this way, such as the State Family Planning Commission or the Chinese Family Planning Association.

In making this linguistic distinction, I do not mean to reduce the entire Chinese program to the birth planning project. Though strict state regulation of childbearing has been the primary mission of the Chinese program, in its other guise it also encompasses a broad array of family planning services that have contributed significantly to maternal and infant health, as well as reproductive health. An examination of those services, however, is beyond the scope of this book.

17. See, for example, Central Document 13 (1986), "Zhonggong zhongyang pizhuan 'guanyu liu wu qijian jihua shengyu gongzuo qingkuang he qi wu qijian gongzuo yijiande baogao' de tongzhi," in *Shiyi jie sanzhong quanhui yilai jihua shengyu zhongyao wenjian xuanbian* (Beijing, 1989), 27–35; Yuan Huarong and Wu Yuping, "Lun renkou, tizhi he jiezhi shengyu," *Renkou yu jingji* 5 (1994): 40–43.

2

Jihua Shengyu:
The Origins of Birth Planning

When the People's Republic was established in 1949, the Chinese Communist Party had the immediate tasks of completing political consolidation, restoring social order, and reconstructing the economy. Beyond that, it was committed to a second revolution—the transformation of China's backward, agrarian society into an advanced socialist society. In Marxist-Leninist terms, the first steps toward that goal were the destruction of existing class relationships, the expropriation of private property on behalf of the proletariat, the transformation of the agricultural sector along socialist lines, and the extraction of the rural "surplus" to fuel urban industrialization and development. In practical terms, however, the first step was to provide a basic level of subsistence for more than five hundred million people.

Outside China, observers were skeptical about the ability of the CCP to accomplish the basic goal of feeding its people.[1] Mao Zedong's response was to condemn this "pessimistic view" emanating from the capitalist West as reactionary, Malthusian, and "utterly groundless" and to insist instead that China's large population was a great asset.[2] Though this aggressive public stance no doubt hid some private anxieties, in 1949 Mao was basically confident that, absent the class exploitation, foreign imperialism, and bureaucratic corruption that had burdened previous regimes, the new

---

1. This position was set forth by Secretary of State Dean Acheson in the *China White Paper,* the official U. S. State Department document on China that was issued in 1949. See United States Department of State, *The China White Paper, August 1949* (a reissue) (Stanford, 1967).
2. Mao Tse-tung, "The Bankruptcy of the Idealist Conception of History," *Selected Works of Mao Tse-tung,* vol. 4 (Beijing, 1975), 451–59.

people's dictatorship could feed, clothe, educate, and gainfully employ China's growing population while simultaneously maintaining a high rate of investment in social and economic development. His confidence was the predictable stance of one who had prevailed against enormous odds to win a revolutionary victory. It was not long, however, before the buoyancy began to fade as the leadership watched its rapid economic gains be consumed by an expanding population base. Nevertheless, in the early years of the People's Republic the party remained publicly committed to a pro-natalist policy.

This pro-natalist stance is generally understood to have been dictated by the ideological position articulated by Mao. Ideology was not the only force at work, however. During the Yan'an period (1937–45) and throughout the civil war, the CCP had maintained a pro-natalist policy in order to offset the effects of disease, infant mortality, and high death rates in the base areas. At the same time, the party had encouraged young people to delay marriage and childbirth so that they could devote all their energies to the work of the revolution. When victory was won in 1949, this position was reversed, and there was a euphoric rush of marriages and pregnancies that contributed to the pro-natalist momentum.[3] Also important was the effect of Soviet policy on China during this period. In the aftermath of World War II, the Soviet Union adopted a pro-natalist policy to compensate for the tremendously heavy casualties inflicted by the war. Women were encouraged to be "mother-heroes" by giving birth to many children. The CCP, which was leaning heavily on the Soviet Union for guidance during this period, initially adopted a similar line in 1949.[4]

Ideology, then, was not the only factor shaping CCP policy in 1949. The predictable postwar baby boom had its own momentum and was reinforced by China's adoption of the Soviet line on childbearing. Mao's public attack on "pessimistic" population assessments set the ideological standard on population questions, however, so much so that it became politically dangerous even to broach the issue of birth control, much less question the party's pro-natalist policy. Nevertheless, between 1952 and 1957 three factors converged to bring about a fundamental policy reversal. The first was pressure from women in elite ranks to expand access to contraceptive methods and loosen restrictions on abortions and sterilizations. The second was the movement toward a comprehensive economic planning process, which required some measure of population size and expected growth. The third

3. Shi Chengli, *Zhongguo jihua shengyu huodong shi* (Urumuchi, 1988), 53.
4. Ibid.

was growing anxiety about economic growth and economic performance, particularly in the agricultural sector.

Women and Contraception

For Mao and other senior leaders, the only real population issue in 1949 was the macro one: whether population growth would outpace food production and retard economic growth. For women within the CCP, however, there was another population issue: whether they would have control over childbearing decisions, including access to contraceptives, sterilization, and abortion.

For women within the party, particularly those from elite intellectual ranks who had been in Yan'an, access to contraceptives was one part of a larger issue they had confronted in the 1930s and '40s. As a party, the CCP had committed itself to the liberation of women and equal rights for men and women. During the war years, therefore, women were participants in the workforce. By engaging in the work of the revolution, it was argued, women would bring about their own liberation from a feudal society.[5]

In practice, the women of Yan'an struggled to cope with the short-term reality of "liberation." They were freed to work equally with men, but they remained responsible for the household—caring for husband and children. They were given a new burden as the price (and reward) of liberation, but the old burden of domestic obligations and expectations was not lifted.[6] This classic dilemma of woman's double burden raised serious questions about the relationship between women's liberation and revolution, questions that went beyond the specific issue of party policy on population and birth control. Nevertheless, the issue of how to raise children while simultaneously serving the revolution made access to contraceptives a crucial piece of the agenda for women.

---

5. On the role of women in the revolution, see Kay Ann Johnson, *Women, the Family, and Peasant Revolution in China* (Chicago, 1983); Margery Wolf, *Revolution Postponed* (Stanford, 1985); Christina Kelley Gilmartin, *Engendering the Chinese Revolution* (Berkeley, 1995).

6. As Ding Ling put it in her essay, "Thoughts on March 8" (International Women's Day), "If women did not marry, they were ridiculed; if they did and had children, they were chastised for holding political posts rather than being at home with their families; if they remained at home for a number of years, they were slandered as backward. Whereas in the old society they were pitied, in the new one they were condemned for a predicament not of their own making." Ding Ling, "Thoughts on March 8," in *The Yenan Way in Revolutionary China*, Mark Selden (Cambridge, 1971), 165–66. The essay may also be found in Tani E. Barlow, with Gary J. Bjorge, eds., *I Myself Am a Woman* (Boston, 1989).

During the 1930s and '40s, the official party policy on population growth was pro-natalist; high birthrates among the peasantry were encouraged to offset losses due to war, disease, and high infant mortality. At the same time, the demand for access to birth control by urban intellectual women led to an official policy advocating delaying marriage until the end of the war with Japan. For married couples, birth control was sanctioned as a means to delay childbirth.[7] This policy did not go unchallenged, however. Opponents writing in the newspaper *Liberation Daily* (*Jiefang ribao*) stressed that birth control surgery—sterilization and abortion—was dangerous and bad for women's health. Others opposed birth control on moral grounds, arguing that giving birth was a natural human phenomenon that should not be artificially regulated.[8] In the face of this opposition, restrictions were placed on access to abortion and sterilization, but birth control after marriage was officially sanctioned.

At liberation, this birth control policy remained in force, despite the adoption of a pro-natalist line. With the party leadership absorbed with more pressing issues, decision making on birth control devolved to the newly created Ministry of Health (hereinafter MOH). Dominated by Western-trained medical professionals inclined by tradition and training to be conservative on contraception, the ministry drew up regulations that imposed severe restrictions on access to contraception, abortion, and sterilization. In April 1950, regulations were issued governing access to abortion by female cadres in party, government, and military posts in the Beijing District. The regulations severely limited access, and those who met the strict conditions were required to obtain a series of written approvals before the procedure could take place.[9] By May 1952, national regulations had been drafted; they were approved at the end of the year and disseminated on a trial basis.[10] The regulations outlawed sterilization or abortion except in cases of severe illness or threat to the woman. In addition, no woman was eligible for sterilization unless she was thirty-five years old, had six or more

7. Shi, *Zhongguo jihua shengyu huodong shi,* 52–53. See also Liu Shaoqi, "Tichang jieyu," in *Zhongguo renkou nianjian, 1985,* ed. Zhongguo shehui kexueyuan renkou yanjiu zhongxin (Beijing, 1985), 4–5.

8. Shi, *Zhongguo jihua shengyu huodong shi,* 50–51.

9. First, the woman's husband had to authorize the abortion in writing. Second, the head of the department or organ where the woman worked had to authorize the procedure. And third, the attending physician had to approve the decision. Failure to obtain all the necessary approvals would result in administrative punishment. Shi, *Zhongguo jihua shengyu huodong shi,* 111.

10. The regulations were entitled "Provisional Method for Limiting Birth Control Surgery and Abortion" (Xianzhi jieyu ji rengong liuchan zanxing banfa). Shi, *Zhongguo jihua shengyu huodong shi,* 113.

children, and had one child aged ten or above.[11] Reinforcing this strict line, the MOH also moved to limit access to contraceptives. In January 1953, only days after the regulations were approved, the ministry notified customs officials to stop the import of contraceptives.[12] This ban, combined with the restrictive policy that discouraged the production of contraceptives domestically, meant that even the rudimentary and unreliable contraceptive supplies available would continue to be extremely scarce.

By early 1953, then, the combined forces of social conservatism and ideological radicalism had produced a set of official state regulations that virtually eliminated access to birth control. Just as they were coming on line, however, the logic of the women's movement in China was moving in the opposite direction, leading some women, particularly cadres, to press for increased access. For female cadres the new regulations were a setback and posed a threat to their pursuit of active political careers. During the 1940s, the party had quietly maintained a two-track policy—allowing urban, educated women to practice birth control while encouraging childbearing among peasant women. The MOH was now moving to establish uniform regulations that would abolish the two-track policy, and it was doing so just as the size of the female cadre and labor forces were beginning to expand. As a result, women in the party's senior ranks began to press for a change in policy, linking access to birth control to the larger movement for women's liberation that was already under way.

The question was how to change the restrictive regulations on access to contraception. Fortuitously, advocates of birth control were aided in the spring of 1953 by the "three-anti" (*sanfan*) campaign. The campaign was directed against corruption and bureaucratism in government, but more generally it was designed to prevent a widening of elite-mass cleavages by keeping the bureaucracy open to mass input. As a result, people were encouraged to write letters to government officials or visit government offices to voice their opinions or complaints.[13] Taking advantage of this climate, women in the labor force and female cadres began to send letters to the Women's Federation, the official trade union, and party and government headquarters complaining of the tight restrictions and requesting access to contraceptives.[14] It is unclear just how many complaints were registered in

11. Deng Lichun and Ma Hong, eds., *Dangdai zhongguode weisheng shiye, xia* (Beijing, 1986), 231.

12. Shi, *Zhongguo jihua shengyu huodong shi*, 115.

13. On the encouragement of citizen participation in the three-anti campaign, see Harry Harding, *Organizing China* (Stanford, 1981), 83.

14. Deng and Ma, eds., *Dangdai zhongguode weisheng*, 231; Shi, *Zhongguo jihua shengyu huodong shi*, 117. For an oblique reference to the receipt of letters regarding marriage and

1953, but in response Zhou Enlai undertook an investigation of living conditions in worker households, comparing the situation of working couples with many children to those with fewer children.[15] The results, which favored households with fewer children and thus access to contraceptives, were passed on to health cadres.[16]

By August 1953, central policy began to shift. The policy changes were set forth by Vice Premier Deng Xiaoping, whom Zhou Enlai would later claim had the "inventor's patent" (*famingquan*) on the birth control issue.[17] In a report to the Women's Federation, Deng instructed the federation members to promote birth control; he also instructed the MOH to revise its regulation banning the import of contraceptives and to publicize the new policy of promoting birth control to all medical personnel.[18] Shortly thereafter, the ban was reversed, and new, more liberal regulations were issued by the ministry in July 1954.[19]

These revisions did not solve the problem of access, however. The liberalization of birth control policy stirred controversy and resistance within the ministry and among medical personnel. Some resisted promoting birth control, while others delayed giving the necessary approvals for sterilizations or abortions, which were still subject to tight controls. Still others opposed the new policy, arguing that contraceptive use would have negative effects on society and the family. In May 1954 these problems prompted Deng Yingzhao (wife of Zhou Enlai) to write Deng Xiaoping to complain of these difficulties.[20] She urged that the matter of birth control be raised in the re-

---

public health, see "North China Organs Strengthen Measures in Dealing with Public Complaints," *New China News Agency* (hereinafter *NCNA*), January 30, 1953, in *Survey of China Mainland Press* (hereinafter *SCMP*) no. 505, 17–19.

15. Deng and Ma, eds., *Dangdai zhongguode weisheng,* 231–32.

16. Ibid.

17. Zhou Enlai, "Jingji jianshede jige fangzhenxing wenti," in *Zhou Enlai xuanji, xia* (Beijing, 1984), 231. Zhou goes on to say that "later on [after Deng had raised it], Mr. Shao Lizi discussed it at the National People's Congress." Since Shao Lizi (a non-CCP or non-Communist Party delegate to the first National People's Congress) is known to have raised the issue at the congress in September 1954, Zhou's comments confirm the sequence of events in 1953–54 as reported above. This sequence gives less credit to Shao for initiating the first birth control discussions than earlier studies have suggested. Indeed, it is quite possible that Shao was following Deng Xiaoping's more private lead when he publicly spoke to the issue. For earlier interpretations of this period and Shao's role, see H. Yuan Tian, *China's Population Struggle* (Columbus, 1973), chap. 5; Leo A. Orleans, *Every Fifth Child* (London, 1972), chap. 2.

18. Li Honggui, "Zhongguode renkou zhengce," in *Zhongguo renkou nianjian, 1985,* 217; Editorial, "Yinggai shidangde jiezhi shengyu" [There should be appropriate birth control], *Renmin ribao* People's Daily, March 5, 1957, reprinted in *Zhongguo renkou nianjian, 1985,* 10–11.

19. Deng and Ma, *Dangdai zhongguode weisheng,* 232.

20. For the text of Deng Yingzhao's letter and the reply, see Peng Peujun, ed., *Zhongguo jihua shengyu quanshu* (Beijing, 1996), 146. At the time, Deng Yingzhao and Deng Xiaoping

sponsible leading organs, adding that they should "work out a way to help *cadres* solve the question of contraception."[21] Her emphasis on the burden on cadres came at a time when the Yan'an-style supply system for cadre compensation was being phased out in favor of a wage system based on one's assigned cadre rank. This change meant that cadres who had received cash supplements for extra dependents no longer could count on the supplemental income, a change that could seriously affect living standards in the households of low-ranking cadres.[22] Whether or not he took this factor into consideration, Deng Xiaoping wrote in response that "contraception is completely necessary and beneficial."[23] Shortly thereafter, he instructed the MOH to find more effective measures for addressing contraceptive needs. The response was a third set of revised regulations issued in November 1954. They promoted the voluntary use of birth control methods, but they continued to express reservations about abortion and sterilization, maintaining strict regulation. Hospitals and health units were instructed to give full guidance on contraception; the Ministry of Light Industry was ordered to speed up production of contraceptives; and the State Pharmaceutical Company was made responsible for their distribution. Contraceptives were to be sent directly to supply outlets for marketing; access would no longer be controlled by medical personnel. Following up on the question of supply and sale, the ministries of commerce and health issued a separate circular in late November. The circular stated that, in general, contraceptives should not be sold in minority nationality districts nor would supplies be sent to rural areas.[24]

By 1954, central policy on access to contraception had been relaxed dramatically. Most urban women could go to women's health units at their local hospitals or clinics and expect to receive guidance on birth control issues. Alternatively, they could go to pharmaceutical retail outlets to purchase such contraceptives as might be available (condoms, spermicidal jellies, diaphragms); a doctor's prescription was no longer necessary. In practice, birth control remained extremely controversial, medical personnel remained generally hostile to disseminating information, cadres delayed giving the necessary approvals, and contraceptives were extremely scarce

both served on the Standing Committee of the Chinese People's Political Consultative Conference (CPPCC), she as a committee member and he as a vice chairman.

21. Deng and Ma, *Dangdai zhongguode weisheng,* 232; Shi, *Zhongguo jihua shengyu huodong shi,* 117 (emphasis added).

22. On the shift from the supply system to the wage-scale system, see Harding, *Organizing China,* 39–40 and 72–73.

23. Deng and Ma, *Dangdai zhongguode weisheng,* 232; Shi, *Zhongguo jihua shengyu huodong shi,* 118; Peng, ed., *Zhongguo jihua shengyu quanshu,* 146.

24. Shi, *Zhongguo jihua shengyu huodong shi,* 119.

and of very poor quality; abortion and sterilization remained the primary methods of birth control. In short, access for many people was more theoretical than real. Nevertheless, an official policy supporting access to birth control had been established in principle.

Although entreaties from women of high rank helped to create momentum for the change in policy, despite the opposition of the MOH, their arguments might well have been ignored by the leadership had their campaign not converged with two other crucial developments—the gradual move toward a comprehensive process of economic planning and growing anxiety about agricultural production. Both led back to the question of China's population growth, and the consequences of rapid growth for China's economic performance.

The First Five-Year Plan and State Advocacy of Birth Control

By the end of 1952, the CCP had basically completed the task of consolidating its power nationwide. In addition, the first stage of the rural revolution—implementing land reform and waging class struggle against the landlord class—was nearing completion. With those accomplishments, the Chinese leadership began to concentrate more intensively on how to bring about rapid industrialization and development, an issue that required two sets of decisions. The first was substantive—what mix of policies would yield the most rapid pace of development at the lowest political, economic, or social cost. The second was administrative—how was the new Communist government to oversee and administer a socialist economy. The substantive question proved so controversial that it devoured the remainder of the decade; I will return to this question later. The administrative question was more straightforward, at least at the outset. The Soviet experience with centralized economic planning and administration had allowed Stalin to industrialize rapidly, and it was the model of choice for the Chinese leadership. Beginning in 1952, China began to create the central organs necessary for development of a nationwide planning process and apparatus. The State Statistical Bureau was established in October, and by the end of 1953 each province had established a statistical department.[25] Similarly, the State Planning Commission (SPC) was established in November, and similar organs were set up in the provinces. The SPC was given responsibility for both short-term (annual) and long-term (five-year) economic planning. Its job

25. Audrey Donnithorne, *China's Economic System* (London, 1981), 458.

was to coordinate the production and distribution needs of individual economic organs and to set priorities for investment and growth.

The creation of these and similar economic organs gave China the semblance of a central planning apparatus, but in practice the system was loose and incomplete, lacking both hard data and the coordinating mechanisms necessary for efficient planning. Nevertheless, these steps paved the way for the development of the first five-year plan (FYP), which spanned the years 1953–57 but was not officially launched until 1955. The plan included basic targets for industrial and agricultural production, as well as targets for related work in such areas as health, education, and scientific development. To set those targets, the leadership needed reliable figures on indicators such as the size of the urban and rural work force, the likely growth in employment needs over the coming five years, and the number of students who would be enrolling in schools and graduating, to cite only a few examples. Most fundamentally, they needed a reliable figure on the overall size of the Chinese population, as well as data on its composition and age structure.

Since 1949, the Chinese Communists had used a population figure of 475 million in all public statements. By the end of 1952, however, the leadership knew that the actual number was much higher. In 1951, the State Statistical Bureau estimated that the Chinese population (including Taiwan) exceeded 564 million at the end of 1950; in 1952, the Internal Affairs Ministry estimated a population of over 575 million at the end of 1951.[26] Though far closer to the actual number than the official figure of 475 million, these estimates were inadequate for long-term economic planning. As a result, in late 1952 the CCP Central Committee ordered a census to be taken on June 30, 1953. The State Statistical Bureau was put in charge of carrying it out, and Premier Deng Xiaoping oversaw the process for the central leadership.

The completed census results were not published until more than a year after the census, in November 1954.[27] In preparation for elections to local people's congresses, however, the preliminary total was announced in June of that year. As head of the General Election Commission, Deng Xiaoping announced that 583 million lived in the People's Republic; the total Chinese population, including Taiwan and overseas Chinese, numbered 601 million. This population total confirmed the crude population estimates made in 1951 and 1952, suggesting a population growth rate of 2 percent per year.

26. Shi, *Zhongguo jihua shengyu huodong shi*, 114.
27. See Ma Qibin, Chen Wen Wu, Lin Yunhui, Cong Jin, Wang Nianyi, Jiang Tianrong, and Bu Weihua, eds., *Zhongguo gongchandang zhizheng sishinian, 1949–1989* (Beijing, 1989), 84.

This high rate of population growth raised serious questions about how to meet the performance goals of the first five-year plan.

The centerpiece of the plan was the development of heavy industry. With Soviet assistance, 156 new plants were to be built, and industrial growth was to expand at a rate of more than 14 percent per year. Investment in agriculture, by comparison, was extremely modest; nevertheless, expectations for agricultural growth were set at 4.3 percent annually. Although meeting these targets would mean impressive gains over the five-year period, it was not at all clear in 1953 that they would resolve basic problems left over from the period of reconstruction (1949–52). One of those problems was unemployment and underemployment. In mid-1952, more than two million laborers remained unemployed, despite the creation of three million new jobs after 1949.[28] In the countryside, land reform left many households without sufficient land to employ all members of the household. As a result, many peasants began to migrate to urban areas in 1952 and 1953, in anticipation of the high-paying jobs in new industries to be created during the First Five-Year Plan.[29] Despite a government directive to prevent this migration, their influx contributed to a jump in urban population of nearly 28 percent between 1952 and 1953, increasing substantially the pressures on cities to expand the employment base.[30] More important, the influx also contributed to the second major problem that confronted planners—continuing food shortages.

Between 1949 and 1952, the CCP's rural policy concentrated on implementing land reform, overthrowing the landlord class, and restoring stable agricultural production. By 1953, however, the party began to look to collectivization as the long-term solution for China's agricultural sector. In 1953, the party proposed a fifteen-year transition from private farming to socialist collectives, a timetable that, under pressure from Mao, would accelerate dramatically in 1955. But in the short-run rural private markets continued to flourish, and peasants were able to choose to sell to rural traders or state purchasing agents. This system of private and voluntary rural marketing quickly proved inadequate, however. Despite the successful economic recovery efforts after 1949, the cities continued to suffer food shortages, which were increasingly blamed on the low peasant sales to state

28. Liu Suinian and Wu Qungan, eds., *China's Socialist Economy* (Beijing, 1986), 93.

29. On the problem of peasant migration, see Chen Yun, "Dongyuan chengshi renyuan xia-xiang," in *Chen Yun wenxuan, 1956–1985* (Beijing, 1986), 152–54.

30. Chen Yun, "Dongyuan chengshi renkou xianxiang," 153; "GAC Directive on Dissuasion of Peasants from Blind Influx into the Cities," *NCNA*, April 17, 1953, in *SCMP* 554 (April 18–20, 1953), 24–25.

purchasing agents.[31] To solve this problem, some within the leadership advocated the creation of a system of mandatory purchases and sales of food grains. Such a system would add stability and predictability to the overall planning process, allowing state planners to better estimate the availability of grain for food, exports, and industrial production, and to better regulate grain supplies and food prices in the cities.

Others argued against this policy, advocating that food prices be readjusted to give the peasants greater incentives to sell to the state. By October, though, this approach was rejected. With state grain sales exceeding purchases by 38 percent, the food supply and the economy as a whole were in peril. Accordingly, the system of unified procurements was implemented in the winter of 1953–54, with each locality assigned a procurement quota by the next higher administrative level. All private trading in grain was made illegal and only designated grain shops or supply and marketing co-ops were allowed to sell grain. Urban residents would be supplied grain through their workplace, with purchases made at low, state-subsidized prices; enterprises that needed grain for business purposes (like restaurants and factories that produced commercial agricultural products) were given a set quota for grain purchase at state-run grain shops.[32]

The system of unified procurements resulted in a dramatic increase in grain purchases in late 1953 and 1954, solving the immediate problem of food-grain shortages.[33] Its very success, however, created a new problem. By late 1954 and early 1955, so much grain had been sold to the state for supply and reserves that the low level of reserves left in the villages was a source of growing anxiety for the peasantry. Peasants were due to receive grain for consumption in the spring of 1955, but before the designated time of distribution arrived, many began to complain of hunger and inadequate supplies of grain. Some claims of hunger were bogus, but the general anxiety over supplies was very real. Moreover, peasants expected to see an increase in their quota for sale in 1955, which would increase production pressures and potentially draw off more of the surplus. Responding to those fears, some peasants began to cut back on their grain production or simply neglect it, concentrating instead on other crops. Recognizing this threat, the state took steps to allay peasants' fears, including fixing grain quotas and prices for three years. Despite their efforts, however, a "grain supply crisis"

31. Vivienne Shue, *Peasant China in Transition* (Berkeley, 1980), 217.
32. For discussions of the short- and long-term effects of the unified procurement and sales system, see Shue, *Peasant China in Transition,* chap. 5, and also Oi, *State and Peasant,* chap. 3.
33. Shue, *Peasant China in Transition,* chap. 5.

emerged in spring of 1955, forcing the leadership to mobilize party leaders at all levels to go into villages to stabilize the situation.[34]

It was in this context—with census results that showed a rapid rate of population growth, and a growing conflict between the ambitious plans for development and the short-term dilemmas of rapid urban growth, tight food supplies, and an uncertain rural political climate—that the CCP formally (though temporarily) shifted to an anti-natalist policy. In July 1954, just as the more liberal regulations on contraception were being drafted, the MOH submitted the first outline plan for controlling birthrates to the State Planning Commission.[35] And in December, a special government group was convened to discuss population and birth control questions. Demonstrating how rapidly the thinking of central leaders had evolved, Liu Shaoqi made a remarkable speech before the group.[36] He acknowledged the ongoing debate within the party over birth control, noting that articles opposing birth control continued to be published. He argued that it was time to bring that debate to an end by announcing officially that "the party endorses birth control." He went on to use Soviet history and the CCP's Yan'an policies to construct a rationale for adopting a policy that would permit open access to contraception. Arguing that the Soviet Union's policy toward birth control had changed to fit changing circumstances, Liu made a similar case for China. He claimed that the pro-natalist Yan'an slogan "People and livestock are flourishing" (*renshu liangwang*) was adopted as a response to the high infant mortality rate (over 50 percent) during the Yan'an period, and that it was adopted only after the party had made an unsuccessful effort to introduce new birth methods that would reduce this figure. When the peasantry resisted, the party resorted instead to encouraging more births.[37] Now that the CCP was out of the hinterland and in power, he argued, circumstances had changed dramatically:

> Of the population increase in the entire world, in China it is the fastest, today the annual rate of increase is two per cent. Without birth control, the increase would be even faster. Will we or will we not have difficulties after the population increases? We'll have difficulties, many difficulties, and they cannot be

34. The classic study of the 1955 grain supply crisis remains Thomas Bernstein, "Cadre and Peasant Behavior under Conditions of Insecurity and Deprivation: The Grain Supply Crisis of the Spring of 1955," in A. Doak Barnett, ed., *Chinese Communist Politics in Action* (Seattle, 1969), 365–99.

35. Shi, *Zhongguo jihua shengyu huodong shi,* 118.

36. Liu Shaoqi, "Tichang jieyu," 4–5.

37. To support his claim, he notes that party cadres were never encouraged to increase births. Liu, "Tichang jieyu," 4.

solved all at once. In Beijing, for example, grain, clothing, and medicines are all insufficient. Our country has a great burden in this respect, and many individuals have difficulties. In short, the difficulties of giving birth to many children are very great, the parents, household and the child itself all [experience] difficulties, as well as the society and the country. Clothing, food, medicine, schools, etc., are all insufficient. . . . Because of this, we should endorse (*zancheng*) birth control, not oppose it. None of the opposing arguments hold water. It is incorrect to say that birth control is immoral. To say that birth control has a bad influence, this is not a real problem.[38]

Liu then gave instructions that reveal the true depth of the controversy over propagating birth control and his determination to prevail over the opposition. He called on the health department to publish guidance manuals on birth control and to educate health workers on the subject. He also called for using every means available to increase the production and supply of contraceptives, including more research, private factory production, purchases in Hong Kong, and imports from capitalist countries. And he called for propaganda and study first within the party, to unify thinking among cadres, with only oral propaganda for public consumption. Most tellingly, he advocated extending this propaganda campaign into the countryside, noting that "it is not the case that there is no demand for birth control in the countryside." He called on cadres involved in "women's work" to find ways to discuss birth control with rural women. But he made clear that a mobilization campaign would be premature, explicitly ruling out a print campaign in newspapers and periodicals.[39]

Liu's instruction to concentrate first on educating party members and cadres was a sensible and measured approach to the revolutionary idea of encouraging contraception and providing birth control guidance on a massive scale. During the 1950s contraception and reproductive control remained extremely controversial, even in the industrialized world. It is hardly surprising that many members of the peasant-based Chinese Communist Party found the idea of mass contraceptive education and distribution unpalatable, or that the initiative would provoke resistance throughout Chinese society, including from medical professionals. Before going forward with a public campaign, therefore, it was essential to first propagate the new line within the party and to translate Liu's speech into a formal party directive.

After Liu's speech, a special small group for research on birth control is-

38. Ibid.
39. Ibid.

sues was organized, with members drawn from the ministries of health, light industry, commerce, and foreign trade, and from mass organizations such as the Women's Federation. The group met four times in early 1955 and submitted a report to the Central Committee on January 31, detailing steps needed to promote birth control.[40] The report was approved by the Central Committee on March 1 and released as "Directive on the Question of Population Control." The directive argued for the promotion of birth control on explicitly economic grounds, stressing that birth control was directly related to the people's livelihood and to the welfare of the country, individual households, and the next generation. Unlike policy statements that began to appear in the 1970s, this one made no effort to link the policy specifically to women's health. Instead, the general welfare of parents (*fumu*) was stressed. Moreover, the use of the language "population control," or *renkou kongzhi*, left no question about the state's decision to adopt an anti-natalist policy, or the subordination of population policy to the state's economic goals. Women's demands for contraceptive access were a secondary consideration.[41]

These steps marked the initial phase of China's first birth control campaign. The only remaining question was how this policy would be put into operation. Before that could be fully addressed, however, a political backlash erupted that challenged the political and economic premises of the population policy and placed it at the vortex of the escalating debate over the first principles of China's development strategy.

The Development Strategy Debate and Birth Planning

By the time the anti-natalist policy was adopted in late 1954, the debate over the pace and shape of socialist transformation in China had begun to overtake and reshape it. Over the next few years, China's leaders would confront the consequences of excessive centralization of decision making, rapid growth in the state bureaucracy and the state payroll, excessive growth in the urban population (with a consequent drain on food supplies and consumer goods), and, most troubling, very sluggish growth in the agricultural sector. By 1955, two distinct viewpoints were emerging about how to resolve the problems of agricultural performance—one favoring a slow to moderate pace of transformation over many years, the other favoring a more aggressive approach and an accelerated pace of collectivization.

40. Ma Qibin et al., eds., *Zhongguo gongchandang zhizheng sishinian*, 91.
41. Ibid.; Li Honggui, "Zhongguode renkou zhengce," 217.

By the spring of 1955, the Chinese countryside had been thoroughly penetrated by the CCP, and a foundation for collectivization had been put in place. Land reform had been followed by the organization of mutual aid teams; the private grain market had been abolished and a system of unified purchase had been instituted; and a small number of cooperatives and collectives had been formed. Although the leadership agreed that these were only preliminary stages toward the goal of collectivized agriculture, the question was how and at what pace to proceed toward that goal. Those responsible for agricultural work argued for a slow transition, adhering to the fifteen-year timetable set out in the first FYP. Faced with widespread difficulties resulting from the excessive extraction of grain in 1954, these officials feared that speeding up collectivization would further dampen peasant enthusiasm and undercut their incentives to produce. To avoid that possibility and assure an adequate food supply, they advocated price increases for grain and a relaxation of quotas. Those responsible for overall economic planning, in contrast, argued for a moderate increase in the pace of cooperativization. From their perspective, price increases and relaxed grain quotas would be far too costly, politically and economically, and concessions to agriculture would delay the rapid development of heavy industry. Only steady movement toward collectivization could remove this threat, by securing state access to the agricultural surplus at a minimal cost.[42]

By midsummer, Mao Zedong had rejected both positions in favor of an accelerated plan for cooperativization. In July 1955, he summoned provincial leaders to a work conference and called for the completion of cooperativization by the end of the decade and for accelerated collectivization. The "high tide" that followed exceeded even Mao's expectations. By the time the Central Committee met in October to reconsider the issue, collectivization was moving ahead at a speed vastly exceeding even Mao's goals, and within a year the process was complete.[43] Building on that example, in late October 1955 Mao called for a similar acceleration in the industrial sector. Rather than abide by previous plans that called for the complete nationalization of industry over a twelve-year period, he proposed that it be done in two.

Behind Mao's press for more rapid transformation was a growing belief that the main barriers to progress were ideological rather than practical. He concluded that the "conservative work style" and "right deviationist mistakes" of the party and state bureaucracy were responsible for the slow pace of rural transformation, a belief that was apparently confirmed by the

42. On these and subsequent policy debates, see David Bachman, *Bureaucracy, Economy and Leadership in China* (Cambridge, 1991).
43. On the rural collectivization process, see Kenneth R. Walker, *Agricultural Development in China, 1949–1989*, ed. Robert F. Ash (Oxford, 1998), chap. 1.

swift completion of the process under his direction. To solve this leadership problem, Mao called for the cultivation of a "progressive work style," a leadership style that emphasized three basic elements: (1) more investigations of local conditions; (2) better and more rapid communication within the bureaucracy; and (3) comprehensive planning.[44] The last element irrevocably refocused China's approach to population policy.

In pushing for a progressive work style, Mao's goal was to foment the mobilizational momentum that had been developing since July. Impatient with Soviet-style bureaucratic methods that seemed to breed pessimism and caution in the party and government, Mao saw the campaign approach as a superior alternative. Adopting mobilizational methods did not imply a deemphasis on planning, however; planning per se was no obstacle to progress, only pessimistic planning. Nor did Mao see planning as a threat to mobilizational methods. If properly led and executed, the planning process could be the means for honing the positive gains of mobilization. Rather than taking the lowest common denominator or the poorest performing units as the basis for setting goals and targets, progressive planning would be based on the most advanced achievements and ambitious targets. And rather than a rigid top-down process of centralized planning and dissemination of targets, progressive planning would involve the mobilization of each sector and each governmental level in comprehensive, bottom-up planning and implementation. In short, Mao saw comprehensive planning as an organic fusion of the best elements of systematic planning and mass mobilization—disciplining mobilization to the needs of the plan and infusing the planning process with the potential for mobilizational breakthroughs.

In response to Mao's call, each ministry and each province began to lay out short- and long-term plans ranging from three to twelve years. To avoid the errors of "right-deviationism" or conservatism, each organ proposed ambitious targets, and lower-level governments pushed their targets even higher as a statement of their political resolve. Calls came forth to complete the first five-year plan by the end of 1956, a year ahead of schedule, and under Mao's guidance, work began on a twelve-year comprehensive plan for agricultural development.

It was in the context of this "planning campaign" that the focus of population policy began to shift from *birth control* to *birth planning*. In late 1954 and through the summer of 1955, birth control advocates took the opportunity presented by the change in official party policy on contraception to begin to write and speak about the subject. They stressed that indi-

44. Harding, *Organizing China*, chap. 4.

vidual couples should *plan* their children and use birth control to prevent early or unwanted pregnancies.[45] In other words, while linking the need for family planning to the larger issue of China's long-term development, they called for family planning in the liberal sense—individual couples taking advantage of new contraceptive techniques to make conscious decisions about the timing and spacing of children. Some proposed that the state encourage fewer births by advocating delayed marriage (age twenty-three for women and twenty-five for men) and providing economic incentives.[46]

Within a year, however, this liberal approach to "planned childbirth" had become fused to the very different concept of comprehensive socialist planning that was being promoted in the larger economic and social sphere. The result was a profound change in the meaning and implications of China's birth control policy. The first step was the insertion of a provision on birth planning into the draft twelve-year plan for agricultural development. The draft, which Mao Zedong submitted to a meeting of the Supreme State Conference in January 1956, had forty articles. Article 29 emphasized the need to "propagandize and popularize" birth control (*jiezhi shengyu*) in all densely populated areas, and "to promote childbirth according to plan" (*tichang you jihuade shengyu zinu*).[47] Rather than justify these measures on grounds of maternal and infant health, they were justified on grounds of reducing household burdens, improving children's education, and most revealingly, realizing the national goal of full employment.[48] The plan was followed in March and August by two directives from the MOH, one loosening restrictions on abortion and sterilization, and the other instructing all health departments and health personnel on methods of disseminating contraceptive knowledge and measures.[49]

To birth control advocates and all who were familiar with the language being used to encourage individual couples to adopt birth control, the phrase "to promote childbirth according to plan" could be understood to refer to household-level decision making about the number and spacing of

45. Shi, *Zhongguo jihua shengyu huodong shi*, 119. For an example of this line of argument, see Shao Lizi, "Planned Parenthood," *Renmin ribao*, March 20, 1957, in *Current Background* (hereinafter *CB*) 445 (April 5, 1957), 9–13.

46. Ma himself reveals this incident in his 1957 tract "A New Theory of Population." The tract appeared in *Renmin ribao* on March 20, 1957, and is translated in *CB* 469 (July 25, 1957).

47. For the relevant excerpt from the draft plan, see *Zhongguo renkou nianjian, 1985*, 13.

48. Ibid.

49. "Weishengbu guanyu rengong liuchan ji jueyu shoushude tongzhi" (March 30, 1956) and "Weishengbu guanyu biyun gongzuode zhibiao" (August 6, 1956), in *Zhongguo renkou nianjian, 1985*, 6–7.

children. To rank-and-file party cadres, however, the nuances of meaning were completely lost. For them, planning was a collective activity, and in early 1956 they were in the midst of a campaign to achieve more comprehensive planning. If births needed to be planned, they would set birth targets and mobilize to achieve them on a mass scale, shifting the planning process from the individual to the state. Accordingly, over the next two years various localities began to draw up plans relevant to the birth control effort. Guangdong and Hebei provinces drew up formal twelve-year plans for birth control work, while Hunan and Sichuan provinces issued directives on strengthening birth control work. Shanghai announced that it planned to reduce its birthrate by half during the second five-year plan (1958–62)—from 40 births per 1,000 to 20 per 1,000; Changsha committed itself to a birthrate of 30 per 1,000 by 1962, with a further goal for the third five-year plan—a birthrate of 21 per 1,000. Women workers in some localities were required to sign "birth plans" of their own; women with two children agreed to have no more during the second five-year plan, and women with one child or none agreed to have only one. Even a few rural cooperatives pledged to cut their birthrate drastically by the end of the second five-year plan.[50]

As a result of this activity, by 1957 the concept of "births according to plan" (*you jihuade shengyu zinu*) was rapidly becoming the doctrine of planned births (jihua shengyu), even though most senior leaders continued to advocate birth control rather than birth planning. In September 1956, for example, Zhou Enlai's report on China's second five-year economic plan endorsed birth control measures and propaganda, but made no reference to "birth planning," and in November he expanded on the issue in a Politburo talk on the 1957 annual plan.[51]

> At yesterday's Politburo meeting I said we should promote birth control. . . .
> It is now clear that we will not be able to employ everyone within a short period of time, and wage increases will not enable workers to support the popu-

50. Zhu Yuncheng, ed., *Zhongguo renkou, Guangdong fence* (Beijing, 1988), 399; Wang Mingyuan, ed., *Zhongguo renkou, Hebei fence* (Beijing, 1987), 460; Mao Kuangsheng, ed., *Zhongguo renkou, Hunan fence* (Beijing, 1987), 435–36; Liu Hongkang, ed., *Zhongguo renkou, Sichuan fence* (Beijing, 1988), 400; Hu Huanyong, ed., *Zhongguo renkou, Shanghai fence* (Beijing, 1987), 360. See also John S. Aird, "Population Policy and Demographic Prospects in the People's Republic of China," in *People's Republic of China*, ed. Joint Economic Committee, Congress of the United States (Washington, D.C., 1972), 247.

51. Zhou Enlai, "Guanyu fazhan guomin jingjide disange wunian jihuade jianshede baogao," in *Zhongguo renkou nianjian, 1985*, 9; Zhou Enlai, "Jingji jianshede jige fangzhenxing wenti," 229–38.

lation of many households. I believe that going so far as to promote late marriage even has some advantages.[52]

Similarly, in August 1957 China's leading economic planner, Chen Yun, spoke pointedly about pressing economic problems, including the large peasant migration to urban areas in search of employment. The migration threatened to put additional pressure on the central budget, since urban residency entitled migrants to a variety of state subsidies, and it also put pressure on the urban food supply. Noting that the current problems were directly related to the rapid pace of population growth and that the effects of birth control measures would only be seen after ten to twenty years, Chen called on each province and municipality to create a specialized committee to handle this work. Acknowledging the difficulty of promoting birth control in Chinese society, he called for widespread propaganda to overcome the "shyness" (*paxiu*) of both men and women about buying contraceptives. In a more practical vein, he said the price of contraceptives would be lowered *again,* even to the point of free distribution (*baisong*), and that the government was prepared to spend "several tens of millions" a year on subsidies. Most striking, he made what is perhaps the first reference to a specific limit on childbearing, suggesting that they "call on Communist Party members not to give birth to a third child."[53] Yet he does not make any reference to the formula of "birth planning."

In contrast, Mao Zedong used the language of birth planning in 1956 and throughout 1957, laying the foundation for an official doctrine of comprehensive birth planning. In October 1956, Mao told a women's delegation from Yugoslavia that couples should make a "family plan" (*jiating jihaa*) for childbirth that was consistent with the national five-year plan, and he compared reproduction to material production.[54] Mao's February 1957 speech, "On the Correct Handling of Contradictions among the People," spoke more fully about the issue. He notes that employment plans for 1956 called for an increase of eight hundred thousand workers, but that approximately three million were employed at the state's expense. In education, four million primary school graduates could not be accommodated in middle schools, another eight hundred thousand lower middle school stu-

52. Zhou, "Jingji jianshede jige fangzhenxing wenti," 231.
53. Chen Yun, "Bixu tichang jiezhi shengyu," in *Chen Yun wenxuan, 1956–1985,* 59. This text dates these comments August 20, 1957, while the party administrative history puts them on August 26. See Ma et al., *Zhongguo gongchandang,* 133.
54. Yang Kuixue, Liang Jimin, and Zhang Fan, eds. *Zhongguo renkou yu jihua shengyu dashi yaolan* (Beijing, Zhonngguo renkou chubanshe, 2001), 12.

dents could not go on to higher middle school, and ninety thousand higher middle school graduates could not advance to university. Apart from the educational loss that entailed, these former students now became a part of the unemployed labor pool.[55] In the context of these problems, he goes beyond the advocacy of birth control to call for comprehensive population planning:

> Our plans, work, [and] thinking all should start from the [awareness] that we have a population of 600 million. Here [we] need birth control; it would be great [if we] could lower the birth [rate] a bit. [We] need planned births. I think humanity is most inept at managing itself. It has plans for industrial production, the production of textiles, the production of household goods, the production of steel; [but] it does not have plans for the production of humans. This is anarchism, no government, no organization, no rules. (Loud laughter) If [we] go on this way, I think humanity will prematurely fall into strife and hasten toward destruction. If China's population of 600 million increases tenfold, what will that be? Six billion: at that time [we] will be near destruction. There'll be nothing to eat; and with advances in hygiene, sanitation, inoculations, the babies will be so many that it will be disastrous, with everyone being of venerable age and eminent virtue. (Loud laughter). . . . Perhaps this government should establish a department, establish a planned birth department—would that be a good idea? (Loud laughter) Or how about establishing a committee, a birth control committee, to serve as a government organ, [or we could] organize a people's group? Organize people's groups to advocate [birth control]. Since [we] need to solve a few technical problems, [we will have to] provide funds, think up methods, propagandize.[56]

In October 1957, Mao reiterated these views at the Third Plenum of the Eighth CCP Central Committee, with provincial, municipal, and county cadres in attendance. By this juncture, the anti-rightist campaign was well under way, intellectuals who had advocated birth control were under attack, and leftist political momentum was building rapidly. Yet Mao's growing ambition for exceptionally rapid economic gains had not altered his views on birth planning. In summary comments at the plenum, Mao said:

55. See Mao Zedong, "On the Correct Handling of Contradictions among the People," in Roderick MacFarquhar, Timothy Cheek, and Eugene Wu, eds., *The Secret Speeches of Chairman Mao* (Cambridge, 1989), 160–62.
56. MacFarquhar et al., *Secret Speeches,* 159–60. The fact that Mao's comments elicited loud laughter should not be misinterpreted. Even in the early 1980s male party cadres were still prone to giggle and titter when the subject of family planning was raised. The high-level cadres who heard this speech were most likely moved to laughter by a combination of Mao's manner, their own embarrassment, and their generally dismissive attitude toward the subject. For high-level male cadres, birth control not only remained a highly controversial subject, it left them nervous and embarrassed when raised in public. Birth control might be an appropriate topic for the Women's Congress, but not for them.

[As for] population control, [if we] have three years of experimental propaganda, three years of popularization, and four years of universal implementation, this is also a ten year plan. Otherwise, if we wait until the population reaches 800 million to carry it out, it will be too late. [We must] achieve planned births step by step.

He elaborated in a second speech:

In the future, China will become the country with the highest production level in the world. Currently, some counties have already reached 1000 *jin* per *mu*, are we capable or not of raising it to 2000 *jin* per *mu* in half a century? In the future will it be 800 *jin* per *mu* north of the Yellow River, 1000 *jin* per *mu* north of the Wei River, and 2000 *jin* per *mu* south of the Wei River? To reach that target by the beginning of the twenty-first century, we still have several decades; perhaps we don't need that much time. We rely on intensive cultivation in order to eat. If there are a few more people, there will still be food to eat. I think a per capita average of three *mu* of land is too much. If in the future there are only a few *fen* [per capita] there will be enough to eat. Of course, there still must be birth control, I don't mean to encourage births.
   . . . There is also a ten-year plan for planned births. There is no need to go propagate it in minority regions and sparsely populated localities. Even in places with a large population, [we] must carry out experiments, gradually popularize [it], gradually achieve universal planned births. [We] must carry out public education on planned birth, nothing other than a free airing of views, a great debate. With respect to births, mankind is in a state of anarchy, the self is unable to control the self. In the future we want to achieve the complete planning of births, but without a societal strength, unless everyone agrees, unless everyone does it together, then it won't work.[57]

Mao's insistence on the need for birth planning, not simply birth control, and his description of human reproduction as an anarchic and uncontrolled process, set his words apart from those of other leaders and mark him as the author of the birth planning doctrine. By framing the issue in this way, birth planning as a goal was separated from the question of whether China's large population was or was not an asset and from the increasingly rancorous debate over China's economic development strategy. If population planning was desirable for the same reasons that economic planning was desirable, if anarchic and unregulated human reproduction was as "anti-socialist" as anarchy in the economic realm, then the issue was no longer

---

57. Mao Zedong, "Zuo gemingde zujinpai," in *Mao Zedong xuanji*, vol. 5 (Beijing, 1977), 469, 471. A *jin* is 500 grams or 1.1 pounds; 1000 *jin* is about half a ton. A *mu* is one-sixth of an acre.

"overpopulation." The question was how to bring birth planning and material planning into balance.

The passage also demonstrates that Mao's commitment to birth control and planning coexisted with his growing optimism about rapid agricultural advances. It is true that Mao was far more sanguine about China's large population than other leaders were. Rather than showing Mao as torn between his faith in the masses as a productive asset and his advocacy of birth planning, however, the passage reveals his singular confidence in the combined processes of unified planning, propaganda, and grassroots party mobilization as key to the overall mission of socialist development. Birth planning was not to be equated with a pessimistic view of China's productive capacity or with the need for a fertility reduction campaign or even with the special needs and burdens of women in the revolution. Birth planning was one part of a desired pattern of unified social organization that Mao increasingly believed to be within reach.

Mao's vision began to crystallize in 1958, when the combined momentum of progressive planning and the anti-rightist campaign culminated in the Great Leap Forward, a utopian political and economic movement that relied on mass mobilization and decentralization to achieve exaggerated and unrealistic production goals.[58] As momentum for the Great Leap started to build, it became increasingly difficult to express reservations about China's capacity for a rapid breakthrough to advanced socialism and communism. As a result, those who had warned of the negative consequences of population growth became vulnerable politically, and high-level party opponents of the birth control policy went on the attack, denigrating supporters of the anti-natalist policy as reactionary enemies. Most birth control advocates retreated from their positions in an effort to blunt the force of the attack, but Ma Yinchu, a nonparty intellectual, a delegate to the National People's Congress (NPC), and the author of a 1957 tract entitled "New Population Theory," refused to back down. As a result, he was targeted by Mao and took the brunt of the attack. In 1959 Ma was branded as a rightist.[59]

In similar fashion the political momentum created by the Great Leap Forward led to exaggerated estimates for increased agricultural production, leading Mao to greater optimism about China's population and the capacity to maintain an adequate food-grain supply. In contrast to his statements in 1957, by August 1958 his public stance on population had shifted.

58. These principles are discussed in detail in Harding, *Organizing China,* 169–77.
59. For the text of Ma's *New Population Theory,* see Ma Yinchu, "Xin renkou lun," in Peng Peiyun, ed., *Zhongguo jihua shengyu quanshu* [Encyclopedia of birth planning in China] (Beijing, 1996), 551–57.

Rather than emphasizing the need for state intervention to promote birth control and planning, at the Beidaihe conference he advocated a more relaxed approach:

> [Our] views on population should change. In the past I said that [we] could manage with 800 million. Now I think that one billion plus would be no cause for alarm. This shouldn't be recommended for people with many children. When [people's] level of education increases, [they] will really practice birth control.[60]

This newfound optimism, and the overall tenor of the Great Leap Forward, account for the collapse of the birth control campaign in 1958. Yet Mao never went so far as to fully repudiate either birth control or birth planning, just their anti-natalist goals. When the grand mobilizations of the Great Leap subsided, therefore, the idea of birth planning remained intact. With its impeccable political credentials—Mao's personal endorsement—it provided the perfect ideological defense for a renewed attack on population growth.

60. Mao Zedong, "Talks at Beidaihe Conference," August 17, 1958, in MacFarquhar et al., *Secret Speeches*, 403.

3

Planning Population Growth: The Political Economy of State Intervention

The economic collapse that occurred in the wake of the Great Leap Forward brought an end to the overt debates on population control. There were two reasons for this.

First, by the early 1960s more fundamental issues preoccupied Beijing. In the aftermath of the Great Leap, the debate over China's development strategy was even more charged and divisive than it had been in the 1950s, so much so that basic questions about what direction to take on economic and social policy were closely linked to fundamental political questions about the purity and discipline of the party and the future of the revolution. In that larger context, the issue of promoting birth control, however strong the sentiments it evoked, became peripheral to the major political struggles of the day.

Second, proponents of population control now had a theoretical rationale on which they could securely base an anti-natalist policy. The doctrine of birth planning, coined by no less an authority than Mao himself, could not be attacked as a Malthusian, reactionary, and pessimistic stance. On the contrary, with its utopian vision of a society in which reproduction would adjust to collective needs and economic capacities, it was the epitome of revolutionary socialist thinking. Anti-natalist arguments were still vulnerable to political attack, but the principle of birth planning was not.

Freed from that political threat, and motivated by mounting economic concerns, systematic steps were taken during the 1960s and '70s to translate principle into practice, to make birth planning an integral part of comprehensive economic planning. During the most radical period of the Cultural Revolution (from 1966 through 1969), those efforts were suspended, but these years were the exception, not the rule. For despite the escalating radicalism of this era, key central leaders remained fixed on one particular economic fear, the same fear that had been a motivating force behind the first birth control campaign, and a fear now dramatically reinforced by the devastating famine during the Great Leap. They feared that they could not feed the people; that they could never escape the shadow of hunger and malnutrition. The most immediate and important measure of progress on this problem was the grain supply. When grain production per capita was improving, fears receded and pressures for birth control relaxed. When per capita supplies of grain declined, fears escalated and pressures for birth control intensified dramatically. It was not just politics—the waxing and waning of radicalism—that had a decisive impact on the evolution of China's birth control program during this period. Both the revival and expansion of birth control efforts in the 1960s and the subsequent transition from advocacy of birth control to mandatory birth limitation in the 1970s were tied directly to China's unstable performance on grain production. The logic of state intervention became ever more transparent: if grain production could not be raised rapidly enough to meet the growing demand, then birthrates had to be lowered.

The Great Leap Disaster

The Great Leap experiment brought famine and economic dislocation on an unprecedented scale. In 1960, official figures for grain production were 26 percent lower than they were in 1957 and average caloric intake dropped by 29 percent. No one knows the exact figures, but most estimates calculate that twenty to thirty million people died from famine or related causes in the 1958–60 period; in turn, the birthrate dropped precipitously.[1] As a result of these combined mortality and fertility shocks, in 1960 China suffered a net decline in population (see table 1). To cope with the disaster,

1. On the catastrophic impact of the Great Leap famine, see Jasper Becker, *Hungry Ghosts* (New York, 1996). See also Edward Friedman, Paul G. Pickowicz, and Mark Selden, with Kay Johnson, *Chinese Village, Socialist State* (New Haven, 1991), chap. 9; Basil Ashton, Kenneth Hill, Alan Piazza, and Robin Zeitz, "Famine in China, 1958–61," *Population and Development Review* 10, no. 4 (December 1984): 613–45; Judith Banister, "Shortage of Girls in China Today," *Journal of Population Research* 21, no. 1 (May 2004): 19–45; Dali Yang, *Calamity and Reform in China: State, Rural Society, and Institutional Change Since the Great Leap Famine* (Stanford: Stanford University Press, 1996); Xizhe Peng, "Demographic Consequences of the Great Leap Forward in China's Provinces," *Population and Development Review* 13 (1987): 639–70; Vaclav Smil, "China's Great Famine: Forty Years Later," *British Medical Journal* 319 (December 18, 1999): 1619–21; and Penny Kane, *Famine in China, 1959–61* (Basingstoke, Eng., 1988). For a demographic analysis of population data related to the Great Leap famine, see Judith Banister, *China's Changing Population* (Stanford, 1987).

TABLE 1. Population size and vital rates, 1949–2003

Year	Population (millions)	Birthrate (per thousand)	Mortality (per thousand)	Rate of natural increase (per thousand)	Total Fertility Rate
1949	541.67	36.00	20.00	16.00	6.14
1950	551.96	37.00	18.00	19.00	5.81
1951	563.00	37.80	17.80	20.00	5.70
1952	574.82	37.00	17.00	20.00	6.47
1953	587.96	37.00	14.00	23.00	6.05
1954	602.66	37.97	13.18	24.97	6.28
1955	614.65	32.60	12.28	20.32	6.26
1956	628.28	31.90	11.40	20.50	5.85
1957	645.63	34.03	10.80	23.23	6.41
1958	659.94	29.22	11.98	17.24	5.68
1959	672.07	24.78	14.59	10.19	4.30
1960	662.07	20.86	25.43	−4.57	4.02
1961	658.59	18.02	14.24	3.78	3.29
1962	672.95	37.01	10.02	26.99	6.02
1963	691.72	43.37	10.04	33.33	7.50
1964	704.99	39.14	11.50	27.64	6.18
1965	725.38	37.88	9.50	28.38	6.08
1966	745.42	35.05	8.83	26.22	6.26
1967	763.68	33.96	8.43	25.53	5.31
1968	785.34	35.59	8.21	27.38	6.45
1969	806.71	34.11	8.03	26.08	5.72
1970	829.92	33.43	7.60	25.83	5.81
1971	852.29	30.65	7.32	23.33	5.44
1972	871.77	29.77	7.61	22.16	4.98
1973	892.11	27.93	7.04	20.89	4.54
1974	908.59	24.82	7.34	17.48	4.17
1975	924.20	23.01	7.32	15.69	3.57
1976	937.17	19.91	7.25	12.66	3.24
1977	949.74	18.93	6.87	12.06	2.84
1978	962.59	18.25	6.25	12.00	2.72
1979	975.42	17.82	6.21	11.61	2.75
1980	987.05	18.21	6.34	11.87	2.24
1981	1000.72	20.91	6.36	14.55	2.63
1982	1016.54	22.28	6.60	15.68	2.87
1983	1030.08	20.19	6.90	13.29	2.42
1984	1043.57	19.90	6.82	13.08	2.35
1985	1058.51	21.04	6.78	14.26	2.20
1986	1075.07	22.43	6.86	15.57	2.42
1987	1093.00	23.33	6.72	16.61	2.59
1988	1110.26	22.37	6.64	15.73	2.31
1989	1127.04	21.58	6.54	15.04	2.25
1990	1143.33	21.06	6.67	14.39	2.17
1991	1158.23	19.68	6.70	12.98	2.01
1992	1171.71	18.24	6.64	11.60	1.86
1993	1185.17	18.09	6.64	11.45	1.85
1994	1198.50	17.70	6.49	11.21	1.84
1995	1211.21	17.12	6.57	10.55	1.7/2.1[a]

TABLE 1. Population size and vital rates, 1949–2003 (*continued*)

Year	Population (millions)	Birthrate (per thousand)	Mortality (per thousand)	Rate of natural increase (per thousand)	Total Fertility Rate
1996	1223.89	16.98	6.56	10.42	
1997	1236.26	16.57	6.51	10.06	
1998	1248.10	16.03	6.50	9.53	
1999	1257.86	14.64	6.46	8.18	
2000	1267.43	14.03	6.45	7.58	1.4/2.1[a]
2001	1276.27	13.38	6.43	6.95	
2002	1284.53	12.86	6.41	6.45	
2003	1292.27	12.41	6.40	6.01	

Sources: Zhongguo tongjiju (National Bureau of Statistics), *Zhongguo tongji nianjian, 2004* [Statistical Yearbook of China, 2004]. *Zhongguo renkou he jihua shengyu nianjian, 2004* [2004 China Population and Family Planning Yearbook], 643.

[a]Because of the deteriorating quality of the data from the mid-1980s, the official figures for the 1990s and early 2000s, provided by the National Bureau of Statistics, are believed to underestimate substantially the total fertility rate. The total fertility rate for 2000 was initially estimated at 1.4, well below the replacement level of 2.1. Chinese demographers estimate that the actual total fertility rate was about 1.8 in the early 2000s. On the deteriorating quality of the data, see "Report on the Deterioration of Chinese National Population Statistics and Analysis of Potential Policy Responses," *Zhongguo jihua shengyu nianjian, 1996* (Beijing: Guojia jihua shengyu weiyuanhui, 1996), 207–8. For a summary of this report and the problems of data collection, see U.S. Embassy, Beijing, "PRC Census Misses One-Third of Births: Chinese Demographers Explain Why," online at http://www.usembassy-china.org/sandt/fert12b.htm.

Liu Shaoqi, Zhou Enlai, Chen Yun, and Deng Xiaoping—the architects of the post-Leap recovery, turned away from the Maoist "high tide" approach to economic construction. Their immediate task was to bring an end to suffering, scarcity, and fear by increasing grain supplies and improving the distribution system. Difficult as that was, the long-run task was much harder—how permanently to improve living standards and consumption levels at a time when agricultural production could not keep pace with population growth.

To ease the immediate food problem, the leadership relaxed radical agricultural policies and reorganized the people's communes created during the Great Leap. The communes had been created by combining several or many collectives into a single territorial unit with a unified administration for political and economic work. In the martial atmosphere of the Great Leap, the commune was subdivided into units called production brigades (roughly equivalent to the preexisting collectives), and brigades were further divided into production teams (often corresponding to the natural villages of the pre-Communist era, or, in other areas, to neighborhoods within the villages). By 1960, however, the famine and dislocation was so severe that the collective organization broke down in many areas and private agriculture reemerged spontaneously. To cope with this organizational collapse, new regulations were issued in 1962 establishing the production team as the primary unit of accounting and distribution and prohibiting commune and brigade cadres from unauthorized requisitions of team labor and resources.[2] To further stimulate the agricultural economy, household and cooperative sideline activities were also encouraged. Banks, credit cooperatives, and taxation offices were instructed to develop policies conducive to the growth of agricultural sidelines.[3]

Emergency steps were also taken to stem the flow of peasants to the cities. Between 1957 and the end of 1960, the urban population increased from 99 million to 130 million; a year later, it had climbed to 149 million.[4] To prevent this "blind" migration, in 1958 the state had adopted new regulations on household registration designed to control rural-urban migration.[5] The regulations established a system to monitor peasant movement and ration access to food grain and other basic supplies. Under this system, peasants who could not produce an authorized work or study permit were ineligible for urban ration coupons that were required for local purchases. Deprived of food and other necessities, they had no choice but to return to, and remain in, the village.

Under normal conditions, these regulations might have been effective in containing peasant migration. But the period between 1958 and 1961 was anything but normal. Under the pressures of the massive mobilization of labor in 1958–59 and the subsequent economic collapse, the regulations could not prevent a desperate flow to the cities, putting tremendous pressure on the state to increase grain procurement for urban areas. Increased procurement not only meant increased cost at a time of financial disaster. More important, it meant an increased demand for grain in urban areas at a time when per capita production had sunk below 1949 levels. With rural consumption at famine levels, increased state procurements placed peasant lives in greater jeopardy and undercut the new policies designed to boost rural production. Although the state had drawn on grain reserves to supplement procurements in 1960 and 1961, by mid-1961 the reserves were in danger of depletion. In addition, increased procurements reduced the

2. The document is known as the "Sixty Articles on Agriculture." For a draft of the text, see "Regulations on the Work in the Rural People's Communes (Revised Draft)," *Issues and Studies* 15, no. 10 (October 1979): 93–111; and 15, no. 12 (December 1979): 106–15.

3. Liu and Wu, eds., *China's Socialist Economy*, 297–98.

4. Chen Yun, "Dongyuan chengshi renkou xia xiang," in *Chen Yun wenxuan, 1956–1965*, 154.

5. "Zhonghua renmin gongheguo hukou dengji tiaolie," in *Zhongguo renkou nianjian, 1985*, 83–84. Earlier versions of these regulations, plus an explanation of the 1958 regulations by the minister of public security, may be found in the same source, 79–82 and 86–89.

amounts retained in the countryside for seed fodder and sidelines, and forced the state to increase the level of grain imports.[6]

To cope with this procurement crisis, two initiatives were undertaken. First, the leadership decided in May 1961 to reduce the urban population by twenty million over three years, with ten million being transferred back to the countryside during 1961 alone. A year later they revised the target, calling for a reduction of an additional twenty million in 1962 and 1963.[7] At the same time, a new campaign was launched to encourage students to leave their urban homes and resettle in rural areas. Although this campaign was promoted as an opportunity for young people to demonstrate their loyalty to the Chinese revolution through rural service, it was linked closely to the economic crisis. Drastic declines in the agricultural sector led to a slowdown in industrial production during the 1961–63 period. This, in turn, led to a series of decisions to reduce the size of the urban labor force, both administrative staff and workers. Those conditions virtually eliminated employment prospects for graduates, while food shortages made it imperative to reduce the urban population. It was in that context that the _xiafang_ ("down to the countryside") campaign was launched. Urban youth were urged under heavy political pressure to volunteer for rural relocation, while rural youth who had completed their education were "returned" to their villages or townships. As a result of the campaign, about a million urban youth were "sent down" between 1962 and 1966, while many more rural youth were returned to the countryside.[8]

Complicating the food crisis was China's determination to pay off debts to the Soviet Union as rapidly as possible. Between 1957 and 1960, Sino-Soviet relations had progressively deteriorated, culminating in the withdrawal of all Soviet personnel and assistance in 1960. Coming at a time of economic crisis, the Soviet withdrawal placed new pressures on the domestic budget just when China was least prepared to take the burden. As tensions continued to escalate under Mao's accusations of Soviet revisionism, China sought for political reasons to pay off its debt as quickly as possible. Yet payment came primarily in light industrial and agricultural goods, straining supplies of staple foods and goods at a time of great scarcity.[9]

The combined burden of debt repayment, urban food consumption, and

6. Chen Yun outlined each of these dilemmas in his 1961 speech at a government work meeting. See Chen Yun, "Dongyuan chengshi renkou xia xiang," 154–56.

7. At the same time, urban grain rations were reduced in order to increase rural consumption. Liu and Wu, _China's Socialist Economy_, 290–91 and 294.

8. On the _xiafang_ campaign, see Thomas Bernstein, _Up to the Mountains and Down to the Villages_ (New Haven, 1977).

9. For a discussion of changing export-import patterns during this period, see Carl Riskin, _China's Political Economy_ (Oxford, 1987), chaps. 6 and 7.

reduced output severely strained the economy in 1961–62, but by the end of 1962 the worst of the crisis had passed. Progress was slow, however, and the depth and gravity of the setback was clear. Per capita grain consumption in 1962 averaged only 81 percent of the 1957 level, and pork and cotton cloth supplies averaged only 43 and 57 percent, respectively.[10] Industrial output value continued to decline, and the shortage of goods continued. It was not until 1966 that grain production surpassed 1957 levels, and even then, there was little to cheer about. Per capita grain production still lagged behind the levels that had been achieved a decade earlier, despite the death toll from famine and disease during the Great Leap (see table 2).

The Revival of Birth Planning

It was in this context that the issue of population growth reemerged on the central agenda. In the spring of 1962, the leadership publicly reaffirmed birth planning work, and a directive on urban work issued in October 1962 called for the promotion of birth control.[11] In December of that year, a Central Committee directive ordered the revival of birth control programs nationwide.[12] The directive, entitled "On Enthusiastically Promoting Planned Births," began by declaring:

It is the set policy during our country's socialist construction that birth control be promoted in the cities and in densely populated rural areas, and that there be appropriate control of the rate of population growth, *in order to gradually move the birth problem from a state of anarchy to one of planning.*[13]

The directive went on to establish the link between birth planning and the process of planned socialist development, and to refute any allegation that the policy was Malthusian. It also called on party committees and governments at all levels to place birth planning at the top of their work agenda, and it gave a mandate to party committees to organize all relevant departments in the development of a comprehensive birth planning program.

The new birth planning directive was a direct outgrowth of the 1958–60

10. Liu and Wu, *China's Socialist Economy*, 299.
11. Shi, *Zhongguo jihua shengyu huodong shi,* 147; Ma et al., *Zhongguo gongchandang zhizheng sishinian,* 233.
12. Ma et al., *Zhongguo gongchandang zhizheng zishinian,* 226. An abbreviated text of the directive, "Zhonggong zhongyang, guowuyuan guanyu renzhen tichang jihua shengyude zhishi" [Central Committee and State Council instructions on enthusiastically promoting planned birth], may also be found in *Zhongguo renkou nianjian, 1985,* 14.
13. *Zhongguo renkou nianjian, 1985,* 14 (emphasis added).

TABLE 2. Grain production and population growth, selected years

Year	Grain production (million tons)	Grain output per capita (kg)	Grain output per capita index (1957 = 100)
1952	112.18	288	94
1957	195.05	306	100
1960	136.83	215	70
1962	160.00	240	70
1965	194.52	272	89
1967	194.55	283	92
1970	239.96	291	95
1972	240.41	269	88
1975	284.52	307	100
1977	282.73	297	97
1978	304.77	320	105
1979	304.75	325	106
1980	332.20	328	107
1981	325.02	328	107
1982	354.50	341	110
1983	387.28	376	122
1984	407.31	395	129
1985	379.11	360	118
1986	391.51	367	120
1987	402.98	371	121
1988	394.08	357	117
1989	407.55	364	119
1990	446.24	393	128
1991	435.29	378	124
1992	442.65	379	124
1993	456.48	387	126
1994	445.10	373	122
1995	466.61	387	126
1996	504.53	414	135
1997	494.17	401	131
1998	512.29	412	134
1999	508.39	406	134
2000	462.18	366	120
2001	452.64	356	116
2002	457.06	357	117

Sources: For years 1949–87, Zhongguo tongji nianjian, 1988, 248; for 1987 to present, *Zhonghua renmin gongheguo nongye bu, Zhongguo nongye fazhan baogao*, 2003, Table 11, at http://www.agri.gov.cn/sjzl/baipsh/WB2003.htm.

grain and food crisis and a key component of the economic recovery strategy. Rather than merely revive the 1955–57 birth control policy, this directive marked a turning point in several respects. First, during the 1950s, birth control efforts had been directed toward "densely populated areas" and had focused overwhelmingly on a few major cities. The language of the new directive made clear that all urban areas were now included in the birth control and planning efforts. More important, it stated specifically that birth control work was to be propagated in densely populated *rural* areas. In the short run, this shift did little more than encourage the extension of birth planning into the suburbs of major cities, but it nevertheless signaled an intent to spread the birth control campaign to the countryside. Second, the directive unequivocally legitimized birth control and birth planning by stating that it was the established policy for the period of China's socialist development. This blanket endorsement, coming so closely on the heels of the anti-Malthusian diatribes that permeated the Great Leap Forward, left little room to doubt the seriousness of the central leadership's intentions. Any doubt that did remain was quashed by the demand that all party and government leaders make birth planning part of their most urgent business and organize accordingly. Third, and most important, the directive formally embraced the concept of "birth planning" and advocated birth control as a means to "appropriately control the rate of population growth."[14] Using Mao's own words to reject the anarchy of unplanned human reproduction in a planned economy and society, the leaders of the economic recovery were able to fortify themselves against the inevitable opposition from leftist critics.[15]

The implications of the new state strategy of planning rates of population growth had immediate and far-reaching consequences. Party and government leaders, as well as all relevant sectoral departments and mass organizations, had been ordered to place this work at the top of the agenda; they had also been directed to pursue birth control with the goal of controlling population growth. But how were these directions to be implemented? How was progress to be measured? And how were basic-level cadres to be mobilized to carry out this work? Answers to these questions were provided nine

---

14. Ibid.

15. I do not wish to imply that Mao was among the potential critics of this more radical deployment of the birth planning concept, but given the ferocity of the attack on birth control during the Great Leap Forward, it is inconceivable that all opposition had died away. I have found no evidence that Mao objected, however, either at this juncture or subsequently. Mao, of course, was increasingly preoccupied with what he considered to be more fundamental political questions.

months later, at the second urban work conference held in September 1963. Convened by the Central Committee and the State Council, the monthlong meeting produced the first set of short-term and long-term planning targets for urban population growth, setting the stage for all subsequent planning. Propelled by sample surveys in 1962 and 1963 indicating a fertility rebound from the losses suffered during the Great Leap Forward (with the annual population growth rate up to 33 per 1,000 in 1963, and a total fertility rate of 7.5), it was agreed that during the remaining three years of economic readjustment (1963–65) the annual rate of urban population growth should be brought under 20 per 1,000.[16] During the third and fourth five-year plans (1966–70, and 1971–75, respectively), urban growth rates were scheduled to continue their descent, with an average annual drop of 1 per 1,000. By the end of the third five-year plan, the target was set for under 15 per 1,000; the fourth five-year plan target was under 10 per 1,000.[17] The plan, in short, would unfold in two stages: first, a three-year campaign to induce a rapid drop in urban birth rates, and second, a steady annual decrease in the population growth rate of 1 per 1,000 over the following ten years.

To support these goals, several additional steps were taken. First, a work conference on population statistics was convened by the Ministry of Public Security and the State Statistical Bureau in December 1962; in March 1963, new regulations on statistical work were drawn up, and population was listed as the first of twelve major categories of statistics that were to be covered by the bureau.[18] Second, at a work conference on the health of women and children, it was decided that "birth planning technical work" was the most important task for guaranteeing women's health. This led to another conference in early 1964 on "birth planning technical work," where new, less restrictive regulations on "birth control operations" (sterilizations, abortions, IUD insertions) were drawn up and the prices for contraceptives reduced.[19] Third, the Birth Planning Office in the State Council was established in early 1964, and similar offices were established in some provinces and municipalities.[20] And fourth, a propaganda campaign promoting late

16. Deng and Ma, eds., *Dangdai zhongguo weisheng*, 234; Fang Weizhong, ed., *Zhonghua renmin gongheguo jingji dashiji, 1949–1980* (Beijing, 1984), 366–67.
17. Fang, *Jingji dashiji*, 367.
18. "Jianguo sanshiwunianlai renkou huodong dashiji," in *Zhongguo renkou nianjian, 1985*, 1266.
19. Deng and Ma, eds., *Dangdai zhongguo weisheng*, 235.
20. Shi, *Zhongguo jihua shengyu huodong shi*, 148; Deng and Ma, eds., *Dangdai zhongguo weisheng*, 235.

marriage and a two-child family was launched. Justification for the campaign was provided by the second national census (1964), which registered a population of 694.5 million.[21]

The driving force behind this mobilization drive was Premier Zhou Enlai. Between 1963 and 1966, Zhou spoke frequently and forcefully on the issue of birth control, seeking to reinforce the Maoist concept of birth planning against leftist attacks. In February 1963, for example, he defended it in a speech to the National Agricultural Science and Technology Work Conference, arguing that it was a "shortcoming" (*duanchu*) of the socialist system that it did not have a "population plan." Zhou explained this by noting that neither Marx nor Lenin had confronted the problem; their writings therefore offered no guidance or solutions. He called for further research on the question, and stressed the importance of the issue not just for health work but also for agricultural work. He also called for a major propaganda effort, focusing on four benefits of birth planning: improving the health of mothers, improving the health of infants, strengthening the education of children, and reducing national burdens. This formulation downplayed the embarrassing problem of stagnant grain production and continuing food shortages, while acknowledging obliquely the economic and social burden of population growth. It was easier and more positive to claim the benefits of the program for women and children, and opponents would find it difficult to challenge a program justified as an improvement to maternal and infant care. Zhou's real concern, however, was to reduce population growth and regulate it in predictable ways. This concern was most clearly revealed in his concluding remark: "In my opinion, after having two children, it is best to undergo sterilization." He went on to advocate male sterilization, urging propagandists to "create the right atmosphere" for it.[22]

Speaking at a meeting of the Standing Committee of the National People's Congress in July 1963, Zhou pressed his theme, stressing the importance of late marriage and childbirth. He argued that the postponement of marriage would allow young people to concentrate their energy on socialist construction, and he called for the repeal of all policies that encouraged early marriage and childbirth, including the distribution of cloth rations on a per capita basis and the provision of additional rations upon marriage. Later that month, in a speech to high school graduates, Zhou raised the issue again. On this occasion, speaking to young people approaching marriage age, he defended the birth control policy against charges that it was Malthusian. Noting that Malthus relied on war and

21. Shi, *Zhongguo jihua shengyu huodong shi*, 150.
22. Ibid., 145–46.

pestilence to solve the population problem, Zhou said, "We can't rely on war to solve the population problem, and we can't rely on pestilence, and we certainly can't rely on overseas developments. . . . [Instead] we must study advanced experience."[23] Remarkably, he cited Japan as a country whose achievements in reducing birthrates deserved China's attention. He advocated sending experts to Japan to study their methods or inviting Japanese experts to China. He stressed that China could not simply borrow another model, however, but would have to create one suited to its own conditions.

By late 1964, Zhou seemed to have fixed on the Japanese experience as the yardstick for measuring China's progress toward birth planning. In particular, he was struck by the fact that Japan's annual population growth rate had dropped to about 10 per 1,000.[24] During 1965 he spoke on several occasions about striving for a similar goal in China by the end of the twentieth century. Speaking to a September 1965 meeting of the Chinese Medical Association devoted to obstetrics and gynecology, Zhou is reported to have said:

> We need to carry out propaganda and education on birth planning. On the one hand, we need to have some special regulations, for example, on salaries, housing, supplies, and the like. On the other hand, we need voluntarism, and absolutely should not resort to coercion. We need both voluntarism and some restraint. How to enable our country's population to be capable of planned birth, this is a great undertaking. If the entire society, based on the needs of birth planning, is able to control the rate of net population increase at 1 percent by the end of the twentieth century, that would be terrific.[25]

This same message was given at the National Planning Conference later that month; and at a central work meeting in October, Zhou stressed that achieving this goal would require extending birth planning work to the countryside.[26]

Zhou's shift of emphasis to rural implementation in late 1965 was the product of three developments. The first was the continued increase in birthrates between 1962 and 1965, peaking at 38 per 1,000 in 1965. This

23. Ibid., 146.
24. For a brief overview of Japan's family planning program between 1945 and 1965, see Minoru Muramatsu, "Japan," in *Family Planning and Population Programs*, ed. Bernard Berelson et al. (Chicago, 1967), 7–20. See also Tiana Norgren, *Abortion before Birth Control* (Princeton, 2001).
25. *Zhou Enlai xuanji*, 2:445; Shi, *Zhongguo jihua shengyu huodong shi*, 152.
26. Shi, *Zhongguo jihua shengyu huodong shi*, 151–52.

translated into an average fertility rate of six births per woman of childbearing age and contrasted sharply with figures for grain production. In 1965, per capita production still lagged significantly behind 1953 levels (see table 2). These trends demonstrated all too well the effect of population growth on economic performance and revealed the great gap between policy-making efforts at the center and practical results at the grassroots. Despite the propaganda about birth control and the authorization of public health units to disseminate birth control information and supplies, resistance and apathy were rampant among health workers, a climate that discouraged couples from approaching the subject. To make any progress toward reducing birthrates, that climate had to change, and more important, the birth control effort would have to be extended to the rural population.

The second development was the prospect of an improved rural health care delivery system. Fed up with the urban bias of the Ministry of Health (MOH) in June 1965 Mao demanded a shift of emphasis from advanced research to providing primary care for workers and peasants. He proposed the creation of medical teams to be sent to the countryside to serve the peasantry. This concept emerged full blown in 1968 as the "barefoot doctor" system, in which young people with minimal training functioned as paramedics in villages, living in the community they served. Although the primary motivation for the barefoot doctor system was to provide rudimentary health care to the peasant population, during 1965 both Mao and Zhou linked the development of the system to the birth planning policy, instructing medical teams bound for the countryside to offer birth control services.[27]

The third development was the decision to launch a socialist education campaign (SEC) and, more generally, the growing tension in 1963–66 over the direction of China's development policy. Despite the success of the recovery program, by 1962 agricultural policies had come under attack for their emphasis on material incentives. Mao and his allies criticized the household contracting arrangements that had developed in some regions, as well as the new emphasis on small-scale private sidelines, free markets, and other material incentives. More fundamentally, the Sino-Soviet split had led Mao to become increasingly preoccupied with the threat of revisionism. His critique of the Khrushchev regime led him to conclude that the CCP was vulnerable to degeneration from within and that the revolution was vulnerable to a capitalist restoration. As his anxiety grew, he stressed the primacy

27. Ibid., 150–53. On developments in the Ministry of Health during this period, see David M. Lampton, *The Politics of Medicine in China* (Boulder, Colo., 1977), chaps. 6–8.

of class struggle, political education, and cadre rectification, concerns that were targeted by the SEC.[28]

A primary focus of the SEC was grassroots cadres in the countryside. Work teams were sent in to villages to "rectify" party branches and cadre ranks, rooting out cadres and peasants found guilty of petty corruption or capitalist economic activity. More broadly, however, the SEC was part of a resurgent leftism that threatened the moderate economic policies and developmental goals that had fueled the post-Leap recovery. The architects of the recovery, Liu Shaoqi, Deng Xiaoping, and Zhou Enlai sought to dampen the effect of the campaign, channeling it through the party organization to control its content and political effect. One example of that approach was Zhou's effort in 1965 to use the SEC to promote the less political and more pragmatic agenda of birth planning. On two occasions, Zhou called for adding birth planning to the content of the "socialist education" being given to rural cadres and peasants. Moreover, there is some evidence that Mao lent his support to the idea. Speaking to a medical team from Tianjin, Mao applauded their local initiative to provide birth control free of charge and urged them to carry birth planning to the countryside after they developed a rural health network.[29]

In short, the focus on rural health care delivery came at an auspicious time, providing an opening through which Zhou could push for the extension of the birth planning campaign into the countryside and simultaneously push for including birth planning in the national planning process. In March 1965, he called on the MOH to develop a comprehensive plan for birth planning, and at the National Work Conference in September he reiterated the call to bring population growth down to under 1 percent annually by the end of the century. This call was repeated at the National Planning Conference in November. It is clear, however, that Zhou continued to encounter resistance. At a Politburo meeting held during the National Planning Conference, Zhou felt compelled to make theoretical arguments again, distinguishing among birth planning, Malthusianism, and capitalist-style birth control programs. Arguing that China must "carry out birth control and oppose Malthusianism," he called birth control "progressive" and "communist," insisting that "proletarian birth planning" was "not the same as capitalist-style birth control for the sake of individual pleasure."[30]

28. For complete descriptions of the socialist education campaign, see Richard Baum and Frederick Teiwes, *Ssu-Ch'ing* (Berkeley, 1968); see also Anita Chan, Richard Madsen, and Jonathan Unger, *Chen Village* (Berkeley, 1984), chap. 2.
29. Shi, *Zhongguo jihua shengyu huodong shi*, 151.
30. Ibid., 152.

Continuing bureaucratic and political resistance prevented the incorporation of birth control goals into the third five-year plan (1966–70). Instead, a Central Committee directive was issued in January 1966 stating that the overall population goal of the third five-year plan was to hold the population within eight hundred million by 1970, a figure in keeping with the goals outlined in 1963.[31] The decision to issue a directive, while omitting the goals from the FYP, suggests that birth planning remained controversial in the increasingly tense political climate of 1965. Placing birth planning goals in the economic plan would have fully legitimized the concept and made cadres at all levels formally responsible for population targets. That mandate would have forced them to create an oversight apparatus to manage childbearing and to go public with a major propaganda campaign. This step also would have forced cadres in county towns and other urban districts to address birth planning, something that many were unwilling to do. Moreover, such a nationwide campaign would have severely taxed an already inadequate birth control and contraceptive supply system, while further investment in that system would have detracted from investment in the training of barefoot doctors and the treatment of basic diseases.

The Cultural Revolution and the Deepening of Birth Planning

Disagreements over the pursuit of birth planning were marginal to the more fundamental issues that split the leadership in 1966. By May of that year, the Great Proletarian Cultural Revolution, Mao Zedong's revolutionary assault on revisionists and capitalist-roaders, had been launched. Mao's open call for waging class struggle against capitalist-roaders in the highest reaches of the party marked the ascendancy of the radical line on politics and economics, the descent of Chinese society into a witch hunt for political "ghosts and monsters," the breakdown of regular governmental activity, and the takeover of local party organs by Red Guard factions of various political stripes. By late 1968, the scope of disorder and factionalism led Mao to decide to rein in the revolutionary movement, but the radical line espoused by Mao's Cultural Revolution allies was institutionalized in state policies that were enforced until the mid-1970s.[32]

Despite the political instability of this period, the birth planning program

31. Ibid., 153.
32. On the politics of the Cultural Revolution, see Roderick MacFarquhar, *Origins of the Cultural Revolution 3: The Coming of the Cataclysm, 1961–1966* (New York, 1997); William A. Joseph, Christine P. W. Wong, and David Zweig, eds., *New Perspectives on the Cultural Revolution* (Cambridge, 1991); White, *Policies of Chaos.*

survived and, after 1969, flourished. In a reversal of the experience of the 1950s, when radical economic policies brought a quick end to the birth control campaign, the late 1960s and early 1970s was a period when birth planning went hand in hand with the implementation of radical economic policies. The first attempts to revive birth planning work came in 1969, as the most intense and violent phase of the Cultural Revolution was coming to an end.[33] During the remainder of the Cultural Revolution decade (1966–76), steady progress was made in creating a birth planning bureaucracy and implementing an increasingly aggressive birth limitation program.

Birth planning survived and gained new urgency in this radical climate for several reasons. First, it received the aggressive support and patronage of Zhou Enlai and, after his political rehabilitation in 1974, of Deng Xiaoping. Mao initially remained quiet on the subject, but he put up no resistance.

Second, radical policies adopted during the Cultural Revolution strained the economy and made population control appear more urgent. Introduced in the late 1960s, these policies marked a shift from the recovery policies of the 1961–65 period in favor of more radical measures emphasizing moral over material incentives, self-sufficiency over specialization, and collective power and investment over private gain and consumption. In agriculture, the result was an emphasis on grain production as the "key link," that is, increasing grain production in order to make grain-deficit areas self-sufficient. This grain-first policy reduced the sown area of cash crops; the extreme hostility toward private economic activity led to the elimination of private plots and all sideline activities. There was also renewed pressure to advance to higher levels of collective organization, and the model Dazhai brigade emerged as the new symbol of successful rural development.[34] These policies did not achieve their intended results (see table 2). Grain production per capita dropped by 9 percent between 1966 and 1969, and then stagnated at 1966 levels between 1970 and 1972.[35]

Third, the threat of war with the United States or the Soviet Union led to a decision to mobilize capital and human labor for the development of major industrial projects in China's interior. A key goal of this "third front" was to strengthen national security by adding a third layer to China's military preparedness. Rather than predicate survival on the ability to withstand assaults on the industrialized coastal region (the first front), or the agricultural heartland just inside that region (the second front), developing a third front in the deep interior regions of China (stretching from Yunnan

33. Shi, *Zhongguo jihua shengyu huodong shi*, 155–56.
34. The definitive study of this issue is David Zweig, *Agrarian Radicalism in China, 1968–1981* (Cambridge, 1989).
35. *Zhongguo tongji nianjian, 1983* (Beijing, 1984), 158 and 393.

and Sichuan in the south to Gansu and Ningxia in the north) would disperse China's economic assets and maximize the ability to withstand a major assault. To facilitate rapid development, decision-making authority was decentralized to regional or local officials, resulting in a loss of central control over labor movement and the degree and pace of local investment.[36] As a result, between 1964 and 1975 the urban nonagricultural population grew by at least fifteen million more than population growth rates alone would predict, even though the *xiafang* campaign to relocate students to the countryside reduced the urban population by about fifteen million during those same years. The state-employed labor force grew by nearly 80 percent during the same period. During the third FYP period, workers and employees added to the state payroll exceeded the planned figure by 7.5 million, and the trend of excess hiring continued in the early 1970s.[37]

The jump in urban population and state employment placed further strain on the food-grain supply system, which was already under tremendous pressure. In 1971, with per capita grain production stagnating, supply pressures in urban areas forced the state to procure far more grain than planned. The 1971 plan called for sales of 39.7 million tons of grain; in fact, 42.75 million tons were sold in 1971, and the figure increased to 44.9 million tons in 1972, a bad harvest year.[38] Meanwhile, the numbers of rural localities that were self-sufficient in grain were declining, forcing the state to resell an increasing amount of grain to grain-deficit villages.[39]

It was in this troubled economic climate that birth planning reemerged on the agenda in 1970. This was the third time an incipient grain crisis gave new urgency to the need for population control. But this time there was no ambiguity about the rationale behind it. Population control was now explicitly viewed as an economic issue and as a remedy for economic problems. If the numerator in the economic equation—the grain supply—could not be made to rise with sufficient speed, the denominator—the population base—would have to be squeezed. When economic planning resumed in

36. On the contours of this "third front" investment strategy, see Barry Naughton, "Industrial Policy during the Cultural Revolution: Military Preparation, Decentralization, and Leaps Forward," in Joseph, Wong, and Zweig, eds., *New Perspectives on the Cultural Revolution,* 153–82.

37. Liu and Wu, *China's Socialist Economy,* 366. During 1970 and 1971, 9.63 million new laborers were hired, more than three times what had been planned. Of these, six million came from the countryside. In 1972, the excessive hiring continued, despite central orders prohibiting local governments from exceeding hiring guidelines. In that year, three million more were added to the payroll, placing severe pressures on state finances by increasing the wage bill. Liu and Wu, *China's Socialist Economy,* 374.

38. Ibid., 374–75.

39. See Nicholas R. Lardy, *Agriculture in China's Economic Development* (Cambridge, 1983).

1970, therefore, Zhou Enlai included birth planning work in the draft outline program of the fourth five-year plan (1971–75), and he spoke pointedly at the National Planning Conference in February about the rapid growth of urban population in the late 1960s.[40] Later that year, he put the matter bluntly, arguing that "birth planning isn't a health question, it is a planning question. If you can't even plan the rate of population increase, how can you have any national plan?"[41] The outline FYP set a goal of reducing urban population growth to under 10 per 1,000 by 1975 and reducing the rural population growth rate to under 15 per 1,000. Given the failure to meet the population targets of the third FYP, meeting these targets would require a full percentage point drop in the rural growth rate, a feat that could only be accomplished through a massive campaign.

To help enforce this new standard, couples were urged to delay childbirth, wait longer between births, and have fewer children and healthier children (*wan, xi, shao*). Under this "later, longer, fewer" campaign, urban couples were urged to have no more than two children, and rural couples no more than three. Two parallel initiatives were launched during the early 1970s. First, a specialized birth planning apparatus was created, extending from central to local levels. In July 1971, the State Council issued a directive calling for the establishment of birth planning offices (*jihua shengyu bangongshi*) within the public health bureaucracy at each level of government.[42] Prior to that time, birth planning work had been coordinated through the Office of Maternal and Infant Health within the Ministry of Health. When the directive was issued, the immediate effect in most places was to divide the office into two separate units, upgrading the bureaucratic standing of birth planning work and personnel.

Second, beginning in August 1970 the government moved to subsidize family planning by providing free birth control supplies and offering reimbursement for the cost of medical procedures. Achieving that goal was complicated by the economic adjustments under way during this period, however. In the early 1970s, provinces controlled substantial revenues outside the central budget; they were instructed, therefore, to find revenues to cover the costs of contraceptives from their own nonbudgetary revenues. Not all provinces did so however, leading Zhou to complain in 1971 that contraceptives were being produced but not distributed in some areas, while in other areas there was no propaganda or birth planning effort. By 1974, Zhou had taken steps to recentralize financial power, and a new document

40. Shi, *Zhongguo jihua shengyu*, 157.
41. Liu Zheng, *Zhongguode renkou* (Beijing, 1982), 22; Shi, *Zhongguo jihua shengyu huodong shi*, 158.
42. Shi, *Zhongguo jihua shengyu huodong shi*, 160.

was issued allowing provinces to bill the central government for the full cost of contraceptives.[43] This policy sped up supply and distribution, since provinces had no budgetary reason for limiting the supply of contraceptives.

Despite these initiatives, however, it took three crucial, final steps to achieve full mobilization. The first was one final step toward integrating birth planning into the economic planning process. Although the outline fourth FYP included population targets, this plan had to be revised during 1971 and 1972 to compensate for overly ambitious economic targets. As a result, the annual plans for 1971 and 1972 were revised each year, and apparently they did not include specific annual targets for population growth. This omission left local leaders without clear-cut annual targets that could be used as a performance yardstick. In 1973, however, population growth targets were included in the annual economic plan for the first time, providing explicit instructions to all local governments to make birth planning a priority.[44]

The second step, also taken in 1973, was the creation of "birth planning leading small groups," that is, ad hoc committees of party and government leaders who were responsible for overseeing the work of birth planning in their area of administration. Unlike the specialized birth planning offices established in 1971, the leading small groups were made up of leading party and government cadres, usually deputy party secretaries and vice-governors. Whereas the birth planning offices were hampered by being just one more governmental bureau that reached only as far as the county bureaucracy, the leading groups put senior party and government leaders directly in charge of birth planning at each governmental level. Subordinate staff offices were created to support their work. They included representatives of every bureaucratic system involved in birth planning work and of relevant mass organizations such as the Women's Federation and the Communist Youth League.[45] Their function was to provide planning and joint coordination of birth planning work within their territorial jurisdiction and to guarantee that local officials would provide leadership to the effort, something that the birth planning offices could not do. To solve the problem of grassroots work, a similar form of ad hoc group was established within basic-level units. Factories, enterprises, neighborhoods, rural people's communes, and production brigades were all required to create a "birth planning work network" (*jihua shengyu gongzuo wang*). Most of the cadres who staffed this extensive system of offices lacked specific training in

---

43. Ibid., 167.
44. Ibid., 163; Deng and Ma, eds., *Dangdai zhongguo weisheng*, 236.
45. Shi, *Zhongguo jihua shengyu huodong shi*, 165–66; Ma et al., *Zhongguo gongchandang zhizheng sishinian*, 364.

birth planning work, and many had concurrent responsibilities in other government jobs. Nevertheless, the creation of this top-to-bottom party-led network was a critical step in promoting universal birth planning. It placed the party in command of birth planning work, increasing the pressure on party leaders to give birth planning a higher profile and take the plan targets seriously.

The final step toward full mobilization was Mao's unequivocal endorsement of birth planning work. At crucial moments Mao made statements that gave added weight to central instructions to carry out birth planning. In October 1972, for example, he indicated that providing birth control free of charge was not enough to speed the acceptance and use of birth control devices. It was also necessary, he argued, to provide home delivery of such devices. And at the National Planning Conference in December 1974, Mao made clear that it was "unacceptable not to control population" (*renkou fei kongzhi buxing*).[46] Although these may sound like inconsequential comments, no comment of Mao's was inconsequential in the political climate of the day. The Mao cult was at its height during these years; each utterance, regardless of context, stood instantly as a directive that demanded action. After Mao's comment on free contraceptive supplies, for example, a document was issued making the policy mandatory nationwide. Similarly, after his 1974 comment (inexplicably made before a group of foreign affairs officials), a central party document was issued within a month, demanding that all party members take the lead in practicing and promoting birth control. For those who had hesitated on moving ahead with this work, the unambiguous statement that "birth planning was promoted by Mao Zedong" was impossible to ignore.[47]

Toward a One-Child Policy: The Post-Mao Transition

The period of political transition between September 1976 and September 1980 saw a marked shift from the radical political and economic program of the late Maoist era to the comprehensive reforms associated with Deng Xiaoping's rise to power. In the midst of that political turbulence, the birth planning program steadily evolved and intensified. By the end of the decade, a one-child limit had been set, and the state resolved to enforce compliance in the countryside as well as the cities.

The deradicalization of Chinese politics occurred in roughly two stages.

46. Shi, *Zhongguo jihua shengyu huodong shi*, 162 and 168.
47. Ibid., 168–69.

From October 1976 until the Third Plenum of the Eleventh Central Committee in December 1978, Hua Guofeng, Mao's bland successor, pursued a modified Maoist line in both political tone and policy content. A campaign to eliminate the "pernicious influences" of the Gang of Four was waged. A grandiose ten-year plan for economic development was launched, and a mobilizational atmosphere laced with fear and foreboding permeated the party hierarchy. The source of anxiety was the ongoing struggle to determine the nature of the political crimes of the "Gang," which was composed of Mao's wife, Jiang Qing, and three of her associates who had risen to power during the Cultural Revolution. How their crimes were defined had profound implications for those who had benefited from the Cultural Revolution. Hua Guofeng, himself closely associated with the leftist policies of the "Gang" and of Mao, fought to contain the campaign by charging that the "Gang" was guilty of "ultrarightist" deviations. This strategy was designed to protect the leftist policies associated with Mao and Hua and to rally the support of the millions of cadres who had carried them out during the Cultural Revolution.

From the Third Plenum until his resignation as party chairman in June 1981, however, Hua Guofeng struggled unsuccessfully against the reform forces led by Deng Xiaoping, who eventually succeeded in having the "Gang" branded as "ultraleftist." The shift of label from ultraright to ultraleft made it possible to rehabilitate the most prominent victims of the Cultural Revolution and placed Hua and his supporters in jeopardy. Simultaneously, Deng Xiaoping's open door foreign economic policy and agricultural decollectivization campaign had their genesis during this period, paving the way for a slow deradicalization of Chinese politics and a new era of reform. Between 1976 and 1980, however, the threat of a political reversal was more or less constant, as virtually every policy area and work unit became an arena of political battle. Despite the deradicalizing objectives of the Dengist reforms, the struggle for power that they provoked created the climate of a political mobilization campaign.

The one-child policy was adopted and first implemented against the backdrop of this post-Mao succession struggle. First proposed in 1978 during Hua Guofeng's tenure, the universal one-child limit became official state policy in September 1980, just as the Deng coalition was consolidating its power and preparing to oust Hua from power. The adoption of that policy goal reinvigorated the birth planning campaign and led to one of the most extensive rural mobilizations in the history of the People's Republic.

The adoption of a one-child policy, and the scale and intensity of the one-child mobilization, is explained by three interrelated factors. First, the strict birth limitation policy was one of the few issues that stood above the politics of elite struggle, a rare area of leadership consensus. This political consensus was the result of a shared economic calculus. Decades of collective learning about the economic consequences of unchecked population growth left the contenders for power in general agreement about the need for state intervention to reduce fertility rates. The only questions were how best to achieve those goals, how quickly progress in fertility reduction had to be achieved, and how state-regulated birth planning could be justified by Marxist theory. For sociologists, demographers, and the staff of the State Family Planning Leading Group, these were significant and highly debatable issues, but for China's senior leaders the extended struggle over who would lead China and where he would lead dominated the political landscape. Birth control was important only because unchecked population growth threatened China's modernization goals, a threat that had become more urgent with time. Hua and Deng had profoundly different visions of the path to China's modernization; but both were mobilizing under the banner of modernization, and neither was prepared to let population growth stand in the way. As a result, the general line on birth planning was not dependent on the outcome of the succession struggle, and the particulars of policy planning were left to expert advisers. When those advisers urged the adoption of a one-child policy, the leadership decided to accept this proposal.[48]

A second explanation for the one-child escalation is the economic agenda of Deng Xiaoping and his allies among the leadership. Although Hua and Deng were both committed to rapid modernization, their divergent economic strategies shaped their degree of emphasis on birth planning, if only in relatively subtle ways. Whereas Hua Guofeng was committed to a neo-Stalinist economic development plan that placed primary emphasis on heavy industrial development and gross output indicators, Deng's reform program called for the development of the agricultural and commercial sectors, the enlivenment of the market sector, and increased personal consumption.[49] His preoccupation with alleviating China's essential poverty and bringing about rapid improvement in standards of living inclined him to be particularly concerned about per capita indicators of growth. With the large cohort of children born in the 1960s beginning to enter their child-

48. On the role of Song Jian, Liu Zheng, and other advisers to central leaders, see Susan Greenhalgh, "Science, Modernity, and the Making of China's One-Child Policy," *Population and Development Review* 29 (June 2003): 163–96. See also H. Yuan Tian, *China's Strategic Demographic Initiative* (New York, 1991).

49. On the differences between the economic programs of Hua Guofeng and Deng Xiaoping and Chen Yun, see Barry Naughton, *Growing Out of the Plan: Chinese Economic Reform, 1978–1993* (Cambridge, 1996), chap. 2.

bearing years, and with a rural and urban unemployment crisis already at hand (made worse in major cities by the return of millions of "sent-down" youth), population control became a priority.

Both of these explanations capture important aspects of the calculus of decision making surrounding the one-child policy. There was strong consensus on the continuing need to enforce strict childbearing limits, and the input of advisers like Liu Zheng and Song Jian was crucial in determining what specific level of childbearing was acceptable given the leadership's modernization goals.[50] Similarly, Deng's economic vision, however blurry in the early days of 1978, placed great emphasis on eliminating poverty and hunger and improving living standards as the first steps toward modernization. The third and central element driving policy evolution during this period, however, was the economic planning process.

By 1975, the goal, structure, and content of China's birth planning program had been firmly established. Zhou Enlai's preliminary planning for the fifth five-year plan (1976–80) set a goal of reducing China's population growth rate to 10 per 1,000 through annual, incremental reductions of one-tenth of 1 percent. The structure of the program paralleled that of China's state-planned economic sector, with the family planning organs of the MOH bureaucracy responsible for national oversight and coordination, and administrative regions (provinces, municipalities, counties) acting as aggregate production units with specific targets to fulfill. The content of the program was to delay childbirth, reduce the average number of children per couple to two (or three in rural areas), and increase their spacing to at least four years apart.

It was this ongoing program that Hua Guofeng inherited in 1976, and despite the disruptive political events of the 1976–77 period the program continued to function for a time on automatic pilot. As in other areas, there were ritual condemnations of the Gang of Four for sabotaging birth planning work, but reports of central and provincial work conferences in 1976 and 1977 indicate that routine planning and administration continued to occur. The extent of policy continuity became clear in February 1978, when Hua Guofeng addressed the First Session of the Fifth National People's Congress. Laying out an ambitious ten-year development plan (1976–85), Hua called for reducing the population growth rate to under 10 per 1,000 by 1980, with a further but more modest decline to 9 per 1,000 by 1985.

Those goals were entirely consistent with Zhou Enlai's preliminary planning for the fifth FYP, continuing a basic pattern of annual reductions of 1 per 1,000 through 1980. By 1978, however, it was increasingly clear that

50. Greenhalgh, "Science, Modernity."

the official policy of promoting "later, longer, fewer" (*wan, xi, shao*) births was too lenient to meet that goal. Data available in 1978 indicated that third or higher-order births had already declined to only 30 percent of rural births annually, and 10 percent of urban births. Further reductions in third births were possible, but given the large childbearing-age cohorts that were on the horizon for the 1980s, it did not appear that a two-child standard would be sufficient to stabilize annual population growth rates in the 10 per 1,000 range, much less induce further declines. To meet future planning targets, policy goals had to be escalated accordingly. Following that logic, in January 1979 the State Council adopted a "one is best, two at most," birth control policy, rewarding couples for limiting themselves to one child and penalizing third or additional births with fines and other economic measures.[51] Provinces began to develop regulations that rewarded a one-child limit, tolerated two, and penalized a third.

By June 1979, however, the goals had become more ambitious. Reporting to the Second Session of the Fifth National People's Congress, Hua reiterated the goal of reducing the population growth rate to under 10 per 1,000 by 1980, but he raised the goal for 1985 from 9 per 1,000 to 5 per 1,000. Shortly thereafter, *Jiankang bao* (Health News) ran an article stating that with hard work it would be possible "to lower the population growth rate to zero in the year 2000."[52] Two months later in *People's Daily*, Vice Premier Chen Muhua, head of the State Family Planning Leading Group, identified two stages to the reduction of population growth rates, the first extending to 1985, the second from 1985 to 2000. In the first stage, population growth would drop to a level of 5 per 1,000, as Hua Guofeng had announced. In the second stage, population growth was scheduled to drop to zero.[53] These goals could not be achieved with a two-child birth limit, advisers insisted. Rather than revisit the planning targets, the leadership embraced a one-child family norm for all childbearing-age couples.

The demographic projections of Song Jian, a scientist and state minister, are usually cited to explain this escalation of policy goals in 1979.[54] In con-

---

51. Liu Zheng, Wu Cangping, Lin Fude, "Dui kongzhi woguo renkou zengzhangde wudian jianyi," in *Renkou yanjiu* 3 (1980): 5.

52. *Jiankang bao*, 21 July 1979, in *Foreign Broadcast Information Service—Daily Report, China* (hereinafter *FBIS*), 24 July 1979, L9.

53. *Xinhua*, August 11, 1979, in *FBIS*, August 16, 1979, L15–16.

54. The most detailed and valuable study of the role and influence of Song Jian during this period is Greenhalgh, "Science, Modernity." Greenhalgh sees Song's computer-modeled population projections as key makers of a turn to science and cybernetics to shape population policy to China's economic goals. The one child birth limit, she argues, was a direct result of this scientific intervention, and a departure from earlier, less quantitative approaches to birth control. As I have shown, however, a two-child limit for urban China was encouraged as early as

junction with a research team, Song used computer modeling to devise five future scenarios for China's population growth based on variable average fertility rates. Starting with the assumption that the achievement of zero population growth by the year 2000 was the short-term goal, Song concluded that only if the average fertility rate was reduced to one by 1985 could this goal be attained.[55] Armed with this "scientific model," the State Council Office for Birth Planning recommended that the birth limitation policy be revised to advocate only one child per couple and impose penalties on those who had a second child.

There can be no doubt that Song Jian's projections and recommendations were influential in the decision to adopt a one-child policy. But their degree of influence was strongly affected by the political and economic climate of late 1978 and 1979. Between the Third Plenum of the 11th Central Committee in December 1978 and the June 1979 session of the National People's Congress, the reform coalition succeeded in undermining Hua Guofeng's development strategy. At the Third Plenum, Deng launched a campaign against the radical agricultural strategy, initiating several reforms and opening the window for others. In March 1979, Deng and Vice Premier Chen Yun stressed the necessity of a three-year period of "readjustment and restructuring" to shift investment away from heavy industrial development toward other sectors of the economy. Arguing that steel production and grain production were not the only indicators of economic development, Deng stressed the need for increased purchase prices for agricultural products to stimulate agricultural production. At the same time, he and Chen Yun repeatedly stressed the poor living standards of China's huge rural population and the continuing problem of rural hunger and called for improved standards of living.[56] Deng also set forth the goal of turning China into a "well-off" (*xiaokang*) society by the year 2000, with a per capita income of

---

the mid-1960s and was explicitly endorsed in the "later, longer, fewer" campaign launched in 1972. Song's computer models, however crude, gave the illusion of precision in calculating how variable fertility rates would influence economic growth and income levels, making them very persuasive to China's senior leaders. The inclination to quantify, however, was already deeply embedded in the birth planning doctrine itself, which treated human reproduction as the functional equivalent of material production and subject to the same levels of planning, regulation, and statistical manipulation.

55. According to Song Jian's computer-modeled projections, sustained average fertility levels of three children would result in China's population peaking at over 4.2 billion in 2080; sustaining a two-child fertility level would result in a peak population of over 1.5 billion by 2052; a 1.5 fertility level would result in a population peak in 2027 at 1.172 billion; and a one-child fertility level by 1985 would result in a population peak in 2004 at just over 1 billion. *Xinhua*, February 13, 1980, in *FBIS*, February 15, 1980, L11–15.

56. Ma et al., eds., *Zhongguo gongchandang zhizheng sishinian*, 440–41; Naughton, *Growing Out of the Plan*, chap. 2.

$1,000. These themes persisted during 1979 and 1980, laying the foundation for the economic reforms to follow.

All of this activity took place against the background of the short-lived war against Vietnam in February 1979. The war worsened the budgetary difficulties created by Hua's massive investment program and was a primary factor in the decision to retreat from that program. Chen Yun was put in charge of sorting out China's finances during the readjustment period, and he and Deng stressed the need to reduce central government expenditures. The emphasis on cutting costs made effective population control even more compelling. Calculations by the demographer Liu Zheng showed that the state had spent nearly 4 trillion yuan (about one trillion U.S. dollars at 1980 exchange rates) on the six hundred million people born since 1949. This figure, and similar calculations regarding food, housing, and employment, underscored in a new way the full cost to the state of high rates of population growth during the 1960s and early 1970s. It also underscored the burden looming ahead, as the children of the 1960s matured and gave birth in the 1980s and 1990s. Reacting to these figures in the spring of 1979, Deng insisted on the need to bring population growth down to 0.5 percent by 1985.[57]

This tightening of goals could be justified in terms of China's long-term modernization goals, but it ran counter to Deng's efforts on other fronts to foster more realistic planning and balanced growth. Nor did it conform with China's actual performance during 1979. Although the official figures showed a continued decline in the population growth rate to 11.6 per 1,000, that figure was still in excess of the target. More important, it was not at all clear that the growth rate could be brought under 10 per 1,000 in 1980, as called for in the economic plan. These shortcomings raised serious questions about the possibility of further reductions during the 1981–85 period. As a result, by the time of the Third Session of the Fifth National People's Congress in September 1980 two decisions had been made. One, the leadership announced the need for a "crash drive" to promote only one child per couple and hold population to 1.2 billion by the year 2000.[58]

57. Shi, *Zhongguo jihua shengyu*, 159.

58. See Hua Guofeng's speech to the Third Session of the Fifth National People's Congress, *Beijing Review* 38 (September 22, 1980): 18. The figure of 1.2 billion appears to have resulted from a simple calculation by Liu Zheng and his demographic team. In a report prepared for State Council consideration, the authors wrote: "From liberation to the end of 1978, six hundred million people were born. From the beginning of the 1970s, this group of people began to enter the marriage age in succession, so even if you calculate on the basis of each couple having two children on average, from the beginning of the 1970s to the end of the twentieth century, this generation of six hundred million born after liberation will give birth to nearly six hundred million." Liu, Wu, and Lin, "Dui kongzhi woguo renkou zengzhangde wudian jianyi."

Provinces subsequently began to amend their regulations to impose economic penalties on those who gave birth to a second child without the permission of local cadres. Two, the population target for 1981 was relaxed slightly, rising to 1 percent from the original target of 0.8 percent set in November 1979. The longer-range, more radical targets of 0.5 percent by 1985 and zero population growth by the year 2000 were quietly abandoned.[59]

This dualistic, apparently contradictory pattern—tightening limits on having a second child while adjusting and lowering goals—was driven by several considerations. First, the adjustment of the 1981 target was necessary to bring targets closer into line with likely outcomes, a change consistent with the broader readjustment of the economic plan in 1979–80. At the same time, however, the failure to contain population growth within 1 percent by 1980 raised growing concerns about the weight of population on China's economic indices, concerns that made the one-child limit seem imperative. At this critical moment, the reform coalition stood poised to push forward a fundamental set of rural reforms, which they hoped would do more than simply increase grain production. Their efforts were focused on improving rural living standards and rural incomes, a focus that would later be sloganized as "It is glorious to get rich." Deng's goal of increasing per capita GNP to $1,000 by the year 2000 could only be met if one assumed twenty years of steady economic growth and an average of 1.5 children per couple.[60] The rush was on, therefore, to set population targets at levels commensurate with Deng's economic vision. This shifted attention to the numerical total of 1.2 billion, which was used to set plans for provincial and lower-level administrative areas, and away from the question of what would happen after the turn of the century, that is, whether, how much, or how long population would continue to increase in the next century.

The Calculus of State Intervention

By the end of 1975 the conceptual and policy shift that had begun with Mao in the 1950s had been cemented. As a result, population goals were redefined as part of the centralized state plan and the crucial prerequisite to successful economic planning. In theory, the health and welfare of women and children continued to be the primary justification for family planning

---

59. In addition to Hua's speech, which does not refer to a goal of zero population growth, see Yao Yilin's report on the national economic plan for 1981 in *Beijing Review* 38 (September 22, 1980): 37; and the "Open Letter" on family planning to all party cadres and youth league members, *Renmin ribao*, September 26, 1980.

60. See, for example, the discussion in Yu Youhai, "U.S. $1,000 by the Year 2000," *Beijing Review* 43 (October 27, 1980): 16–18.

and birth control programs until after Mao's death. In practical terms, however, from the early 1960s onward the logic of centralized economic planning provided the rationale for population control plans. This meant applying to birth control goals the same target-oriented approach that was the standard tool of policy implementation in the material sector, where numerical targets were routinely used to set production levels and determine standards of performance in production units. With population planning thus linked to the primary obligation of the socialist state—the production, allocation, and distribution of material goods—childbearing became subject to those same mechanisms of centralized planning.

This underlying conception of birth planning as the reproductive corollary to planned material production immunized it from the destructive impulses of the Cultural Revolution. And the deep commitment to a radical agrarian strategy protected it thereafter. During the 1966–75 decade, the ideological commitment to agrarian radicalism ruled out any fundamental shift in rural policy, even when it became clear that grain production would not keep pace with population growth. Rather than abandon the agrarian program, the leadership focused ever more urgently on the other side of the coin—reducing population (consumption) pressures on the harvest. Once government work began to function again in late 1969, therefore, Zhou Enlai pressed forward quickly with a birth planning initiative. His goal was rapid progress in creating a supply of high-quality contraceptives, in building an effective delivery system, and in disseminating information on contraception and birth planning. He also wanted a responsive party and government apparatus, one that would take seriously the need for sustained attention to population issues. By 1975, when his illness forced him to turn over most of his work to Deng Xiaoping, Zhou had accomplished all of these organizational goals.

In the end, however, his persistent pressure over two decades to achieve a sustained organizational approach to population planning had resulted in a dangerous equation of intervention: that what could not be achieved through economic policy levers (increasing grain production) could be accomplished through planned population growth (mandating strict birth limits). Rather than pursue the goal of lower birthrates as an independent good, that is, as a bonus that might enhance the positive effects of economic growth, birth planning was increasingly coming to be seen as a necessary condition for economic planning and a compensation for shortfalls in agricultural performance. By the mid-1970s, this shift of paradigm was complete, and one of the most extensive and penetrating mobilization campaigns of the entire Maoist era was well under way.

The one-child policy that emerged at the end of the decade was the final expression of this calculus of state intervention. Outside China, where the context and background for this announcement were largely hidden from view, the announcement of a one-child limit seemed to signal a sudden and radical escalation of China's population goals. Certainly, the drive for a one-child limit was a radical example of social engineering, even for a regime that was given to breathtaking ventures in that direction. In another sense, however, it was not radical at all. The truly radical step had been taken long before, when Mao Zedong embraced the principle of subjecting childbirth to direct socialist planning. In 1979, Mao's heirs carried this principle to its logical and disturbing extreme.

4

The Architecture of Mobilization

It took more than a shift of conceptual paradigm to bring about a rapid fertility decline during the 1970s and maintain it through the reforms of the early 1980s. It took a massive mobilization campaign that was unsurpassed in its scope, complexity, and organization.

By the time the state began to call for a one-child limit in 1979, two types of campaign had become a standard part of China's policy process. The first, which I call transformation campaigns, were those designed to transform some aspect of the political, social, or policy climate. Such campaigns could be negative, designed to eliminate a problem or threat (e.g., the antirightist campaign); or they could be positive, designed to achieve socialist goals (e.g., the Great Leap Forward). They could also claim to combine negative and positive goals, as was most obviously the case in the Cultural Revolution. Whatever their intent, these campaigns were typically characterized by a massive mobilization of party and society for a distinct period of time in a climate pervaded by insecurity, unpredictability, fear, and violence.

The second form of campaign I call a routine production campaign. This campaign grew up side by side with the transformation campaign and mimicked its methods. Unlike the transformation campaign, however, which was self-consciously disruptive of routine and extraordinary in its goals, the production campaign was devoted to the achievement of material production targets or concrete administrative targets in a predictable fashion and on a reliable timetable. Routine production campaigns were designed to fulfill the goals and targets of the national economic plan.[1]

1. These two campaign types are the rough equivalents, on a smaller scale, of Lowell

The one-child campaign was an amalgam of these two campaign types, one that joined the ongoing organizational requirements of a production campaign to the mobilizational techniques of the most effective transformation campaign. Like a production campaign, birth planning targets were set alongside grain and steel targets in the annual and five-year economic plans and were disseminated along with other local economic targets. Yet unlike other production campaigns, birth planning targets could not be achieved in a single mobilizational sweep. They required an ongoing administrative process, one in which there was regular monitoring and inducement of compliance. Manipulating childbearing-age couples into compliance with birth limits was a vastly more complex task than mobilizing workers or peasants to fulfill material production quotas, however. Achieving birth planning targets required a radical alteration of the childbearing behavior of an entire nation, and not just for a brief period but for decades to come. The one-child campaign thus qualified as a major transformation campaign, one that required a climate of radical political mobilization and the frenzied methods characteristic of that climate. Yet without the administrative infrastructure to sustain a birth planning effort, without a means to routinize and institutionalize the policy, even the most massive and successful short-term campaign would mean little over the long run.

Over the course of the 1970s, the Chinese state succeeded in joining the tactics of political mobilization to routinized methods of control and administration. The result, by 1980, was a stunning campaign performance. Between 1971 and 1980, the natural rate of population growth was cut in half, a feat that was achieved by a precipitous drop in birthrates in both the urban and rural sectors (see table 3). Following the progressive tightening of childbearing limits, the percentage of annual births that were first births increased dramatically, while the percentage of third or higher order births was cut in half (see table 4). Although some of this fertility decline was attributable to pent-up demand for contraceptive services, implying voluntary compliance with the campaign, other data for this period suggest the strong influence of state policy.[2] One example is the sudden increase in age at mar-

---

Dittmer's "storming" and "engineering" approaches to revolution. See Dittmer, *China's Continuous Revolution*.

2. For a demographic analysis of the impact of state policy on fertility decline, see Griffith Feeney and Wang Feng, "Parity Progression and Birth Intervals in China: The Influence of Policy in Hastening Fertility Decline," *Population and Development Review* 19, no. 1 (March 1993): 61–101. The authors conclude (95) that over half of the fertility decline between 1970 and 1990 is attributable to government intervention. See also Ronald Freedman, Xiao Zhenyu, Li Bohua, and William Lavely, "Local Area Variations in Reproductive Behavior in the People's Republic of China, 1973–1982," *Population Studies* 42 (1988): 39–57. Using data from China's 1982 One-per-Thousand Fertility Survey, the authors conclude that exceptionally rapid fertility declines between 1973 to 1976 and 1979 to 1982 among women and across

TABLE 3. Crude birthrates and total fertility rates for urban and rural population, 1962–1985 (per thousand population)

Year	Crude birthrate	Urban birthrate	Rural birthrate	Total fertility rate	Urban fertility rate	Rural fertility rate
1962	37.22	35.98	37.43	6.02	4.78	6.30
1963	43.60	45.00	43.38	7.50	6.20	7.78
1964	39.34	33.02	40.27	6.18	4.39	6.56
1965	38.06	27.61	39.54	6.08	3.74	6.59
1966	35.21	—	—	6.26	3.10	6.95
1967	34.12	—	—	5.31	2.90	5.84
1968	35.75	—	—	6.45	3.87	7.02
1969	34.25	—	—	5.72	3.29	6.26
1970	33.59	—	—	5.81	3.26	6.37
1971	30.65	21.30	31.86	5.44	2.88	6.01
1972	29.77	19.30	31.19	4.98	2.63	5.50
1973	27.93	17.35	29.36	4.54	2.38	5.00
1974	24.82	14.50	26.23	4.17	1.98	4.64
1975	23.01	14.71	24.17	3.57	1.78	3.95
1976	19.91	13.12	20.85	3.24	1.60	3.58
1977	18.93	13.38	19.70	2.84	1.57	3.11
1978	18.25	13.56	18.91	2.72	1.55	2.96
1979	17.82	13.67	18.43	2.75	1.37	3.04
1980	18.21	14.17	18.82	2.24	1.14	2.48
1981	20.91	16.45	21.55	2.63	1.39	2.91
1982	21.09	18.24	21.97	2.87		
1983	18.62	15.99	19.89	2.42	1.3	2.2
1984	17.50	15.00	17.90	2.35		
1985	17.80	14.02	19.17	2.20		

Source: 1990 Zhongguo tongji nianjian (Beijing: Guojia tongji chubanshe, 1991), 89; Zhongguo funü tongji ziliao, 1949–1989.

riage during the 1970s. The percentage of newly married women complying with the "late marriage" policy tripled between 1970 and 1977, and by 1980 nearly 53 percent of all newly married women were twenty-three years of age or older, compared with only 14 percent in 1970. In rural areas, the late marriage rate rose from 10 to 45 percent of all newly married women (see table 5).

Going into 1980, the Deng regime had staked its reputation and will on achieving a per capita GNP of $1,000 by the end of the century. With end-

villages at all educational levels can only be explained by the impact of the birth planning program. Referring to data from Sichuan Province, the authors conclude that "the magnitude of the declines . . . across educational levels for a short period and for such a large population . . . is probably unprecedented in history, apart from periods of famine, epidemics, wars, or other overwhelming disasters" (57).

TABLE 4. Proportion of total births by parity, selected years

Year	First births (% of Total births)	Second births (% of Total births)	Third and higher order births (%)
1970	20.7	17.1	62.2
1975	24.8	23.7	51.5
1977	30.9	24.6	44.5
1980	42.7	27.2	30.1
1981	46.6	25.3	28.1
1985	50.4	30.1	19.5
1988	56.8	29.6	13.6
1989	51.9	32.5	15.6
1990	49.5	31.2	19.3
1991	55.2	30.9	13.9
1992	60.5	27.5	12.0
1993	61.3	27.5	11.2
1994	62.8	27.6	9.5
1995	67.0	25.6	7.4
1996	67.9	25.5	6.6
1997	70.9	24.0	5.1
2003	72.4	26.2	1.5

Sources: Song Yuanzhu, Shi Yulin, and Zhang Guichao, "Funu shengyu taici zhuang-quang" [Situation with women's birth order], in *Quanguo qianfenzhiyi renkou shen-gyulu chouyang diaocha fenxi* [Analysis of the national one-per-thousand population fertility survey] (Beijing: *Renkou yu jingji* chubanshe, 1983), 56; Yu Gang, "1997 nian woguo renkou jixu pingwen cengzhang" [Our country's population continued to steadily increase in 1997], in *1998 Zhongguo renkou tongji nianjian*, 439; Peng Peiyun, ed. *Zhongguo jihua shengyu quan shu* [Encyclopedia of Birth Planning in China] (Beijing: Zhongguo renkou chubanshe, 1997), 887.

Note: This table draws on data compiled by the State Statistical Bureau and the birth planning bureaucracy. These two different streams of statistical reporting and calculation result in minor variations in reported annual figures.

less uncertainty lying ahead in the newly launched reform process—both domestic uncertainty and global political and economic uncertainty—population growth seemed to be the one area where control and predictability could be imposed. The more firmly and thoroughly control was exercised over population growth, the leadership believed, the more room China gained to cope with unpredictable developments elsewhere in the reform process. As in the past, then, the regime intensified the birth limitation campaign in order to compensate for lagging economic performance. This time, however, the staggering implications of having already hit the one billion population mark created a heightened sense of urgency.

However much China's elite were divided by issues of the pace and scope of political and economic reform, they were united in their resolve to do whatever was necessary to prevent the enormous rising generation from having more than one or two children. This unity and resolve was signaled

TABLE 5. "Late Marriage Rate"
(percentage of newly married women who
deferred marriage until age 23 or older)
1962–1982.

Year	Total	Urban	Rural
1962	10.7	27.7	7.6
1963	10.4	29.2	7.1
1964	10.4	35.1	6.6
1965	12.0	41.0	7.4
1966	12.2	44.3	7.7
1967	12.6	43.1	7.5
1968	13.2	40.5	8.4
1969	14.1	38.7	10.0
1970	13.8	40.1	10.1
1971	14.0	46.1	9.9
1972	16.3	50.7	11.8
1973	20.1	55.8	15.2
1974	24.5	61.7	18.6
1975	31.0	68.4	25.0
1976	38.9	77.1	32.2
1977	42.2	81.4	34.9
1978	48.0	84.0	41.4
1979	52.9	88.8	45.3
1980	52.8	86.1	44.8
1981	50.9	79.0	42.9
1982	47.8	81.6	38.9

Source: Wen Zhifu and Wei Cen, "Jianguo
yilai funude wanhunlu he zaohunlu dongtai
fenxi" [An analysis of trends in the rate of late
marriage and early marriage for women since
the founding of the country], in *Quanguo
qianfenzhiyi renkou shengyulu chouyang diaocha fenxi* [Analysis of the national one-per-
thousand population fertility survey] (Beijing:
Renkou yu jingji chubanshe, 1983), 126.

in September 1980 by the unprecedented decision to publish an "Open Letter" from the Central Committee to all party cadres, urging them to take
the lead in accepting and implementing the one-child limit.[3] The letter,
which was printed in all newspapers and broadcast repeatedly, marked the
beginning of an intensive rural campaign that would draw and build on the
well-honed methods of the 1970s. What those methods were—how they

3. "Open Letter of the CCP Central Committee to the General Membership of Communist
Party and the Chinese Communist Youth League on the Problem of Controlling Population
Growth in Our Country," *Renmin ribao*, September 25, 1980. The full text of the "Open Let-
ter" may be found in Tyrene White, ed., "Family Planning in China," *Chinese Sociology and
Anthropology* 24, no. 3 (Spring 1992): 11–16.

blended transformative and routine campaign elements into an effective and durable architecture of mobilization—is the focus of this chapter.

The Rural Setting

Whatever factors conspired to bring about an unpredictably rapid decline in birthrates over the course of the 1970s, it would not have occurred without aggressive state intervention. Even in urban areas, where population density, housing shortages, educational levels, and generational changes surely contributed to the speed of the fertility decline by leading younger couples to prefer fewer children and eagerly accept free contraceptives, the sudden sharp reduction in birthrates during the first half of the 1970s points to the strong influence of administrative measures in workplaces and neighborhoods (see table 3). In the volatile political climate of the late Cultural Revolution era, where opposition to birth control could be construed as a political offense, resistance to birth limits could be dangerous.[4] In the countryside, where traditional childbearing attitudes, marital customs, educational levels, and economic backwardness conspired to maintain preferences for more children and sustain high population growth rates, state intervention to limit births was the key to swift fertility decline.

The capacity of the state to enforce rural birth limits, and the means it used to do so, were conditioned by two basic aspects of the rural setting. The first, childbearing attitudes and preferences of the peasantry, worked against the state. The second, the structure of the rural collective, worked in its favor.

The Determinants of Childbearing Preferences

As China's leaders prepared to launch a rural birth limitation campaign, the most formidable obstacle they faced was a set of deeply ingrained childbearing attitudes and habits. Life in the Chinese countryside made rural couples prefer more children than their urban counterparts and especially to strongly prefer sons. These preferences were reflected in traditional sayings like "The more children, the more wealth" and "Men are superior to

4. One Shanghai woman vividly illustrated the power of this political climate by noting that in 1979, after the Cultural Revolution had ended, she felt compelled to accept the new one-child policy: "How would anyone rebel? No way! You could be labeled as an enemy of the state. There is no way you can go against the policy. That would be going against the Party. You would suffer severely. No one rebelled, no one rebelled. The whole society was a tight society. If they handed down an order, that was it. No going against it and no second opinions." Quoted in Yilin Nie and Robert J. Wyman, "The One-Child Policy in Shanghai: Acceptance and Internalization," *Population and Development Review* 31, no. 2 (June 2005): 313–36.

women" and in data on rural fertility. As the birth control campaign and birth control services slowly made their way into the countryside in the 1970s, rural fertility began to decline; but in 1979, as in 1970, rural fertility was about twice as high as urban fertility (see table 3).

Several factors in combination help to explain these preferences. First is the role of culture and tradition. The importance of producing offspring, especially sons, was an inherited part of the Confucian ethic. Only a son could carry on the ancestral line of the family, and it was the filial obligation of each generation of men to produce ancestral heirs. Giving birth to at least one son, therefore, was the single most important act a woman could perform, and failure in this regard brought social ostracism, humiliation, and rejection. Despite the revolutionary transformation of the countryside after 1949, including the repudiation of Confucianism and the emphasis on women's equality, the impact of these attitudes remained strong, embraced by men and women alike within the village.[5]

Like other peasant communities, however, traditional cultural norms and rational economic calculations were mutually reinforcing. Children, particularly sons, were an economic resource. They provided labor power from an early age through their adult years, bringing additional income into the household, and they were a guaranteed source of old-age support. Although daughters contributed to the household during their younger years, when they married they left the family and village to become part of the groom's family, taking their economic potential with them. Sons, on the other hand, were not only more valuable contributors to the family during their youth, they remained at home and brought another person into the family when they married.[6]

Certain aspects of the collective system of agriculture reinforced this economic calculus. Under the collective, peasant income accumulated in work points, with each laborer assigned a standard number of work points per day of labor. After the harvest, households "paid" for the grain distributed to them by having its value deducted from their work point accounts. This work-point system influenced childbearing preferences in two distinct ways. First, it reinforced the preference for sons. A strong adult male typically earned ten work points per day, while younger or less able males earned nine or eight. A woman generally earned only 60 to 80 percent of the income of her male counterpart, averaging anywhere from six to eight work

5. Elisabeth Croll, *Chinese Women since Mao* (London, 1983); Johnson, *Women, the Family, and Peasant Revolution in China;* Wolf, *Revolution Postponed.*

6. William L. Parish and Martin King Whyte, *Village and Family in Contemporary China* (Chicago, 1978); Fred Arnold and Liu Zhaoxiang, "Sex Preference, Fertility, and Family Planning in China," *Population and Development Review* 12, no. 2 (June 1986): 221–46.

points per day.[7] This work-point differential made daughters less economically valuable than sons even before they were married, and, as noted above, their income was lost altogether after their marriage.

Second, it reinforced the economic incentive to have more children. Under the work-point system, labor-rich families fared much better than labor-poor families. Moreover, local authorities allocated grain to households on a per capita basis, often making no distinctions between infants, small children, and adults. Since the per capita rations were meager at best, childbearing could be a vehicle for increasing a family's food supply. Even those without sufficient work points to cover the cost of a new infant's rations could benefit from this strategy, since each person was guaranteed a basic ration of grain. The debt was carried on the household's work-point accounts, on the understanding that it would be repaid when the family's children grew old enough to enter the work force.[8] For those who gambled on this strategy, it was clearly preferable to have a son rather than a daughter. In the short run, a baby boy or baby girl brought the same benefit of increased rations. As the child matured and became a full-time member of the labor force, however, the boy would be able to earn more income than would the girl, and provide long-term income security for his parents.

Long-term security was critical in rural China, where the collective maintained only a skeletal social insurance system to assist the neediest households, primarily the elderly without offspring to care for them.[9] Although the basic guarantee of food rations and help with everyday chores provided by this system was a laudable aspect of collective support, the poverty and dependency of such households only reinforced the message that it was critical to have sons to provide old-age support. The pitiable condition of the childless elderly was to be avoided at all cost.

The combined power of traditional attitudes and economic considerations in shaping childbearing preferences was illustrated by the results of a survey conducted in 1981. Of the 728 women of childbearing age (20–49) interviewed, only 5 percent wanted one child, 51 percent wanted two children, 28 percent wanted three, and 15 percent wanted four. In what the author referred to as "hilly districts where traditional ideology is compara-

7. Hong Ying, "Women in China Making Headway to Full Equality," *China Daily* (March 6, 1982), 5. Wu Naitao, "Rural Women and the New Economic Policies," *Beijing Review* 10 (March 7, 1983): 19. Interview File 821014.

8. Parish and Whyte, *Village and Family*, chaps. 5 and 9; Oi, *State and Peasant in Contemporary China*, chap. 2.

9. This system was generally referred to as the "five guarantees"—food, clothing, medical care, housing, and burial expenses—and recipients were commonly referred to as *wubaohu*, or "five guarantee households."

tively dense," however, the numbers climb to 27 percent wanting two or three children, and nearly 72 percent wanting four.[10] Asked which sex child they prefer, a sample of 100 women in one brigade responded as follows: 2.2 percent wanted a girl, 36.7 percent wanted a boy, and 61.6 percent were neutral. In hilly districts, however, the number desiring a male soared to 77 percent. Asked what they would do if the first child was a girl, 61 percent said that they would try to have another child.[11] In a separate article based on the same survey, fully one-third of 710 women said they wanted to have a boy even if they already had two girls. Only 2.21 percent of a sample of 548 said they wanted to have only one girl.[12]

The survey concluded that the desire for more children is caused by factors such as the "social economy," "ideology," and "traditional habits." The data make clear, however, that economic calculations were the primary determinant of childbearing preferences. Of 808 people who were asked why they wanted additional children, the responses were: additional labor power, 21 percent; old-age security, 51 percent; preserve the ancestral line, 25 percent; enjoy the pleasure of children, 3 percent.[13] The problem of old-age security clearly predominated. This category, taken together with those who cited the desire for additional labor power, drew 70 percent of all responses.

Power and Politics in the Collective

If rural childbearing preferences stood as a major impediment to the birth limitation campaign, the organization of the collective was a major asset. During the collective era, grassroots cadres at the commune, brigade, and team levels served as agents of state authority and wielded tremendous political and economic power. This accumulation of power left the peasantry deeply vulnerable to arbitrary rule and unpopular policies, including birth limits. Although the rural reforms began to undermine this system just as the one-child campaign got underway (see chapter 5), the structure of the collective and the enforcement methods molded to that structure continued to be utilized.

10. Cheng Du, "Hubei sheng nongcun shengyulu diaocha," *Renkou yanjiu* 5 (1982): 36–38 and 31. The survey was conducted in five production brigades in five counties of Hubei Province.

11. Cheng's article does not make clear that the number of respondents to the questions about sex preference was only 100, not 728. This information was gained from an interview with a scholar from Wuhan University who participated in the investigation. Interview File 831125.

12. Cheng Du, "Nongcun renkoude zaishengchan—dui yige diaocha baogaode fenxi," *Jingji yanjiu* 6 (1982): 56.

13. Cheng Du, "Hubei sheng," 31.

One source of cadre control lay in the pervasive administrative apparatus at the local level. The three-tiered commune system was designed to organize rural work along military lines, with each commune divided clearly and organized efficiently into constituent production brigades and teams. Each unit had its own cadre force, and each group of cadres was primarily oriented toward the tasks of political control and economic management. Communes were staffed with state cadres, often brought in from outside the commune territory, and collective cadres, who were employed and paid by the commune itself. State cadres were professionals on the state payroll, while collective cadres were paid well by commune standards and relieved of the burden of agricultural work. The division of authority was fairly specialized and the cadre force relatively large. Brigades were staffed by a less professional force. Led by a party secretary and brigade leader who were native to the community, brigades were staffed by several (mostly male) deputy leaders with special portfolios; one female leader in charge of women's affairs; and technical personnel, including accountants, bookkeepers, and security men. All were collective cadres, paid by the income generated within the village. Because they were full-time administrative cadres, they too were usually relieved of their responsibility for agricultural production. At the team level, team leaders were usually joined by one to five male cadres, plus the female women's leader. At this level, the cadres received subsidies for the time they spent in administration, but they were not entirely divorced from agricultural work. On the contrary, the job of the team leader was to remain intimately acquainted with the production process in the village and to share the work burden with the peasantry. Nevertheless, team cadres were separated from the peasantry by their status, and their status and authority was enhanced by the long tenure in office that they frequently enjoyed.[14]

The second source of cadre power was their monopoly of economic power. Not only was peasant income tightly controlled through the workpoint system but cadres also controlled the work assignments within the brigade or team. Labor was organized within the team on a daily basis, and team leaders had full decision-making power over how to use the labor force on any given day. Cadres therefore had it in their power to assign peasants to the least desirable tasks, such as hauling night soil, or the most desirable, such as operating the team tractor. They also exercised control over the use of collective assets. Agricultural machinery, farm animals, and

14. For two detailed descriptions of the organization and functions of each level of commune administration, see Barnett, *Cadres, Bureaucracy, and Political Power in Communist China,* and Steven Bailey Butler, "Conflict and Decision-Making in China's Rural Administration, 1969–1976," PhD diss., Columbia University, 1980.

other agricultural inputs were owned by the collective and administered by local cadres. Similarly, cadres administered buildings, vehicles, land, and other physical assets, deciding how and when they would be used.[15]

Although the concentration of economic power in the hands of cadres was crucial to their power within the village, that power would have been diluted substantially if the peasantry had a means of escape from the village or an alternative source of employment. During the collective era, however, there was no means of escape, and this was the third major source of cadre power. Control of the movement and migration of peasants was extremely tight. To stem the spontaneous flood of peasants into the cities during the mid-1950s and early 1960s, tight controls had been put into place to restrict peasant travel and migration. A system of household registration gave every peasant (and city dweller) an official place of residence, or *hukou*. This system was administered by the state public security organs, which maintained a detailed set of files on the composition and characteristics of each household. With this control system in place, disgruntled peasants did not have an exit option. Even short-term travel was difficult to arrange; it required the permission of local cadres and the public security bureau, and on arrival at one's destination it was necessary to register with the local street committee. Migration, particularly to an urban area, was virtually impossible. Only in rare cases were peasants allowed to change their official residency, and without an official residency permit one could not obtain the ration coupons necessary to purchase food, cotton cloth, or other staples.[16]

This tight system of economic and administrative control left peasants with little means to resist the state's incursions, unless they were supported, directly or indirectly, by brigade and team cadres. Most village cadres were natives of their communities, individuals who shared a social identity with their fellow villagers. At the same time, they were the formal agents of the party-state, responsible for the conduct of the state's business at the grassroots. As a result of this dual role, they were set apart from their fellow villagers, who were required to subsidize their work and submit to their authority. They were equally set apart from the party-state, however, by their

15. In some areas of rural China, collective decision making was more collegial, with peasant participation tempering and constraining the power of team and brigade cadres. See John Burns, *Political Participation in Rural China* (Berkeley, 1988), and Marc Blecher, "Consensual Politics in Rural Chinese Communities: The Mass Line in Theory and Practice," *Modern China* 5, no. 1 (January 1979): 105–26.

16. As Jean Oi has noted, coupons for grain and other commodities were "place-specific." When peasants were given permission to travel, they were issued food coupons that were valid only at their place of destination. Oi, *State and Peasant*, 30.

status as "collective" rather than "state" cadres and by their deep ties to their home villages.

In the early years of Communist state-building, the extension of the Communist state into the village through the recruitment of indigenous village leaders was a conscious strategy on the part of central leaders. By recruiting village members to cadre roles and instilling party loyalty and discipline, the state was able to permeate rural villages in pursuit of its goals, while maintaining open organizational boundaries and close ties with the peasantry.[17] It was also able to extract the "rural surplus" to fuel urban development and contain cadre deviations through political discipline.[18] In so doing, the new state overcame the "involutionary" pattern characteristic of the republican state, whereby the formal expansion of the state apparatus was not accompanied by control over an increasing proportion of societal resources.[19] Over time, however, the Communist state's monopoly of resources placed a premium on the development of personal ties and connections with higher-level cadres at the commune and county levels and with activists and ordinary peasants within the village.[20] Grassroots leaders relied on these patron-client networks to survive the demands and dangers of their job, and at times the networks aided in the implementation of state policies. When vested local interests were at stake, however, these ties could also be used to subvert, distort, or deflect central directives, creating a gap between central initiatives and local results.[21] The threat of distortion was much greater in cases where cadres themselves were the target of state policy, or where policy changes affected their vital political or economic interests.

In the case of birth planning, grassroots cadres, like all peasants, were targets of the campaign, either directly or indirectly. If they were still in their childbearing years, they were direct targets of the policy. If they were beyond their childbearing years, it was likely that their children were targets of the policy, or else other relatives in the village. But even if their families were not directly affected, brigade and team cadres were still peasant-cadres, sharing with fellow villagers the set of attitudes, preferences, biases, and interests that stood in the way of the birth planning effort. Overcoming

17. Victor Nee, "Peasant Entrepreneurship and the Politics of Regulation in China," in *Remaking the Economic Institutions of Socialism,* ed. Victor Nee and David Stark (Stanford, 1989); Siu, *Agents and Victims in South China.*

18. Oi, *State and Peasant.*

19. Prasenjit Duara, "State Involution: A Study of Local Finances in North China, 1911–1935," *Comparative Studies in Society and History* 29, no. 1 (January 1987): 132–61; Duara, *Culture, Power, and the State* (Stanford, 1988).

20. Jean C. Oi, "Commercializing China's Rural Cadres," *Problems of Communism* (September–October 1986): 1–15.

21. Oi, *State and Peasant.*

the obstacle posed by this solidarity of interest and opinion was the greatest challenge the state faced in attempting to limit births over a sustained period. To meet that challenge, it was necessary to garner the attention of a vast and generally resistant corps of local officials, build a specialized organizational network to coordinate the complex array of tasks involved in a comprehensive and sustained birth planning campaign, and deploy an array of campaign methods to assure grassroots compliance.

Party Mobilization and Organizational Development

The first steps toward mobilizing the cadre force came in the early 1970s, when broad efforts were underway to revive government organs that were paralyzed or destroyed by the Cultural Revolution. In that context, a series of decisions were made to place birth planning on a sound administrative footing. In the fall of 1970 the MOH was ordered to set up a birth planning office within its organization, formally separating birth planning work from the Office for Maternal and Infant Health (*fuyou baojian ke*). The instruction was included in the draft of the fourth five-year plan in 1971, which specified the provision of operating funds for the Birth Planning Office. Simultaneously, the Family Planning Leading Group of the State Council was reestablished on a temporary basis.[22] In July 1973, it was given permanent standing through a State Council document. In addition, a birth planning office was established under the jurisdiction of the MOH.[23] Governments down to the county level were ordered to create similar leading groups and birth planning offices, creating a top-to-bottom governmental system.

The creation of government offices was insufficient to guarantee results, however. Party organs also had to be involved, and the organizational network had to penetrate to the commune and village levels. This was accomplished after the issuing of two Central Committee documents. The first, in February 1975, instructed all party committees to make birth planning a part of their regular work agenda and to appoint a party secretary to take personal responsibility for the work.[24] The second directive, Central Document 69 (1978), ordered the first party secretary of every party committee, down to the brigade and enterprise level, to take personal responsibility for birth planning. Placing the most powerful local figure directly in charge of birth planning sent an unambiguous signal to all party cadres that birth planning was a primary state task, one that they could not ignore.

22. Shi, *Zhongguo jihua shengyu huodong shi*, 158 and 160–61.
23. Ibid., 160–61; Ma et al., *Zhongguo gongchandang zhizheng sishinian*, 364.
24. Shi, *Zhongguo jihua shengyu huodong shi*, 169; *Zhongguo renkou—Guizhou* (Beijing, 1988), 432–33.

Central Document 69 also included several crucial provisions that demonstrated the growing climate of urgency in the late 1970s. It instructed all localities to strengthen their birth planning offices by giving them independent and higher bureaucratic status. The practical effect of this change was to take birth planning out from under the jurisdiction of health bureaus at each governmental level and give them equal standing as independent bureau-level units. At the same time, personnel in these offices were given the status of "administrative" (*xingzheng*) cadres, and governments at all levels were given authorization to increase the staff size (*bianzhi*) of the office. These changes meant that office personnel were no longer treated as health care workers. Instead, they were given the status of state cadres, with the ranks, privileges, and career opportunities that went with that status.[25]

Most important, each commune, each urban neighborhood district, and each unit, enterprise, or factory with more than one thousand people was instructed to appoint a cadre with specific responsibility for birth planning, and the number of authorized personnel in grassroots organs was increased.[26] This change gave birth planning higher visibility at the commune level and was the first step toward developing a specialized birth planning apparatus that penetrated to every workplace. The specialized birth planning cadres became a part of the state birth planning bureaucracy, with an obligation to follow the leadership of the birth planning office on all substantive policy matters. Grassroots cadres remained under the leadership of the local party secretary for their administrative area, but the professional linkage with the centralized birth planning organization enhanced the likelihood that local leaders would support and respond to birth planning directives from higher levels.

These documents dramatically strengthened the administrative organization for birth planning. In Hubei Province, for example, there were 145 specialized cadres (*zhuanzhi ganbu*) assigned to birth planning in 1972, 132 at the county level and 13 at the prefectural and provincial levels. By 1980, the number of cadres had increased to 2,395, the bulk of whom were assigned to basic-level units (communes, factories, and neighborhood committees).[27] Similarly, in Guizhou Province, the number of cadres jumped from 49 in 1971 to 4,300 in 1979.[28] In two other cases, Guangdong and Hunan, personnel increased similarly. Guangdong had 395 cadres assigned to birth

25. Shi, *Zhongguo jihua shengyu huodong shi*, 175–76; *Zhongguo renkou—Anhui* (Beijing, 1987), 385; *Zhongguo renkou—Fujian* (Beijing, 1988), 339.

26. Shi, *Zhongguo jihua shengyu huodong shi*, 175.

27. *Zhongguo renkou—Hubei* (Beijing, 1988), 362, 364–65.

28. *Zhongguo renkou—Guizhou*, 432–33.

planning in 1964, a number which most likely remained stable until the early 1970s; by the late 1970s, staff had increased to more than 3,000.[29] In Hunan, the provincial office had a staff of ten in the 1960s, prefectural offices had a staff allocation of three to five, and county offices had an allocation of two or three. By the late 1970s, the latter two administrative levels had higher staff quotas, nine to thirteen for prefectures and five to ten for counties.[30]

Despite this penetration to the commune level, however, the key to enforcing rural birth limits ultimately lay at the brigade and team levels, where the vast majority of peasant households were located. With the countryside organized into about 670,000 brigades and five million teams during the mid-1970s, there was no question of extending the formal bureaucracy to that level. What was possible, however, was to mobilize the network of cadres and activists already in place. At the brigade and team levels, that cadre force consisted principally of the party secretary and all other members of the brigade party branch, all brigade and team cadres, all party members, and all active members of mass organs (e.g., the Women's Association, the local militia, or the Youth League).

Although the senior leaders in the village (the brigade party secretary, the brigade leader, and the team leaders) played a crucial role in enforcing birth limits, the key to the grassroots network was rural women. Each brigade and team had at least one woman on the cadre force—the women's leader. At the brigade level, she was responsible for representing, organizing, and mobilizing women in the brigade; and the post she occupied was mandated by the central government. She was often a member of the brigade party branch committee, usually (but not always) a party or Youth League member, and usually a leading member of the commune branch of the Women's Federation, a nationwide mass organization for women. The brigade leader often began her career at the team level, where a cadre position was also reserved for women's affairs. Like other brigade cadres, brigade women's leaders were usually engaged in full-time work as grassroots cadres, whereas team women's leaders, like all team cadres, were part-time cadres and part-time agricultural producers. These women constituted the backbone cadre force for implementing birth planning in the village. Although they had no special expertise in this area, they were in a position to monitor all village childbearing-age women. This capacity for grassroots penetration and surveillance was crucial to the success of the birth planning

29. In Guangdong, all commune-level cadres were given state cadre status. *Zhongguo renkou—Guangdong* (Beijing, 1988), 402, 404.
30. The quota was linked to the population size of the administrative area. *Zhongguo renkou—Hunan* (Beijing, 1987), 438, 443–44.

campaign, and rural women's leaders quickly became the nonprofessional appendage to the birth planning bureaucracy. Without the cooperation and aggressive assistance of these women, the birth planning campaign could not have succeeded.

Building Momentum

By the early 1980s, this top-to-bottom organization had a well-developed set of routines that structured its activity. Those routines were designed to accomplish seven basic tasks: (1) collecting population data; (2) disseminating birth targets; (3) monitoring childbearing-age women; (4) distributing contraceptives; (5) holding organizational work meetings; (6) conducting investigations of grassroots work, and (7) educating cadres.

The Collection of Population Data

The first and most basic job of the birth planning apparatus was to provide basic population data and maintain population records. These records were transmitted to the commune, where cadres tallied and forwarded them to the district birth planning office. By 1982, county-level birth planning offices maintained detailed population records that included the following categories: total population; age structure and composition; birth, death, and population growth rates; number of childbearing-age couples and number of children per couple; the birth order (i.e., first, second, third, or higher) of each birth during the year; and the number of couples using each type of birth control technique. Data were compiled on the basis of records kept at the brigade and team levels and records maintained by the local public security officials. Brigade women's leaders, with the assistance of their team-level counterparts, kept records for births, pregnancies, and contraceptive use, including IUD insertions, sterilizations, and abortions. Once initial records were set up for each childbearing-age woman, her status could be updated periodically. The records were transmitted to the commune birth planning cadre, who compiled them for further transmission to the county office. Once compiled, the records provided a detailed picture of grassroots compliance with birth plans.

Although grassroots women's leaders compiled data on contraceptive use and on planned and unplanned births (i.e., births formally approved by cadres in accordance with the local birth plan, and births not approved within that plan), public security officials supplied the official figures for births and deaths. A public security office was located in each commune and was responsible for maintaining official household residence files. These files were carefully maintained and updated periodically, registering changes in the size or composition of a household in the village, including births, deaths, and permanent changes of residence (due to marriage or employment, for example). From those records, birth planning officials could calculate rates of birth, death, and population growth.

Once county-level records were compiled, birth planning cadres at that level were responsible for submitting them to the next-higher office (municipal or prefectural), which in turn was responsible for submitting records to the provincial office. In Hubei, a reporting system of this sort was created as early as 1970, requiring county offices to report to municipal or prefectural offices before the tenth of each month. In turn, municipalities and prefectures had to report to the province by the fifteenth of the month.[31] This system of monthly reports was supplemented by a set of quarterly reports that focused primarily on birth control measures.[32] Finally, comprehensive midyear reports were compiled and submitted to the provincial office by July 15. These reports allowed the organization to project year-end totals for births and birth control measures, and to zero in on localities or areas of work where their performance appeared weak.[33]

The Dissemination of Birth Targets

The detailed population records maintained by brigades and communes made it possible to allocate numerical birth planning targets to each locality, but it took some time to develop a comprehensive system for translating national goals to local targets. Beginning in 1973, population growth targets were included in the national economic plan. As a result, by 1974 all governments down to the county level had specific annual targets for population growth. Working from that figure, they were able to develop a target for the annual birthrate and calculate the approximate number of births that could be allowed countywide. In the early 1970s, specific targets were sometimes distributed to communes and brigades, who allocated birth permits to individual couples.[34] In other cases, grassroots cadres were told to work primarily to prevent individual couples from exceeding the number of children allowed under state policy.[35] For example, couples with three or more children were pressured not to have another; after 1977, those with two children were also urged to stop.

31. Interview Files 840608, 840607, 840606, 840613, 840602.
32. Interview Files 840607, 840606, 840613.
33. Interview Files 840607, 840606.
34. *Ming Bao,* September 10, 1974, in *Joint Publications Research Service* (hereinafter *JPRS*) 63369, November 5, 1974, 3. See also Pi-Chau Chen, *Population and Health Policy in the People's Republic of China* (Washington, D.C., 1976).
35. Interview File 920801.

By the mid-to-late 1970s, the more sophisticated practice of setting birth targets had been implemented nationwide. This process began with the designation of national targets for population growth and year-end population size. Those targets were then divided by province, based on relative population size, to be further divided to cities, counties, and communes. In Hubei, for example, targets for 1980 and 1985 were set in the mid-1970s. The targets for 1980 were to reduce population growth to 10 per 1,000 and to hold total population to forty-six million. By 1985, population growth was to slow to about 8 per 1,000, and population was to be held to about forty-nine million.[36] Based on these figures, population targets were calculated and distributed to each city, county, commune, and brigade.

Once the commune-level population growth target was calculated in terms of a specific number of births, it was the job of the commune officials to distribute the quota to individual brigades. Brigade cadres, in turn, allocated specific birth quotas to production teams or to individual couples. At the brigade and team levels, specific local factors, such as the anticipated number of marriages and the number of married couples yet to give birth, could be used to negotiate some leeway in the target. But the official target for planned births could not be increased, even if it was not high enough to cover all eligible couples. In such circumstances, cadres relied on the probability that some eligible women would not become pregnant to compensate for pregnancies elsewhere.

In Donghu (a pseudonym meaning East Lake) Commune, for example, which is located in the distant suburbs of Wuhan, commune leaders were given birth quotas of 430, 398, and 404 for 1981, 1982, and 1983, respectively. These quotas were divided among the commune's nineteen production brigades according to relative population size and the anticipated number of births during the year. Commune and brigade cadres negotiated over the exact birth allocation, and the actual brigade allocation sometimes varied significantly from year to year. Once brigade quotas had been set, they were distributed to production teams, with most teams receiving a quota of only one or two births.[37] Those who had permission to give birth under the plan were given an official birth permit. The permit, which was issued by brigade cadres, was valid only for the year of issue and was nontransferable. In the event that the couple did not give birth during that year, their permit could be transferred to another couple with an unplanned pregnancy. Only the brigade cadres were authorized to make this change, however.[38]

36. *Zhongguo renkou—Hubei,* 362.
37. Interview Files 821014, 821201, 820523, 821012, 821028, 821104, 821109.
38. In 1982, the birth permit read: "Based on the nationally issued population plan targets, combined with the need for late marriage, late birth, and fewer births, it is agreed that you may

The Monitoring of Childbearing-Age Women

Brigade and team women's leaders were responsible for more than simply reporting on the situation within their jurisdiction. They were also responsible for keeping close records on all women of childbearing age and for continually monitoring those in their peak childbearing years to ensure that they did not become pregnant outside the plan. Women's leaders lived and worked in the small and close-knit community of the production team and thus found it easy to monitor their friends, neighbors, and relatives. In this setting, it was virtually impossible to remain undetected if one were pregnant outside the plan. In some villages, women's leaders went so far as to post public records of women's menstrual cycles, a system that required monthly examinations to determine each woman's status.[39] This capacity to maintain close surveillance within the village was the key link in the top-to-bottom organizational system.

The Distribution of Contraceptive Supplies

During the 1970s, an increasing proportion of rural couples relied on the IUD for contraception. IUD insertions, as well as abortions and sterilizations, were performed at commune clinics or county hospitals. Many couples continued to rely on condoms, spermicides, and other forms of contraception, however, and those supplies had to be provided directly to rural couples. To assure a stable supply, birth planning cadres at higher levels relied on quarterly reports from brigades and communes indicating the number of birth control procedures that had been performed in the locality and the number of couples relying on different forms of birth control. Those reports were compiled and sent to the provincial and central levels, becoming the basis for annual and quarterly planning for the production and supply of various types of contraceptives. Placing orders for contraceptives was the responsibility of the State Family Planning Commission. On the basis of nationwide reports, the SFPC notified the State Pharmaceutical Bureau (SPB) about the quantity and type of supplies needed, as well as the schedule for distribution. The SPB then coordinated the production and distribution of contraceptives through the network of pharmaceutical companies located in various provinces and municipalities. The companies distributed supplies to local pharmaceutical retail outlets, where county birth planning cadres collected them. In Wuhan, commune officials were required to travel to the district birth planning office once a month to collect the supplies.[40]

---

give birth to a child during the year [198X]; the quota is valid for this year and cannot be transferred." Interview File 820406.

39. Interview Files 820406, 900722.
40. Interview File 821014.

Beginning in the early 1970s, all contraceptives were supplied by the state free of charge. As a result, local officials did not pay for contraceptive supplies. Funds for that purpose came out of the central budget. They did pay management fees, however. The SPB received a management fee from the State Family Planning Commission equal to 2 percent of the sales price. Provincial-level pharmaceutical companies and distribution stations received a fee equal to 5 percent of the sale price, and county-level companies received 1.5 percent.[41]

Similarly, local hospitals under the jurisdiction of the MOH did not charge directly for the birth control procedures they performed. Individuals scheduled for procedures were accompanied by brigade or commune birth planning officials. Quarterly reports recording these procedures were forwarded to higher levels and were used to determine the amount of compensation due the MOH from each locality.[42]

The Holding of Organizational Work Meetings

One of the principal methods for maintaining organizational cohesion was conducting frequent work meetings to discuss policy and report results. Large annual work conferences were held at the national and provincial levels, attended by representatives of all lower-level administrative units. These meetings, generally held in the first quarter of the year, reviewed performance during the previous year, discussed the work situation for the current year, and planned for the work of the following year. Instructions communicated at these conferences set the agenda for local birth planning work in the coming year.

At the municipal and local levels, meetings were held more frequently. In Wuhan, for example, municipal work report meetings (*gongzuo huibao hui*), attended by district and county-level officials, were held quarterly. Lasting from one to three days, the purpose of the meeting was to hear reports about the status of local-level work. District and county cadres prepared for these meetings by holding their own one-day meetings with commune-level officials on a monthly basis. These meetings, combined with the statistical reporting system, ensured that birth planning cadres could monitor progress toward fulfilling the plan in different localities and attempt to intervene in areas doing poorly.

Municipal offices also conducted meetings to disseminate information on the experience of a particular locale in carrying out birth planning. Dubbed "experience communication meetings" (*jingyan jiaoliuhui*), such meetings

41. Yang Deqing, Su Zhenyu, and Liu Yuangu, *Jihua shengyu xue* (Nanjing, 1984), 154–55.
42. Interview File 821014.

were usually held in localities that had done especially well. Occasionally, however, they were used to single out a backward area as a negative example, a strategy that was designed to force senior leaders in the area to make a greater commitment to the work.[43]

Meetings were also held to disseminate new policy guidelines or educate grassroots cadres. Within Wuhan municipality, county-level "study" meetings were held once a month for commune-level cadres in charge of birth planning.[44] Less frequent, but equally important, were "specialized cadre meetings" (*zhuanzhi ganbuhui*), attended by commune-level party secretaries, commune directors or deputies, and any other cadres with direct oversight responsibility for birth planning. They were joined by the regular birth planning cadres.[45]

At the grassroots, periodic work meetings were also held. In Donghu, a commune "women directors' meeting" (*funu zhuren hui*) was held once a month. Attended by the commune birth planning official, the Women's Federation director, all brigade women's leaders, plus the commune director and party secretary, this meeting was used to hear reports on brigade performance, to study relevant documents or instructions from higher levels, and to discuss concrete problem cases among peasant households. Once every three months, all team women's leaders attended the meeting as well.[46] At the brigade level, discussions of birth planning were integrated into regular meetings on women's affairs. Women's leaders put birth planning on the agenda at regular meetings of the Women's Representative Congress (*funu diabiao weiyuanhui*), a local mass organization for women that met once a month. In addition, periodic mass meetings for all brigade women were held on an irregular basis. These meetings focused on political indoctrination and education, tackling such practical issues as local attitudes toward childbearing. In one brigade, three such meetings were held in 1981, the first year in which the one-child policy was pressed vigorously for rural couples.[47]

Conducting Investigations of Grassroots Work

To check the quality of the information they receive from lower levels, birth planning cadres at all levels conducted investigations on a regular basis. At the Hubei provincial level, investigations of overall work performance were conducted two to four times a year. In addition, two investiga-

---

43. Interview File 840607.
44. Interview Files 821014, 821201.
45. Ibid.
46. Interview Files 821014, 820406.
47. Interview Files 820523, 820516, 820521, 821028.

tions of statistical reporting were conducted, covering four municipal neighborhoods and thirty-eight brigades.[48] In turn, the Wuhan municipal office conducted two types of investigations annually. In January of each year, office cadres spent three weeks to two months investigating the results of the previous year's work, and in July, they traveled to localities with good and poor records to evaluate the situation and prepare for the second half of the year.[49]

Similar investigations occurred at the grassroots. County cadres visited commune sites at least once a year and selected specific sites for more extensive investigation twice a year.[50] Commune cadres in Donghu made investigative trips to each brigade every three months. With nineteen brigades in the commune, she thus averaged slightly more than one field trip per week just to cover each brigade on a quarterly basis.[51]

Cadre Education and Training

Another function of the birth planning organization was to educate and train cadres, a process that was intended both to inform them about the birth planning policy and mobilize them to enforce it. Between 1975 and 1978, several provinces held extensive training classes in population theory. The classes, which were offered at party and cadre training schools at each level, reached large numbers of cadres and individuals. In Hunan, for example, four major training classes were held between 1977 and 1981, each of which trained cadres to offer classes at lower levels. In 1978 alone, more than 910 population theory classes were held at all levels, with more than 970,000 people participating. In the same year, birth planning was discussed 1,378 times at classes in party and cadre schools and in other meetings, with over 360,000 people in attendance, and there were eighty special broadcasts with nearly two million listeners. Finally, another twenty-four million were exposed to population theory at political study classes.[52] In Guangdong and Sichuan, a similar process occurred. In Guangdong, between 1975 and 1978, over two hundred thousand cadres took population theory classes. In addition, 40 percent of all communes and 38 percent of all brigades also participated in such classes, with 3.25 million people receiving instruction.[53] In Sichuan, 1,174 population theory classes were held

48. Interview File 840608.
49. Interview File 840607.
50. Interview File 840606.
51. Interview File 820406.
52. *Zhongguo renkou—Hunan*, 442.
53. *Zhongguo renkou—Guangdong*, 405. Other provinces report holding similar classes without giving details. See *Zhongguo renkou—Hubei* (Beijing, 1988), 466–467; *Zhongguo renkou—Sichuan* (Beijing, 1988), 402–3.

between 1976 and 1978, with more than one hundred thousand cadres in attendance.[54]

As important and effective as the basic organizational system was, the seven elements described above were insufficient alone to gain peasant compliance on a mass scale. The key was grassroots enforcement within the village, and enforcement could only be guaranteed if two requirements were met. First, party and state cadres throughout the system, but especially at the grassroots, had to be persuaded that the center had made birth planning a priority. If they were not persuaded, they would put little effort into enforcement and they would violate the birth limits themselves. Getting sustained cadre compliance was the necessary condition for successful implementation. Second, specific measures for encouraging peasant compliance and deterring offenders had to be crafted, measures that grassroots cadres could rely on within the existing administrative framework of the collective. To meet these two requirements for campaign success, central and local cadres saw no need for crafting new techniques for implementation. Instead, they turned automatically to the campaign methods that had become a ritualized part of the implementation process. It is to these methods that we now turn.

Propaganda, Education, and Training

One of the earliest and most important signals that a new campaign was being launched was a shift of media attention to a new topic and intensive coverage of that topic. Propaganda and education were important not only for establishing and publicizing the party line on the issue but were also designed to increase pressures for action throughout the political system and to communicate the rewards and sanctions to be used to garner compliance.

The propaganda campaign for birth planning followed this general pattern, becoming more intense as the 1970s wore on. It reached its zenith with the "Open Letter" from the CCP that made the one-child limit universal. At the central and provincial levels, the principal propaganda activities were conducting radio and newspaper campaigns and holding meetings designed to popularize the experience of a particularly successful locality. At the grassroots, broadcasts were made over the public address (loudspeaker) system, and movies and slides were produced locally and shown once a month. At all levels, birth planning slogans were painted on walls, hung on public banners, and written on big character posters.[55]

54. *Zhongguo renkou—Sichuan,* 403–4.
55. Interview File 821014.

The content of these campaigns is well illustrated by a series of reports that appeared in local newspapers or on radio broadcasts in the 1978–80 period. During those years, local broadcasts and articles stressed two basic themes that were set at the central level. First, given the attacks on birth control in the 1960s, an effort was made to explain the underlying theory of socialist political economy that justified birth planning. Far from being Malthusian and non-Marxist, it was argued that population planning was necessary because of the shifting balance of productive forces and labor power in modern society. Whether a large population size was "good" could only be calculated in relation to economic capacity and technological level. As China's socialist development progressed in tandem with continued technological innovation in the capitalist world, the need for labor power fell, making population control essential. Without it, China's developmental gains, no matter how impressive, would continue to translate into economic losses or stagnation on a per capita basis.

The Marxist basis for this argument was actually a quote from Frederick Engels:

> According to the materialistic conception, the decisive factor in history is, in the last resort, the production and reproduction of immediate life. But this itself is of a two-fold character. On the one hand, the production of the means of subsistence, of food, clothing and shelter and the tools requisite thereto; on the other, the production of human beings themselves, the propagation of the species.[56]

If material production and human reproduction are two halves of the same fundamental productive process, it was argued, both should be integrated into the planning process. "Jointly grasp two kinds of production" (*liangzhong shengchan yiqi zhua*) thus became a key slogan over the next several years.[57] The phrase proved especially valuable in bridging the gap between theory and practice in birth planning work, operating as a departure point for mass education and cadre instruction. The masses could be instructed in the immediate links between economic development and population growth, and cadres could be reminded of their obligation to treat local planning targets for population control with the same seriousness as production targets.

56. Frederick Engels, *The Origin of the Family, Private Property, and the State* (1884), in Robert Tucker, ed., *The Marx-Engels Reader* (New York, 1978), 734–59.
57. Sun Jingzhi, "Jiejue zhongguo renkou wentide genben tujing," *Renkou yu jingji* 1 (1980): 6; "Beijing dierci renkou lilun taolunhui zhuanti zongshu," *Renkou yu jingji* 3 (1980): 17; Liang Wenda, "Makesi zhuyide 'liangzhong shengchan' guan shi jihua shengyu gongzuode lilun jichu," *Renkou yanjiu* 3 (1980): 35. *Xinhua*, December 22, 1979, in *FBIS*, December 28, 1979, L7–9.

The theoretical argument laid the groundwork for the second theme during this period—explaining why the state had a vested interest in controlling childbearing. To those who argued that childbearing was a private choice, not a public one, the state responded with rough calculations about the cost to the state of raising each child to the age of sixteen, the point at which one could be considered a full-time laborer. According to estimates, in 1978 a rural couple spent 1,600 yuan, a town (*zhen*) couple spent 4,800 yuan, and a city (*cheng*) couple spent 6,900 yuan.[58] With about six hundred million births since 1949, it was calculated that "the state, the collectives, and individual families" had therefore spent about one thousand trillion yuan, equal to 30 percent of all national income since 1949.[59] Of that amount, about 30 percent, 396 trillion yuan, was absorbed by the state in direct and indirect subsidies. Once put in those terms, the state could argue its legitimate and rational interest in population growth, and it could make everyone more aware of the economic consequences of childbearing.

Provincial media reports were blunter about the economic consequences of excess population growth. Focusing on per capita declines in arable land and grain production, and the rising costs of childbearing, newspaper articles and radio broadcasts directly linked the drive for modernization and the burden of population growth.[60] In Hubei, for example, the provincial daily newspaper used the stagnant figures for rural development to encourage fertility control.[61] Days later, a follow-up report on Hubei's Huanggang County reported a decline in arable land from 1.6 to 0.95 mu per capita, and a per capita drop in grain rations of 34 jin between 1965 and 1977. The report also linked investment in birth planning work directly to increased local income, claiming that one commune's three-year birth control expenditure of 26,752 yuan (1975–78) reduced the rate of birth sufficiently to increase local income by 97,536 yuan.[62]

Apart from these educational themes, the propaganda campaign also focused on model cases for emulation and targets for criticism. National and local reports took pains to acknowledge and praise progressive individuals and units and to condemn those that were backward and set bad examples. In Hubei, for example, five types of model cases were reported in the

58. *Xinhua* Domestic Service, "How Much Money Is Needed to Bring a Baby to Full Growth?" June 8, 1989, in *FBIS*, June 13, 1989, L16–17.

59. *Xinhua*, August 11, 1979, in *FBIS*, August 16, 1979, L15–17.

60. For example, Shandong Provincial Service, August 7, 1979, in *FBIS*, August 10, 1979, p. O-8–9; Wen Yinggan, "To Do Well in Controlling Population Growth is an Important Item of Work," *Nanfang ribao*, August 1, 1979, 3, in *FBIS*, August 10, 1979, P2–3.

61. Li Sheng, "Jihua shengyu yu nongye xiandaihua," *Hubei ribao* (June 19, 1978), 3.

62. "Huanggang xian shi zemyang zhuajin jihua shengyu gongzuode?" *Hubei ribao* (June 23, 1979), 3.

provincial paper between February and June 1979, paralleling other provincial newspaper reports. They are summarized below.[63]

1. *Persuading the reluctant husband.* A peasant woman with one daughter tells of how she persuaded her husband, who wanted a son, that she should have an operation. The woman had been an only child and had been able to care for her mother. Variations on this story include withstanding an evil husband's brutality in order to comply with the policy.
2. *The good mother.* A mother of seven who encouraged her eldest daughter to have an operation after giving birth to one son is praised as a model. Variations include the good mother-in-law and the evil mother-in-law.
3. *Progressive feminism.* A rural couple with two girls faced a decision when the wife becomes pregnant for a third time. They decided to have a late-term abortion, followed by sterilization (no explanation is offered for why it is a late-term, or third trimester, abortion). The bad neighbors urged them to reconsider, as did the mother-in-law, who complained that she had two sons and five granddaughters, but no grandsons. They didn't listen to these backward views. Variations included a progressive woman with one daughter, an evil husband who insisted on having a son, but a good mother-in-law who was happy with her one granddaughter.
4. *Leadership sets example.* In one model production brigade, fifty-three party members and fifteen brigade leaders underwent sterilization, including six women who had daughters but no sons. Everyone got a 50 yuan reward. Variations include all brigade women's leaders undergoing sterilization.
5. *Model cadre.* A brigade women's leader uses her free time to take care of those undergoing birth control procedures. Variations include selfless cadres who persist in their work despite the threat of abuse or no pay.

Positive role models were not enough, however. Publicizing the political and economic distress suffered by noncompliant workers, peasants, and especially cadres sent a more pointed and threatening message. Again, a selection of reports from Hubei and other localities illustrates the range of bad examples.

---

63. The five model cases are based on articles in *Hubei ribao* for the following dates: June 23, 1979, 3; May 8, 1979, 3; February 20, 1979, 3; June 23, 1979, 3; May 8, 1979, 3.

1. *"Woe is me."* A peasant bemoaned the fact that she did not heed the call for limiting family size. Instead, she had six children, became indebted to the team, and had to borrow over 40 yuan from the state for grain.[64]

2. *Party member punished.* A peasant was thrown out of the party for one year for having a sixth child.[65]

3. *Uncooperative cadres criticized.* A cadre in the propaganda department in Hengyang County, Hunan, wrote to a Hunan radio station to complain about cadres in urban units who were uncooperative when the rural wives of their employees fled to the units for refuge against sterilization.[66]

4. *Defiant cadres punished.* A deputy director of the People's Liberation Army (PLA) department in Xiangtan County, Hunan, was dismissed and demoted when his wife refused to abort her pregnancy. The couple already had three daughters.[67] Similarly, a Beijing couple, both party members and cadres, incurred penalties totaling 3,000 yuan for having a fourth child.[68]

5. *Sterilization as the ultimate sanction.* In Guizhou, two county-level cadres who were married defied the birth limits to have a third child. Their first two children were daughters. They were severely criticized for their backward, feudal thinking, and the wife was dismissed from her post. The husband suffered more intrusive punishment.[69] He was required to undergo sterilization. Also in Guizhou, more than one hundred party and municipal officials in Zhijin city underwent sterilization to "take the blame" for their failure to enforce the regulations, after being criticized by provincial authorities. They were not charged with violating the regulations themselves but rather with failing to require others in the city to comply.[70]

Linking Campaigns

Linking campaigns—giving a policy-oriented campaign added urgency and significance by linking it to an ongoing political campaign—was a standard part of campaign politics during the Maoist era. It remained a common

---

64. *Hubei ribao,* June 23, 1979, 3.
65. *Hubei ribao,* February 1, 1980, 2.
66. Hunan Provincial Service, September 23, 1979, in *FBIS,* September 26, 1979, P2–3.
67. Hunan Provincial Service, December 8, 1979, in *FBIS,* December 13, 1979, P6.
68. Beijing City Service, April 12, 1980, in *FBIS,* April 21, 1980, R1.
69. *Kyodo,* March 24, 1980, in *FBIS,* March 25, 1980, Q1.
70. *Kyodo,* June 26, 1980, in *FBIS,* June 27, 1980, Q1.

practice during the 1970s, when radical politics and elite instability made every policy initiative a political battleground.[71] Apart from the momentum created by the birth planning propaganda itself, central or local officials could increase the probability of grassroots compliance by linking it with political campaigns. Birth planning was linked to four major campaigns during the 1970s: (1) the "prepare for war" campaign of the early 1970s; (2) the "anti-Confucius—anti-Lin Biao" campaign of 1974–76; (3) the "learn from Dazhai" campaign (1969–76); and (4) the "anti–Gang of Four" campaign of 1976–80.

The "prepare for war" campaign began in the late 1960s in response to U.S. and Soviet threats. The campaign was the focal point for all national planning during the 1970–72 period, and accordingly the birth planning campaign that reappeared at this time was linked to this strategic political line of Chairman Mao. The following selection from a medical pamphlet on birth planning illustrates how the linkage was constructed:

> The work on planned parenthood has a vital bearing on the national economy and is an important matter of changing customs and transforming the world, and a major measure for implementing Chairman Mao's great instructions on "be prepared for war, be prepared against natural disasters, and do everything for the people," and on "grasp revolution to promote production, work, and combat readiness." Our country is a socialist country, and its economic and construction programs are carried out according to plans and ratios. Therefore, increase in population must be regulated by plans. The enthusiastic use of scientific methods for birth control and a successful program for planned parenthood are good for the health of mothers and children, and what is more important is that they make it possible for those concerned to concentrate more of their energy on the study of Chairman Mao's works and on changing their world outlook.[72]

Although the link between birth planning and the "prepare for war" strategy was of the most general sort, this example demonstrates how essential it was to forge linkages across policies and campaigns. Connecting birth planning to the most important revolutionary task of all, national survival and transformation, gave it legitimacy and weight that it otherwise would not have had. Without any attempt to link birth planning with larger strategic or political goals, the initiative would have been lost in bureaucratic indif-

71. For a discussion of campaign linkage in rural policy during the 1970s, see Zweig, *Agrarian Radicalism*, 41–43.

72. The pamphlet from which this selection was taken was issued by the Shanghai Municipal Publications Revolutionary Team in July 1970 as the seventieth issue of *Yiliao weisheng ziliao* [Medical and Health Materials]. See "Pamphlet Promoting Planned Parenthood and Late Marriage," *JPRS* 52013, December 17, 1970, 7.

ference; by making the link, cadres were put on notice that birth planning work mattered.

More concrete linkages were made between birth planning and the other three campaigns. The campaign to criticize Confucius and Lin Biao (Mao's ally and minister of defense until his death in 1971 after leading a military coup attempt) was intended, among other things, to repudiate the conservative and reactionary ideas espoused by both, and more generally, to eliminate feudal habits and customs. Those ideas were said to comprise a "reactionary ideology" with tenets such as "having no children is the biggest of the three unfilial acts" and "men are superior to women."[73] Although Confucius and Mencius were identified as the authors of these views, it was charged that Lin Biao had espoused them as well. Those who refused to comply with birth plans could therefore be threatened with a reactionary political label, as the following report from Shandong Province illustrates:

> In [Lushan] production brigade of [Huichi] commune, Changtao County, one bad element attempted to undermine late marriage and planned parenthood. He was exposed through the movement to criticize Lin Biao and Confucius. Later, the party committee and party branch of the commune and the brigade used this bad element as a live target for criticism. By mobilizing the masses to criticize his crimes, tear off his mask, expose his true nature and vigorously criticize Lin Biao and Confucius, the party committee and party branch guided all commune members to further raise their awareness of the need to carry out Chairman Mao's revolutionary line. The percentage of the people willing to submit to birth control in the commune has increased sharply, from 75 to 82 percent.[74]

This report shows vividly the power of linking a policy campaign to a political campaign and how political campaign tactics—identifying and exposing the enemy to mass criticism—could be imported into other types of campaigns and used to great effect.

In similar fashion, the "learn from Dazhai" campaign, which called for emulation of the radical Dazhai production brigade and its advanced collectivist and egalitarian policies, also became a vehicle for birth planning. At the Second National Conference on Learning from Dazhai, convened in December 1976, conference delegates were told to integrate birth planning into their work. This reference provided the basis for linking birth planning work to the ongoing "emulate Dazhai" campaign. To be designated an advanced unit in learning from Dazhai, a designation that brought commendation to local cadres, communes and production brigades had to meet cer-

73. Canton City Service, March 4, 1974, in *FBIS*, March 15, 1974, D4.
74. Shandong Provincial Service, March 25, 1975, in *FBIS*, April 2, 1975, G8.

tain specific targets in political and economic work. After 1975, some localities added birth planning to the list of targets that had to be fulfilled. In 1978, for example, Henan Province decreed that only those units with a population growth rate under 8.5 per 1,000, a very high target, could be designated as advanced Dazhai units.[75]

Birth planning was also linked to the campaign against the Gang of Four. The campaign against the Gang of Four, which raged during the 1976–78 period, was the litmus test for political loyalty in the immediate post-Mao period. The Gang was charged with crimes conducted during the Cultural Revolution and with sabotaging every policy initiative of the previous decade. Ritual criticism of the Gang was therefore a necessary part of every government and party meeting, regardless of the agenda. Birth planning was no exception, even though the most rapid gains in this area had occurred during the period when the Gang's power was supposedly at its peak. Their "pernicious influence" was said to have done great damage to birth planning work, and Jiang Qing (Mao's second wife and leader of the Gang) was charged with having propagated the wild idea that women were superior to men. She was also charged with rejecting the need for birth control and late marriage, while the Gang in general was blamed for the mistake of allowing three children per couple instead of two.[76] Failure to meet escalating goals in these areas, therefore, posed a serious political problem for grassroots cadres. A *People's Daily* editorial of July 8, 1978, for example, attributed lingering high birthrates and other problems in birth planning work to "the pernicious influence of the fallacies of the Gang of Four" thus drawing a direct connection between poor performance and political standing. At a time when many cadres were scurrying to align themselves with the new reform-minded regime of Deng Xiaoping, and when leftist opponents were being purged, the language of the editorial put everyone on notice that opposition to a tightening childbearing policy, no matter what the motive, might make one vulnerable to the dangerous charge of having pro-Gang sympathies.[77]

Apart from these linkages to political campaigns, birth planning was also linked with other, more practical campaign goals. The ultimate linkage in this category was that between population control and the achievement of the "Four Modernizations" (the modernization of agriculture, industry, science and technology, and national defense) by the year 2000. But other, more obscure, linkages were also made. In one area, birth planning was

75. Henan Provincial Service, July 16, 1978, in *FBIS,* July 21, 1978, H1.
76. Guangdong Provincial Service, December 12, 1976, in *FBIS,* December 15, 1976, H15–17; Anhui Provincial Service, February 4, 1978, in *FBIS,* February 7, 1978, G1–2.
77. *Renmin ribao,* July 8, 1978.

linked with a pest eradication and disease control campaign, and in another it was linked with "patriotic sanitation" campaigns.[78] Unlike the linkages to political campaigns, where the linkage added weight to the campaign efforts, linkages to these types of practical campaigns were simply efficient ways to mobilize the public health bureaucracy and grassroots cadres to do several things at once. A single meeting could be called to send down instructions on birth planning and pest control; a single set of documents could be sent down to organize sanitation work and birth planning. This concentration of work gave it more import at the grassroots and allowed grassroots cadres to organize their work around the simultaneous accomplishment of multiple tasks.

Cadre Targets and Territorial Assignments

If propaganda campaigns and political pressure were insufficient to persuade rural cadres to enforce birth limits, two additional mechanisms, both commonly used to enhance administrative zeal, were put into place to hold them personally accountable. First, cadres at the commune, brigade, and team levels had specific birth planning targets issued by higher levels. In Donghu commune, for example, five targets were set for 1981: achieving a birthrate of 13.5 per 1,000, persuading 85 percent of all single-child couples to sign a certificate guaranteeing not to have another child, achieving a 90 percent rate for late marriage (aged twenty-three for women, twenty-five for men), assuring that 90 percent of all births were within the plan, and assuring that all couples of childbearing age were using birth control.[79] Cadres who met the targets received cash awards and bonuses along with political commendation. Those who failed to meet the targets received no bonuses or smaller bonuses, their political record suffered, and by placing the performance of their superiors in jeopardy, their relations with those at higher levels could also suffer. In 1978, birth planning targets were officially included in the list of important performance targets that would be used to evaluate cadres, determine promotions and salaries, and award the title of "advanced" cadre or unit.[80]

In addition to birth targets, per capita economic targets were sometimes issued as well. In Huaide County of Jilin Province, for example, cadres had to meet three targets annually: (1) increase in grain production, (2) increase in per capita income, and 3) decrease in population growth. Cash rewards

78. Shanghai City Service, February 25, 1975, in *FBIS*, March 3, 1975, G6–7; Sichuan Provincial Service, December 22, 1974, in *FBIS*, December 24, 1974, J1–2.

79. Interview File 821014.

80. *Zhongguo renkou—Hubei*, 363.

were given for each target they completed, and penalties were imposed for those they did not.[81] A similar set of joint targets was implemented in Liaoning Province. Known as the *liang, qian, ren* (grain, money, and people) system, cadre salaries and bonuses depended on their joint achievements in economic production and birth planning.[82]

Second, at the county level and below, cadres entered into pledges or contracts to be personally accountable for the performance of a certain administrative territory.[83] Senior county leaders, for example, pledged themselves to be responsible for the work of a certain group of subordinate county officials. Each member of that group, in turn, pledged personal responsibility for the performance of certain communes within the county. At the commune level, senior cadres, assisted by groups of subordinates, were assigned responsibility for certain brigades—the same brigades that they normally oversaw during production campaigns or for other work. And brigade leaders, in turn, divided responsibilities for the production teams within the brigade. The advantage of such a system was that it did not reward or punish all cadres equally for the performance of the region as a whole. Instead, because cadres at each level had different areas to cover, some cadres might be rewarded for meeting the targets for their area of responsibility, while those who failed to meet theirs were penalized. This increased visibility and risk heightened cadre attention at every level. Moreover, since county leaders were completely dependent on their subordinates to turn in a performance that would net them a bonus and commendation, this method tended to produce intense pressures from higher levels to meet and exceed campaign targets. Under such pressures, grassroots leaders had little alternative but to push the campaign forward aggressively.

Rewards and Penalties for Compliance

The threat of political punishment for violating birth planning was one of a whole range of rewards and penalties that were adopted and implemented over the course of the decade. Rewards were either economic or political in nature and were applicable either to childbearing-age couples or to cadres responsible for implementation.

The first step toward creating an incentive system for birth planning was

---

81. Jin Chao, "Shixing jihua shengyu, youxiaode kongzhi renkou cengzhang," *Renkou yu jingji* 2 (1980): 43. (This journal, which was published by Jilin University and was renamed *Renkouxue kan* in 1981, should not be confused with the *Renkou yu jingji* published by the Institute of Population Economics of the Beijing College of Economics.)

82. *Zhongguo renkou—Liaoning* (Beijing, 1988), 332.

83. This system was referred to as *fenpian baogan,* or simply *baopian.*

TABLE 6. Schedule of vacation allowances for birth control procedures, 1973

Procedure	Vacation period
IUD insertion	2 days
IUD removals	1 day
First trimester abortion	14 days
First trimester abortion; simultaneous IUD insertion	14 days
First trimester abortion; simultaneous tubal ligation	1 month
Second trimester abortion	1 month
Second trimester abortion; simultaneous tubal ligation	10 days
Female sterilization	21 days
Sterilization after childbirth	regular maternity leave plus 14 days*
Male sterilization	7 days

Source: Shi, *Zhongguo jihua shengyu huodong shi*, 163–64.
*During the Maoist era, women were generally entitled to a three-month maternity leave.

the decision to provide generous vacation periods to all who underwent birth control procedures. In March 1973, the MOH issued a document entitled "Regulations on Birth Control Operations."[84] The document urged all units to give paid vacation leave to all individuals undergoing sterilization and to all women undergoing abortions or IUD insertions (see schedule in table 6). Because local governments, work units, and production teams would ultimately be responsible for providing this economic benefit, the MOH could not mandate the implementation of these guidelines. It is unclear, therefore, how widely these guidelines were enforced during the mid-1970s, but they reappeared at the end of the decade in trial regulations on birth planning that were issued by local governments and sanctioned by the center.

Trial regulations on birth planning were enacted by provincial revolutionary committees or people's congresses over a period of about one year, with Sichuan and Anhui provinces developing "one-child" regulations in early 1979 and Guangdong delaying until February 1980. The regulations varied slightly from province to province, but all followed a general formula approved at the January 1979 national meeting of birth planning office directors. Apparently, Guangdong and Tianjin had already developed draft regulations by that time. The regulations, which offered incentives for having only one child and invoked penalties against those who had a third child, were "popularized" by the State Council Office for Birth Planning,

84. Shi, *Zhongguo jihua shengyu huodong shi*, 163.

triggering other provinces to adopt similar regulations without delay. In turn, municipalities and other local governments adopted their own regulations, providing a regulatory framework for the policies that extended to the grassroots.

The regulations of Hubei Province and Wuhan municipality provide examples of the general format and content of the regulations. In September 1979, *Hubei ribao* published the "Trial Regulations for Hubei Province for the Implementation of Family Planning," which had been adopted at a full session of the provincial revolutionary committee.[85] Prior to 1979, regulations for birth planning had been based on the results of a 1972 meeting in Huanggang Prefecture, at which time it was agreed that a standard of two children in urban areas and three in rural areas would be promoted. The new regulations, issued as Provincial Document 82 (1979), consisted of ten articles. With the exception of Article 1, which reiterated the need for a population policy and introduced the regulations, the articles detailed procedures for implementing the "one is best, two at most" policy in effect at that time.

Rewards were divided into three categories. First were the rewards for undergoing birth control procedures. The regulations reaffirmed that men and women of childbearing age were entitled to free birth control supplies and devices, as well as free "birth control operations," that is, abortions, sterilizations, and intrauterine device insertions. Workers and peasants were to receive paid vacations after undergoing a "birth control procedure," and bonuses were not to be adversely affected by the vacation time. Specific guidelines for vacations were not given, but presumably the MOH guidelines served to set standards in this area.

Second were the economic preferences to be given to one-child couples. Parents of single children were to receive health care fees (*baojianfei*) totaling 30–40 yuan per year in urban areas and 400 work points in rural areas. These health subsidies were to be allocated until the child reached fourteen, but only those parents who underwent sterilization after the first child received the subsidy from the date of birth. Those who "adopted effective measures" and guaranteed not to have a second child received the subsidy for ten years, beginning with the child's fourth birthday. Anyone who received the bonuses and later had a second child was required to repay the health subsidies received. Single children under age fourteen were also guaranteed preferential treatment in admission to nursery, kindergarten, elementary, and middle schools, obtaining work as an adult, and entering university, "other things being equal."

85. *Hubei ribao*, September 27, 1979.

Parents of single children were guaranteed retirement income. Workers were to receive the standard retirement pay offered by their unit plus an additional 5 percent, except where such pay already equaled 100 percent of a worker's salary at the time of retirement. Peasants were to receive a monthly subsidy of 3–5 yuan, in addition to any retirement privileges already in effect under local regulations.[86]

Third were housing and grain allotment benefits. In cities and towns, residents who complied with late marriage regulations were guaranteed priority in housing; single-child couples were guaranteed a housing allotment equivalent to that of a two-child household. In rural areas, couples with a single child were entitled to receive a grain ration equivalent to that for three adults. This provision counteracted the effect of a 1978 change in grain allotment policy that mandated that children receive smaller allotments of grain than adults. Similarly, couples with one child were entitled to a private plot equivalent to that of a two-child family; however, the regulations did not mandate village redistribution for this purpose but referred instead to future landholding adjustments.

In addition to specifying these rewards, the regulations also outlined penalties for noncompliance. Anyone who exceeded two children had to pay an "excess-child fee" (*duo zinu fei*) consisting of 10 percent of the salary of each parent for fourteen years. Exceptions were to be made in cases of twins or multiple offspring resulting from the second pregnancy. Workers' pay would be docked and the funds deposited in the unit welfare fund. Peasants would be assessed by the production team during the year-end distribution process, those funds also to be diverted to the team welfare fund. Especially in the countryside, where peasant households lived with little or no margin of income beyond subsistence, an economic penalty amounting to 20 percent of a couple's income for fourteen years was an extremely serious threat. All such penalties were to become effective six months from the date of publication of the regulations, presumably to allow time for women to terminate pregnancies that would result in "excess" children.

---

86. Elaborate procedures were outlined regarding how local units would pay birth planning benefits. In urban areas, unit welfare funds were to be drawn on for this purpose. For temporary workers, however, unit operating funds were to be used. This distinction insured that the unit welfare fund would not be unfairly depleted by workers who had not paid into the fund. In rural areas, brigade and team welfare funds (*gongjijin*) were the source of family planning rewards. If both parents worked, each unit was to pay half. If one parent was a full-time worker and the other a commune member, a temporary worker, or without work, the worker's unit was responsible for the rewards. Finally, if the parents lived in two separate provinces, the unit where the child lived was responsible for arranging the subsidies and preferential treatment, unless the parent was unemployed. In that case, rewards were to be drawn from the operating expenses of the local birth planning office.

Only days after the publication of the provincial regulations, the Wuhan municipality "Provisional Regulations on Birth Planning" were issued.[87] These regulations became the departure point for crafting specific regulations for the rural communes within the jurisdiction, including Donghu. The municipal provisions were more detailed than the provincial regulations and included specific conditions under which medical personnel became eligible for rewards. According to the regulations, "technical cadres" who performed one thousand or ten thousand birth control procedures without accidents (*shigu*) or mistakes (*chacuo*) were to receive rewards, though the amount was not stipulated. In addition, the regulations dealt with three other issues that were not covered under the provincial regulations. First, they mandated the creation of courses dealing with "puberty, biology, and hygiene" (in other words, sex education), as well as courses in birth control, late marriage, and population theory. Second, Article 8 stressed the importance of marriage registration, denying maternity benefits or compensation for birth control to those who failed to register. It also reiterated a longstanding prohibition against marriage for those studying as apprentices or in school and called for lengthening the periods of apprenticeship or delaying work and study for those who violated the provision. Finally, they mandated the use of a birth planning "card system" (*kapian zhidu*) that would require the presentation of a card with relevant birth planning information, along with a birth permit, in order to register a child at the local public security bureau.

Both the provincial and municipal regulations also stated when the regulations would take effect. However, whereas the provincial regulations called for a six-month delay, the municipal regulations allowed only a two-month delay. Because the municipal regulations were published only days after the provincial regulations, the municipality cut the delay in enforcement by four months. The implications of this decision were clear. All those pregnant with a third or additional child, as well as those expecting a second child within three years of their first, had to make a rapid decision about whether to try to carry the child to term. While the provincial regulations left time for women in the second or third trimester to give birth without suffering economic sanctions, women in Wuhan did not have that luxury. Those expecting a third child had to choose between a late-term abortion and stiff economic penalties.

Both sets of regulations passed on to local jurisdictions the right to shape or alter the regulations to suit local conditions. This caveat was essential, in

---

87. They were published in *Changjiang ribao* on October 10, 1979, and were composed of thirteen articles.

that it was impossible for the regulations to cover every possible contingency. Nevertheless, the caveat also carried some risk, since local governments had explicit power to modify the regulations, as long as they worked within the general framework of the guidelines and achieved their birth planning work quotas. As we will see, this leeway was later utilized at the grassroots to stretch the policy in favor of local preferences.

Shock Attacks

At the grassroots, rural cadres supplemented the array of mobilization techniques outlined above with methods designed specifically for the target population—women who were pregnant outside the plan or who had not adopted effective birth control.

By issuing regulations that outlined the economic rewards and penalties, the state implied that couples would be left to choose whether to comply with birth limits. Yet this presumption of choice, constrained only by the political and economic incentive structure, was an illusion. The purpose of the regulations, and the campaign as a whole, was to reduce birthrates. That goal could not be achieved by passively allowing couples to choose to absorb penalties for excess births. Instead, cadres were urged to use "shock attacks" to mobilize the peasantry for swift and total compliance.

Like other elements of the campaign process, the "shock attack" or "crash drive" (*tuji*) was a standard part of campaign practice by the 1970s. Conceived as a uniquely socialist method of achieving quick results through intense mobilization and politicization, a way to break through routine administrative barriers, by the 1970s the shock attack itself had become routine and predictable. A shock attack constituted an intense period of campaign activity, during which the emphasis was on achieving quick results. During this period, a wide array of tactics would be used, ranging from escalated economic and political threats to the use of physical force.

Campaigns in China have sometimes been defined solely in terms of these shock attacks. The preparation for, and implementation of, a shock attack, it was argued, constituted a campaign cycle. Campaigns have been defined in this way because they are understood to be irregular and extraordinary administrative phenomena—the exact opposite of administrative routine. Shock attacks, more than any other part of the process, meet that definition. Shock attacks could also become ritualized in their use, however, and this quickly became the case in the birth planning campaign. Like production campaigns, birth planning was an ongoing process in which production targets (or, in this case, reproduction targets) were clearly specified on a seasonal or annual basis. During the 1970s, birth planning shock attacks occurred once or twice a year—in the early summer (May–June) and the late fall and early winter (December–January).[88] They also entailed a fairly standard set of tactics that could be calibrated closely to the level of resistance encountered.

One of those tactics, orchestrated at either the county or commune level, was to send in special "shock teams." Shock teams had the dual mission of conducting education, propaganda, and persuasion and achieving practical results. Made up of county and/or township-level cadres and activists, plus a medical team capable of performing birth control procedures, these teams moved from commune to commune and village to village to enforce the new birth limits.

Shock teams of this sort helped to compensate for deficiencies that remained in the rural medical network despite state emphasis on rural health care. By 1975, over one million barefoot doctors and over three million part-time medics and midwives had been trained in maternity and infant care and birth planning. In addition, over one hundred thousand urban doctors had been relocated to the countryside to reinforce this basic-level contingent.[89] The result was a dramatic increase in the capabilities of local-level hospitals and clinics to perform the "four procedures"—IUD insertions, abortions, and male and female sterilizations. In Guangdong, for example, 49 percent of all communes had the capability to perform these procedures by 1978, while 38 percent of all brigades were able to perform IUD insertions and removals. Similarly, Shandong reported that the majority of communes were able to perform "three or four" of the procedures by 1978, and a "large group of brigades" were able to perform IUD insertions and abortions.[90]

Effective as this medical contingent was, however, it evolved over a period of years during the 1970s and was inadequate to meet the growing demand. Mobile medical teams from counties or cities had the dual objectives of conducting a large number of contraceptive procedures in a single sweep and training local medical personnel.[91] In Hebei, for example, mobile teams conducted 1.1 million procedures in 1972 and 1.98 million in 1973.[92] In Shanxi, mobile teams carried out 161,000 IUD insertions and 43,000 tubal

88. Shandong Provincial Service, March 25, 1979, in *FBIS*, April 2, 1975, G7–8; Hebei Provincial Service, November 21, 1973, in *FBIS*, November 26, 1973, F1–2.

89. *NCNA*, June 19, 1975, in *FBIS*, June 24, 1975, E2–3.

90. *Zhongguo renkou—Guangdong*, 406; *Zhongguo renkou—Shandong* (Beijing, 1989), 454.

91. *Zhongguo renkou—Liaoning*, 331; *Zhongguo renkou—Hebei* (Beijing, 1987), 464–65; *Zhongguo renkou—Shanxi* (Beijing, 1988), 348; *Zhongguo renkou—Qinghai* (Beijing, 1988), 430.

92. *Zhongguo renkou—Hebei*, 464–65.

ligations in 1972.[93] And in Qinghai, mobile teams were organized in 1972–73 to carry out birth control procedures and train local personnel and were used throughout the decade.[94]

Shock teams did more than reinforce the medical staff, however. Timed as part of the annual or biannual drive to meet population quotas by targeting offending couples, outside shock teams brought great pressure to bear on brigade and team cadres and forced them to attend to the work. Left to their own devices, brigade and team cadres sometimes attempted to deflect the campaign away from couples with whom they had special sympathy, for example, those who had three or four daughters but still wanted a son. Once an outside work team composed of higher-level officials descended on them to check local implementation efforts, however, it was difficult not to cooperate in full.

An alternative to the shock team strategy was to organize entire villages or birth planning offenders for intense "persuasion" meetings. When local campaigns got underway in the mid-1970s, they often began with a series of village-wide meetings to educate about birth control and to urge compliance with national policy.[95] Couples who resisted abortion or sterilization could be required to attend all-day meetings at the brigade or commune headquarters until they agreed to the procedure. While attending the meetings, they received no pay, and couples were often separated into two groups—husbands and wives. In other cases, only women were required to attend the meetings and they were forced to pay fines for each day they did not attend. Away from the pressures of husbands and family members, they were subjected to a constant harangue by the local women's leader or senior brigade and commune leaders, a harangue that was alternately imploring or threatening. Worn down by the pressure after several days of such meetings, most women eventually gave in to the demands that they undergo abortion or sterilization, including women in the eighth or ninth month of pregnancy.[96]

If intimidation meetings of this sort were insufficient to gain compliance, more direct forms of coercion could be used. One approach was to seize and hold family members until the couple had complied. In one Shandong commune, for example, a woman's mother was held captive by brigade leaders until the woman agreed to an abortion. Where other forms of pres-

93. *Zhongguo renkou—Shanxi*, 348.
94. *Zhongguo renkou—Qinghai*, 430.
95. Yan Yunxiang, *Private Life under Socialism* (Stanford, 2003), 190–91.
96. The single best account of one such meeting can be found in Steven W. Mosher, *Broken Earth* (New York, 1983). Third-trimester abortions were a common feature of the campaign. Interview Files 820410, 920801.

sure had failed, this tactic worked very quickly.[97] Another effective tactic was also employed in this commune. A woman who had locked herself in her home and refused to undergo an abortion found her home surrounded by armed members of the brigade militia. When they threatened to take her by force, and demonstrated their will by firing into the air outside her house, she gave herself up.[98]

Limits to Enforcement

By 1980, when China was poised to enter a new era, the capacity of the state to enforce childbearing limits was impressive. Over the course of a decade, a comprehensive and specialized bureaucracy had been created to oversee routine administration, a grassroots medical corps had been developed and trained, and the party apparatus had been indoctrinated for enforcement. A two-child, then a one-child, family became nearly universal in urban areas, and a growing number of rural couples were having fewer children. Transformative campaign goals were wed to routine production techniques, and the power of the state to shape individual childbearing was growing.

Impressive as this capacity was, however, it was inadequate to the task on the horizon. As the one-child limit was extended to the countryside and pressure for compliance intensified, peasants and cadres alike began to resist the radical policy. The Deng regime tried to override this resistance by increasing campaign pressures to a mobilizational frenzy in the early 1980s. Ideological exhortation, economic and political intimidation, and the threat or use of physical coercion were joined in a formula that produced moments and pockets of spectacular success.

The combined effect of the increasingly disruptive rural reforms, on the one hand, and campaign pressures, on the other, however, created an implementation paradox. In some places, at some moments, the capacity of the state to enforce birth planning was ruthlessly complete. Yet in other places, at other moments, the campaign had little force at all, as the architecture of enforcement began to buckle and corrode.

97. Interview File 920801.
98. Interview File 920801.

5

Two Kinds of Production: Rural Reform and the One-Child Campaign

The one-child policy, taken alone, would have been one of the greatest implementation challenges the Communist regime had ever faced. To attempt it in a climate in which the very premises of rural life and collective agriculture were being rapidly transformed, however, was nothing short of brazen. Central leaders could and did create a climate of extreme mobilization—even hysteria—by arguing that the one-child policy was the essential precondition for the success of China's entire modernization project, the program on which all other gains would finally depend.[1] But such arguments could not alter the fact that local leaders were wholly absorbed with the process of agricultural reform in the early 1980s and with the broader reform agenda of the Deng regime. Whether those reforms were received as opportunity or resisted as a threat, they disrupted rural administration and challenged cadre authority all across the countryside. To compensate for the disruption, cadres were exhorted by Beijing to "jointly grasp two kinds of production," agricultural production and human reproduction. Because there was no question of altering the agricultural reforms to fit the needs of birth planning, however, those responsible for birth planning were expected to adjust to the fluctuating conditions created by each new wave of rural reform. This was a formidable—and at times impossible—task, one that left rural cadres reeling.

1. See, for example, the editorial in *Renmin ribao*, January 27, 1979, which states, "If we only pay attention to economic development planning and not to population development planning, our economic development plans will be adversely affected and may even fail."

Rural Reforms, 1979–1985

The reform program included four core elements that had great bearing on the one-child campaign. The first element, and the centerpiece, was the process of decollectivization. Between 1979 and 1984, a variety of new "responsibility systems" for agricultural production were introduced, and collective organization of agriculture was gradually phased out. By 1984, it was replaced by a new system of household contracting, in which land remained collectively owned but was divided for use by individual households. Each household entered into a production contract that obliged them to meet certain state and local obligations, including a grain quota and other taxes. Beyond those obligations, they were gradually freed to organize their agricultural work as they chose and to reap income in direct proportion to their own labor and success. When this reform was coupled with significant increases in grain prices and expanded opportunities for small-scale, sideline entrepreneurship, it led to a rapid expansion of the rural economy.[2]

With the decollectivization campaign basically complete by mid-1983, the second element of reform was introduced: the rural people's commune was slowly phased out in 1983 and 1984.[3] The groundwork for the change had been laid in 1981 and 1982, when the commune was criticized for stifling the autonomy of the production team, for encouraging a concentration of arbitrary power in the hands of a single party secretary, and for impeding economic development and scientific management.[4] After trial tests at several experimental sites in Sichuan and Anhui, it was replaced by a new, con-

2. Before arriving at a nationwide system of household contracting by 1984, many preliminary forms of "responsibility system" were first implemented. A full description of these forms, and the process of transition to household contracting, can be found in David Zweig, "Context and Content in Policy Implementation: Household Contracts and Decollectivization, 1977–1983," in Lampton, ed., *Policy Implementation,* 282–83. See also Kathleen Hartford, "Socialist Agriculture Is Dead; Long Live Socialist Agriculture! Organizational Transformations in Rural China," in *The Political Economy of Reform in Post-Mao China,* ed. Elizabeth J. Perry and Christine Wong (Cambridge1985), 31–62, and Jonathan Unger, "The Decollectivization of the Chinese Countryside: A Survey of Twenty-Eight Villages," *Pacific Affairs* 58 (Winter 1985–86): 585–606.

3. For preliminary critiques of the commune system, see Lin Tian, "Inquiry into the Question of the System of People's Communes," *Jingji guanli* [Economic Management] 1 (February 1981): 10–13, in *FBIS,* March 12, 1981, L20–L26; *Xinhua,* August 25, 1981, in *FBIS,* August 26, 1981, K1–2.

4. Zhang Chunsheng and Song Dahan, "Separation of Government Administration from Commune Management Required by the Development of the Rural Economy and the Buildup of State Power," *Renmin ribao,* July 30, 1982, in *FBIS,* August 5, 1982, K2–3; *Xinhua,* August 25, 1981, in *FBIS,* August 26, 1981, K1–3; Wu Min, "From Integration to Separation of Government Administration and Commune Management," *Shanxi ribao,* June 7, 1982, in *FBIS,* June 23, 1982, R6; Zhong Gao, "On an Investigation into the Conditions of Structural Reform in Kaocheng Commune in Fengyang County," *Guangming ribao,* September 19, 1983, in *FBIS,* October 5, 1983, K15.

stitutionally prescribed institutional structure that was designed to separate political and economic work and to strengthen local government.[5] Communes were replaced by township-level governments, and their status as the basic organ of local government was guaranteed under the 1982 Constitution of the People's Republic of China.[6] Economic committees, sometimes called "joint agro-industrial-commercial companies" or "economic management committees," were created to manage township-run enterprises and other township economic activities. The party committee was streamlined but retained its leading role in overall policymaking and political guidance. At lower levels, production brigades were replaced by villagers' committees; their economic functions were transferred to village-level economic committees; and teams were replaced by villagers' small groups.

The third element in the reform program was the drive to promote commercialization and entrepreneurship. Party documents issued in 1983 called for specialization and commercialization in the agricultural sector, and the new reform slogan, "It is glorious to get rich," made profit making a heroic socialist enterprise.[7] With the collective structure dismantled, households were encouraged to specialize in particular lines of production and to join with neighboring households in developing cooperative enterprises. Township and village leaders were urged to give these new "specialized households" privileged access to loans and other resources and to "take the lead" in developing sideline activities and cultivating entrepreneurial habits that would lead their villages to wealth.[8] Entrepreneurs were allowed to hire laborers, although tight controls were exercised over employment practices. The state monopoly of supply and distribution was progressively scaled back, and the unified procurement system for agriculture was abolished, allowing a freer flow of goods across territorial boundaries.[9]

---

5. *FBIS,* October 27, 1981, K14; *Kyodo,* January 3, 1982, in *FBIS,* January 4, 1982, K3–4. Vivienne Shue, "The Fate of the Commune," *Modern China,* 10, no. 3 (July 1984): 259–83.

6. *Zhonggua renmin gongheguo xianfa, 1982* (Beijing, 1982), Article 8. In some localities, particularly in Hubei, Guangdong, and Yunnan, communes were not converted into a single township. In Guangdong and Yunnan brigades were initially converted into townships and communes into administrative districts. Guangdong changed the organization several years later, turning the prereform commune-level administration into township governments. In Hubei, each commune, on average, was divided into three townships. A description of the different patterns can be found in Wang Zhenyao, "Nongcun jiceng zhengquande zhineng fenhua taishi yu zhengce xuanzu," *Zhengzhixue yanjiu* 4 (1987): 29–33. See also Guangdong Provincial Service, June 26, 1986, in *FBIS,* July 2, 1986, P1.

7. For the texts of the major rural reform documents of 1983 and 1984, see *Renmin ribao,* April 10, 1983, in *FBIS,* April 13, 1983, K1–13; *Xinhua,* June 11, 1984, in *FBIS,* June 13, 1984, K1–K11.

8. Wan Li, "Developing Rural Commodity Production," *Beijing Review* 27, no. 9 (February 27, 1984): 18; *Zhongguo nongmin bao,* April 24, 1984; Interview Files 840514, 840615.

9. See Central Document 1 (1985), in *Renmin ribao,* March 25, 1985.

Fourth, fiscal and budgetary reforms made townships and villages responsible for their own budgets. To be able to maintain local services, rural governments were encouraged to develop township- and village-run enterprises. Local factories could benefit their communities by employing labor, but more important, they could yield revenues that could be used to subsidize local governments. With these new fiscal arrangements and other incentives, township and village industry began to expand rapidly, and local officials translated their new economic power into greater local autonomy.

In retrospect, China's rural reforms appear to have unfolded logically and in neat sequence. What appears neat in retrospect, however, was a protracted, incremental, and hard-fought process that took its toll on rural stability and cadre morale. Neither policymakers nor rural cadres knew at the outset where the reforms would ultimately take them. Nor could they be sure the reformers would prevail in the political struggle under way in Beijing. Even among reformers, there were important differences over how far and how fast rural reform should go. During these years, therefore, rural cadres and peasants operated in a climate of confusion, uncertainty, and fear. Some were afraid that a familiar pattern would be repeated: they would embrace reforms that repudiated the radical policies of the Cultural Revolution decade, only to be attacked for their mistakes when those policies were later reversed. Others were afraid the policies would succeed, undercutting their relatively privileged economic positions and political power. Still others pushed for reform, or were willing to be loyal agents of central directives, but they were left bewildered by a flood of documents calling for ever more radical administrative and economic changes, and by contradictory signals coming from Beijing and from their immediate superiors. Others simply abandoned their administrative duties to concentrate on getting rich. By 1982, grassroots organs in many areas were said to be in disarray or paralyzed. Other reports complained that a "laissez-faire" attitude had set in as cadres abandoned their work.[10] Through it all, one thing was constant—the unrelenting pressure of the one-child campaign and the enormous difficulty of enforcing it in the volatile rural climate.

The Impact of Reform on the One-Child Campaign

If the rural reforms were ultimately a grand economic success for the Deng regime, in the 1980–84 period they were an unfolding nightmare for birth control officials (and during campaign mobilizations, all local officials be-

10. *Hebei ribao,* March 19, 1982, in *FBIS,* March 31, 1982, R1–3; Beijing Domestic Service, March 18, 1982, in *FBIS,* March 19, 1982, K1–2.

came birth control officials). The reforms had an impact on the campaign in four important ways: (1) land distribution patterns benefited larger, labor-rich households; (2) welfare systems collapsed, drying up funds to reward single-child households; (3) penalties against policy violators became much harder to enforce; and (4) cadre discipline declined as incentive structures changed.

Patterns of Land Distribution and Childbearing Preferences

The new household contracting system, like the collective work-point system before it, rewarded labor-rich households, especially households with several healthy sons, with extra land. As household contracting spread, therefore, and incomes became more directly linked to family production, rural couples wanted to increase their household labor power by having more children rather than fewer. This preference was fueled in part by the traditional belief that labor-rich households were the most prosperous and secure. But it was strongly reinforced by the process of dividing land among households.

In most areas, land was divided on a per capita or per laborer basis, or some combination of the two, a system that privileged larger households and those rich in male labor power. How much advantage could be gained? An example from one team in Donghu commune illustrates. When one brigade implemented the household contract system in 1983, production team five had 169 mu of land to distribute among 42 households with 163 people. The land was divided into three grades, each grade having a different quota attached: for grade one, 1,100 jin of rice per mu; for grade two, 1,000 jin per mu; for grade three, 900 jin per mu. Of team five's land, 66 percent was grade one, 23 percent grade two, and 11 percent grade three. In dividing the land, each household was to receive proportionate amounts of each grade of land.[11]

Step one was to distribute one-third of the arable land on a per capita basis in order to provide for personal consumption. In this team, each person received 0.311 mu of "grain-ration land" (*kouliang tian*). Step two was to distribute "labor-power land" (*laoli tian*) to all agricultural laborers, adjusting the allotment to account for the laborer's work-point standard under the old collective system. Healthy adult males usually received ten work points for a day's labor, while younger men or the infirm received proportionately fewer points. Women typically earned anywhere from six to nine work points a day, with most falling in the seven to eight point range. In this production team, most received eight points a day. The labor-land

11. Interview File 821104.

allotment for female laborers was therefore only 80 percent of that for male laborers.

Although the allotment differences appear to be relatively small, they could translate into a sizeable difference in annual income for households of different size and composition. In 1983, each household in team five had to sell 25.3 percent of its rice quota to the state, at a price of 12 yuan per jin. Another 1.3 percent was to be turned over to the team without compensation for collective use. After harvest, each household was responsible for paying the agricultural tax of 4 yuan per mu of contracted land, and contributing 3 yuan per mu to the team welfare fund. Finally, brigade cadres estimated that average grain consumption was 600 jin per capita, and that household expenses toward agricultural production averaged 15 yuan per mu of contracted land. If we assume that actual yields are equal to quota levels, that investment and consumption levels are the same for each household, and that all excess production was sold to the state at its above-quota price of 18 yuan per 100 jin, it is possible to calculate average household incomes from rice production, assuming different household compositions. A couple with two working sons would earn about 200 yuan more per year than a couple with two working daughters and more than 400 yuan more than a couple with one son. A couple with one daughter would fare worst, earning only 75 percent of the income going to the two-son household.

In short, the immediate effect of the contract system was to reinforce the preference for, and the value of, male offspring. Moreover, as per unit yields increased, so did the value of each additional increment of land. In this example, I assumed only that production quotas were met. In 1981, however, average yield brigadewide was 25 percent higher than the specified quota levels. If this figure were used to calculate income, the relative value of more labor power and more sons would increase significantly.

The male-biased system of land distribution was only one factor that led peasants to resist the one-child limit, but its effect was immediate and transparent. It reinforced resistance to the one-child limit, and it reinforced the perception that household survival and security depended on having a son. Birth planning officials responded in two ways. First, they embarked on a propaganda campaign to show the economic benefits of having only one child. Press articles stressed the costs of raising children, the burdens on households with too many children and too few laborers, and the economic successes of single-child couples. Academic journals reinforced this line of argument by publishing articles purporting to prove the economic advantages of having only one child.[12] Second, and more important, couples who

12. See, for example, Zhang Xinxia, "Dusheng zinu hu ye you tiaojian fufuqilai," *Renkou yanjiu* 5 (1982): 32–33 and 43.

had only one child, and who agreed to sign a "one-child certificate" pledging not to have another, were promised an extra allotment of "responsibility fields." They were also given a private plot equivalent to that of a family of four.

These efforts were largely undercut, however, by the simultaneous effort to promote the rural reforms. Not mindful of the implications for the birth planning program, media reports on the agricultural reforms frequently focused on the successes of large households. Those reports competed with reports on successful one-child households and reinforced peasant impressions that large, multi-son households benefited more from the process of land division than did small households.[13] In theory, providing one-child households with an additional plot of land could partially offset this inequality, but it could not compensate fully for large differences in the number of laborers in the household. For example, where all land was divided on a per capita basis, a family of three received the same land allocation as a family of four. However, per capita allocation was most common in villages where arable land was very scarce. Only by dividing the land on a per capita basis could they assure that each person had sufficient land to provide for their own food. While an extra allotment for a one-child couple would provide some cushion, the small size of the extra portion did little to boost income. In villages where a portion of the land was divided as *kouliang tian* (for personal consumption) and the remainder was divided among laborers, a family of three received a small additional allotment for consumption, but they did not receive the laborer allotment.

Whatever value this benefit had, it was quickly undermined by a more fundamental problem. In some areas, land was contracted to the households before the one-child benefit took effect. As a result, there was no land available to serve as an incentive for complying with the one-child policy. In other areas, the initial division of land took into account one-child households, allocating them an extra portion of land. For those who gave birth and signed a one-child certificate after land division, however, no additional land was available to apportion. In theory, readjustment was to occur annually to shift lands from families whose size was reduced (through death, marriage, or relocation) to those whose size increased. In practice, such a policy was not only cumbersome and time consuming, it was in conflict

13. This problem was emphasized by Bo Yibo in a speech to the Family Planning Propaganda Work Conference in November 1982. Bo related a conversation with Wang Wei of the State Family Planning Commission, in which Wang had complained about a radio broadcast that began with a report on birth planning but ended with an item about a peasant household that had gotten rich. The household included several healthy sons and a total of seven laborers. Bo Yibo, "Ba shixian hongwei mubiao tong kongzhi renkou lianxichilai," *Renkouxue kan* [Demography Journal] 1 (1983): 11.

with the state's desire to stabilize landholding. That conflict became more pronounced in 1983 when the state extended peasant contracts for fifteen years.[14] This step was taken to encourage peasant investment in the land and to defuse rumors about a reversal of policy, but it made it extremely difficult to reapportion land to couples willing to sign one-child certificates. In Donghu commune, for example, brigades that had divided the land in 1982 had made no effort at readjustment by the spring of 1984. Brigade leaders confirmed that land transfers had occurred, but the transfers were negotiated by the families involved for economic reasons. No effort had been made to provide land for one-child households.[15]

Brigade leaders sometimes argued that instead of land, young couples should take jobs in brigade or commune industries and be given priority for them. According to national policy, however, priority in job assignments should have been offered to one-child households in addition to the extra land allotment.[16] Although several brigade leaders insisted that the failure to allocate additional land had no impact on their birth planning performance, one brigade women's leader made clear that it did. In her village, one-fourth of those who gave birth to their first child in 1983—eleven out of forty-four—refused to sign a one-child certificate because they were not given an extra land allotment. According to the women's leader, with no land to divide, the couples "didn't care" about any other benefits.[17]

Welfare Funds and the Incentive System

As the reforms pushed villages toward household contracting, rural collective organization disintegrated rapidly. Farm animals and machinery were divided among peasants, buildings were dismantled for their wood or bricks, public works and irrigation projects were mismanaged or neglected, and financial accounting work was left "in confusion," with "nobody to straighten it out."[18] In the service sector, the drive to reduce "peasant burdens" (*nongmin fudan,* or the sum of all taxes, fees, and levies extracted

14. Central Document No. 1 (1984). See *Xinhua,* June 11, 1984, in *FBIS,* June 13, 1984, K1–K11.

15. Interview Files 840228, 840303, 840306, 840310, 840313, 840317, 840320, 840324, 840611.

16. See the "Open Letter," *Renmin ribao,* September 25, 1980, and Central Document 11 (1982), "Zhonggong zhongyang, guowuyuan guanyu jinyibu zuohao jihua shengyu gongzuode zhishi," in *Jihua shengyu zhongyao wenjian,* 8–14.

17. Of the eleven couples who refused to sign, nine had sons. This rules out the most likely alternative explanation for their refusal to sign, i.e., refusing to accept having only a daughter. Interview File 840310.

18. *Renmin ribao,* April 3, 1982, in *FBIS,* April 15, 1982, K3; *Xinhua,* March 2, 1981, in *FBIS,* March 3, 1981, L27; *Yunnan ribao,* March 11, 1981, in *FBIS,* March 31, 1981, Q1.

from peasant income) led some localities to cut all service personnel from the payroll, including barefoot doctors and teachers, or to reduce their already meager wages.[19]

Cadres no longer controlled collective income, and as a result, they were no longer in a position to extract taxes (in cash or in kind) before villagers received their income. Instead, they were forced to become tax collectors. Responsibility contracts obliged peasants to pay fees to the collective, often a fixed tax levied per unit of land, but many resisted payment.[20] Where it was collected, it was rarely enough to cover local expenses. In one Donghu brigade, for example, the fund was cut in half between 1979 and 1981, declining from 12,000 to 6,000 yuan. In a second brigade, the 1981 welfare fund of 4,648 yuan was only 36 percent of the 1979 level of 12,974 yuan.[21]

The strain on collective resources had a direct effect on birth planning. The collective welfare fund was the primary source of funds for paying benefits to one-child couples. As the fund was depleted, villages could not make good on their promises. This default discouraged newly married couples from complying with the one-child limit, and many refused to sign a one-child pledge.[22] To compensate for the decline in withholding, brigade and team leaders were told to use fines for unplanned births to supplement the fund, but that did not always solve the problem. In areas where birth planning was rigorously enforced and the one-child rate was high, for example, the economic burden for one-child benefits hit hardest, placing strain on the local budget. Precisely because of the successful enforcement, however, there were no fines for unplanned births that could be used to underwrite the benefits program. In teams with many one-child households, then, peasants began to understand that they were paying taxes into the col-

19. As a result of these pressures, in 1979 the Ministry of Health was forced to make a public case for the retention of barefoot doctors on the payroll. Beijing Domestic Service, February 6, 1979, in *FBIS*, February 12, 1979, E15. Liaoning Provincial Service, October 11, 1981, in *FBIS*, October 22, 1981, S3. *Renmin ribao*, September 9, 1981.

20. In Donghu, for example, peasant contracts in 1983 required a welfare tax payment of 3 yuan per mu of responsibility fields. Interview File 821104. See also *Renmin ribao*, September 1, 1981, in *FBIS*, September 9, 1981, K9. Some peasants were reported to refuse payment with a quip: "I don't owe a cent of tax, and besides, I don't have a tael." See Zhang Huaiyu and Dong Shigui, "New Problems in the Control of Population in the Rural Areas Brought About by Implementation of Agricultural Production Responsibility Systems," *Renkou yanjiu* 1 (1982): 31–34, in *JPRS* 80709, April 30, 1982, 19–46.

21. This drop cannot be attributed to decreases in the overall solvency of the brigades. In both cases, the total production value, net income, and per capita income all increased between 1979 and 1981. Interview Files 821012, 821102.

22. On fund depletions, see Liang Naizhong, "Nongye shengchan zerenzhi yu renkou kongzhi," *Xibei renkou* 2 (1982): 3; Zhang Yongchen and Cao Jingchun, "Shengchan zerenzhi yu kongzhi nongcun renkou zengzhang," *Renkou yu jingji* 1 (1982): 13; Zhu Mian, "Nongye shengchan zerenzhi yu nongcunde jihua shengyu gongzuo," *Renkou yanjiu* 5 (1982): 27.

lective in order to get benefits out of the collective, and that for all practical purposes, their "benefit" was no benefit at all.[23]

Decollectivization and Penalty Enforcement

Under the collective, one of the most serious penalties imposed on those who violated birth plans was a 10 percent income deduction levied against both parents. Though the length of time for enforcing this penalty varied from place to place, most provincial regulations called for a seven-year penalty for a second child, and a fourteen-year penalty for a third. In the countryside, these penalties were to be deducted from the total work points earned by both parents, even if it left them in debt to their team. The work-point reduction was a foolproof system. Since cadres controlled work-point accounting and year-end distributions within the production teams, they had absolute control over the amount of income, whether in cash or kind, distributed to the peasants. Household contracting dismantled this control system.

Collecting fines for unplanned births was even more difficult than collecting taxes.[24] Cadres were instructed to penalize unplanned births, but this was impractical and unworkable in the new rural context. Cadres had little patience for such a prolonged and unwieldy enforcement scheme, and some brigade leaders refused outright to levy any economic penalties.[25] In others, cadres shifted to a flat fine. The amount of the fee varied from place to place; it also varied depending on whether the offending couple had a second child, a third, or a higher order birth. In 1982 and 1983, the fines were often set at 200 yuan for a second birth and 300 yuan for a third.[26]

Levying a flat fine did not solve the problem of how to get the peasants to pay, however, nor did it always serve as a deterrent. When peasant income derived entirely or primarily from the collective sector, the work-point system and the collective withholding system allowed cadres to know quite precisely the income of each household. As the reforms took hold, however, the proportion of peasant income from collective sources began to decline, and opportunities for private or cooperative entrepreneurship increased.[27]

23. Liu Haiquan, "Cong guoqing chufa, ba kongzhi renkou zengzhangde zhongdian fang zai nongcun," *Renkou yanjiu* 6 (1983): 11.
24. Zhang Huaiyu, "Lun renkou yu jingji jianji dangqian nongcun renkou kongzhi wenti," *Jingji yanjiu* 12 (1981): 37; Zhang and Cao, "Shengchan zerenzhi yu kongzhi nongcun renkou zengzhang," 13.
25. Interview Files 821012, 821028, 840313, 840310, 840303.
26. Interview Files 840228, 840310, 821109.
27. The percentage of peasant income from collective sources declined from approximately 60 percent in 1980 to only 10 percent in 1984. *Zhongguo nongye nianjian, 1985* (Beijing: Nongye chubanshe, 1986), 236; *Zhongguo nongye nianjian, 1986* (Beijing: Nongye chubanshe, 1987), 289.

As a result, not only did cadres find it difficult to extract collective fees from such income, they had difficulty even determining how much income had been earned. For some couples, a fine of 200 yuan might be a major deterrent to unplanned births; for other couples more flush with cash, 200 yuan might constitute a much smaller portion of household income and be seen as a good investment in the household's future. In Donghu, for example, several brigade women's leaders reported that fines of 200, 300, or 500 yuan were willingly paid by couples who wanted another child. In at least one case, the couple was allowed to pay on an installment plan, since they could not pay in one lump sum.[28]

Disruption of the Rural Cadre Force

By 1985, the rural reforms had dismantled the economic and political institutions that constituted the core of Mao's developmental model. What had not changed, however, was the party's determination to control the process and direction of change at the grassroots. The party center normally relied on the rural cadre force to maintain local order and implement its policies effectively. During the reform process, however, rural cadres were targeted as a major part of the problem, as well as the solution. Among other things, they were criticized for abuses of authority and arbitrary infringements on production team rights during the commune era, errors that had undermined cadre-mass relations. They were also criticized for their numbers; press articles complained that the peasants had to support too many "unproductive" cadres. During 1980 and 1981, this criticism was necessary to build momentum for reform, encourage peasant enthusiasm, and to break the iron grip of cadres on the collective economy of the village. By mid 1982, however, that grip was largely broken, and in its wake came a variety of "disintegrative tendencies" that undermined efforts to enforce birth limits.[29]

In some cases, cadres quickly abdicated their leadership responsibilities to pursue their own economic interests. In other cases, cadres who initially sought to maintain local order simply gave up in the face of peasant indifference, opposition to their authority, or in protest of what they labeled "retrogressive" reforms.[30] The decision to "exit" was especially common at

28. Interview Files 840310, 820406, 821109, 840611, 840228.
29. On the problem of disintegrating rural organizations, see Thomas P. Bernstein, "Reforming China's Agriculture." Paper prepared for the conference titled "To Reform the Chinese Political Order." Harwichport, MA, 18–23 June 1984, 50.
30. "Rapidly Implement and Stabilize the Agricultural Production Responsibility System," *Shanxi ribao*, March 17, 1981, in *FBIS*, March 18, 1981, R2; Zhong Yan, "Washing One's Hands of the Whole Business and Passive Resistance," *Sichuan ribao*, May 9, 1981, in *FBIS*, May 26, 1981, Q1.

the production team level, where cadres had continued to be engaged in agricultural production throughout the collective era and were usually not party members, but brigade-level organizations were also affected.[31] Their withdrawal encouraged the collapse of all semblance of local organization in some localities, leaving no one to monitor land use, economic contracts, or other regulatory work. It also led to the deterioration of party branch organization and to a decline in new recruits. A survey of twenty villages in Henan, for example, revealed that six out of twenty party branches had not recruited a single new member between 1978 and 1985.[32]

By early 1982, as household contracting began to spread to more villages, concerns about grassroots organizations became more pronounced. Although the collapse of political leadership was important in its own right, press articles reveal that the primary concerns of central leaders at this juncture were economic. Great stress was placed on the continuing importance of the planned economy and the secondary role of the market. In addition, the perennial fear of declining grain production translated into complaints about reductions in the area sown to cereal and grain.[33] To persuade cadres that they still had a job to do, long lists of job responsibilities were compiled. In addition to collective economic work, such as the management of household contracts, cadres were reminded of their responsibility to maintain financial accounts and records, oversee any collective sideline or industrial enterprises, and to aid higher authorities in carrying out other programs, including birth planning.[34]

There is no way to estimate just how many cadres abandoned their posts, either formally or informally, during this period. What is clear, however, is that a much larger number of essentially responsible cadres remained in their posts but were confused by an uncertain policy and political environment that brought their authority into question.[35] Many cadres simply did not know how to conduct themselves under the new conditions, or what the

31. John Burns, "Local Cadre Accommodation to the 'Responsibility System' in Rural China," *Pacific Affairs* 58, no. 4 (Winter 1985–86): 614–19. On the concept of "exit," see Albert O. Hirschman, *Exit, Voice, and Loyalty* (Cambridge, 1970).

32. Rural Economic Survey Leading Group of the Rural Policy Research Center, Secretariat, CPC Central Committee, and the Rural Development Research Center of the State Council, "Rural Primary Organizations, Party Members and Cadres," *Nongmin ribao* [Farmer's Daily], May 16–17, 1986, in *JPRS* 86064, August 19, 1986, 33. The survey covered 25,159 cadres at all three levels of rural organization.

33. Commentator, "Communes and Production Brigades Must Take Charge of the Things That Ought To Be Taken Charge Of," *Banyue tan* [Semi-Monthly Talk] 4 (February 25, 1982): 8–9, in *FBIS*, March 11, 1982, K11–12.

34. Ibid.; "Give Full Play to the Leadership Role of Rural Basic Level Organizations," *Renmin ribao*, February 19, 1982, 1, in *FBIS*, March 2, 1982, K8–11.

35. *Ningxia ribao*, April 8, 1982, in *FBIS*, April 30, 1982, T2.

new conditions were supposed to be.[36] In these circumstances, some chose to concentrate on taking advantage of the new economic policies, to the neglect of other administrative tasks like birth planning. Prior to the reforms, grassroots cadres received all or part of their income from the collective to compensate for their administrative work. Under the reforms, that was no longer the case. Subsidies were cut back and cadres were encouraged to become more engaged in agricultural production. Like other households, theirs received allotments of land for contractual production, and whether they liked it or not, their income became more dependent on their agricultural prowess,[37] Many cadres took advantage of their opportunity to withdraw from administration to concentrate on "getting rich." Others had little interest in agriculture, but they were quick to develop other sources of household income. Either way, grassroots cadres who in the past had given their undivided attention to administrative organization and control now had to divide their time between administration and productive work. With less time for administration at the brigade level, and fewer lieutenants at the team level, the system of supervision and surveillance was relaxed and weakened. Birth planning work suffered accordingly.[38] According to two county-level birth planning officials in Hubei Province, the disruption caused by cadre laxity was the single most damaging consequence of the responsibility system.[39]

Apart from turning their energies elsewhere, the cadre force was further weakened by a reduction in personnel. Two campaigns led to cutbacks during this period. In 1979, a campaign was launched to reduce "peasant burdens," which included all fees, taxes, or other assessments deducted by the

36. Report, "Hebei Provincial CCP Committee Rural Work Department's 'Opinions on Regularly Grasping the Work of Perfecting the Agricultural Responsibility Systems'," *Hebei ribao,* June 12, 1981, in *FBIS,* July 9, 1981, R7. See also *Xinhua,* March 2, 1981, in *FBIS,* March 3, 1981, L23. A second *Renmin ribao* editorial also raised the issue, noting that some cadres "do not sufficiently understand the party's current policies" or "know how to manage the economy by economic means." "It Is Necessary to Show More Concern for and Assist Grassroots Cadres in Rural Areas," *Renmin ribao,* July 15, 1981, in *FBIS,* July 23, 1981, K8.

37. In three brigades surveyed on this issue, two brigade leaders got land allotments 50 percent the size given to a full-time laborer, and one got 30 percent of the allotment. Team-level cadres got 50 to 100 percent allotments. Interview Files 821008, 821104, 821109. See also Zong Xin and Bai Jian, "Shilun nongcun shengchan zerenzhi yu jihua shengyu," *Renkouxue kan* 1 (1982): 10; Zhang and Cao, "Shengchan zerenzhi yu kongzhi nongcun renkou zengzhang," 13.

38. The survey undertaken by the Rural Policy Research Center reported an average decrease in brigade-level cadres of 12.9%, dropping from 6.2 to 5.4 cadres. Rural Economic Survey, 32. Liaoning Provincial Service, October 25, 1981, in *FBIS,* October 28, 1981, S3; Zhu Mian, "Nongye shengchan zerenzhi," 27, 29; Cui Fengyuan, "Guanyu wo guo nongcun funu shengyu lu wenti," *Renkou yu jingji* 2 (1982): 50.

39. Interview File 840613.

brigade and team to cover collective expenses, including cadre salaries. The campaign called for a reduction in all nonproductive personnel, that is, administrative cadres who did not contribute directly to the income of the unit. This campaign undercut the birth planning directive of 1978 that ordered all communes to add a cadre for birth planning work, and it led some localities to take women's leaders off the payroll, along with doctors, teachers, and other collectively funded personnel. Although many localities added birth planning personnel between 1978 and 1980, while the campaign was under way, those that did not wish to spend their money in this way or did not have funds to pay for birth planning cadres could use the peasant burden campaign to justify their inaction.

The commune structural reform also affected grassroots staffing. One goal of the reform was to streamline administration and reduce the number of personnel. By 1984, the team level of administration had collapsed in all but name. According to one large survey, between 1978 and 1984 the average number of personnel at the production team level dropped from 3 to 1.4, a decline of 69 percent.[40] The organizational responsibilities and power of team leaders largely ceased to exist, and those who did not abandon administration right away were left without purpose once the new system was stabilized. Some localities continued to hire team leaders, but women's leaders who were crucial to grassroots implementation were often the first to be laid off. In other places, women were kept on staff, but they were asked to serve as accountants as well as women's leaders, reducing their attention to birth planning.[41]

The township level was also affected. Specialized birth planning cadres at the township level were classified as collective cadres and were paid out of local collective funds. With the reforms emphasizing streamlining personnel and cutting administrative costs, however, township leaders did not necessarily choose to hire such personnel. In other cases, the township reform resulted in the division of one commune into two or more townships, with a division of collective township funds. Although the original commune's birth planning cadre remained in place at one of the townships, newly formed townships sometimes failed to hire their own cadre. This division of communes into multiple townships was especially pronounced in Hubei Province, and the effect was immediate. According to a birth planning official in one county, for example, in 1984 there were no county funds to hire

40. Rural Economic Survey Leading Group of the Rural Policy Research Center, Secretariat, CCP Central Committee, and the Rural Development Research Center of the State Council, "Rural Primary Organizations, Party Members and Cadres," *Nongmin ribao,* May 16–17, 1986, in *JPRS* 86064, August 19, 1986, 31–37.

41. Interview Files 840306, 840317, 840313.

grassroots personnel, but some township governments refused to use their own funds for this purpose. As a result, thirty-one of the fifty-five townships in this county had no birth planning cadre by the middle of 1984.[42]

Dual Contracts and Responsibility Systems

To compensate for the administrative problems caused by the rural reforms, the state began to promulgate "responsibility contracts" that linked birth planning targets directly to economic work and production targets. Where peasants entered into agricultural production contracts, officials inserted birth planning clauses directly into those contracts or drafted separate documents linking birth planning compliance to the terms of the agricultural contracts. These "dual contracts" (*shuangbao hetong*) gave concrete reality to the campaign slogan "jointly grasp two kinds of production."

The dual contract came in several forms, depending on the agricultural responsibility system in effect in an area. The first was applied in production teams that had implemented the system of assigning production quotas to work groups (*baochan daozu*). Under this system, the laborers of a production team were divided into two or more subgroups, and each group was given a production contract detailing all production obligations. Where dual contracts were in place, the group contract held the entire work group responsible if any individual in the group had an unplanned birth. In Mianju County, Sichuan Province, for example, work groups assigned contracts specifying the total bonus to be allotted if agricultural and birth planning quotas were both met. Of the total bonus, 70 percent was contingent on meeting the agricultural production target, while 30 percent was tied to performance in birth planning. If one member of the group had an unplanned birth, therefore, all members forfeited 30 percent of the bonus. If both targets were met, on the other hand, an additional 10 to 20 yuan was given as an extra bonus.[43]

The second system was utilized where the household quota system was in effect. Here, land was divided among the households according to family size, and production quotas were fixed under a contract. Contracts also specified whether the household was authorized to have a birth during the year and what penalties would apply in the event of an unplanned birth. Rather than levy cash penalties, this form of contract usually penalized the couple by raising their state production and sales quota. In one Jiangsu

---

42. Interview File 840609.
43. Zhang Wen and Xin Hai, "Nongye baochan daozu hou jihua shengyu gongzuo ruhe kaizhan," in *Zhongguo renkou kexue lunji,* ed. Beijing jingji xueyuan renkou jingji yanjiusuo (Beijing, 1981), 189.

county, for example, offending couples were penalized with a 20–30 percent increase in state production quotas for a period of fourteen years.[44]

Under household contracting or *dabaogan,* peasants were required to sign two contracts—one each for agricultural production and birth planning—or one contract that included a birth planning clause. Violation of the contract could entail one or more of the following penalties: financial penalties, increased state sales quotas, or forfeiture of a portion of land contracted out to the household. Two cases from Jilin Province are illustrative. In the first, those who had an unplanned child paid a fine of 50 yuan and forfeited a percentage of their contracted land according to a fixed schedule. For an unplanned first child, 15 percent of the land was forfeited, for a second, 30 percent, and for a third or additional birth, 50 percent was forfeited. Regardless of the amount of land to be forfeited, however, the couple's state sales quota would remain the same. At a minimum, this provision ensured that the couple giving birth to a second or third child would have little produce available for sale after meeting its state obligations. For those forced to forfeit 50 percent of their "responsibility fields," this provision raised the possibility that they would be forced to purchase grain and other staple foods for their own consumption.[45] This system had two undesirable consequences, however. First, withdrawing the land affected the couple's income so greatly that they were unable to pay the cash fine to the team or brigade. Second, the plots of land seized were small and scattered, and thus difficult to reallocate. In a second case, therefore, offenders were allowed to keep their contracted land, but their production quotas were raised. This method was billed as superior to the former because it avoided problems related to land redistribution.[46]

Responsibility systems and contracts were also extended to grassroots cadres through "cadre job responsibility systems" (*ganbu gangwei zerenzhi*). Cadre pacts of this sort emerged in some areas in the mid-1970s, spreading rapidly as the reforms took hold.[47] This system was designed to spread the burden of responsibility for birth planning from grassroots birth planning officials and women's leaders to party branch secretaries and brigade or team leaders by tying job evaluations and bonuses to birth plan-

44. Zhu Mian, "Nongye shengchan zerenzhi," 27–31.
45. Wang Yaqin, "Nongcun shixing shengchan zerenzhi zhihou jihua shengyu gongzuo yinggai zemma ban?" *Renkouxue kan* 12, special issue (September 15, 1982): 51–52.
46. Siping shiwei xuanchuanbu, Siping renda changwei wenjiaoban, Siping shi weishengju, Siping shi jishengban, "Shixing liangzhong shengchan 'shuangbao' zhi, jihua shengyu gongzuo jian chengxiao," *Renkouxue kan* 4 (1983): 57–58.
47. For example, according to birth planning officials, cadre job responsibility systems emerged in Huangpi County in Hubei in 1975–76, then later spread to other areas. Interview File 840608.

ning performance. In one Jilin commune, for example, contracts covering all three levels of commune cadres were established in 1981. At the commune level, 30 percent of cadre bonuses were tied to birth planning work, which was evaluated according to their performance on three targets: the birth control utilization rate (*jieyulu*), set at 90 percent of all childbearing-age couples; the natural rate of population growth, set at 7 per 1,000; and the one-child rate (i.e., the percentage of all births that were first births), set at 90 percent. Each target was worth 10 percent of the total bonus value, and failure to meet any one or all would result in the forfeiture of that portion of the bonus. The remaining 70 percent, however, would be unaffected by the results of birth planning work.[48]

Brigade cadres were collectively responsible for three targets: a birth planning rate (*jihua shengyulu*) of 100 percent, implying that there could be no unplanned births in the brigade, a birth control rate of 100 percent, and a one-child rate of 100 percent. These targets were worth 50, 30, and 20 points, respectively. For each target that was met, the point value was multiplied by 2 yuan and divided among the cadres. For each target they failed to meet, 0.60 yuan was subtracted per point. If all targets were met, therefore, brigade cadres received a 200 yuan bonus to be divided among them. If one target was missed, a penalty was deducted. If the birth control target was missed, for example, the 70 points earned on the other two targets were worth a 140 yuan bonus (70 points multiplied by 2 yuan), but the missed target resulted in an 18 yuan penalty (30 points multiplied by 0.60 yuan). After subtracting the penalty, 122 yuan remained for distribution among the cadres. If all targets were missed, no bonus was given. Instead, a collective penalty of 60 yuan was imposed, to be deducted from other bonuses or basic cadre subsidies. At the team level, cadres operated under the same system. The value of each point was reduced, however. At this level, each bonus point earned was worth only 1 yuan, for a maximum potential bonus of 100 yuan. Points subtracted as penalties were valued at 0.30 yuan, for a maximum penalty of 30 yuan.[49]

Variations on this pattern were in force around the country in the early 1980s, but the monetary rewards at stake were not necessarily high. In Donghu, for example, the party secretary, commune director, and birth planning cadre each received 20 yuan if they met the five targets for the

---

48. Bai Yuwen and Cao Hui, "Shixing jihua shengyu zerenzhi shi gaohao jihua shengyu gongzuode zhongyao cuoshi," *Renkouxue kan* 12, special issue (September 15, 1982): 47–50.

49. Ibid. The authors reported that brigade and team cadres did not like this arrangement because their target quotas were set at 100 percent, allowing no margin of error. Targets for commune cadres were set lower, however, allowing commune cadres to receive bonuses for a less that perfect performance.

TABLE 7. Responsibility targets for two brigades, Donghu commune, 1984

	Brigade 1		Brigade 2	
Target	Target (%)	Target Value (% of total)	Target (%)	Target Value (% of total)
One-child rate[a]	90	50	98	50
Birth planning rate[b]	87	20	96	25
Contraception rate[c]	95	20	95	25
Late marriage/Birthrate[d]	80	10	—	—

Source: Interview Files 840310; 840303.
[a]percentage of all births that are first births.
[b]percentage of all births that are approved within the plan.
[c]percentage of all childbearing-age couples using contraception (excluding those who have permission to not use contraception, due to illness, spousal separation, and so forth).
[d]percentage of all marriages in which the woman has reached age 23, the man age 25; percentage of all births that are delayed until age 25.

year. If they missed any one of the targets, a portion of the bonus was deducted, depending on the assigned value of the target. In 1982, the five targets were: (1) a birthrate of 13.5 (or less) per 1,000 (valued at 40 percent of the total), (2) a one-child certificate rate of 85 percent (worth 30 percent), (3) a late marriage rate of 90 percent (worth 10 percent), (4) a planned birthrate of 90 percent (worth 10 percent), and (5) a birth control utilization rate of 100 percent (worth 10 percent).[50]

Brigade cadres also had responsibility targets. Targets for two Donghu brigades are listed in table 7. As shown, the targets varied slightly from brigade to brigade, as did the value assigned to the target. In these two cases, if all targets were met brigade cadres received a collective bonus of 50 yuan. If a target was missed, the bonus was reduced accordingly. Birth planning was only one of several targets to be met, however. For the brigade women's leader, birth planning represented only about half her work under the responsibility contract. She was also held responsible for other aspects of women's work, civil mediation, primary school performance, and health work.[51] For senior brigade leaders, birth planning comprised a much smaller part of their overall work target. In one case, birth planning ac-

50. Interview File 821014. The second target implies that 85 percent of all one-child couples should sign a certificate. The third target implies that 90 percent of all marriages during the year should be late marriages, i.e., the woman should be at least twenty-three years of age, and the man twenty-five. The fourth target implies that 90 percent of all births during the year should be "within the plan." The fifth target implies that all couples of childbearing age should be using an approved form of birth control unless officially excused from doing so.
51. Interview Files 840303, 840310.

counted for only 15 percent of the total, while the other 85 percent was devoted to different aspects of economic production and political work.[52]

The third type of responsibility system that emerged during the 1980–82 period was a technical responsibility system (*jishu zerenzhi*). This system was used to hold health and medical workers accountable for the quality of their work in carrying out birth control procedures. Concern and anxiety about poor medical care was a constant problem in birth planning work during the 1970s, but as the volume of procedures rose over the course of the decade those anxieties grew. Rural medics, barefoot doctors, and commune doctors were hastily trained to conduct all types of procedures, from IUD insertions to sterilizations, and in some cases the quality of their work was very poor. "Accidents" that resulted in death or injury occurred frequently, particularly during periods when large numbers of procedures were performed. In addition, medical workers often had little sympathy with those who complained of complications or sought outpatient care. In some cases, this attitude was the result of poor coordination between hospitals and birth planning officials. In other cases, medics were indifferent to complaints because they were being poorly compensated for their work.[53] The agricultural reforms exacerbated this problem. Many barefoot doctors were taken off brigade payrolls as "nonproductive personnel," just as the number of procedures being performed began to escalate. Other medical workers concentrated on making an income from their responsibility fields, increasing the case load on health workers at the commune level.[54]

The technical responsibility system was designed to address these problems by offering doctors and medics economic incentives to improve the quality of their work, and by assuring an appropriate level of funding. A typical example is the system used in Peng County, Sichuan Province, where contracts specified medical targets, expenses, and rewards and penalties.[55] Four targets were specified. The first was the IUD utilization rate, which was set at 80 percent of all one-child couples, except for those who were medically exempt. Second was the sterilization rate, set at 30 percent of all couples with two or more children. The third target was the IUD failure

52. Interview File 840303.
53. *Xinhua*, January 10, 1983, in *FBIS*, January 13, 1983, K15; *China Daily*, January 4, 1983, 1; Shaanxi Provincial Service, May 3, 1981, in *FBIS*, May 4, 1981, T5; Changling xian weishengju, "Baizheng guanxi, kejin zhize, jiji zuohao jihua shengyu jishu zhidao gongzuo," *Renkouxue kan* 12 (September 15, 1982): 53–55 and 50.
54. *Xinhua*, March 24, 1981, in *FBIS*, March 25, 1981, L18–19.
55. Xin Dan and Peng Zhiliang, "Sichuan sheng peng xian shixing jieyu jishu zerenzhide jiangyan," *Renkou yanjiu* 6 (1982): 29–31.

rate, set at 10 percent or less of all wearers. The fourth target was the failure rate for vasectomy, which was set at 3 percent or less.

Assuming that all quotas were met and that medical standards were maintained, compensation was provided on a "piecework" basis—0.10 yuan for an IUD insertion, 0.20 yuan for a vasectomy, and 0.30 yuan for a tubal ligation. To encourage fewer abortions, no compensation was offered for this procedure. Conversely, those who demonstrated a poor attitude or acted "irresponsibly" were fined 1 yuan per occurrence, and those who made errors (*chacuo*) during operations were to be punished based on the severity of the error and their attitude toward it. The contract also included provisions for more serious offenders. Those who "practiced fraud" (*nongxu zuojia*) or "engaged in malpractice for selfish ends" (*yingsi wubi*) were to be deprived of half of the annual bonus money, with additional penalties for more serious offenses.[56]

To underwrite this system of rewards and penalties, the contract also required that commune leaders agree to provide secure funding for birth planning work. The commune agreed to set aside 0.10 yuan per capita as a birth planning operating expense fund. This fund guaranteed an annual income for doctors and other health workers and assured that the promised rewards would materialize at the end of the year.[57]

These various forms of the responsibility system spread rapidly after 1980, and they were officially sanctioned in a new central document on birth planning issued in February 1982.[58] Where they were rigorously implemented, they were very effective in mobilizing cadres and deterring peasant violations. They were not implemented universally, however, even among brigades within the same commune. And implementation was sometimes in name only. In Wuhan, for example, birth planning officials reported that the dual contract system had been implemented in every commune and village in their rural district, which included Donghu. When officials in Donghu were asked about the system in late 1982, however, they said they had never heard of "dual contracts."[59] District officials explained that although the system had been sanctioned and endorsed, only three of the district's twelve communes had taken the lead in implementing it, and in those three communes, 90 percent of the villagers were covered,

56. Ibid., 29–30.
57. Ibid.
58. See "Zhonggong zhongyang, guowuyuan guanyu jinyibu zuohao jihua shengyu gongzuode zhishi," in *Shiyizhou guanhui yilai jihua shengyu zhongyao wenjian*, ed. Guojia jihua shengyu weiyuanhui xuanchuan jiaoyusi, Zhonggong zhongyang dangxiao jihua shengyu weiyuanhui (Beijing, 1989), 8–14.
59. Interview File 821012.

but 10 percent were not. In other words, most brigades and teams were participating, but a few were not. Of the remaining nine communes, eight had adopted the system, and 80 percent of their commune members were covered. According to district officials, the commune in which interviews had been conducted was the only one that chose not to adopt it, and district officials could not compel them to do so.[60]

Eighteen months later, in June 1984, the same district officials downplayed the importance of dual contracts. They confirmed that the system had been implemented in many brigades, but they argued that the contracts were really no different from the local regulations that had been binding before the contracts were enforced. In other words, dual contracts in this area did not link production quotas or landholding to compliance with birth planning. Instead, where birth planning provisions were inserted into production contracts, they simply specified the rewards and penalties in effect in that village and indicated whether the contracting party had permission to give birth during that year.[61] This trend was confirmed by a second round of brigade-level interviews. Of the eight villages surveyed within one commune, only one reported using increased state sales quotas as a penalty to deter unplanned births, and none reclaimed responsibility fields.[62]

What had changed between 1982 and 1984? Dual contracts had been effective tools to cope with the erosion of collective administration between 1980 and 1982, but by the time they were officially sanctioned their utility had already peaked.[63] Once household contracting became the basic organizational framework for rural agriculture, the very provisions that had made dual contracts effective were in growing conflict with evolving priorities in the agricultural sphere.

What made dual contracts effective in controlling peasant childbearing behavior was the threat to increase quotas or reduce land allotments as penalties for unplanned births. They were also effective when they threatened to penalize the entire village for the errant behavior of one couple. As rural policy evolved, however, these methods were increasingly at odds with the economic and political goals of the state. The overriding goal of the agricultural reforms was to provide every incentive for peasants to boost production rapidly. To achieve that goal, the state increased the price of agricultural products, offered even higher prices for above-quota produc-

60. Interview File 821201.
61. Interview File 840606.
62. Interview Files 840303, 840310, 840320, 840228, 840313, 840611.
63. Dual contracts were first legitimized by an article in *People's Daily* in June 1981. The article focused on the use of dual contracts in Chuxian Prefecture, Anhui, one of the model regions for implementing the agricultural responsibility system. *Renmin ribao,* June 16, 1981.

tion, and committed itself to buying all that the peasantry wished to sell. Decollectivization, by linking economic rewards directly to household effort, was also designed to spur production. For the new organizational arrangements to work properly, however, peasant contracts had to be fair. Production contracts specified penalties for failing to meet production quotas. If large numbers of peasants failed to meet those quotas in the first year or two and were forced to pay penalties, the incentive value of household contracting would be lost. It was important that the quotas for state sales were perceived as reasonable and appropriate in light of historic patterns of local productivity. Similarly, fees for collective services and agricultural inputs also had to be fair. Fees had to be set at rates or price levels that ensured peasants' ability to make more income than in previous years. Only in that way would the reforms translate into greater peasant enthusiasm and effort and, in turn, higher production levels. When the land was divided and the first contracts were signed, therefore, production quotas were pegged to average productivity levels for the previous three to five years. And to calm fears that any increases in production would translate into higher quotas the following year, peasants were guaranteed that the quotas would not increase for a period of several years.

As the majority of peasant households shifted to household contracts and production, however, two problems arose that required further action. First, peasants feared the possibility of a policy reversal, a fear that was all too real given the continuing opposition to radical reform. That fear, plus the desire to cash in on the reforms as quickly as possible, led some to use their land for maximum short-term gain rather than long-term productivity. To prevent that trend and to encourage reinvestment in the land, the state tried to calm fears of a policy reversal and to stabilize landholding. It extended land contracts to fifteen years beginning in 1984, and major efforts were made to persuade peasants that their contracted lands were secure.[64]

A second problem was that cadres in some localities refused to treat the newly devised contracts as binding documents. Cadres arbitrarily increased quotas, levied additional collective fees, and made other changes to the contract after it was signed. In instances in which peasants leased land for sideline activities that began to generate large profits, cadres sought to negate the contracts or to raise the fees payable to the collective. These actions not only undermined peasant confidence in the contract arrangements, they also undermined production incentives.[65] To counter this problem, cadres were

64. *Xinhua*, June 11, 1984, in *FBIS*, June 13, 1984, K1–K11.
65. *Xinhua*, March 2, 1981, in *FBIS*, March 3, 1981, L24; Jilin Provincial Service, October 11, 1981, in *FBIS*, October 15, 1981, S2; Jilin Provincial Service, September 27, 1981, in *FBIS*, September 29, 1981, S2.

instructed to treat the contracts as binding documents.[66] More important, as part of the state's broader effort to reinvigorate the legal system and govern according to law, peasants were urged to seek legal redress against arbitrary attempts to alter the terms of the contract, and some began to do so.[67]

Dual contracts were in direct conflict with these efforts to create the best possible environment for agricultural growth. The distinctive characteristic of such arrangements was that birth planning offenders were penalized by altering the terms of their economic contract, either by depriving them of a portion of their responsibility fields or by increasing their production quotas. Confiscating a portion of their land, however, undermined efforts to stabilize landholding and build confidence in the contract system. Increasing their quotas dampened their enthusiasm for production by reducing the profit margin. More important, increasing quotas for birth planning offenders also played into peasant anxieties about the power of local cadres to alter contracts at will. Emboldened by the state's argument that they seek legal redress for arbitrary changes to contracts, peasants began to challenge the birth planning provision, and legal departments in local governments began to question the legal standing of such provisions.[68]

As a result of these concerns, dual contracts in their most potent form began to disappear from the scene in 1984. Villages continued to enforce a system that they referred to as a dual contract, whereby household contracts included a provision on birth planning or separate birth planning agreements were signed. In practice, however, the two were delinked. Penalties were generally enforced through levying "excess-birth fees" (*chaoshengfei*), not through land confiscations or increased quotas. Charging fines for excess births was no solution, however, since the fees were often an inadequate deterrent.[69] Extracting penalties from the proud parents of an above-quota child was not the goal of the state. Preventing births was the goal. By late 1982, therefore, the focus for implementation shifted to a surer and more permanent solution to excess births—mandatory sterilization.

but this ignores consumption.

---

66. See Central Document 1 (1984).

67. For a revealing and entertaining look at peasant efforts to get legal redress for their complaints, see the six cases that are summarized in David Zweig, Kathy Hartford, James Feinerman, and Deng Jianxu, "Law, Contracts, and Economic Modernization: Lessons from the Recent Chinese Rural Reforms," *Stanford Journal of International Law*, 23, no. 2 (1987): 319–64.

68. Interview File 840606.

69. A new central document on birth planning issued in April 1984 stated that it was "impermissible" to "wreck the basic means of production or means of livelihood of the peasants" as a penalty for violating birth planning regulations. See Zhonggong guojia jihua shengyu weiyuanhui dangzu, "Guanyu jihua shengyu gongzuo qingkuangde huibao" [Report on the situation in birth planning work], in *Jihua shengyu zhongyao wenjian*, 21.

6

The Politics of Mass Sterilization

By the middle of 1982, China's leaders were afraid that the disruption caused by the rural reform process was compromising their population goals. To prevent that, they launched a mass sterilization campaign at the end of that year, with the goal of sterilizing by 1985 all childbearing-age couples with two or more children. For more than a year, this radical Maoist-style campaign was prosecuted with ruthless efficiency, driven by the illusion that the problem of "excess births," especially third or higher order births, could be solved once and for all. The Chinese phrase "one cut of the knife" (*yidaoqie*), which is used to refer to an overly rigid and uniform approach to policy implementation, was never so chillingly apt as in this campaign.

By the end of 1983, however, the political context that had buttressed the campaign began to shift. As worries about rural unrest grew and a party rectification campaign was launched, criticism of the harsh methods used in the sterilization campaign gained more ground. That change was reflected in a 1984 party document on birth planning, Central Document 7 (CD 7), which repudiated the use of coercion and "shock tactics" to enforce birth control targets, stressing instead the need for routine and patient work in order to gain compliance.

Although the sterilization campaign continued in some areas into 1984 and 1985, the issuance of Central Document 7 marked a significant shift in central policy. Over the next five years, birth limits in many rural areas were progressively relaxed, allowing a growing number of couples to have a second child "within the plan." And though overzealous cadres often committed the same abuses rejected by CD 7, the emphasis shifted after 1984 to the hard work of building an effective organization that could manage childbirth according to local regulations. This shift, it was believed, would not only help the sagging morale of birth planning cadres, it was the only way to square the hard work of birth planning with the rapidly changing environment produced by the reforms. If the documents and speeches on birth planning continued to insist on the primacy of meeting population control targets, those on rural reform placed even greater stress on economic performance. The message to local cadres was that in any conflict between birth control and economic reform goals, it was the birth control program that had to adjust and adapt. The politics of this cycle of campaign mobilization and retrenchment is the subject of this chapter.

The Sterilization Option

Prior to 1983, there were two episodes of increased use of sterilization to achieve birth planning goals. The first, in 1973–75, was the result of the decision to launch an aggressive birth planning campaign and to make campaign goals a part of the fourth five-year plan. Compared with preceding years, the number of sterilizations, IUD insertions, and abortions were much higher in these years and especially so in 1975, the final year of the five-year plan (see table 8). The second episode came in 1979–80, the final years of the fifth five-year plan (1976–80) and the inaugural years of the one-child policy. Campaigning under the slogan of "prevention first" (*yu-fang wei zhu*), couples with two or more children were urged (or required) to undergo sterilization, and sterilization after only one child was also encouraged. This mobilization produced a second spike in birth control procedures. Compared with 1978, the number of tubal ligations doubled in 1979, and abortions were performed in record numbers (see table 8).

This pattern was reflected at the local level (table 9). Of the four brigades in Donghu commune for which comparative information is available for the 1979–82 period, three show a heavy concentration of sterilization procedures in 1979. In the fifth brigade, no comparative information is available, but more than 70 percent of all sterilizations performed between 1979 and 1982 occurred in 1979. The brigade women's leader explained this burst by revealing that she and all the team women's leaders had undergone sterilization that year in order to set a good example.[1] Apart from the pressure on all cadres and party members to take the lead in accepting sterilization, one-child couples were encouraged with the offer of substantial economic re-

---

1. Interview File 820523.

TABLE 8. Numbers of contraceptive procedures, 1971–2003 (in millions)

Year	IUD insertions	Tubal ligations	Vascetomies	Abortions
1971	6.17	1.74	1.22	3.91
1972	9.22	2.09	1.72	4.81
1973	13.95	2.95	1.93	5.11
1974	12.58	2.27	1.44	4.98
1975	16.74	3.28	2.65	5.08
1976	11.63	2.71	1.49	4.74
1977	12.97	2.78	2.62	5.23
1978	10.96	2.51	0.77	5.39
1979	13.47	5.29	1.67	7.86
1980	11.49	3.84	1.36	9.53
1981	10.33	1.55	0.65	8.70
1982	14.07	3.92	1.23	12.42
1983	17.76	16.40	4.36	14.37
1984	11.75	5.42	1.29	8.89
1985	9.58	2.28	0.57	10.93
1986	10.64	2.91	1.03	11.58
1987	13.45	4.41	1.75	10.49
1988	12.23	3.59	1.06	12.67
1989	15.52	4.22	1.51	10.38
1990	15.88	6.93	3.09	13.49
1991	12.29	6.75	2.38	14.10
1992	10.09	4.50	0.86	10.42
1993	13.46	3.58	0.64	9.49
1994	13.21	3.73	0.67	9.47
1995	9.34	2.82	0.51	9.78
1996	8.79	2.72	0.54	8.71
1997	8.35	2.47	0.44	8.20
1998	7.66	1.99	0.33	7.38
1999	7.20	1.83	0.32	6.76
2000	9.98	2.56	0.48	1.49
2001	9.52	2.50	0.46	1.28
2002	9.25	2.21	0.37	1.34
2003	9.58	2.10	0.31	1.66

Sources: Zhongguo weisheng nianjian [China Health Yearbook], 1988 and 2004 editions. For 1971 and 1972 figures, see Zhang Lizhong, "Birth Control and Late Marriage," in Liu Zheng, Song Jian et al., *China's Population: Problems and Prospects* (Beijing: New World Press, 1981), 113.

wards. In 1979, those rewards included a sewing machine from the commune, a cash subsidy of 30 to 100 yuan from the brigade, a small subsidy or gift from the team, and an extended paid maternity leave of two to three months. In addition, one-child couples were given priority for jobs in commune and brigade enterprises. At a time when annual per capita incomes in these localities ranged from 200 to 300 yuan and nonagricultural jobs were

TABLE 9. Sterilizations in nine production brigades, Donghu commune, 1979–1985

Brigade	#CBW[a]	1979	1980	1981	1982	1983	1984	1985
1	295	37	17	17	—	—	121	—
2	219	45	13	2	5	—	109	—
3	149	24	—	2	0	—	39	—
4	296	120+	—	—	—	—	170	—
5	181	9	—	11	3	61	—	80
6	299	113	0	0	1	52	—	166
7	360	—	—	8	6	99	—	162
8	98	—	—	—	—	34	—	48
9	255	—	—	—		63	—	96

Sources: Interview Files 821104, 840310, 840320, 840228.

[a]CBW refers to childbearing-age women. For brigades one through four, the number of childbearing-age couples was accurate as of late 1982. For brigades five through nine, they were accurate as of early 1984. These figures illustrate the rough ratio between numbers of childbearing-age women and numbers sterilized annually. Exact figures on the number of childbearing-age women during each year are unavailable.

scarce and highly sought after these material rewards were genuinely tempting to some young couples.

By late 1982, sterilization again became the solution of choice, but this time a truly massive rural campaign was envisioned. There were several reasons for this. First, rural birthrates remained unacceptably high and were climbing. Despite the policy prohibiting third or higher parity births, 28 percent of all births in 1981 fell into that category. Moreover, the results of the national census taken on July 1, 1982, confirmed that the population growth rate for 1981 had been significantly higher than previous estimates. As late as August 1982, the growth rate for 1981 was estimated at about 12 per 1,000. According to the census, however, the actual figure was 14.55 per 1,000.[2] Second, while the overall number of couples willing to sign a one-child certificate continued to show an increase nationwide, in some areas the certificate rate among the rural populace was declining.[3] Similar problems were evident in the data on provincial birth planning rates (the proportion of total births considered "within the plan"). In highly populous provinces such as Hunan and Hebei, the rural birth planning rate declined significantly between 1980 and 1982. In other provinces, including Guangdong and Sichuan, birth planning rates had stagnated. Sichuan Province, one of the leading performers since the mid-1970s, also began to register a

2. *Xinhua*, August 17, 1982, in *FBIS*, August 18, 1982, K7; *Renmin ribao*, October 28, 1982.

3. *Xinhua*, August 17, 1982, in *FBIS*, August 18, 1982, K7.

decline in its one-child rate.[4] Third, leaders were also concerned about the high failure rate of birth control methods, including IUDs, and the increased numbers of abortions that resulted.[5] They were also disturbed about the growing incidence of unauthorized IUD removal, seeing it as part of the overall lapse in grassroots control brought about by the reforms. In the middle of 1981, senior leader Hu Qiaomu was so distressed over reports of IUD removals that he wrote a letter to Chen Muhua (then head of the SFPC) to urge her to have strict laws drawn up that would impose heavy penalties.[6]

All of these concerns took on heightened importance in 1982. In the first half of the year, a final draft of the sixth FYP (1981–85) was prepared. Premier Zhao Ziyang presented the plan to the National People's Congress in November, setting the goal for agricultural growth at 4–5 percent annually, and setting the population growth rate goal at an average of "under 13 per 1,000" annually. By the summer of 1982, the prospects for meeting the agricultural target looked quite good, but population growth continued to top 14 per 1,000, and *duotai* (third or higher parity births) continued to represent 24 percent of all births, down from 28 percent in 1981 but still too high.[7] Only 22.7 percent of China's 1,209 counties had *duotai* rates— the percentage of total births that were third or higher parity—of 10 percent or less, and in "some counties," the rate exceeded 40 percent.[8] The leadership continued to fear that production increases, particularly grain production, would be undercut by population growth, slowing the growth of personal income that was necessary for economic expansion. Even more important was a growing fear among central leaders about losing control of the birth planning effort. Serious concerns were raised about the "laxity" and "paralysis" of grassroots party organs in the wake of the reforms. Reports of rising birthrates and grassroots resistance fed fears that a "laissez-faire" attitude toward birth planning was taking hold as peasants dared to grow more defiant of the one-child limit.[9]

4. Sichuan Provincial Service, May 24, 1982, in *FBIS*, May 27, 1982, Q2.
5. Yang Jishun and Xu Peng, "The Principal Measure to Implement Birth Control Is the Practice of Contraception," *Renkou yu jingji* 5 (1982): 15, 13, in *JPRS* 84994, December 21, 1983, 95–97; Qi Wen, "Adopt Effective Measures to Stop Multiple Births: Learning from the Experience of Premier Zhao's 'Government Work Report'," *Hebei ribao*, July 18, 1983, in *JPRS* 84590, October 24, 1983; *China Daily*, January 4, 1983, 1.
6. Shi, *Zhongguo jihua shengyu huodong shi*, 221. See also *Yunnan ribao*, April 17, 1982, 1, in *JPRS* 81380, July 28, 1982.
7. Liang Jimin and Peng Zhiliang, "Quanmian zhunquede lijie he zhixing dangde jihua shengyu fangzhen zhengce," *Renkou yanjiu* 3, no. 12 (1984): 14.
8. Liang and Peng, "Quanmian zhunquede lijie," 12.
9. In November 1981, for example, Premier Zhao Ziyang stressed that the problem of rising birthrates could not be allowed to "drift." Shi, *Zhongguo jihua shengyu huodong shi*, 228.

The new head of the State Family Planning Commission, Qian Xinzhong, shared that fear. Speaking to a national meeting of birth planning cadres in May, he emphasized that China had suffered from earlier mistakes in population policy and that it could not afford to make another one.[10] He reiterated that view at the national birth planning work meeting held in August. Qian announced that emphasis had to be placed on "seriously controlling second births and resolutely putting an end to third births."[11] This language differed from that which had been in use earlier in the year. In the central document issued in February, for example, it was stressed that for those with "practical difficulties," such as rural couples living in remote districts who worked larger tracts of land and needed extra household labor, second births could be permitted if approved by birth planning officials. Regarding third births, the document stated that "no matter what the circumstance, no one may give birth to a third child."[12] The difference between this phrasing and Qian's new language may seem subtle, but the policy implications were not. Qian's language suggested a harsher policy line on all unplanned births, and by November, Premier Zhao Ziyang was using the same language.[13]

This harsher line originated in July, when the SFPC held a work meeting in Guilin to draft the sixth five-year population plan and the long-term plan. Two sets of goals were set at that meeting and disseminated to all provinces and autonomous regions. One set was unveiled in the draft of the sixth five-year plan: population was to be held within 1.06 billion, and the average population growth rate was to be lowered to 13 per 1,000.[14] These goals, though ambitious, were not out of line with China's performance over the previous several years. Another set, however, was excluded from the plan. The one-child rate was to be raised to 58 percent of all births by 1985 and to 63 percent by 1990. Third or higher parity births were to fall from 28 percent of total births in 1981 to below 5 percent by 1990 and the population growth rate to 11 per 1,000.[15] These goals revealed that the

10. Shi, *Zhongguo jihua shengyu huodong shi*, 236. Qian relieved Chen Muhua as head of the SFPC in May 1982.

11. Ibid., 240.

12. "Zhonggong zhongyang, guowuyuan guanyu jinyibu zuohao jihua shengyu gongzuode zhishi," in *Shiyizhou sanzhong quanhui yilai jihua shengyu zhongyao wenjian xuanpian*, ed. Guojia jihua shengyu weiyuanhui xuanchuan jiaoyusi, Zhonggong zhongyang dangxiao jihua shengyu weiyuanhui (Beijing, 1989), 11.

13. Zhao incorporated the language into a speech to the Fifth Plenum of the Fifth National People's Congress. Shi, *Zhongguo jihua shengyu huodong shi*, 240; Guojia jihua shengyu weiyuanhui, ed., *Jihua shengyu zhongyao wenjian*, 40.

14. Zhao Ziyang, "Report on the Sixth Five-Year Plan," *Beijing Review* 51 (December 20, 1982): 18.

15. "Strictly Control Population Growth," *Renmin ribao*, August 23, 1982.

basic strategy for achieving China's long-term target was to nearly eliminate all third or higher order births by the end of the decade.

These planning decisions were the prelude to a massive sterilization campaign during 1983. Preparations were made throughout the fall of 1982 to launch a major propaganda drive during the New Year and Spring Festival period. At a November preparatory meeting, Qian Xinzhong called on all localities to send in "technical work teams" of high quality to "carry out permanent birth control measures on those with two or more births."[16] At the same time, Qian sent a letter to the party leaders of the fifteen largest provinces and autonomous districts, those with a population of thirty million or more. Writing in his capacity as head of the party group within the SFPC, Qian was more specific about his expectations for the campaign. He "suggested" that the focus should be on sterilizing *all* couples of childbearing age with two or more children. The only exceptions were minority nationalities and those who had worn an IUD successfully (i.e., without an unplanned pregnancy) for five years. Qian further suggested that this work should be "basically finished" within a year and that while concentrating on sterilizations, abortions should be carried out on all women with unplanned pregnancies.[17]

Qian's letter was reinforced by a joint circular issued by the Chinese Communist Party Propaganda Department, the General Political Department of the PLA, the SFPC, and other related state organs. The circular reiterated the importance of birth planning work for the remainder of the decade and emphasized the importance of the 1983–85 period. Relying on newly released census data, it also pointed out that the goal of holding population to 1.2 billion by the year 2000 could only be met if the average annual rate of population growth did not exceed 9.5 per 1,000 and the annual average population increase did not exceed 10.37 million.[18] These figures, rather than the more liberal goals originally set for the sixth FYP, became the guideposts for the campaign.

Responding to this mobilization call, party leaders at the provincial level held meetings, made conference telephone calls, and used every other standard method to mobilize party leaders below them.[19] Those leaders, in turn,

16. Qian Xinzhong, "Nuli kaichuang jihua shengyu xuanchuan jiaoyu gongzuo xin jumian," *Renkouxue kan* 1 (1983): 9. At about the same time, one of Qian's subordinates on the commission wrote an article extolling the experience of Shifang County in Sichuan in eliminating all third or higher order births. See Xing Peng, "Shifang xian 1981 nian yi wu duotai shengyu," *Renkou yanjiu* 6 (1982): 1.

17. Shi, *Zhongguo jihua shengyu huodong shi*, 251. Sun Muhan, "Kai jihua shengyu gongzuo xin jumiande yijian," *Renkouxue kan* 1 (1983): 22.

18. *Xinhua*, December 9, 1982, in *FBIS*, December 15, 1982, K20.

19. For a series of mobilization speeches at a preparatory work meeting in Jilin, see *Renkouxue kan* 1 (1983): 2–23. Among the speeches included here are those by Zeng Delin, deputy

used detailed birth planning records to set high quotas for sterilizations, IUD insertions, and abortions, and mobilized all cadres, regardless of their post, to participate in the campaign.[20] Medical teams were mobilized and sent to reinforce commune and brigade health workers as part of a larger propaganda work force. Army and people's militia units were also called out to reinforce the effort.[21] During January and February alone, 1.37 million activists and 138,000 medical workers were mobilized, and nearly 8.9 million birth control procedures were performed. Of those, 40 percent were sterilizations.[22] That was only one part of the campaign, however. After the initial winter mobilization, many localities pressed again in the May-June and August-September periods, striving to meet high quotas before the end of the year. Areas that had done poorly in the early months were singled out for pressure in the later months, and local governments were ordered to provide all funds necessary to achieve local goals. If the work in 1983 was poor, despite this pressure, then even greater pressure was brought to bear in 1984-85.[23]

The overall impact of this campaign was far greater than the 1979-80 mobilization and demonstrated the CCPs continued capacity to launch a mass campaign and enforce its very unpopular provisions. More than sixteen million women were sterilized, nearly three times as many as in 1979, and more than four million vasectomies were performed, more than double the 1979 figure (see table 8). In addition to the jump in IUD insertions, there was also a major increase in IUD removals. Much of the increase was due to the instruction that even women with IUDs undergo sterilization, unless they had worn them successfully for at least five years. In some locali-

director of the CCP Propaganda Office; Qian Xinzhong, director of the SFPC; and Bo Yibo, elder party leader and deputy director of the CCP retired cadre committee. See also *Shaanxi ribao,* January 16, 1983, in *JPRS* 83105, March 21, 1983, 113; *Hebei ribao,* January 19, 1983, in *JPRS* 83105, March 21, 1983, 118-19; Gansu Provincial Service, December 21, 1982, in *FBIS,* December 23, 1982, T1; *Xinhua,* January 10, 1983, in *FBIS,* January 13, 1983, K13-14.

20. *Zhejiang ribao,* December 11, 1982, in *FBIS,* January 19, 1983, 72-73; Shaanxi Provincial Service, January 14, 1983, in *JPRS* 82880, February 16, 1983, 42-43.

21. *Dazhong ribao,* December 26, 1982, in *JPRS* 82839, February 10, 1983, 43; Yunnan Provincial Service, December 29, 1982, in *JPRS* 82842, February 10, 1983, 71-72.

22. *Xinhua,* January 10, 1983, in *FBIS,* January 13, 1983, K13-14. Shi Chengli, "Woguo jihua shengyu gongzuode fenqi," *Xibei renkou* 1 (1988): 31. These figures do not reflect statistics from areas that had begun to mobilize in the fall of 1982. In Zhejiang's Jinhua Prefecture, for example, over 69,000 birth control operations were conducted in fifty days between September and November 1982. Of those, more than 54,000 were sterilizations. Zhejiang Provincial Service, November 11, 1982, in *JPRS* 82440, December 10, 1982, 55.

23. *Zhejiang ribao,* October 18, 1983, in *JPRS* 84014, February 10, 1984, 41-43; *Fujian ribao,* August 31, 1983, in *JPRS* 84001, January 3, 1984, 12-13; *Hebei ribao,* January 19, 1983, in *JPRS* 83105, March 21, 1983, 118-19. For a vivid and disturbing description of the campaign being implemented in 1984, see Huang, *Spiral Road,* chapter 10.

ties, even that instruction was ignored. Unable to meet the high quotas for sterilization in their locality, local cadres turned to women wearing IUDs for more than five years or to women nearing the end of their childbearing years.[24] In Guizhou, for example, the number of childbearing-age women using birth control increased by 231,000 in 1983. The number of women who had been sterilized increased by 788,000, however, a doubling of the total in a single year.[25] Since this number exceeds the number of women newly practicing birth control of any form by more than 300 percent, it is clear that vast numbers of women were required to shift from other methods to sterilization.

In Hubei Province, the campaign was equally pervasive and thorough. Between 1963 and 1978, the cumulative number of sterilizations was 990,000. In 1979, the year of the previous sterilization campaign, that figure jumped to 1,460,000, a 50 percent increase in one year. By the end of 1983, the cumulative figure had climbed to 3.02 million, and according to provincial officials one million sterilizations occurred in 1983 alone. In other words, the sterilizations carried out in 1983 exceeded the cumulative number performed between 1963 and 1978.[26] Of those one million sterilizations, 70,000 were conducted in the Wuhan municipal area. All couples with at least two children and under forty years old were mobilized, and over fifty medical teams were dispatched into the countryside.[27]

Data from Donghu commune reveal the scope of this campaign at the grassroots. In this locality, 2,300 sterilizations occurred between 1979 and 1990. Of those, 1,012, or 44 percent, occurred in 1983 alone, when local campaign directives called for the sterilization of all childbearing-age women under age thirty-seven with two children. By contrast, in 1984 there were only 24 sterilizations, and in 1985, 65.[28] Figures on five brigades in the commune reveal how the campaign made an impact (see table 9). In each case, the number of sterilizations during 1983–85 dwarfed the numbers of the previous two or three years.

Several factors help to explain the scale of implementation in this campaign. First and most important, outside work teams composed of provincial, county, and township cadres were mobilized to go into villages after intensive meetings of local party cadres to study the campaign documents

24. The use of this strategy to meet high sterilization targets is revealed in Central Document 7 (1984). See State Family Planning Commission, *Jihua shengyu zhongyao wenjian*, 21.
25. *Zhongguo renkou—Guizhou*, 439.
26. Interview File 840608.
27. Interview File 840607. The medical teams were composed of one surgeon, one doctor, and one nurse.
28. Interview Files 840228, 901123.

and goals. Second, the campaign was made the primary task of the entire party from January 1 to the end of the Spring Festival, or Chinese New Year. Campaign instructions came directly from the first party secretaries of each provincial and local government, and those instructions were neat and specific. There was no ambiguity about who was eligible for sterilization or about the timetable for compliance. In Jilin, for example, cadres were told that the sterilization campaign should be completed within a year, covering all eligible couples. They were also told to work quickly to mobilize the twenty to thirty thousand women with unplanned pregnancies to undergo abortions, and they were given a duotai target of under 3 percent. Birth planning cadres were also given specific targets for the number of territorial units that should achieve the "three no's": no unplanned births, no duotai births, and no late-term abortions. Counties that wanted recognition for excellent work were required to have one to three "three no" communes. More backward counties were told to concentrate on duotai, eliminating all three or higher parity births in several communes. The provincewide target was to have two or three counties in which duotai had been eliminated, and the two major cities in the province were instructed to achieve the "no third birth" target in 1983 and the "no unplanned birth" target within two years.[29]

Third, the campaign was successful because the standard admonition to avoid using "commandism and coercion" was missing from the campaign instructions. On the contrary, strong signals were sent to cadres that they would be judged on the basis of their results, not their campaign methods. At the national birth planning work conference held in August 1982, some of the experts and officials used the growing problem of rural implementation to support their call for a relaxation of rural policy. Such talk was quickly overruled, however. Cadres were instructed to treat all problems that emerged during the course of implementation, including problems of "work style," as secondary to the main task at hand—controlling birthrates.[30] In December, shortly before the campaign began, CCP General Secretary Hu Yaobang, reinforced this message by stating that birth planning work depended "first on political mobilization, second on law, and third on technical measures."[31] At a time when political mobilization had been generally repudiated as a method of policy implementation, Hu's emphasis on it as the first of three crucial ingredients was a clear signal that coercion was acceptable if it achieved quick results. And finally, neither the

29. Sun, "Kaichuang jihua shengyu gongzuo," 19.
30. Shi, *Zhongguo jihua shengyu huodong shi*, 236.
31. Ibid., 256.

mobilization circular nor a second campaign document issued to cadres made reference to cadre work styles or the need to avoid coercion.[32] Cadres were told to carry out patient and thorough education, persuasion, and mobilization, but they were not warned away from coercion, even as a formality, as they had been in previous documents and speeches. On the contrary, cadres were given clear permission to use it. Such warnings would not have been sufficient to prevent the use of coercion, of course, but they might have tempered it. Cadres with long experience in interpreting the subtleties of campaign instructions might have been more cautious had a warning been included.

Despite the reforms, these instructions and the intense pressure from above left even reluctant grassroots cadres with little option but to prosecute the campaign with vigor. Moreover, in many cases the first to be mobilized were party members, youth league members, and activists. After this group recovered from the operation without incident, a second group including all employees of commune and brigade enterprises was mobilized. Ordinary peasants were usually the third and final group to be mobilized. Party members who refused to comply could lose their opportunity for promotion or their current cadre position. Industry workers could lose their jobs and be forced back into agriculture, a fate that young women in particular often sought to avoid. As for ordinary peasants, those who received special contracts to engage in sideline production could have their contracts voided, and those who needed permits to engage in private enterprise could have those permits revoked. Threats were not always necessary, however. Some villages combined political pressure with economic incentives to achieve the same result. In Hubei, for example, one commune used cash subsidies and extended vacations to encourage couples to accept sterilization.[33]

Finally, the campaign worked because China's highest leaders had declared population control one of the two primary tasks for achieving modernization by the year 2000, and there was genuine agreement on this point. At the Twelfth Party Congress in September 1982, Hu Yaobang called birth planning a "fundamental state policy." He stressed that unless population was held within 1.2 billion by the year 2000 China would fail in its mod-

32. "Guanyu kaizhan quanguo jihua shengyu xuanzhuan huodongde tongzhi" and "Guanqie dangde shiyida jingshen, jinyibu kongzhi renkou zengzhangde xuanzhuan yaodian," both in *"Sida" yilai funu yundong wenxuan, 1979–1983* (Beijing, 1983), 156–58 and 159–65.

33. These benefits varied somewhat from brigade to brigade. Generally, women received at least forty-five days of paid vacation time at the rate of 1 yuan per day. In addition, they received a supplemental nursing and support subsidy that ranged from 15 to 35 yuan. Men received fifteen days paid vacation at the rate of 1 yuan per day. Interview Files 840310, 840303, 840320, 840310.

ernization effort. Statisticians and central planners, knowing that the number of childbearing-age couples would peak between 1985 and 1995, argued that if China did not overperform during the sixth five-year plan (1981–85), there was no hope for long-term success. Yet because of the relatively poor results during 1981 and 1982, it was clear that only extraordinary efforts would make it possible to fulfill the plan.

Going into 1983, therefore, two profoundly different impulses were at work. On the one hand, rural economic policy was moving rapidly away from the dictates of administrative planning. Decollectivization and commercialization were beginning to make output quotas and administrative management obsolete. At the same time, however, planning on a higher plane reached a pinnacle, as advisers and officials worked to outline a comprehensive but realistic plan to accomplish Deng Xiaoping's strategic objective of becoming an economic dragon by the end of the century. Having concluded that this could only be accomplished if market activities were allowed some space within the collective economy, it then became necessary to subject population control to the strictest planning and administration. For a brief time, these two impulses—one de-mobilizational, one hyper-mobilizational—were able to coexist. Not for long, however. The campaign led to grave tensions between cadres and peasants that threatened the stability of the reform process, and it made a mockery of reformers' oft-stated goal of eliminating leftist thinking and practice. Even before the campaign was over, therefore, the political retreat was under way.

The New Line: Central Document 7

The sterilization campaign marked the zenith of China's effort to control rural childbearing in a centralized and uniform way. Through some combination of reward, persuasion, intimidation, and coercion, more than twenty-five million people were sterilized during 1983 and 1984. Abortions and IUD insertions also peaked in late 1982 and 1983, and birthrates fell markedly through 1985. By early 1984, however, the most intense period of the campaign had passed. In April, a new central document on birth planning was issued, one whose clear intent was to repudiate the "work style" and excesses of the campaign.

Central Document 7 had two parts—a report by the party group within the State Birth Planning Commission and a statement of concurrence by the Central Committee—and it made clear that strict birth limits would continue to be enforced. At the same time, the need for rural political stability was stressed. Methods that provoked a serious peasant backlash and endangered their enthusiasm for reform were to be modified in a way that would make them "acceptable to the peasants."[34] More specifically, the document signaled a shift in policy in three important respects.

Coercion and Cadre Work Style

CD 7 admitted that coercion was a serious problem in the implementation of birth planning work. The party group took the blame for problems with "coercion and commandism," acknowledging that they had not paid enough attention to their "work style" or adopted "remedial measures." They also admitted that the demands made on localities in the implementation of the sterilization campaign in 1983 were too severe and that the problems began at the top: "In those places where coercion exists, and no immediate solution has been found, the main responsibility is ours. We believed that because birth planning work tasks are heavy, the appearance of coercion was unavoidable." With regard to future work, cadres were instructed to avoid rigid and uniform implementation (*yidaoqie*). Births outside the plan were to be "resolutely checked," but handling the problem "simplistically" or "rashly" was deemed unacceptable. For example, in a provision regarding economic penalties for policy violators, the document explicitly prohibited "infringing upon or destroying the masses' basic means of production or basic means of subsistence" as a penalty.[35]

Sterilization was still to be "promoted" for those with two or more children on the "principle of voluntarism." Cadres were instructed not to carry out this policy by enforcing "arbitrary uniformity," and lower levels were not to be pressured with unrealistically high sterilization targets. In one of the most revealing passages, cadres were told explicitly that women who had already passed their peak childbearing years need not be required to undergo sterilization. Those who adopted other forms of effective birth control were also made exempt. These passages confirm that a significant number of women in both categories had been mobilized in 1983.

Allowances for Second Births

CD 7 also marked a turn in policy by increasing the proportion of one-child households that would be allotted a second child. In 1982, the quota for second births had been limited to "under 5 percent" of all couples; in

34. Central Document 7 (1984) is titled "Guanyu jihua shengyu gongzuo qingkuangde huibao" [Report on the situation in birth planning work]. The complete Chinese text of this document may be found in State Family Planning Commission, *Jihua shengyu zhongyao wenjian*, 15–25, and in Peng Peiyun, ed., *Zhongguo jihua shengyu quanshu*, 24–27. An English translation is in Tyrene White, ed., "Family Planning in China," *Chinese Sociology and Anthropology* 24, no. 3 (Spring 1992): 11–16.
35. Ibid.

1984, the quota was expanded to "about 10 percent."[36] On its own, this small increase was little more than a cosmetic adjustment to the one-child limit, one much too small to address peasant grievances. The document went further, however. It stated that additional concessions would be made as the rate of forbidden duotai declined. This policy became known as "opening a small hole to close a large hole" (i.e., increasing allotments for a second birth in order to reduce the number of third or higher parity births).[37] This provision opened the door to further relaxation of the one-child limit after 1984, including experiments in some localities with a rural two-child policy.

The document was also notable for abandoning the language coined by Qian Xinzhong regarding third births. Rather than state that third births had to be "absolutely eliminated," the document returned to the early 1982 formula, stating that "no one may have a third birth, no matter what the circumstances." Referring to both unplanned second births and third births, cadres were informed that they had to be "resolutely stopped" but that they "could not be handled simplistically."

The Relationship between Modernization and Fertility Levels

The document departed from previous official statements by inverting the standard argument on the relationship between economic development and birth planning. Over the previous five years, propaganda on the one-child policy had stressed that China's modernization effort was dependent on induced fertility control: without strict birth limits, the CCP insisted, China's development gains would be largely offset by increases in population. In CD 7, however, a more complex relationship was implied. The text stated that "high birthrates are a reflection of economic and cultural backwardness" and that "the reasons why the masses demand additional births are many-faceted."[38] This tentative acknowledgement that a decline in fertility levels in the countryside might *result* from the process of development, not *fuel* it, implied that less developed areas should be treated more leniently than more developed areas.

The new line represented by CD 7 resulted from the convergence of two sets of developments in late 1983. The first was the growth within the birth planning community of a vocal opposition to the radical rural program and

36. Ibid
37. On the 1984 decision and the implications of a one- or two-child policy, see Susan Greenhalgh, "Shifts in China's Population Policy, 1984–1986: Views from the Central, Provisional, and Local Levels," *Population and Development Review* 12, no. 3 (1986): 494–515.
38. Ibid.

its extremely disturbing consequences. The second was the launching of a party rectification campaign which, by emphasizing the necessity of opposing leftism and improving cadre–mass relations, raised serious questions about the methods used in the sterilization campaign. This political countercurrent, which reflected ongoing leadership struggles over the scope, pace, and consequences of reform made rural stability the top priority and forced birth planning leaders to adjust accordingly.

The Internal Debate on Birth Planning

As preparations were being made to launch the propaganda and sterilization campaign in late 1982, special attention was also being given to a profoundly disturbing consequence of the program. With couples limited to only one child, or perhaps two, reports of female infanticide, infant abandonment, and violence against women who gave birth to girls began to rise dramatically. Although many of those reports came from backward rural areas, there were urban cases as well, suggesting a deeply ingrained sex bias.[39] That bias transcended socioeconomic and educational status and could not be eliminated by the ongoing propaganda campaign denouncing "feudal" preferences for sons over daughters.

The results of the 1982 census showed a nationwide male-female sex ratio of 106.3 to 100, within the range demographers consider normal for a national population (based on historical data and cross-national comparisons). That did little to reduce concerns about an increase in female infanticide, however.[40] Those concerns grew during 1981 and 1982, but they peaked in the spring of 1983 during the sterilization campaign. Women's Federation offices, as well as birth planning offices, were receiving reports of female infanticide and abandonment, cases that were frequently going unpunished by local cadres. Reports also appeared in the Chinese press, and the international press picked up the story as well.[41]

39. For a review of historical patterns of son preference and an analysis of data on son preference based on the 1982 one per thousand survey, see Arnold and Liu, "Sex Preference, Fertility, and Family Planning in China." On female infanticide in the republican era, see Lillian M. Li, "Life and Death in a Chinese Famine: Infanticide as a Demographic Consequence of the 1935 Yellow River Flood," *Comparative Studies in Society and History* 33, no. 3 (July 1991): 466–510.

40. For a report on the findings of the 1982 census, see Cheng Fenggao, "Zhongguo renkou xingbie jiegou," in *Zhongguo renkou nianjian, 1985*, ed. Zhongguo shehui kexueyuan renkou yanjiu zhongxin (Beijing, 1986), 222–36.

41. See, for example, Yang Fan, "Save the Baby Girl," *Zhongguo qingnian bao*, November 9, 1982, in *FBIS*, December 7, 1982, K55–56; "Drowning Baby Girls Is a Criminal Offense," *Guangming ribao*, January 12, 1983, in *FBIS*, January 19, 1983, K22; Li Jianguo and Zhang Xiaoying, "Infanticide in China" (*New York Times*), April 11, 1983, A25; Michael Weisskopf, "China's Birth Control Policy Drives Some to Kill Baby Girls," *Washington Post* (January 8,

Of all the ways in which peasants were attempting to sidestep the one-child policy, this was the most cruel and disturbing. It was also politically embarrassing, raising new questions at home and abroad about the social impact of the one-child policy and peasant resistance to it. By the spring of 1983, two different responses to those questions were being put forward. One was a demand for urgent attention to the problem and a solution for it, even if it meant adjusting the birth planning policy. The other was to deny or minimize the problem, attributing it to feudal thinking rather than current policy.

The organization most immediately concerned with the problem was the Women's Federation, the official party organ for women's affairs. By 1982–83, the reform process had given rise to a wave of criminal activity targeted at women. Growing prosperity, the return of markets, the mobility of the population, and growing corruption among local officials made it easy to profit at the expense of women. The abduction and sale of women as brides and prostitutes, the maiming of women by individuals who offered to remove IUDs illegally, and sexual assault, including rape, all increased after 1978.[42] The reform process, combined with population and employment pressures, had also created a climate in which employers discriminated openly against women—refusing to hire qualified women, pressuring current employees to "retire" to the home, and passing over women who sought leaves of absence for additional education or training. Some officials and experts went so far as to advocate a general policy of returning women to the home as the solution to unemployment.[43]

These trends produced a new wave of women's activism in the early 1980s, one aspect of which was an increase in the number of complaints received by Women's Federation offices, many of them put forward by lower-level female cadres. This activity, in turn, provoked the Women's Federation to push more aggressively for attention to the serious problems women were facing. By 1982, the federation was proposing new laws to protect women and infants, and at its annual conference in March 1983 this was the major issue on the agenda.[44]

1985), A1; Philip J. Hilts, "Chinese Statistics Indicate Killing of Baby Girls Persists" (*New York Times*), July 11, 1984, A14.

42. *FBIS*, December 28, 1982, Q1; *FBIS*, March 4, 1982, P13–14; *FBIS*, October 28, 1982, S2–3.

43. References to all of these problems may be found in the various documents and speeches included in Zhonghua quanguo funu lianhehui, ed., *"Sida" yilai funu yundong wenxuan, 1979–1983*, 182–86. On the particular issue of sending women home to solve the employment problem, see "Quanguo fulian shujichu wei funu jiuye wenti gei Wan Li, Peng Chong tongzhide xin (gaoyao)," in *"Sida" yili funu yundong wenxuan*, 86–89.

44. Kang Keqing, "Weihu funu ertong hefa quanyi shi fuliande guangrong zhize" and "Quanguo fulian disizhou diqici changwei kuoda huiyi guanyu 'Renzhen guanqie zhongyang

It was in this context that the decision was made in August 1982 to launch the sterilization campaign at the end of the year. That decision was reached at the national conference of birth planning directors, and it overrode the concerns of some participants about problems being encountered in their work, including female infanticide. The final report of the conference drew a distinction between the first priority problem—reducing the rate of population growth—and second priority problems, such as infanticide, violence against women, and the use of coercion in enforcement. Those problems, it suggested, should be dealt with, but they could not be allowed to interfere with the central goal of controlling population growth.[45] In the lead-up to the year-end campaign, therefore, local cadres were signaled to focus exclusively on population and sterilization goals. At the same time, however, the problem of female infanticide and abuse of women was made an important part of the propaganda and education campaign.[46]

The line adopted by the conference was not unanimous, however. Ever since the one-child policy had been put forward in 1979, there had been serious reservations about such a strict rural birth limit. Those concerns had grown in the intervening years. Some conference participants argued for relaxing the policy somewhat in the countryside, taking into account the economic needs and cultural norms of the population. A relaxation of the one-child policy, or a standard two-child policy with an interval of five years between births, would address the most basic peasant concerns and reduce problems with infanticide and violence. Others sought to find a middle ground—a way to solve the infanticide problem without altering the policy on birth limits. For example, in November 1982, after the Twelfth Party Congress and before the sterilization campaign, Politburo member Hu Qiaomu wrote to Qian Xinzhong suggesting a revision of regulations that rewarded single-son and single-daughter households equally. He urged that the prejudices of peasants be addressed directly and pragmatically, by giving preferential benefits to single-daughter households.[47] His rationale was that such preferential treatment would make it easier for peasant couples to accept having only one daughter, thereby reducing the likelihood of infanticide. Providing extra rewards for single-daughter households would undercut the argument that men and women were equal and reinforce arguments for son preference. Nevertheless, this option was promoted beginning in

zhishi jingshen, jianjue weihu funu ertong hefa quanyi' de jueyi," in *"Sida" yilai funu yundong wenxuan*, 337–39 and 340–42.

45. Shi, *Zhongguo jihua shengyu huodong shi*, 241.

46. See the "Xuanchuan yaodian" [Main propaganda points] for the 1983 campaign, in *"Sida" yilai Funu yundong wenxuan*, 159–65.

47. Shi, *Zhongguo jihua shengyu huodong shi*, 248.

early 1983, and individual localities began to apply a differential benefit system.[48]

This tactical policy adjustment, whatever its merits, was seen by many as insufficient. What was needed was a more serious intervention, one that would acknowledge the direct link between tight rural birth limits and female infanticide. The ongoing propaganda campaign provided an opportunity for one such intervention, and in late 1982 and early 1983 a flurry of articles appeared denouncing infanticide. In February 1983, just as the initial phase of the sterilization campaign was concluding, *People's Daily* published an article on reported cases of infanticide in Anhui Province. The report was particularly compelling because it was based on letters written by fifteen women in provincial and county offices, detailing cases of infanticide, abandonment, and abuse of women. The article condemned the "feudal mentality" that led to this pattern and called for "a second liberation" to bring an end to this sort of oppression.[49]

The report triggered an investigation by the Anhui provincial Women's Federation. The results were reported in April. In a comparison of two counties in Anhui, the investigators discovered that one county showed a serious imbalance in the male-female sex ratio, while a second county had a much more balanced ratio. Because their findings were limited to a single county, the outcome may have been a natural occurrence. The report referred to specific cases, however. In one commune in Huaiyuan County, forty female infants were drowned over a two-year period. In one production brigade, three female infants were drowned and two abandoned in the first quarter of 1982. The three remaining babies born during that period, all male, survived and were healthy.[50]

These and other reports, combined with the international attention they attracted, gave greater urgency to the issue in 1983. At its April conference, the All-China Women's Federation declared war on this problem, vowed to press for legal remedies, and declared that it had the full support of the party secretariat.[51] At a plenary meeting of the Sixth National People's Congress in June, a Women's Federation official and congressional deputy spoke about the issue at a small group session, arguing that the problems of female infanticide and attacks on women were of utmost concern to the

48. Beijing Domestic Service, "Special Preferential Treatment Should Be Given to the Female Infants of Only-Child Couples," January 22, 1983, in *JPRS* 83105, March 21, 1983.
49. *Renmin ribao*, February 23, 1983; Shi, *Zhongguo jihua shengyu huodong shi*, 263.
50. *Renmin ribao*, April 7, 1983.
51. Chen Pixian, "Quandang quanshehui yao wei funu yundong qianjin er fendou," in *"Sida" yilai funu yundong wenxuan*, 182–86.

people. She called for immediate action on a law for the protection of women and infants and a law on women's rights.[52]

The momentum developing around this issue did not go unanswered. Articles appeared rebutting foreign reports that linked infanticide with the one-child policy.[53] Statisticians were called out in April to explain that the census data from 1982 showed a sex ratio within normal bounds nationwide and to rebut criticisms of the one-child policy appearing in foreign newspapers.[54] They also responded directly to the Anhui case, pointing out that one could not draw conclusions about the sex ratio based on the small population sample offered by a single brigade or commune.[55] These efforts to quash the issue failed, however. Provincewide and nationwide sex ratios might be within normal bounds, but the large volume of evidence about individual cases of infanticide and violence against women was irrefutable.

Responding to this debate, Hao Jianxiu, alternate member of the party secretariat and former head of the Women's Federation, spoke to a conference on population theory in March 1983, urging the delegates to make a greater effort to link their study of population theory with the practical problems, needs, and preferences of the people. She also urged them to study the impact of the reforms on the concrete circumstances of rural life and to link that reality with their theoretical work.[56] This message was a very different one from that delivered at the national work meeting the previous August, and Hao's comments took on special significance in the context of the meeting. The Secretariat had designated Hao as its liaison with the State Family Planning Commission.[57] This role placed her between Qian Xinzhong, the director of the SFPC and a strong supporter of the sterilization campaign, and the senior decision-making body of the party, led by General Secretary Hu Yaobang. Her emphasis on linking theoretical work with practical circumstances was effectively a directive from the Secretariat to think more concretely about how to solve the problems that had emerged during the course of implementing the one-child policy.

That call went out to a group of theorists who had been engaged for some time in an obscure and highly theoretical debate on the true meaning of Marx's theory of "jointly grasping two kinds of production." On the sur-

52. Shi, *Zhongguo jihua shengyu huodong shi,* 275.
53. "Zhongguo renminde jihua shengyu gongzuo burong waiqu," *Jiankang bao, jihua shengyu ban,* May 3, 1983.
54. *Xinhua she,* April 15, 1983; Shi, *Zhongguo jihua shengyu huodong shi,* 269.
55. *Xinhua she,* April 17, 1983; Shi, *Zhongguo jihua shengyu huodong shi,* 270.
56. *Xinhua,* March 1, 1983, in *FBIS,* March 3, 1983, K10; Shi, *Zhongguo jihua shengyu huodong shi,* 265.
57. This decision was made on October 11, 1982, after the conclusion of the Twelfth Party Congress. Shi, *Zhongguo jihua shengyu huodong shi,* 244.

face, the debate appeared to be about how to interpret Marxist writings on the relationship between material production and human reproduction. By late 1982, however, the debate had intensified, become more rancorous and urgent, in large part because it was increasingly seen as having important practical implications for China's birth planning policy. At the core of the debate was an argument over how human reproduction and material production—together and separately—influenced the overall process of social and economic development. Some scholars argued that population played a determining role, while others argued that material production was the decisive factor. Most agreed on the need for ensuring that population reproduction and material production should be kept in approximate balance, but there were differences over whether the means of subsistence or the production of material goods should be balanced with population.[58] By late 1982 these debates had led to charges and countercharges about the Malthusian character of some of the arguments. Some scholars suggested that the theory of balancing two kinds of production was tantamount to "population determinism" and Malthusianism, while those charged argued vigorously that their argument was well grounded in Marxist-Leninist thought.[59]

There was more than theory at stake in these debates, however. These tedious theoretical arguments had practical policy implications for the conduct of China's population policy and for the lives of women and children. Those promoting the concept of balancing "two kinds of production" argued for understanding the human being not merely as a material being, a producer and consumer, but also as a social being, someone who contributed to, and drew upon, a larger social system. They suggested, in other

---

58. For a brief and rather polite summary of some of the different views being espoused by population theorists, see Zhang Li, "Liangzhong shengchan lilunde taolun zongshu," *Renkou yanjiu* 5 (1982): 2–5. Another summary can be found in Song Fulin, "Wo guo renkou lilun wenti taolun," *Renkouxue kan* 2 (1985): 39–44. Other samples of this voluminous literature include Liu Zheng, "Renkou zai shehui fazhanzhongde zuoyong," *Renkou yanjiu* 5 (1982): 6–7; Cao Mingguo, "Luelun liangzhong shengchan," *Renkouxue kan* 4 (1981): 10–14; Gao Chun, "Lun liangzhong shengchan zai shehui fazhanzhongde zuoyong," *Renkouxue kan* 4 (1981): 15–19; Wang Shengbing, "Guanyu 'liangzhong shengchan' de jige lilun wenti," *Renkouxue kan* 4 (1981): 19–24; Wen Yingqian, "Ye tan gongyoude renkou guilu," *Renkouxue kan* 5 (1982): 9–13; Zhang Guangzhao, "Liangzhong shengchan yu 'wanquan jingji xunhuan'," *Renkouxue kan* 5 (1982): 14–17; Chen Yaozhong, "Wuzhi shengchan jueding renkou shengchan," *Renkouxue kan* 5 (1982): 18–20; Wang Shengduo, "Wei 'renkou jueding lun' zhengming," *Renkouxue kan* 5 (1982): 21–24; Zhang Guangzhao and Yang Zhiheng, "Zai lun liangzhong shengchan tong shi lishi fazhanzhongde juedingxing yinsu," *Xibei renkou* 3 (1982): 23–29.
59. Cao Mingguo, "Qiantan liangzhong shengchan fazhan zhanlue," *Renkouxue kan* 3 (1984): 14–17.

words, that the relationship between human reproduction and material production was exceedingly complex and not merely a question of balancing the production of material goods with human reproduction. To assure success in social and economic development, one had to consider patterns of social development, education, employment, age distribution, the composition of the labor force, and similar factors. In short, one had to focus on the quality of the population in relation to the material base, not just the size of the population. This argument earned them the misleading label of "population determinists." In fact, it was their critics who were more single-minded in their focus on population size and population growth as the determining force, or at least the prohibitive force, in the social development process.

Although the theoretical debate remained unresolved, in 1983 momentum began to build for approaching the question of rural birth limitation in a more comprehensive way. The decision to promote a near-universal rural one-child limit had been unpopular in some quarters from the beginning. By mid-1983, with abundant evidence of peasant resistance to the policy, scholars met in Shandong to confer on rural population theory. The theme of the conference was how to undertake "comprehensive management" (*zonghe zhili*) of the rural population question, considering such issues as labor power and employment, care for the elderly, and education. The conference papers also focused on the factors influencing peasant childbearing preferences, and on how to resolve the contradiction between peasant preferences and state policy.[60] Scholars also discussed whether the one-child policy would produce an "aging population," one in which each child would have two parents and four grandparents to support. The latter theme was part of a broader effort to look beyond the projections about population size in the twenty-first century to a consideration of demographic structure and social demand. Foremost in those calculations was the social burden to come when the huge childbearing cohorts of the 1980s and 1990s began to retire.

Rectification and Reform

The theoretical debates and the concern over female infanticide, violence against women, and an aging population produced a great deal of ferment and discussion, but the birth limitation policy remained on track and the

---

60. Shi, *Zhongguo jihua shengyu huodong shi,* 278. Several of the conference papers were published in *Renkouxue kan* 1 (1984). See, in particular, Li Shuqing, "Nongmin duo shengyu zhu yinsu jiqi shehui duice," 6–10.

sterilization campaign began to heat up again in the fall of 1983. The disputes took on new meaning in October and November, however. In October, the Second Plenum of the Twelfth Central Committee adopted documents on launching a party rectification campaign.[61] At almost the same time, left-leaning members of the elite launched a campaign against "spiritual pollution," raising the specter for a brief time of a reversal of the reform process.

At the first meeting of the Twelfth Party Congress in September 1982, a decision had been reached to launch an intraparty rectification campaign the following year.[62] The campaign was to be focused on the growing problem of corruption and graft within the party, which had become more acute as the reforms had loosened tight economic controls and decentralized economic decision-making power to lower levels. It would also target problems in the political and ideological sphere, "leftist" and "rightist" tendencies within the party, weakness and laxity in party organs, and deteriorating party-mass relations. To calm fears about the campaign, however, central party leaders went out of their way to stress that the campaign would be conducted in an orderly and disciplined fashion. No class struggles were to be waged, nor was the party to be subjected to mass criticism and mass struggle, as during the Cultural Revolution. Intellectuals were also told that they need not fear a new anti-rightist movement.

The prospect of the impending campaign brought to the surface divisions within Deng Xiaoping's reform coalition and provoked an intra-elite struggle over the primary focus of the campaign.[63] Reform-minded officials, advisers, and intellectuals sought to focus the campaign on the remnants of leftism, a tack that would place conservatives and other reform skeptics under pressure to resign their posts and establish a clear party policy in favor of extending the economic reform process. Conservatives, however, particularly those within the military, sought to make "rightism"—that is, bourgeois tendencies in theoretical and intellectual circles, and corrupt behaviors brought on by the economic opening to the West—the principal focus of the campaign. Beginning in the spring of 1983, both sides made ef-

61. For the text of the document and excerpts from the CCP constitution, see "The Decision of the Central Committee of the Communist Party of China on Party Consolidation," *Beijing Review* 42 (October 17, 1983): I–XII.

62. The decision was announced by General Secretary Hu Yaobang in his report to the Congress. See Hu Yaobang, "Create a New Situation in All Fields of Socialist Modernization," *Beijing Review* 37 (September 13, 1982): 11–40.

63. For a complete analysis of this period, see Stuart R. Schram, "Economics in Command? Ideology and Policy since the Third Plenum, 1978–84," *China Quarterly* 99 (September 1984): 437–61.

forts to stake out the content of the campaign to suit their purposes, but at the end of the second plenum in October, leftists had gained the upper hand. The leftists were aided by Deng Xiaoping, who was simultaneously the principal advocate of economic reform and the principal guard of ideological and political orthodoxy. At the Twelfth Party Congress in 1982, Deng's position had been ratified under the banner of building two "civilizations" in China—the material civilization represented by the drive to achieve the Four Modernizations, and a socialist spiritual civilization (*shehui jingshen wenming*), referring to a socialist society of the highest standards, ethics, and discipline.[64] This call had translated into a concrete campaign linking the successful implementation of party policies, including birth planning, to the creation of the socialist spiritual civilization. By October 1983, however, concerns over trends in theoretical circles, including an ongoing debate about the phenomenon of alienation in socialist society, led to a decision to launch a campaign against "socialist spiritual pollution." This decision occurred simultaneously with the launching of the party rectification campaign and provoked a strong leftist wind in the latter months of the year.

The campaign manifested itself in several ways. Intellectuals exploring novel terrain within the confines of socialist thought came under suspicion for their capitalist tendencies. Entrepreneurs who had done well under the reform were pursued and criticized as petty capitalists who had become rich through exploitation and corruption. Individuals who had adopted aspects of "Western" dress were criticized, particularly women with permanent waves, high heels, or jewelry. Young couples who used public parks for intimate walks, holding hands, and kissing were spied on, hunted out, and lectured about corrupting bourgeois notions of love.[65] In short, party cadres throughout China responded to the campaigns much as they had in the pre-reform era. Believing that the campaigns were tests of loyalty and opportunities for advancement, they were quick to respond to the signals from the center and to take action against those with "bourgeois tendencies."[66]

The campaign gained such strength and momentum that intellectuals and some party members began to fear that a new class-struggle movement was unfolding, and that they, and the reforms they had supported, would be la-

64. See Hu, "Create a New Situation," 21–26.

65. On the politics of this campaign, see Richard Baum, "The Road to Tiananmen: Chinese Politics in the 1980s," in *The Politics of China, 1949–1989*, ed. Roderick MacFarquhar (Cambridge, 1993), 351–60; Colin Mackerras, " 'Party Consolidation' and the Attack on "Spiritual Pollution," *Australian Journal of Chinese Affairs* 11 (January 1984): 175–86; and Thomas P. Gold, " 'Just in Time! China Battles Spiritual Pollution of the Eve of 1984," *Asian Survey* 24, no. 9 (September 1984), 947–74.

66. This point is made by Schram in "Ideology and Politics," 440–41.

beled as rightist. Such a movement threatened to bring a halt to the economic reforms and Deng's entire modernization process. By the end of the year, therefore, Deng reversed himself and joined with General Secretary Hu Yaobang to set limits on the campaign and contain its scope.[67] To protect the rural economic reforms, the countryside was declared off limits for the campaign. And at the round of year-end conferences on economic work, where planning for 1984 took place, the general line of reform and opening up to the outside world was reaffirmed, paving the way for new reform initiatives.

The key to fending off the leftist forces was protecting agricultural reform policies. To protect that flank, Hu Yaobang was assisted by Wan Li. Wan, an ardent advocate of rural reform who had presided over the Ministry of Agriculture in the early 1980s. At the Twelfth Party Congress, he was elevated to the General Secretariat, and in October 1983 he was placed on the central party working committee for the rectification process as one of five vice chairmen under Hu Yaobang. At a rural work conference held in late November, Wan came out forcefully in favor of continuing and extending the reform process. Noting the dramatic improvement in economic performance since 1978, Wan called for a rapid expansion of commodity production and for reforms in the state-dominated system of commodity circulation. He called for changes that would allow peasants greater freedom in marketing their own products and in forming cooperative enterprises for that purpose. To make those reforms possible, and to ensure continued high production figures, he called for an extension of peasant responsibility contracts to fifteen years. With that security, peasants would spend less on household consumption and more on agricultural investment. Not only would they take greater care of their contracted land, they would also have a greater incentive to invest in commercial production. Concerned about the "irrational" levies and taxes that peasants were being forced to turn over to village and township governments, Wan also called for restraint in local-level taxation.[68]

In making these arguments, Wan explicitly rejected the notion that these policies would lead to a [income] "polarization" of the peasantry. He conceded that not everyone could be first to get rich but argued that it was appropriate and necessary to provide incentives and encouragement for those who were successful. A successful villager or village enterprise would have a trickle-out effect; those who were successful would be in a position to assist their fellow villagers and help bring prosperity to others. If peasants were

67. Ibid.
68. Wan Li, "Zai quanguo nongcun gongzuo huiyishangde jianghua," in *Zhongguo jingji nianjian* 1984: 44–52.

not allowed to become stratified by income, with some accumulating substantial wealth, he warned, modernization would not be possible.[69]

He also argued that economic development was central to the process of
consolidating and rectifying rural political organs, and he explicitly warned
against using rectification as an excuse to relax economic work. On the contrary, the goal of the rectification process was to strengthen and accelerate
economic work. He reminded delegates that class-struggle methods would
not be used during the campaign and that cadres should rely instead on economic penalties and legal administrative measures.[70] On that same theme,
he warned that the party could not allow itself to become divorced from the
masses in economic or political work and suggested that the best route to
ideological success was economic success. He insisted that "simplistic" and
"rigid" (*shengying*) methods of political work would not bring lasting results, and he instructed the delegates to adopt only those methods that the
peasantry was "able to accept" (*nenggou jieshou*).[71]

The line articulated by Wan Li was affirmed in a 1984 Central Document
on Rural Work (CD 1), issued in January.[72] Although the document was
not released for public consumption until June, a summary of Wan's speech
was published in *People's Daily* in January.[73] The speech, plus the path-
breaking nature of the document, began to reverse the leftist wind of the
previous months, and the spiritual pollution campaign lost its momentum.
In April, the campaign was effectively brought to a halt by an editorial in
People's Daily that was based on informal comments made by Hu Yaobang
to a group of party colleagues. The editorial linked the struggle against
"weakness and laxity" in party organs with residual leftist "poison" and
stressed that the problem of leftism would have to be given the utmost attention in the process of rectification.[74]

Political Context and Policy Change

The rise and fall of leftism in late 1983 and early 1984 provided the unstable political backdrop for the shift in birth planning policy represented

69. Ibid., 46–47.
70. Ibid., 52.
71. Ibid., 45, 52.
72. "Zhonggong zhongyang, guowuyuan guanyu 1984 nian nongcun gongzuode tongzhi,"
in *Xiangcun gongzuo shouce* (Beijing, 1990), 353–65. For the translated document, see *China Quarterly* 101 (March 1985): 132–42.
73. *Renmin ribao*, January 18, 1983.
74. "Suqing 'zuo' de liudu he jiaozheng ruanruo huangsan," *Renmin ribao*, April 1, 1984,
1. On the politics of CD 1 (1984), see Kenneth Lieberthal, "The Political Implications of Document No. 1, 1984," *China Quarterly* 101 (March 1985): 109–113.

by CD 7. This backdrop was much more than a subtle influence, however. In combination, the party rectification campaign, the anti–spiritual pollution campaign, and the new rural reform initiative exercised a determining influence over policy evolution. Peasant anger and cadre frustration over the sterilization campaign had created divisions among central-level birth planning officials and advisers, but until a division opened up within the central elite over the basic party line, those divisions could not translate into meaningful policy change.

Party Rectification and Birth Planning

The rectification campaign was not scheduled to reach grassroots party organs until 1985, but the overall emphasis on party work style and abuses of power put a spotlight on abuses that had occurred in birth planning. While the anti–spiritual pollution campaign was at its peak, the primary emphasis was on corruption and other forms of ideological laxity, rather than the use of coercion. Even during that period, however, one fundamental theme of the rectification campaign was the need to improve party-mass ties and to cultivate an attitude of "serving the people."[75] In preparing for and launching the sterilization campaign, service had been sacrificed in the name of results, and problems in implementation had been declared secondary to the main issue, strategic control of population.[76] Peasant complaints, and the realities of rural life, had been overridden in the short run in order to serve the long-run interests of the peasantry and the country, as seen from Beijing.

By mid-1983, concerns about overly coercive methods were being aired at birth planning conferences, and Qian Xinzhong was well aware of the strong opposition to his policy of achieving universal sterilization of all two-child couples by the end of 1985.[77] In a briefing for President Li Xiannian in July 1983, he reported that there were people inside and outside the party who "did not understand the importance and significance of adopting this measure, even to the point of censure." He insisted on his determination to carry it through by 1985. Li told Qian he had the support of the Standing Committee of the Politburo. He also commented that it did not matter if some problems came up in the process; if they "resisted firmly" (*yingzhe toupi,* literally, "toughen their scalps") and carried it out a

---

75. "Decision on Party Consolidation," *Beijing Review,* II–III.
76. Delegates to the Birth Planning Work Conference in August 1982 were told that it was understandable if some problems emerged in carrying out this work and that cadres should not be "censured too much" for them. These problems, which clearly included the use of coercion, were described as secondary to the main task. Shi, *Zhongguo jihua shengyu huodong shi,* 241.
77. Ibid., 278.

few more years, then things would be more easily managed.[78] Such an attitude was harder to defend by the end of the year, however, when maintaining close ties with the masses and adopting a democratic work style were central tenets of the rectification campaign. In January 1984, the party Secretariat discussed birth planning work and approved a report it had received from the Family Planning Commission that was the precursor to CD 7.[79] Shortly thereafter, a party journal carried a report on the use of coercion to carry out sterilizations in Shaanxi Province. Hu Yaobang attached an instruction to the article requesting that Shaanxi and all other provinces be notified immediately that this was unacceptable. He wrote that work had to be carried out in a "fair and reasonable way" (*heqing heli*) that would earn the "sympathy" (*tongqing*) of the masses, language that would later be reproduced in CD 7.[80]

Spiritual Pollution and Birth Planning

Just as the pressure on Qian Xinzhong was growing, the anti–spiritual pollution campaign appeared to signal a reprieve. With its hard-line emphasis on party discipline and ideological conformity, it provided Qian an opportunity to counterattack his critics. On November 1, Qian published a signed article in the official newspaper for birth planning work, in which he argued that the party line on birth planning was threatened by spiritual pollution. He charged that capitalist theories had permeated theoretical circles and that the theory of "population determinism" (*renkou juedinglun*) posed the greatest threat.[81] The article raised a furor among population theorists and brought a swift counterattack. At a meeting of the China Population Association in late November, the deputy head of the association, Chen Da, publicly challenged Qian by stating that theoretical debates about "population determinism" were just that—theoretical debates that did not fall under the domain of spiritual pollution. And at a meeting on birth planning financial work in early December, Li Zongquan, deputy director of the State Family Planning Commission, repudiated the article, saying it reflected the opinion of one person, not the position of the commission.[82] On December 8, Qian's critics won. At a meeting of the Standing Committee of the National People's Congress, Qian was removed from his post and replaced by Deputy Director Wang Wei.

On its own, the uproar within population circles might not have been

78. Ibid., 276.
79. This occurred at the 108th meeting of the Secretariat on January 19, 1984. Ibid., 289.
80. The censured district was Weinan Prefecture, Shaanxi Province. Ibid.
81. Ibid., 283. See also "Yao juyi fangzhi xifang sichan jieji renkou lilun dui womende yinxiang," *Jiankang bao, jihua shengyu ban,* November 1, 1983.
82. Shi, *Zhongguo jihua shengyu huodong shi,* 284.

enough to bring Qian down. It was aided by the broader counterattack against leftism that began in late November, particularly Wan Li's speech to the rural work conference on November 29. Two aspects of Wan's speech were especially useful for supporters of a more reasonable and flexible rural birth planning policy. First, unlike his speech to a similar conference a year earlier, Wan Li failed to mention birth planning at all. In 1982, Wan had identified birth planning as an important aspect of rural work and insisted that China could not afford to relax its birth control effort. In 1983, his speech was equally wide-ranging, but birth planning was omitted, implying a downgrading of its importance for the year ahead. Second, the 1982 and 1983 speeches also had something in common. In late 1982, at a time when other leaders were consciously avoiding the issue, Wan emphasized the need to avoid the use of "coercion and commandism" or any method that was "seriously divorced from the masses." This returned as one of his principal themes in 1983, and the party rectification campaign gave it new urgency.

Rural Reform and Birth Planning

The rejection of hard-line methods of implementation was also linked to pragmatic considerations. The new Central Committee document on agriculture, CD 1 (1984), represented the beginning of a second stage of rural reform, one in which peasants had to be encouraged to move into commercial undertakings. The initiatives proposed in the document would not succeed unless peasants could be persuaded to take more economic risks and cadres could be persuaded to cede more direct political and economic control. Cadre authority had to be preserved, to be sure, but that authority needed to be rooted in a legal and administrative system that was predictable, reasonably fair in its dispensation of justice, and accessible to peasants seeking legal redress against cadre abuses. The use of arbitrary force and coercion would impede the rural reform process. It was not simply a matter of political discipline; it was a matter of economic strategy.

The new rural economic strategy had another practical implication for birth planning work, one that mitigated against a continuation of 1983 campaign tactics. Unlike Wan Li's speech, CD 1 (1984) made one reference to birth planning work. To boost enthusiasm and reduce the peasant tax burden, the document called for a reform of grassroots finances. Birth planning was one of several "government-subsidized projects" targeted for reform.[83] The goal was to reduce excessive taxes, fees, and levies by requiring

83. Other public programs mentioned were rural education, militia training, and disability programs for retired servicemen and martyrs and their families. Birth planning is listed second within this group. See CD 1 (1984), *FBIS*, June 13, 1984, K7.

township governments and village leadership committees to develop item-ized budgets at the beginning of each year. At the township level, the budg-ets were to be submitted by the township government to the local people's congress for approval. At the village level, the budgets were to be set based on a process of "democratic consultation." Once the budgets had been set, local leaders were not allowed to spend more than planned or to raise more public funds than specified. Nor were they allowed to levy fees or taxes that were not itemized in the budget.

For local leaders, this directive came as a welcome relief, at least with re-gard to birth planning. Beginning in the early 1980s, a series of reforms de-centralized fiscal powers from the center to the provinces. As a result, the sterilization campaign cost local governments a staggering amount in 1983, far beyond what was budgeted for the year. Nationwide, birth planning ex-penses increased 36 percent in 1982 and an astounding 60 percent in 1983, on top of 1982's inflated figure. The proportion of total expenses for which rural governments were responsible remained steady at about 38 percent, however, placing great burdens on rural communities to pick up the tab.[84]

Local governments were ordered to cover the costs of sterilizations, abor-tions, and other procedures that could not be met by regular birth planning budgets.[85] At the grassroots, extra funds had to be allocated for propa-ganda materials and work hours, for the transportation and care of individ-uals undergoing sterilization, and for the benefits they received. In Wuhan municipality, for example, the 1983 annual budget for birth planning was 600,000 yuan, but 1 million yuan was spent on the sterilization campaign alone.[86] In Donghu, one village that had budgeted 2,000 yuan for 1983 spent 6,000 yuan on sterilizations alone, and similar figures were reported by a nearby village.[87] A much larger village reported spending 20,000 yuan in 1983, more than twice the total expenditure of 8,400 yuan for the fol-lowing five years (1984 through 1989).[88] At higher levels of government, fi-nancial organs of local governments were instructed to cover all excess ex-penditures, but at the village level there was no place to turn for a bailout.

In the midst of the campaign, these expenditures were justified on grounds that the large outlay was efficient over the long run. As the number of sterilizations increased, it was argued, the money spent on abortions for

84. Gao Ersheng, Qian Hua, Li Rong, Yang Yiyong, and Yang Juan, "Jihua shengyu yaoju shoufei zhengcede tantao," *Renkou yanjiu* 21, no. 1 (January 1997).

85. On March 31, 1983, the State Birth Planning Commission and the Ministry of Finance issued a document to this effect. Shi, *Zhongguo jihua shengyu huodong shi*, 267.

86. Interview with municipal family planning officials, June 1984.

87. Interview Files 840310, 840228.

88. Interview File 901129.

unplanned pregnancies, and on manpower, declined accordingly.[89] Subsequently, however, the new director of the State Family Planning Commission made precisely the opposite argument, citing the case of a Guangxi county that had reduced annual expenditures by 20,000 yuan by switching from periodic "shock tactics" to the employment of full-time personnel for continuous implementation.[90]

In short, the new rural reform document signaled localities that overall economic growth and financial solvency took precedence over specific programmatic mandates. No matter how important population planning was, it could not be allowed to absorb revenues that might otherwise be invested profitably.

CD 7 was approved in the spring of 1984, but the complete text was not made public at the time.[91] Instead, key phrases and excerpts were used to stress the main points, especially the necessity of making the policy "acceptable to the peasants" and implementing it in a "fair and reasonable" way. This selective reading created a strong impression that the state was responding to peasant anger and frustration and conceding its error in prosecuting the sterilization campaign. That interpretation is not so much wrong as it is incomplete. Peasant hostility to the campaign did contribute to the pressures to relax the policy, but in no sense was CD 7 directly responsive to mass action or backlash. Instead, the backlash was felt indirectly, transmitted by frustrated cadres who could not cope with the pressures they felt from both sides. Their complaints gave support to those within the birth planning community who were already persuaded of the need to relax rural targets and improve the method of implementation, and to those seeking to steer the rectification campaign toward anti-leftism and protect the advancing reform process. Most important, their critically timed complaints contributed to rising fears of political instability in the countryside. For the sake of political order and a smooth and advancing rural reform process, therefore, angry peasants had to be calmed, and demoralized cadres in-

89. Qi Wen, "Adopt Effective Measures to Stop Multiple Births: Learning from the Experience of Premier Zhao's 'Government Work Report'," *Hebei ribao*, July 18, 1983, in *JPRS* 84590, October 24, 1983, 39–40.

90. Wang was referring to Longsheng County, where annual expenditures dropped from 70,000 to 50,000 yuan. Wang Wei, "Jixu tongyi zixiang, jingxin zhidao zhongyang qihao wenjiande quanmian guanqie luoshi," *Renkou yu jingji* 1 (1985): 3–6 and 19 (see p. 6).

91. It was published in the source I have cited above, State Family Planning Commission, *Selected Birth Planning Documents*, a collected volume of documents that was prepared only for intraparty use and thus classified for internal distribution only (*neibu*). Thanks to Nancy Hearst, librarian for the Fairbank Center Library, Harvard University, for finding and acquiring this volume for the library.

dulged. In the absence of this broader context, peasant backlash against the sterilization campaign counted for very little.

Incremental Policy Relaxation

Party rectification campaigns always employ ritual self-criticism as a means of disciplining party members and party organs. Central Document 7 (1984) was the enactment of that ritual. In it, the leading party group within the SFPC admitted to and accepted the blame for ideological and leadership errors. Because the leaders had acted on the assumption that coercion was unavoidable and inevitable, the document confessed, they had set the tone for cadres below them. Because the leaders had adopted an arbitrary policy of uniform sterilization, they had become "divorced from the masses" and contributed to the deterioration of party-mass relations. And because the leaders had single-mindedly and ruthlessly pressed for strict enforcement (*zhuajin*), they had neglected to implement the policy well, or on a sound basis (*zhuahao*).

In the wake of that mistake, the new task of the commission was to accomplish the impossible—define a rural birth limitation policy that would be "fair and reasonable" and "acceptable to the peasants" without conceding any of the state's population goals. What the state saw as reasonable fell far short of peasant hopes, but at least room for negotiation was opened up over having a second child. Under CD 7, the allowance for a second birth in the countryside was officially increased to "about 10 percent" of all single-child households in 1984 and to 20 percent in 1985. But the policy of no third children was nonnegotiable. To drive that point home, enforcement during 1984 and 1985 continued to be very tight, and the sterilization campaign continued in particular localities and regions. Some cadres continued to rely on shock tactics, and tensions in some localities increased rather than decreased. Over the next five years, however, the state became increasingly flexible on the question of how to allocate second births and increasingly willing to tolerate diverse responses to that question. As a result, the power to make and enforce birth planning rules was progressively decentralized. Local policies were revised to better fit local conditions, methods of enforcement were tailored more closely to local political and economic conditions, and more rural couples, primarily single-daughter households, gained the right to have a second child "within the plan." Finally, "regular work" (*jingchang gongzuo*), meaning routine and continuous implementation, was promoted, while campaigns and "shock attacks" were discouraged.

The relaxation and decentralization of birth planning policy after 1984 reflected a subtle shift in central priorities that was the byproduct of economic success. By the end of 1984, agricultural production was booming and commercialization was under way. Grain production reached a new peak in 1984. Production was so high that the state had trouble absorbing all the grain that peasants wished to sell. Although the countryside had only small pockets of true prosperity, the unprecedented performance in grain production and other foodstuffs went far toward eliminating basic hunger, as per capita consumption increased steadily. In 1985, the state took the crucial step of formally abolishing the quota system for most agricultural products, including grain, replacing it with a purchasing system based on guaranteed prices for contracted products and negotiated terms for the purchase of excess production.[92] With this step, plus a simultaneous reform in the industrial sector, the state placed itself halfway between plan and market, still deeply involved in the planning and management of the economy but dependent on market forces as well. Despite difficulties in introducing and implementing the reforms (including inflation, transport problems, and cadre corruption), by the end of 1985 all of the goals of the sixth FYP were fulfilled or exceeded. The growth rates for agriculture and industry far exceeded the planned rates, and rural industry expanded at an extraordinary rate, absorbing sixty million laborers by 1986.[93] This development helped to lessen rural unemployment and underemployment, a key concern of the planners. At the same time, living standards increased significantly, particularly in the countryside, where inflation-adjusted incomes rose by 13.7 percent annually.[94]

This economic success played an important role in recasting the terms of debate on population control. In 1979, birth planning propaganda had stressed that China's economic development was dependent on strict population control. In 1984, however, CD 7 had conceded a more complex relationship between population and development; without abandoning the argument that population growth was a determining factor in the development process, it was now allowed that declining fertility would likely follow, not precede, economic growth. The influence of this perspective can be seen in the seventh FYP (1986–90), which was approved in April 1986, and in a new document on birth planning that was issued in May. Under the

92. See "Zhonggong zhongyang, guowuyuan guanyu jinyibu huoyue nongcun jingjide shixiang zhengce," *Xinhua yuebao* 3 (1985): 52–55. The document was published in *Renmin ribao* on March 25, 1985. A translated version may be found in *Xinhua*, March 24, 1984, in *FBIS*, March 25, 1985, K1–9. As Jean Oi notes, formal abolition did not translate into truly voluntary contracting relations between state and peasant. Purchasing agreements actually differed little from the previous arrangement. Oi, *State and Peasant*, 178–79.

93. "Plan of the CPC Central Committee and the State Council for Rural Work in 1986," *Xinhua*, February 22, 1986, in *FBIS*, February 24, 1986, K6.

94. Zhao Ziyang, "Report on the Seventh Five-Year Plan," in *Beijing Review* 16 (1986): III.

sixth FYP, both the plan and senior leaders made clear that population control was directly linked to the key goal of rapidly improving living standards and incomes, and discussions of population control were placed together with discussions of improving income levels. In contrast, the seventh FYP and Zhao Ziyang's Government Work Report deemphasized that relationship.[95] Both discuss population control under the less distinguished category of "other social projects," and Zhao's report only mentioned birth planning in passing. The plan called for "trying" to keep the annual population growth rate at "around 12.4 per 1,000," and total population by 1990 at 1.113 billion. Despite the rigorous goal of 12.4 births per 1,000, the failure to emphasize birth planning or urge better efforts stands in striking contrast to the tone and content of the 1981–85 period. Zhao Ziyang's speech to the Thirteenth Party Congress in October 1987 was equally light on birth planning. He grouped it with environmental protection as a serious social issue—one that required political commitment but commanded relatively few resources. Finally, in late 1986 China's official population target for the year 2000 was revised; the original goal of holding population "under 1.2 billion" was changed to "about 1.2 billion," a change soon understood to mean 1.25 billion.[96]

That change of tone also permeated Central Document 13 (1986) on family planning.[97] While reiterating the importance of population control in *promoting* economic development, the document reaffirmed the position taken in CD 7 (1984):

The condition of individual localities having differing birth levels illustrates that unequal economic and cultural development influences birth levels, re-

95. For the text of the seventh five-year plan and Zhao's report, see *Beijing Review* 16 (1986). For the reference to birth planning in Zhao's speech at the Thirteenth Party Congress, see Zhao Ziyang, "Advance along the Road of Socialism with Chinese Characteristics," *Beijing Review* 30, no. 45 (November 9–15, 1987): X.

96. The relaxation of the 1.2 billion figure apparently originated in July 1984, when a report was submitted to the Central Committee, "Some Questions On Population Control and Population Policy" [Renkou kongzhi yu renkou zhengce zhong ruogan wenti], in Ma Bin, *Lun Zhongguo renkou wenti* (Beijing, 1987), 2. Subsequently, Wang Wei, then head of the SFPC, used the new formulation of "about 1.2 billion" in a speech at the Central Party School in November 1985. See Wang Wei, "Zai 'Qiwu' qijian ba jihua shengyu gongzuo zhuade geng jin geng hao," in *Jihua shengyu zhongyao wenjian*, 68.

97. Its correspondence to the national plan is clear from the content, but also from the date. It is dated March 23, 1986, and Zhao Ziyang delivered his NPC report on the seventh FYP on March 25, 1986. The document can be found in *Jihua shengyu zhongyao wenjian xuanbian*, 27–35.

flecting the important function of economic development, culture, and education in transforming birthrates.[98]

In other words, economic development was identified as a cause, not merely a consequence, of declining birthrates. This perspective justified a flexible and more relaxed rural policy, one that took into account local economic conditions in determining the appropriate birth limits rather than insisting on a single, uniform limit.

Provinces took advantage of this new flexibility to implement a variety of policies covering allowable second births. By 1988 fourteen provinces and autonomous regions had declared rural single-daughter households to be eligible for a second child, and several more had moved toward a de facto two-child policy, with the births spaced four or five years apart.[99] In May of that year, the SFPC, concerned about rising birthrates, sought to reimpose a uniform standard by declaring that it was national policy to grant a second child to single-daughter households; localities wishing to implement a more restrictive policy, or a more relaxed one, had to apply to the SFPC for approval.[100] By mid-1989, four policy categories had emerged: (1) a two-child policy, operative in six provinces and autonomous regions (Guangdong, Hainan, Yunnan, Ningxia, Qinghai, and Xinjiang); (2) a "one-son or two-child" policy, operative in eighteen provinces, plus less developed areas in Jiangsu and Sichuan; (3) a policy of limited concessions for second births, operative in Beijing, Tianjin, Shanghai, and most rural areas in Jiangsu and Sichuan; (4) a policy of two or more births per couple, operative among minority nationalities.[101]

This localization of policy was also accompanied by a new emphasis on the routinization of birth planning work. After several years of administratively disruptive rural reforms, and in the wake of the excesses of the sterilization campaign, efforts were made to build an organizational structure to stabilize the enforcement process. The birth planning bureaucracy was strengthened and funding and personnel were increased. Supplemental regulations were drawn up to cover various aspects of administration, such as statistical reporting and the use of funds collected as penalties. Efforts also

---

98. Ibid., 31.
99. Hu, "Zhongguo renkou shikongde yuanyin," 51.
100. Peng Peiyun, "Zai quanguo jihua shengyu weiyuanhui zhuren huiyi bimushide jianghua," in *Jihua shengyu zhongyao wenjian*, 108–20; Zeng Yi, "Family Planning Program 'Tightening Up'?" *Population and Development Review* 2 (June 1989): 335.
101. Zeng, "Family Planning Program 'Tightening Up'?" 335.

were made to do a better job in coordinating with related bureaucracies, such as the public health bureaucracy.

In addition, birth planning work was thoroughly professionalized. Demographers, sociologists, and other social scientists were consulted in the policy-making process and hired to write instructional materials and teach classes.[102] By 1990, there were over 160,000 full-time professional cadres on staff, and most had been placed in training classes to increase their professional knowledge and skills.[103] On completion of their training, many were placed at the county and township level to train grassroots personnel and to enhance the quality of grassroots work.[104] In Sichuan, for example, there were 22,663 birth planning workers in 1988, concentrated in 2,076 county-level service stations throughout the province. In addition to providing service to the population, these workers and stations were responsible for training grassroots cadres. Over 30,000 training classes had been held nationally by 1988, with 250,000 cadres participating.[105]

Efforts also were made to decentralize control over birth planning by giving provinces and other local governments greater leeway in the planning process. In keeping with the spirit of CD 7, the seventh five-year plan assigned broad targets for total population size and average population growth rate to each province. Localities were placed on a "target management system," but how they met those targets was up to them. Implementation was to be based on local conditions (*yindi zhiyi*), not on arbitrary uniformity (*yidaoqie*). At the local level, this shift meant that counties and townships were given overall targets for population growth, but they had greater leeway in assigning births to individual couples. Specific birth totals were not set as targets. And although annual target levels were important, greater leeway was allowed for year-by-year fluctuations due to local demographic trends or other factors. As long as local governments remained within the basic framework of the plan, local variation was acceptable. In short, in contrast to the rigid practice of setting detailed numerical targets that was in force during the sixth five-year plan, the 1986–90 plan period introduced greater flexibility into the implementation process. That flexibility was needed to give local cadres the discretion to approve second births

---

102. See, for example, the cadre training volume, Yang Deqing, Su Zhenyu, Liu Yuangu, eds., *Jihua shengyu xue* (Nanjing, 1984).

103. Ai Xiao, "I Hope That Everyone Will Conscientiously Carry Out Birth Planning—An Interview with Peng Peiyun, Minister of the State Family Planning Commission," *Renmin ribao*, April 14, 1989, 5, in *FBIS*, April 19, 1989, 35.

104. For example, two training classes for county-level cadres were held at Wuhan University in 1984 while I was in residence there.

105. *Xinhua*, October 21, 1988, in *JPRS*, December 19, 1988, 49.

and expand the acceptable categories for rural births.[106] These changes were summarized under the new slogan of promoting the "three primaries," that is, ideological education over economic sanctions, contraception over abortion, and regular work (*jingchang gongzuo*) over shock activities (*tuchu huodong*).[107] In CD 13 (1986), the use of "barbaric methods" (*yeman zuofa*) was again condemned, underscoring the persistence of brutal and coercive methods of enforcement.[108]

There was an inherent contradiction in the simultaneous shift toward a relaxation of birth limits and the routinization of work methods, however. Policy relaxation did little in the short run to assuage angry villagers, and it encouraged cadres to believe they could relax their enforcement efforts. Regime goals, however, remained radical—to revolutionize rural childbearing behavior. How that could be accomplished without the use of intensive mobilization was unclear. As leaders and cadres struggled to resolve this contradiction, they settled for a time on a middle ground. While working to build a strong bureaucratic capacity for routine implementation, they relied on periodic campaigns—short, predictably timed bursts of collective administrative effort designed to override resistance and meet the required targets. Rather than disappear, the campaign was gradually domesticated, scaled down to size and carefully tailored to the political and economic realities of a reformed economy.

106. Interview File 901123; Lu Haimu, "Contract Responsibility System in Population Planning to Be Put into Practice Comprehensively," *Nanfang ribao*, January 13, 1986, in *JPRS* 86–036, May 5, 1986, 57–58. Xi Jianwei, "Dui bianzhi 'qiwu' renkou jihuade chubu shexiang," *Renkou yanjiu* 4 (1985): 3–8.

107. Liang Jimin and Peng Zhiliang, "Quanmian junquede lijie he zhixing dangde jihua shengyu fangzhen zhengce," *Renkou yanjiu* 3, no. 12 (1984): 14.

108. See Central Document 13 (1986), in State Family Planning Commission, *Selected Important Documents on Birth Planning*, 27–35.

7

Strategies of Resistance

The reforms that swept rural China during the 1980s had a major effect on the structure of power and relationships of power at the grassroots. This was especially true at the village level, the key administrative level for enforcing birth limits. In the immediate aftermath of decollectivization, powerful village leaders in some localities were still able to rule as "local emperors," with peasants remaining dependent on them for access to collective goods such as preferential loans, permits to engage in sideline or commercial activities, or employment in a village-run enterprise. Cadres were able to use these new powers to maintain their political leverage and to enrich themselves, their families, and their village clients.[1] As the reforms progressed, however, and peasants gained more economic autonomy, village leaders were forced to become far more circumspect in the way they exercised their power. Peasants began to see cadres as officials in their employ and to demand greater accountability. They also complained of corrupt practices that gave cadres unfair economic advantages, and of state demands for grain procurement, tax collection, and birth limits. They gave voice to their frustration by dubbing local officials the "three-want cadres" (*yao qian, yao liang, yao ming*), that is, cadres who "want money [taxes], want grain [state grain requisitions], and want lives [prohibit births]."[2] And

1. Oi, "Commercializing China's Rural Cadres"; Thomas Bernstein, "The Limits of Rural Political Reform," in *Chinese Politics from Mao to Deng*, ed. Victor C. Falkenheim and Ilpyong J. Kim (New York, 1989), 299–330.
2. Yao Minhua and Li Shenye, "Renkou yu fazhan," *Zhongguo renkou bao*, February 16,

compared with ten years earlier, they were far more likely to openly challenge the authority of village and township leaders.[3]

The reforms also challenged the political monopoly of grassroots cadres and eroded their status. Older and more conservative cadres were pushed out of office, and younger cadres began to replace them. In addition, beginning in 1984, village leaders in some areas were elected to three-year terms in office. Although the electoral process was generally tightly controlled by party organs during the 1980s, with time and repetition village elections became more competitive and meaningful as an important mechanism for holding local cadres accountable. The necessity of standing for election and reelection made village leaders nervous lest they be defeated or meet with some embarrassing challenge that would cause them to lose face.[4] As younger leaders came to occupy village offices, therefore, they began to pay more attention to village opinion, especially as the authority of the local party branch began to decline. Policies that provoked peasant opposition were handled with caution, and for good reason. In the new rural climate, peasant retaliation or aggressive resistance was a real possibility, and unlike their township-level superiors, most village cadres were permanent residents of the villages they served. They and their families had to live with the legacy of their tenure in office, and with the often undesirable consequences of decisions made by township or county leaders. As anger mounted during the 1990s, therefore, villages began to suffer from the result of grievances

---

1990, 3. Ren Weijie, "A Profound Call," *Nongmin ribao*, September 12, 1988, in *FBIS*, September 29, 1988, 48; see also Oi, "Commercializing China's Rural Cadres."

3. Xie Zhenjiang, "No Route of Retreat," *Jingji ribao*, January 24, 1989, in *FBIS*, February 15, 1989, 37.

4. Pei Gang, "Thoughts on the Present Disarray in Matters of Population Reproduction and Suggested Improvements," *Renkou yu jingji* 5 (1989): 6–10, in *JPRS-CAR* (*Joint Publications Research Service-China Asia Report*, hereinafter *JPRS*) 90–010, February 7, 1990, 65. On the origins and evolution of the program for village self-rule and village elections, see Tyrene White, "Rural Politics in the 1990s: Rebuilding Grassroots Institutions," *Current History* 91, no. 566 (September 1992): 73–77; Kevin O'Brien, "Implementing Political Reform in China's Villages," *Australian Journal of Chinese Affairs* 32 (July 1994): 33–59; Lianjiang Li and Kevin J. O'Brien, "The Struggle over Village Elections," in *The Paradox of China's Post-Mao Reforms*, ed. Merle Goldman and Roderick MacFarquhar (Cambridge, 1999): 129–44; Tyrene White, "Village Elections: Democracy from the Bottom Up?" *Current History* 97, no. 620 (September 1998): 263–67; Wang Zhenyao, "Village Committees: The Basis for China's Democratization," in *Cooperative and Collective in China's Rural Development*, ed. Eduard B. Vermeer, Frank N. Pieke, and Woei Lien Chong (Armonk, N.Y., 1998), 239–255; Tianjian Shi, "Village Committee Elections in China: Institutionalist Tactics for Democracy," *World Politics* 51, no. 3 (1999): 385–412; Kevin O'Brien and Lianjiang Li, "Accommodating Democracy in a One-Party State: Introducing Village Elections in China," *China Quarterly* 162 (June 2000): 490–512. Guo Zhenglin and Thomas P. Bernstein, "The Impact of Elections on the Village Structure of Power: The Relation between the Village Committees and the Party Branches," *Journal of Contemporary China* 13, no. 39 (May 2004): 257–75.

about land sales, pollution, environmental degradation, excess taxation, corruption, and the illegal manipulation of elections, and collective protests led by village leaders against township governments grew more common and more explosive.

This, then, was the charged and difficult climate in which cadres sought to enforce birth limits after 1985. Families that saw childbearing as their best long-term guarantee of economic strength, respect, and stature in the village (and their best defense against weakness, bullying, and abuse by powerful families or clans) believed that birth limits represented a profound threat to their future security. Some were prepared to take any steps necessary, including the use of force, to protect that future.[5] Cadres were sympathetic to these concerns but labored under relentless pressure to fulfill exacting population targets. Caught between these contending forces, cadres frequently erred on the side of their neighbors, employing an array of tactics designed to avoid, evade, or otherwise sidestep their birth planning obligations.

Resistance to birth planning can be classified into five basic types. Four of those types—evasion, collusion, cover-up, and confrontation—are standard strategies of rural resistance that have been well documented in other studies of rural politics. The fifth type, accommodation, is more unusual. Acts of accommodation are generally seen as signs of resignation, subordination, or defeat, the opposite of resistance.[6] In the case of birth planning, however, where the state insists on the acceptance of birth limits and its justification for those limits, acts of accommodation can be subversive, a challenge to state hegemony.

---

5. Yao Minhua and Li Shenye, "Renkou yu fazhan," *Zhongguo renkou bao* (February 16, 1990): 3; Xie Lianhui, " 'Zhejiang cun' zhuke hude shengyu guan" [The Views of the Host and Guest Households in 'Zhejiang' Village toward Birth Planning], *Renmin ribao,* November 30, 1988, 3; Yang Xudong, "Woguo nongcun jihua shengyu gongzuo zhong xuyao yanjiu jiejuede jige wenti," *Renkou yanjiu* 6 (1989): 62–64. Su Suining, "There Are Many Causes of Strained Relations between Cadres and the Masses in Rural Areas," *Nongmin ribao,* September 26, 1988, in *FBIS,* October 7, 1988, 12–14. Not all of this violence was directed outward toward village officials. It was also directed inward toward the family. Confronted with the prospect of having only one daughter and no male heirs, some men took out their frustration on their wives. When wives gave birth to daughters, men sometimes responded by filing for divorce so they could remarry and try again for a son. Others beat or killed their wives, sometimes with the assistance and participation of other family members. Women who resisted having a second child risked further abuse. On these and similar cases, see pages 353–55 in Jeffrey Wasserstrom, "Resistance to the One-Child Family," *Modern China* 10 (July 1984): 345–74.

6. An exception is James Scott, who sees accommodation as meaningful resistance under the constraints of state structural control. See Scott, *Weapons of the Weak,* chap. 7.

Evasion

The most commonplace forms of resistance to the one-child policy were simple attempts at evasion.[7] The simplest form was the attempt by pregnant women to hide their unplanned pregnancy by timing the pregnancy so that it would not show. Beginning in the fall, rural women wear several layers of clothing, including heavy padded jackets as the weather grows colder. To avoid detection, women attempted to become pregnant in August or September, too early for a fall mobilization campaign to detect them. By the time their pregnancy began to show, the extra layers of clothing would protect them from detection by observation. Only a physical exam would detect the pregnancy, but such exams were more likely to occur during the spring and summer months than at the end of the year. The layers of extra clothing are worn through March and into April, depending on the climate. If they could make it until their eighth or ninth month of pregnancy without detection, it was less likely that they would be placed under extreme pressure to abort.

The effectiveness of this strategy was confirmed by two village women's leaders in Donghu township.[8] One women's leader explained an unplanned birth during the previous year by saying that the pregnancy had not been detected because the woman was wearing padded clothes all winter.[9] When asked whether there were any current unplanned pregnancies, a second women's leader replied that she did not know because the winter was not over. As long as the women were wearing padded jackets, she explained, it was hard to tell whether they were pregnant.[10] This strategy had its limits, however. One women's leader pointed out that she could usually find out about an unplanned pregnancy just by asking around the village. She said pregnant women betrayed themselves by telling at least one person about the pregnancy, often the mother-in-law with whom she lived. Once she knew, the mother-in-law usually could not resist telling a friend, and word began to spread. The women's leader would then discover the pregnancy very quickly.[11] How much pressure was brought to bear on the pregnant

---

7. One form of evasion that I will not explore here is the exit strategy pursued by Chinese emigrants who cite the one-child policy as a major reason for leaving China. For a brief look at this issue and the U.S. response, see "United States Asylum Law and China's One-Child Policy," U.S. Committee for Refugees (September 1999), at http://www.refugees.org. On the notion of "exit" as a response to power, see Hirschman, *Exit, Voice, and Loyalty.*

8. Donghu commune was converted to a township (*xiang*) in early 1984, and its constituent brigades were converted to villages (*cun*).

9. Interview File 840310.

10. Ibid.

11. Ibid.

woman, however, would depend on how quickly the women's leader reported the problem to higher-level authorities. A small delay could mean the difference between getting caught or getting away, that is, leaving the village until it was safe to return, or until the baby was born.

Fleeing the village was a common strategy that was employed most often when township cadres came into the village. Hearing about their impending arrival, couples closed and locked their doors, fled out the back door into the fields, went next door to hide at a neighbor's home, or employed similar tactics to avoid face-to-face contact with cadres. Those who were pregnant sometimes went a step farther, leaving altogether, either before or after a pregnancy had been detected by cadres. In Jinxi city of Liaoning Province, for example, 19 percent of all *duotai* births in 1986 followed this pattern. In each case, the women involved were from villages under the jurisdiction of the city government. After the birth of the child, the offending women returned to the village.[12] Couples who employed this strategy faced two threats from cadres. The first was that cadres would pursue them to catch them before the birth of the child, or they would notify work units where they suspected the woman was going. If cadres did not pursue them in this way, and they had the baby, their main goal was achieved, but they still faced the threat of stiff punishment at home. On returning to the village, therefore, they typically claimed to have adopted a child from outside the village, perhaps the orphan of a dead relative.[13]

Except for those townships that were prosperous enough to employ several birth planning cadres, the chances of being aggressively pursued were slim. Most townships and villages could not afford to send cadres off on individual missions of that sort. And unless couples returned with the baby while it was still an infant, it was highly unlikely that cadres would do anything more than impose a fine. Since the baby was born in someone else's jurisdiction, local officials could ignore it. It would not count against them in the local birth plan. Consider the case of a Yunnan couple who left two children behind in their village to go work temporarily in a nearby city. The couple had two more children after they left the village. When asked how they were allowed to do so, and how they would register these children when they returned home, the laborer replied:

12. In China, cities (*shi*) contain residents with both urban and rural residency status. Jinxi is a county-level city that includes both urban and rural populations. Hu Zhongsheng, "Jiushijiu lie jihuawai chusheng diaocha fenxi," *Xibei renkou* 3 (1987): 4.

13. Letter from Henan sheng nongcun chouyang diaochadui nongjingchu, "Yao duju chao jihua shengyude luodong," *Nongcun gongzuo tongxun* [Rural Work Bulletin] 5 (1988): 46.

Since I am from another locality and my residence is not registered here, nobody here will interfere with how many children I am going to have. . . . [When I go home] I will simply say that I have picked up and adopted an abandoned child here. Even if the residence of the child is not allowed to be registered, it will not matter because the child will then already be two or three years old. Somehow he will be recognized as my son.[14]

This method of evasion became a major problem as the tight network of controls over mobility and food supply that had kept peasant laborers tied closely to the villages during the Maoist era began to erode. To encourage the development and commercialization of the rural economy, restrictions on peasant movement were progressively relaxed, making it more difficult to monitor and control childbearing age couples. With the end of strict rationing of grain and other staple items, basic necessities could be purchased on the free market. As long as migrants had cash savings or were able to find employment, they could remain a part of the migrant community for an indefinite period of time.[15] By 1990, this "floating population" (*liudong renkou*) had grown to more than seventy million, including 21.35 million who had lived outside their native residence for more than one year.[16] Of the total, approximately 25 percent were women of childbearing age.[17] By the end of the century, the number of migrants had risen to more than 140 million, with seventy-nine million moving between provinces or counties, and another sixty-six million moving within counties.[18]

The enormous increase in population mobility vastly complicated the job of enforcing even a two-child limit. Once rural couples were allowed to relocate for long periods of time beyond the jurisdiction of their native village or township, local authorities no longer had the ability or the incentive to monitor pregnancy and childbearing. In towns and cities where migrant laborers congregated, however, local birth planners were also unable to control their behavior. In some areas, the bureaucracy simply did not have the personnel or economic means to deal with the logistical problems posed by

14. Xu Yaping, "Plug Up a Loophole in Planned Parenthood Work," *Renmin ribao,* June 4, 1985, in *FBIS,* June 5, 1985, K3.

15. *Xinhua,* March 3, 1989, in *FBIS,* March 16, 1989, 42–43.

16. These figures were computed from the fourth national census. Shen Yimin, "Disici quanguo renkou pucha jige zhuyao shuzhude kekaoxing pingjia," *Renkou yanjiu* 1 (1992): 16. On China's floating population, see Dorothy Solinger, "China's Floating Population," in Goldman and MacFarquhar, *Paradox of China's Post-Mao Reforms,* 220–40, and Solinger, *Contesting Citizenship in Urban China* (Berkeley, 1999).

17. *China Daily,* February 27, 1991, 1.

18. Zai Liang and Zhongdong Ma, "China's Floating Population: New Evidence from the 2000 Census," *Population and Development Review* 30, no. 3 (2004): 467–88.

a scattered migrant population. In others their work was thwarted by powerful employers anxious to retain cheap peasant labor. Some remote mountain districts saw an influx of prosperous migrants from the south who violated birth planning regulations, but no one wanted to confront them.[19] The result was the growth of an "excess-birth guerrilla corps" that produced a large "illegal" population.[20] Some localities became notorious as "safe havens" for birth planning offenders.[21]

To counter this problem, the state proposed to substitute indirect regulation for direct administrative control. Beginning in 1987, local branches of the state bureaucracy for commerce and industry were instructed to withhold work permits from individuals who violated the birth limitation policy. Peasants were required to present proof of compliance, and local bureaus were forbidden to issue work papers without this evidence.[22] These procedures were easily skirted, however. Local commerce and industry officials had no interest in becoming adjunct family planning officials. Nor were local employers interested in the problem, particularly when they had a special interest in retaining cheap labor. As the number of migrants increased, therefore, fewer and fewer bothered to register locally or acquire the obligatory work permit.[23] Periodic sweeps of districts with large numbers of migrants were sometimes made in an effort to curb violations of the plan, but this was only a temporary solution. Migrant couples could not be prevented from trying again to have another child or from fleeing to a

19. Zhen Huaixin, "Qiongkun shanqu jihua shengyu ruhe zuochu digu," *Zhongguo renkou bao* (February 16, 1990): 3.

20. Guo Xiao, "The 'Population Explosion' Is Drawing Near," *Jingji ribao* [Economic Daily], January 10, 1989, in *FBIS*, February 3, 1989, 51; Fan Xiangguo and Huang Yuan, "Zhongguo 'hei renkou' " [China's illegal population], *Xin guancha* [New Observer] 4 (February 25, 1989): 28–32; "Couples with More Than One Child Seek Shelter along Borders of Hunan, Hubei, Sichuan, and Guizhou," *Zhongguo tongxun she* (January 20, 1989), in *JPRS* 89–014, February 15, 1989, 44–45; *Xinhua*, June 15, 1990, in *FBIS*, June 18, 1990, 37; Zhang Mengyi, "A New Mode of Population Shift and Mobility in China," *Liaowang Overseas Edition* 2 (January 8, 1990): 16–17, in *FBIS*, February 9, 1990, 18–20; Wang Xu et al., "Renkou wenti yao zhuajin zai zhuajin," *Liaowang* 28 (July 13, 1987): 14–15. Xie Lianhui, " 'Zhejiang cun' zhuke hude shengyu guan," *Renmin ribao*, November 30, 1988, 3.

21. "Couples with More Than One Child Seek Shelter"; Xu Xiaoran and Wang Zhigang, "Account of a Visit to the 'Excess Birth Guerrillas'," *Henan ribao*, November 29, 1990, in *FBIS*, December 27, 1990, 71–73; *Xinhua*, March 3, 1989, in *FBIS*, March 16, 1989, 42–43.

22. De Ming, "China's Population Situation Remains Grim," *Liaowang Overseas Edition* 17 (April 1988), 9–10, in *FBIS*, May 11, 1988, 28.

23. Those who did were more likely to have used corruption and bribery to acquire the necessary certificates. Pei Gang, "Thoughts on the Present Disarray in Matters of Population Reproduction and Suggested Improvements," *Renkou yu jingji* 5 (October 25, 1990): 6–10, in *JPRS* 90–010, February 7, 1990, 65.

different locale where surveillance was less effective.[24] Repeated attempts to draft effective regulations to curb migrants' excess childbearing, including national ones issued in 1999, appeared to make little difference.[25] By that time, the regulations required migrants to bring documentation of their birth planning status to their place of employment. Temporary residency permits could not be issued without them. With a booming economy and a demand for cheap labor, employers often ignored this requirement and spent little or no effort monitoring childbearing.

Collusion

A second category of enforcement dilemmas involved more active collusion between cadres and peasants, or between cadres at different administrative levels. In some cases, cadres assisted because of their sympathy for peasant childbearing preferences. In other cases, the collusion was self-interested, or corruption was at work.

One form of resistance was illegal early marriage, followed by early childbirth. Beginning in 1981, a new marriage law made marriage legal for women at age twenty and for men at twenty-two.[26] Compared with the 1950 law, this raised the legal age of marriage by two years.[27] In practice, however, state policy had encouraged late marriage during the 1960s and 1970s, resulting in an increase in average marriage age from 19.8 in 1966 to 23 in 1980. The new law, therefore, lowered the actual age at marriage, even while late marriage and late birth were being urged for birth planning purposes. As rural families took advantage of the new law, the number of marriages increased, and the average age of marriage began to fall. Under-age, or early marriage (*zao hun*, under the legal age of twenty), also contributed to the decline in marriage age, as rural cadres knowingly helped

24. Xu and Wang, "Account of a Visit," 73.
25. For an example of attempts to regulate migrants, see "Liaoning Provincial Regulations on Family Planning Management and Implementation among the Floating Population," *Liaoning ribao*, June 26, 1996, in *FBIS*, June 20, 1996. Online at http://www.unescap.org/esid/psis/population/database/poplaws/law_china/ch_record043.htm. This is the website for the United Nations Economic and Social Commission for Asia and the Pacific. It provides the full text of a selection of central and local documents and regulations. In 1999, new national regulations were issued. See "Measure on the Administration of Family Planning for the Floating Population" (January 1, 1999). Online at http://www.unescap.org/esid/psis/population/database/poplaws/law_China/ch_record031.htm.
26. "Zhonghua renmin gongheguo hunyinfa" [Marriage Law of the People's Republic of China], in *Zhongguo renkou nianjian, 1985*, 73–75. The Marriage Law was passed by the National People's Congress in September 1980 and took effect on January 1, 1981.
27. "Zhongguo renmin gongheguo hunyinfa (1950)," ibid., 65–67.

couples under the legal age to register their marriage, or rural couples and their parents ignored official registration requirements and conducted traditional marriage ceremonies. In Hubei Province, early marriages constituted 13 percent of the total by 1988.[28] In Hunan, they accounted for 20.8 percent of the total.[29] Nationwide, 6.1 million people had married under the legal age by 1988. That figure translated into about 15 percent of all marriages, and those marriages contributed about 10 percent of all births annually.[30] By 1994, the figure for early marriages had risen to 1.6 million annually, representing 75 percent of all illegal marriages, and 16 percent of the ten million marriages annually.[31]

The rural reforms reinforced this trend in several ways. First, peasants were sometimes anxious to find brides for their sons in order to increase the allotment of responsibility fields for the household.[32] Second, by making peasants more independent of the collective, the reforms reduced the practical value of official registration. Prior to the reforms, couples who sought to marry were at the mercy of rural officials, who could grant or deny their request for marriage. To register, couples had to obtain supporting documents from their team leader and brigade leader and then take them to the commune headquarters. At the commune, a local cadre responsible for civil affairs gave them a marriage permit, allowing them to register with the local public security bureau and establish residency together. Prior to the reforms, peasants had used a variety of tactics to circumvent this bureaucratic process.[33] After the reforms, circumvention became even easier, and a growing number of couples took advantage of it. As a result of the reforms, official registration was no longer necessary to gain access to scarce goods or coupons, or to be allotted agricultural land or housing acreage. As a result, peasants saw less need for official registry and were content to hold traditional wedding ceremonies considered valid in the village. This practice, which earned them the label of "firecracker" or "banquet" couples, gained

28. Hubei Provincial Service, February 27, 1988, in *FBIS*, February 29, 1988, 51.
29. Hunan Provincial Service, November 9, 1988, in *FBIS*, December 19, 1988, 49.
30. *China Daily*, January 9, 1988, 1; Zhu Baoxia, "Birth Control Planned for Transient Population," *China Daily*, February 27, 1991, in *FBIS*, February 27, 1991, 35.
31. *Xinhua*, "Government to Curb Illegal Marriages," in *FBIS*, March 1, 1994, 23.
32. This was a factor in the sudden increase in marriages in 1981 and 1982. Not all of the increase was due simply to the implementation of the new marriage law. Because villagers sometimes knew in advance that the land would be divided for contracting at the end of the year or after the current harvest cycle, some rushed to marry to increase the size of their household before distribution. Zhang Huaiyu and Dong Shigui, "New Problems in the Control of Population in the Rural Areas Brought About by Implementation of Agricultural Production Responsibility Systems," *Renkou yanjiu* 1 (1982): 31–34.
33. Parish and Whyte, *Village and Family,* chap. 10.

rapid acceptance as a means to avoid birth controls until the couple gave birth to a son.[34]

The reforms further encouraged peasants to avoid registration by putting pressure on local government offices to find their own sources of revenue. Not wanting to forego any money-making opportunity, township officials began to charge large fees to register officially, leading many to avoid the process.[35] Peasants complained about the charges, and some refused to pay. Others were prepared to pay, but they were below the marriage age. The solution was bribery or corruption. For a price, or as part of an ongoing exchange relationship, village officials were sometimes willing to certify that the couple had reached the appropriate age.[36] With this false certification in hand, township officials rarely questioned its authenticity. If they did, however, they too could be bribed to sign the registration document. Finally, the trend toward early marriage became a reinforcing phenomenon, as parents began to worry that their children would not find suitable mates. To assure they did, engagements were often arranged for young teenagers. Once the engagement was set, however, the couples invariably married, or began to cohabit, prior to the legal marriage age.[37]

Other forms of collusion drew cadres directly into corrupt or illegal activity, as couples who were unwilling to have an unauthorized child went to any lengths to arrange a "legal" birth. In some cases, couples sent their child to relatives without children and informed cadres that the child had been adopted. Without asking too many questions, cadres certified that this was the case, making the couple eligible for another child.[38] A second pattern was to engineer a false divorce. Couples ineligible to have another child bribed or colluded with local officials to obtain a quick divorce decree. The birth rules on divorced couples allowed the couple to carry the pregnancy to term without penalty. After the baby was born, the couple, which had never separated, applied and received permission to remarry. These maneuvers were all legal in the narrowest sense, but given the lengthy process usually required to obtain a divorce in China, the strategy could work only with the assistance of sympathetic or greedy officials.[39] A third pattern involved cor-

---

34. Shi Zhonglin, "A Discussion of the Underlying Causes of and Measures for Concealed Marriages and Births," *Renkou yanjiu* 107 (September 1997): 72–73, in *FBIS*, December 22, 1997.

35. *Xinhua*, March 14, 1990, in *FBIS*, April 13, 1990, 11.

36. Interview File 900722.

37. "Yixie nongcun zaohun zaoyu qingquang yanzhong" [A serious situation for early marriage and early birth in some rural areas], *Renmin ribao*, October 21, 1988, 3.

38. Henan Rural Survey Team, "Yao duzhu chao jihua," 47.

39. Ibid., 47–48.

ruption on the part of medical personnel or birth planning officials. As a general rule, rural women were fitted for IUDs after the birth of their first child. Only under special medical circumstances were they allowed to adopt some other form of birth control, and removal of the IUD was illegal. Some doctors and other medical personnel began to offer their services to remove the IUDs.[40] Others faked examination results for women getting regular checkups on their IUDs; rather than report pregnant women, they allowed them to go undetected.[41] Still others could be paid to tie only one fallopian tube during sterilization surgery, or to provide false certification of having undergone sterilization.[42] In 1994, a former vice president of a county hospital in Hunan was executed for taking nearly 200,000 yuan in bribes between 1986 and 1991 in exchange for falsifying 448 sterilization certificates.[43] Despite the extremity of the penalty in this case, bribery and falsification remained widespread practices.[44]

Medical personnel and birth planning cadres were also implicated in phony permit schemes. Medical personnel could sometimes be persuaded to issue official certificates indicating that a child had a congenital defect that would prevent her from becoming a full-time laborer. With that certificate, couples could then get special permission to have another child legally.[45] This route was especially attractive to couples anxious to find a legal way to skirt the one-child limit. In 1990, for example, while visiting a young village leader's home in Donghu township I noted the presence of three children, the youngest of which was a boy. When I inquired into the matter, he claimed that the first two children, both girls, had congenital defects. Yet all three children appeared to be in good health.[46] Similarly, official birth permits were controlled and issued by birth planning cadres. Peasants who

40. *FBIS*, August 17, 1981, Q2–3; *FBIS*, September 10, 1981, K31; *Hubei ribao*, December 9, 1982, 2; *Summary of World Broadcasts (SWB)*, September 25, 1979, 16; Shi, *Zhongguo jihua shengyu huodong shi*, 218, 221.

41. Henan Rural Survey Team, "Yao duzhu chao jihua," 47.

42. Du Xin and Yu Changhong, "Zhongguo nongcunde shengyu dachao," *Liaowang choukan haiwaiban* 43 (October 23, 1989): 19. See also Li Ching-feng and Ma Chao-yu, "Massive Massacre of Newborn Babes," *Yi chou kan* 230 (August 5, 1994): 52–53, in *FBIS* 94–187, September 27, 1994, 47–51.

43. *Xinhua*, "Henan Province Executes Hospital Official," in *FBIS*, October 24, 1994, 79.

44. The extent of the problem was indicated by the issuance of provincial regulations in the 1990s regarding administrative punishments for party and government cadres who violated procedures. Regulations for Shaanxi and Hainan, for example, promised that medical personnel and other cadres who falsified operations or certificates would be punished. See the translated text of the Shaanxi regulations (published in *Shaanxi ribao*, August 10, 1994) in *FBIS* 94–194, October 6, 1994, 52–53. The Hainan regulations (from *Hainan ribao*, December 20, 1997) are translated in *FBIS*, January 14, 1998.

45. Henan Rural Survey Team, "Yao duzhu chao jihua," 47.

46. Interview File 901204.

could not find other ways around the birth limit sometimes discovered that local officials were willing to sell the permits for the right price. In 1988, officials in some localities were charging 1,600 yuan for a permit.[47]

The fourth and most pervasive pattern of collusion was to levy fines for unplanned births rather than expend extra effort attempting to prevent them. If grassroots women's leaders were unsuccessful in persuading a couple to abort an unauthorized pregnancy, village leaders sometimes did little or nothing to reinforce their efforts. This strategy allowed cadres to fulfill the letter of the law while reducing the risk of major confrontations with villagers. They could make it clear that heavy penalties would be levied after the child was born, but if that threat was not a sufficient deterrent, no further deterrence efforts were made. Leaders in some localities pushed fines as high as possible, but others imposed fines that were lower than those authorized by county or township regulations. In one Shandong township, for example, fines were lowered in 1990 from the official levels of 1,000 yuan for a second birth, and 1,500 yuan for a third birth, to the 500–800 yuan range.[48] In Donghu township in Wuhan, township fines were set at 600 and 1,200 yuan for peasants, and at 800 and 1,800 yuan for collective enterprise workers. At the village level, however, significantly smaller fines were levied. One village reported fines of 400 yuan for a second child and 300 for a third; two others reported fines of 400 yuan and 1,000 yuan.[49]

Cadres were particularly lenient with "single-daughter households" (*dunu hu*), or couples with two or more daughters but no sons. State efforts to change the "feudal" idea that daughters were as valuable as sons were never as aggressive as the effort to prevent births, and the education campaign had little effect. Moreover, the state's official concession to single-daughter households in 1984—allowing the parents of a girl to have a second child after an interval of 3 to 4 years—reinforced peasant beliefs in the importance of male offspring. The state argued that the reforms made it possible for women to earn incomes equal to, or greater than, the incomes of men. But that did not alter the fact that women married out of the household (and often out of the village) and became a part of their husband's household, economically as well as socially. Nor did it alter the social stigma attached to not bearing a son. The threat of that stigma put tremendous pressure on rural women and left them vulnerable to abuse for failing to produce a son to continue the ancestral line. Even beyond that, however,

47. Zhong Cheng, "Delegates and Members Show Concern for Birth Planning," *Zhongguo xinwen she*, April 11, 1988, in *FBIS*, April 13, 1988, 33.
48. Interview File 900722.
49. Interview Files 901123, 901205, 901126.

to produce no sons was to risk a lifetime of vulnerability as a small and weak household at a political, economic, and social disadvantage. These considerations were well understood by village cadres, causing them to look the other way, or "close one eye," to offending couples.[50] A typical attitude was voiced by a village women's leader in Hubei: "They [peasant couples] want to have a son. What can we do?"[51]

That attitude contributed to the poor record of Guangji County in 1983. According to Hubei provincial officials, Guangji County turned in the poorest record in the province that year—4,500 women with two daughters had given birth to a third child. Cadres who were sympathetic to their plight had failed to impose fines or other penalties.[52] Similarly, village leaders in one Shandong township were sympathetic to couples with no sons. In some cases, they made no effort to impose fines on these couples if they gave birth to another girl. If couples violated the policy and had a son, however, payment of fines was transformed into a near-ritual performance. Cadres sent to collect the fines were received happily, and couples paid the fine as part of the celebration over the birth.[53] A similar case was reported for Xincheng township in Shanxi. The report tells of the case of a woman who had three daughters but who was pressured by her husband and mother-in-law to keep trying until she had a son. Birth planning officials tried to dissuade her, but they were not successful. When she gave birth to her fourth child, a son, the entire family pooled its resources to pay the 3,000 yuan fine.[54]

The same pattern prevailed with respect to sterilization. Pressed to meet sterilization quotas for couples with two or more children, many cadres made every effort to avoid couples who had no sons. Even during major mobilizations like that of 1983, village cadres worked to shield couples with no sons from the campaign. Because of the extreme pressures to meet sterilization quotas, they were not always successful, but during less-intense periods they had no difficulty bypassing them. In Xinyu city in Jiangxi Province, for example, more than 82 percent of duotai births in 1985 were to couples with two or more daughters, including those with six or seven daughters. These births occurred despite the major sterilization mobiliza-

50. The phrase is *zheng yiyan, bi yiyan* ("keep one eye open and another closed"). Wu, "Guangyu jihua shengyu houjin danwei," 53.
51. Interview File 821012. For an outstanding documentary film on this subject, see *Small Happiness,* directed by Carma Hinton and Richard Gordon (Philadelphia, Long Bow Group, 1984).
52. Interview File 840608. Wuhan municipal officials also reported that cadres were "of one heart" (*tongxin*) with the peasants, causing problems in enforcement. Interview File 840607.
53. Interview File 900307.
54. Xiao Ming and Chen Yan, "Family Planning: A Tough Nut to Crack," *Women of China,* 11–12.

tion during 1983 and 1984, because cadres had been unwilling to impose permanent birth control measures on couples without a son. Rather than resent the exceptions, other couples, even those with sons who had been mobilized for sterilization, tended to be sympathetic with this discriminating use of power.[55]

Cover-up

One of the most pervasive and deeply entrenched strategies for coping with enforcement pressures was the cover-up—hiding or embellishing the truth when reporting the results of birth planning work to higher authorities. Just as team and brigade cadres had colluded during the collective era to marginally underreport the harvest in order to keep more grain in the village, grassroots cadres used the statistical reporting system for birth planning to hide embarrassing numbers on unplanned births, particularly multiparity births.[56] In estimating vital rates (birth rate, mortality rate, and natural rate of population growth) and tracking birth parity, government officials at all levels had to rely on household registration figures compiled by local public security offices, and on statistical reports compiled by village women's leaders and township government officials. As discussed in chapter 4, village leaders were required to report births and deaths to township officials on a quarterly basis. Township officials compiled those reports and passed them along to county birth planning officials. On the basis of those grassroots reports, birth planning officials at higher levels plotted the progress of the regional campaign and reported to the State Family Planning Commission.

By the end of the 1980s, the erosion of the statistical reporting system was a major problem. Women's leaders were provided with standard forms to fill in showing the number of births and deaths, the number of couples using different types of contraception, and other basic information. If an accurate report would reflect unfavorably on the village, however, they or senior village officials simply altered the data in their favor.[57] Village leaders used any pretext to underreport the number of local births. Women known to have given birth, but who did so outside the village, were left off local birth rolls. Even those who gave birth in the village were sometimes omitted, and the omission covered up by refusing to issue a household registration for the infant. As a general rule, township officials had to assume that

55. Wang Peishu, "Wanshan shengyu zhengce, kaihao 'xiao kouzi' de guanjian shi duzhu 'da kouzi'," *Xibei renkou* 3 (1987): 20–21.
56. On this pattern of behavior, see Oi, *State and Peasant,* chap. 6.
57. *Renmin ribao,* October 12, 1988, 3.

the data were reliable, for they had neither the money nor the manpower to conduct regular investigations of each household in the township. As for the head of birth planning work at the township, there were only so many villages that he or she could visit in any given month, and village investigations did not always produce evidence of irregularities. Glaring discrepancies in the reports might come to his or her attention, but it was much harder to detect the omission of one or two unauthorized births, particularly when the births took place outside the village. Sending township officials into a village did not necessarily increase the likelihood of full disclosure. One former township cadre complained that village leaders did everything they could to obstruct the work of such teams. Village leaders warned peasants about the impending visit by the team, giving offending couples a chance to flee or hide. Village leaders sometimes hid themselves so as to avoid a confrontation. Other cadres welcomed the team and accompanied it into the village, but their assistance was calculated to minimize the team's access to accurate data and to move them quickly out of the village. These tactics were so effective that one cadre concluded that it was impossible for outsiders to know the true state of affairs in the village.[58]

This problem was aggravated by the tendency of grassroots cadres to view population targets as "soft" or secondary targets, less important that the "hard" economic targets that are used by party and government superiors to judge their work performance and make evaluations for promotions, bonuses, or special citations.[59] In theory, birth planning and other soft targets were to be included in the evaluation process in the 1980s. In practice, these targets were often given less weight, or a poor performance was forgiven as long as economic performance was sound. Superiors overlooked these performance weaknesses because these officials were part of their clientelist network and because their own evaluation process resembled that at lower levels. Like their subordinates, they also were evaluated primarily based on their fulfillment of hard economic targets. At each level of the political system, therefore, leaders engaged in the practice of target forgiveness, knowing they would benefit from the same consideration.

During the 1980s and 1990s, persistent efforts were made to force cadres to stop this practice by considering birth planning as a hard target. Throughout the 1980s, local governments were told to make birth planning one of the major criteria for evaluation and promotion, and provinces responded by issuing local regulations to that effect.[60] With the exception of

58. Interview File 900307.

59. Lu Xueyi and Zhang Houyi, "Peasant Diversification, Problems, Remedies," *Nongye jingji wenti* 1 (1990): 16–21.

60. De Ming, "China's Population Situation Remains Grim," *Liaowang haiwaiban* 17, April 25, 1988; Henan Provincial Service, March 30, 1989, in *FBIS*, March 31, 1989, 60.

those cadres who personally violated the birth limit, however, regulations of this sort had little effect.[61] Yet when birth planning targets *were* taken seriously in the evaluation process, the result was fraud. Township cadres found it more convenient to accept questionable village data than to investigate the true state of affairs, and county officials were equally eager to receive good news from their townships. Birth planning officials learned quickly that the local party secretary did not want to receive reports that would reflect badly on the overall performance of the locality or threaten its privileged standing as an "advanced unit." And zealous cadres who sought out fraud learned that they would not be rewarded for "rectifying" a fraudulent statistical report.[62] As one former township cadre put it, an honest report would accomplish nothing but the destruction of one's own career, since higher-level political leaders would be embarrassed and angered by the revelation. He admitted that he had knowingly submitted false reports rather than face the censure that would come with accurate accounting.[63]

By 1988, evidence of these statistical irregularities began to raise alarms over the quality and reliability of China's official statistics for vital rates. According to the State Statistical Bureau, the population growth rate for 1987 was 14.39 per 1,000, a rate that was higher than desired but within acceptable planning limits. In the fall of 1988, however, a detailed 1 percent sampling survey, conducted jointly by several state agencies, concluded that the true rate for 1987 was 16.16 per 1,000, nearly two percentage points higher than the officially reported rate.[64] It also revealed that the majority of all provinces, municipalities, and autonomous regions (sixteen out of twenty-nine) had birthrates at least 30 percent higher than originally reported for 1987, and another six had birthrates at least 20 percent higher.[65] The discrepancy between survey results and the data compiled by the birth planning bureaucracy was attributed to "statistical leakage" (*shuifen*), that is, exaggerated reporting by local-level birth planning officials.[66] Survey data from 1989 were no more encouraging. Provincial figures on unauthorized births and multiparity births in 1988 revealed that fifteen provinces had unauthorized birthrates of 40 percent or higher, and the multiple-birth

61. Pei Gang, "Thoughts on the Present Disarray," 64.

62. Yang, "Woguo nongcun jihua shengyu gongzuo," 64.

63. This cadre admitted to having prepared and filed reports he knew to be false. Interview File 900722.

64. *Renmin ribao*, October 28, 1988, 3. The survey was conducted jointly by the SFPC, the State Statistical Bureau, the State Planning Commission, and the Ministries of Finance and Public Security Bureau, and was based on data obtained from local field work, household reproduction data, and birth planning data.

65. *Renmin ribao*, October 24, 1988, 3; *Zhongguo jihua shengyu nianjian, 1991* (Beijing, 1992), 109.

66. *Renmin ribao*, October 24, 1988, 3.

rate also remained unacceptably high in several provinces (see table 9). The problem was so pervasive that it was captured in a rhyming jingle: "The village deceives the township, the township deceives the county, and so on all the way to the State Council" (*cun man xiang, xiang man xian, yizhi man dao guowuyuan*).[67]

Efforts to clean up statistical reports proved as ineffective in the 1990s as in the 1980s, and the situation grew worse. In the early 1990s, the state made an attempt to get tough on cadres by placing them on a "one-ballot veto" (*yipiao foujue*) system designed to hold their overall work performance evaluations hostage to their success with birth planning targets. Although this led many officials to press for strict local enforcement, others responded to the escalation of pressure by submitting fraudulent reports.[68] By the end of the decade, the problem had grown so pervasive that critics began to compare the situation to the Great Leap Forward, when outrageously inflated figures were reported in response to intense political pressures.[69]

The extent of the statistical exaggeration was laid out in detail by Chinese demographer Zeng Yi. In a 1995 article in one of China's premier population journals, Zeng questioned the very sharp drop registered in the total fertility rate in the early 1990s.[70] In 1989, the total fertility rate was already a low 2.3, very near to replacement level, but by 1991 figures gathered in the annual sample survey of population change showed that it had dropped to 1.65. In 1992 it was reported to have dropped even lower, to 1.52.[71] Zeng attributes this sudden and historically unprecedented drop to the new pressures brought to bear on cadres as a result of the new target responsibility system that made their salary, bonuses, and promotions contingent on fulfilling all birth control targets. This system, he argued, had not eliminated statistical fraud but deepened it, giving leaders at all levels strong incentives to massage the numbers, either by outright suppression of the data or by the more old-fashioned method of building in a margin of error, that is, inflating targets sent down to lower levels to assure that the real target can be met even if the inflated targets are not.

67. Wang Linchun, "Jihua shengyu tongji manbao xianxiang qianxi," *Renkou yu jingji* 5 (1995): 24.

68. When enforcement targets were especially difficult, cadres sometimes had to alter their figures even after launching a harsh new campaign. For a fascinating discussion of how the one-ballot veto system and other factors led to the falsification of statistical reports, see Cui Xianwu and Da Wangli, "Renkou chusheng man, lou bao wenti chanshengde yuanyin jichi fangfan," *Renkou yu jihua shengyu* 5 (1997): 31–34.

69. A Ji, "Who will Stop the 'True Lies'?" *Minzhu yu fazhi* 243 (May 1997): 8–11, in *FBIS*, August 15, 1997; Liu Zhuyu, "Guarding against the Malpractice of Making False Reports and Exaggerating Figures," *Renmin ribao*, December 15, 1999, 4, in *FBIS*, January 12, 2000.

70. Zeng Yi, "Wo guo 1991–1992 nian shengyu lu shifou da da diyu daiti shuiping?" *Renkou yanjiu* 19, no. 3 (1995): 7–14.

71. Ibid., 7.

Based on interviews with persons involved in the annual sample surveys, Zeng raised serious questions about the quality of Chinese population statistics gathered between censuses, charged cadres with continuing to engage in the variety of dubious behaviors that became commonplace in the 1980s, and described the new extremes to which they went. Not only did they warn villagers in advance that the survey team was coming, they coached them on how to respond to questions: "[They] post guards and sentries" to maintain surveillance on team members and use "secret signals" to communicate and "tunnels" to move about secretly.[72] This description confirms the report of a former township cadre in Shandong who, reflecting on his experience in the late 1980s, concluded that it was impossible for township officials to discover the true state of affairs in villages.[73] It is also confirmed by a 1995 report from Shandong that attributed continuing statistical leakage to intense pressures on birth planning cadres and impossibly high performance targets that leave cadres "without any margin of error." These unrealistic expectations create grievances and morale problems for cadres, leading them to "take the crooked path." And if birth planning cadres didn't take the initiative to massage the statistics, their superiors did it for them.[74]

The extent of the statistical leakage resulting from these tactics is suggested by the results of a survey of thirty-two villages in Hebei and Hubei provinces in October 1993. Unlike the annual 1 per 1,000 surveys used to calculate national vital rates and fertility levels, this survey was unannounced, making it impossible for cadres to prepare in advance. In addition, survey takers were selected from outside the township or county in which the villages were located, with the purpose of decreasing villagers' fears that accurate reporting would lead to retribution after the team left. The results showed the actual number of village births in 1992 had been 35 percent higher than previously reported. They also revealed a tendency to report a third birth as a second birth, and a second as a first birth. In Hebei, less than 1 percent of births were reported as third births, whereas the actual figure was 14.7 percent. In Hubei, the figures were 4.2 percent and 14.8 percent, respectively.[75] Drawing on these and other survey results, Zeng Yi estimated a 1991 fertility rate around 2.2, dropping to 2.1 in 1992. Two-thirds of this more modest drop was attributed to a true decline in the birthrate and one-third to a small increase in the age at marriage.[76] Evidence such as that provided by the survey made Chinese demographers

---

72. Ibid., 9.
73. Interview File 900722.
74. Wang Linxiang, "Jihua shengyu tongji manbao xianxiang qianxi," *Renkou yu jingji* 5 (1995): 24–25.
75. See Zeng, "Wo guo 1991–1992 nian shengyulu," 11.
76. Ibid., 12–13.

skeptical when the fertility rate was reported to have dropped to 1.65 by the end of the eighth FYP (1991–95). This skepticism was eventually borne out, and the official data were revised to reflect a fertility rate of 2.1 at the end of the century.

Statistical reporting was not the only way that cadres doctored the books. They also took liberties with funds designated for birth planning work. Fiscal reforms implemented after 1984 encouraged financial neglect of birth planning and created opportunities for graft, embezzlement, and other misuse of funds. Until 1984, the costs of contraceptives and all family planning–related medical procedures (IUD insertions, abortions, sterilizations, etc.) were covered within the central state budget. All other expenses—for example, the costs of preparing and disseminating propaganda materials, work subsidies for village cadres and activists involved in mobilization campaigns, and subsidies and benefits for compliant couples who undergo sterilization or have only one child—were absorbed by local governments or rural villages, whether or not they exceeded budgeted expenditures. As discussed in chapter 6, those costs skyrocketed during the 1983 sterilization campaign, placing unanticipated burdens on local government finances. In 1984, however, Beijing mandated a reorganization of township-level finances. Birth planning was one of several categories of local expenses targeted for reduction and rationalization.[77]

The impetus for fiscal reform was twofold. First, central authorities sought to reduce the total tax burden imposed on the peasantry by the various levels of government and by specific bureaucratic offices (*nongmin fudan*). Still uncertain in late 1983 how rapidly agricultural performance would improve, they feared that licit and illicit extractions by local cadres might stifle peasant entrepreneurship and impede the reform process.[78] Second, the reform of local government expenditures was part of a larger effort to spur local economic investment and growth and reduce central-level budgetary commitments, by decentralizing fiscal authority and allowing local governments to retain more profits. By 1984, new revenue-sharing arrangements had been negotiated with individual provinces, giving them greater control over the structure of local spending and the right to deter-

77. See Central Document 1 (1984). On the costs of birth planning work, see Gao et al., "Jihua shengyu yaoju shoufei zhengcede tantao."
78. On the problem of "peasant burdens," see Lu Xiaobo, "The Politics of the Peasant Burden in Reform China," *Journal of Peasant Studies* 24, no. 4 (October 1997): 113–18; Thomas Bernstein and Lu Xiaobo, "Taxation without Representation: Peasants, the Central, and the Local States in Reform China," *China Quarterly* 163 (September 2000): 742–63; Tyrene White, "Below Bureaucracy: The Burden of Being a Village under the Local State," paper presented at the annual meeting of the Association for Asian Studies, Chicago, April 5–8, 1990.

mine their own fiscal arrangements with local governments under their jurisdiction.[79] In turn, counties eventually gained the right to set fiscal
arrangements with township governments, placing all levels of government
on "harder" budgetary constraints.[80]

This comprehensive reform of the fiscal system had far-reaching implications for the overall pattern of government spending and investment, and
for specific budgetary categories such as birth planning. As governments
gained greater control over their budgetary revenues, governmental bureaus
and commercial enterprises were pressured to balance their budgets and
generate their own sources of revenue for reinvestment or expansion. As
more responsibilities were transferred from the central budget to local authorities, the solvency of local governments came to depend on their entrepreneurial abilities. Government activities that did not generate a profit
were often neglected, while profit-making ventures attracted more investment.[81] Agencies that could not compete on the market were starved for
funds and came under increased pressure to find their own sources of revenue simply to maintain their existing operations.[82]

In that climate, the birth planning bureaucracy found itself strapped for
funds during the seventh FYP, just as the pressures of an increasing
childbearing-age cohort demanded increased investment. After the drastic
increases in birth planning expenses during the 1982–83 sterilization campaign (rising 36 percent in 1982 and 60 percent in 1983), expenditures
went up by only 2 percent in 1984 and 1985.[83] In late 1986, SFPC director
Wang Wei complained about this drop-off in funding. He criticized "some
provinces" for drastically reducing their allocation for birth planning and
called on them to give it higher priority in future budgets.[84] By 1988, delegates to the annual meeting of birth planning commission directors were

79. James Tong, "Fiscal Reform, Elite Turnover and Central-Provincial Relations in Post-Mao China," *Australian Journal of Chinese Affairs* 22 (July 1989): 13–14.

80. The arrangements or contracts between provincial governments and prefectural governments, prefectures and counties, and counties and townships vary over time and by locality. This had created an exceedingly complex set of financial arrangements at the local levels. See, for example, "Hebei sheng renmin zhengfu guanyu gaijin caizheng guanli tizhide jixiang guiding," *Hebei jingji tongji nianjian, 1987,* 488; Zhonggong hebei shengwei yanjiushi nongcunchu, "Fangshou rang xiang zhengfu dang jiali cai," *Nongcun gongzuo tongxun* 6 (1986): 32–33. On the distinction between "hard" and "soft" budget constraints, see Janos Kornai, *Contradictions and Dilemmas* (Cambridge, 1986).

81. On the role of township governments in developing profit-making township enterprises, see Jean C. Oi, *Rural China Takes Off* (Berkeley, 1999).

82. On the impact of fiscal reform, see Christine Wong, Christopher Heady, and Wing T. Woo, *Fiscal Management and Economic Reform in the People's Republic of China* (Hong Kong, 1995).

83. Gao Ersheng et al., "Jihua shengyu yaoju shoufei zhengcede tantao," 23.

84. Wang Wei, "Jihua shengyu gongzuo qingkuang."

pressing central leaders for increased funding and personnel. Premier Li Peng's response, however, was to remind them of the "financial difficulties" with the central budget and request that local governments carry even more of the financial burden for family planning.[85] This was difficult to do at the grassroots level, however, as expenses grew much more rapidly than rural income. Frustrated birth planning officials were left to complain publicly about the lack of support at all levels of government. One provincial Family Planning Commission director was quoted as saying: "During the past few years, we spent half our time lobbying government leaders at all levels. They should take the lead in family planning, but we end up having to push them into action."[86]

The lack of funds to maintain and develop the birth planning bureaucracy, combined with the new pressure on all governmental organs to compensate for declining financial allocations by generating their own revenues, had serious and paradoxical consequences for rural enforcement. First, after 1984, all township governments were supposed to be staffed by a full-time cadre for public health and family planning. In many areas, however, townships refused to pay such individuals out of collective revenues, and the state would not put them on its payroll either. As a result, many townships had no birth planning cadre during much of the 1980s, and many more had one or two who were poorly paid.[87] Second, work was slowed in some areas due to lack of funding for medical support. In areas where the birth planning organization sought to establish or upgrade "family planning service stations" independent of local hospitals, local governments could not or would not provide funds.[88] Third, some state-run hospitals increased fees to cover their own rising costs and to generate profits. They also dispensed unnecessary medicine and services, inflating the charges billed to the birth planning offices.[89] As a result, costs to township governments increased rapidly, and local governments sometimes could not afford

85. Li Peng, "Zai tingchu quanguo jihua shengyu weiyuanhui zhuren huiyi huibao shide jianghua," in *Jihua shengyu zhongyao wenjian*, 62.
86. Zhu Li, "Family Planning to Emphasize Economic as Well as Administrative Methods," *Jingji cankao* [Economic Reference], March 10, 1989, 4, in *JPRS* 89–047, May 17, 1989, 39.
87. Qinghai Provincial Service, February 20, 1987, in *FBIS*, February 27, 1987, T2. See also Liaoning Provincial Service, February 28, 1988, in *FBIS*, March 3, 1988, 38. In some cases, "birth planning cadres" held more than one work portfolio simultaneously. See Shuai Zepeng, "Jihua shengyu ganbu duiwude guanli jidai jiaqiang" [Management of birth planning cadres ranks in urgent need of strengthening], *Renkou yanjiu* 4 (1988): 59. *Tianjin ribao*, March 13, 1990, in *FBIS*, April 11, 1990, 45–46.
88. Cheng Linli and Wu Yousheng, "Jiceng jihua shengyu gongzuode fancha xiaoyi yu sikao," *Renkou yanjiu* 6 (1989): 53.
89. Panshi xian yantongshan xiang jishengban, "Women shi zemyang guanhao, yonghao 'sishu' fei he chaoshengfeide," *Renkou xuekan* 2 (1985): 51–52 and 55.

to reimburse hospitals in a timely way. Hospitals retaliated by refusing to accept additional birth planning patients until the debt was paid, but they did accept women without birth permits if they could pay the 200 yuan procedure fee.[90] One report claimed that "many" provincial governments owed public health departments "up to 10 million yuan" in tubal ligation surgery fees. To place this sum in perspective, one irate official pointed out that 100 million yuan had been spent to renovate the hotel where a birth planning meeting had been held. He added, "How come funds just dry up when it comes to family planning?"[91]

In this strict fiscal context, the birth planning bureaucracy came to rely on the extraction of fines from policy violators to cover ordinary operating costs. Paradoxically, to pursue its bureaucratic mission of preventing excess births, the bureaucracy needed the monies collected as a result of excess births. In one county in Sichuan Province, for example, the gap between budgeted allocations and actual expenditures during the 1979–87 period was 606,000 yuan annually. To cover the deficit, the county relied on the collection of excess-birth fees, making it bureaucratically imperative that couples violate the birth limitation policy.[92] Conversely, counties that were very successful in preventing excess births soon recognized the benefit of turning in a more mediocre performance. The better they did their job, the less money they had to cover their expenses.[93] In one Shandong township, for example, a former cadre reported that the six birth planning workers hired to help in the township office had no interest in anything except the collection of fines, since their salaries were paid directly out of those monies.[94]

The collection of fines by no means guaranteed that the money would be used to reward one-child couples or support birth planning work, however. Township and village leaders often took advantage of murky accounting procedures to divert the funds to other uses. In some cases, funds were embezzled by corrupt cadres, but in many other cases the funds were put to public use. In one case, 57 percent of the fines collected in one county in Jiangsu Province in 1997 were diverted to other uses, with 80 percent of the diverted funds used to pay for new township sedans and another 12 percent

90. Cheng and Wu, "Jiceng jihua shengyu," 53; *Xinhua*, September 22, 1988, in *JPRS* 88–063, October 5, 1988, 33.
91. Zhu, "Family Planning," 39.
92. Cheng and Wu, "Jiceng jihua shengyu," 53–54.
93. Cheng Yicai, "Chaosheng zinufei guanli tanwei," *Renkou yanjiu* 4 (1990): 61.
94. Interview File 900722. This case is doubly interesting because most of the workers were related to senior leaders. Three were daughters of the township mayor, one was a cousin of the mayor, the fifth was related to a county cadre, and the sixth was the son of the manager of the local retirement home (*jinglaoyuan*).

spent on entertaining guests.[95] Others diverted funds to invest in projects that had a more immediate and concrete impact on the village economy.[96] Rather than try to prevent excess births, local cadres used the fine system as a fund-raising tool, collecting penalties for infractions and investing them in local projects. In one report, a village party secretary was quoted as saying that in "four or five days' time" the village had collected 10,000 yuan, "just enough to pave a village road." The reporter condemned this practice of encouraging "fund-raising births" as an "evil embryo" (*guaitai*) that should be terminated.[97]

Although the collection of fines could provide added funds, some or all of the monies raised at the village level had to be turned over to higher levels of government. In Sichuan Province, for example, township governments in one county received 70 percent of all monies collected as fines, the district (*qü*) received 5 percent, the county received 20 percent, and the prefecture received 5 percent.[98] Elsewhere, villages were allowed to retain a portion of the fees, usually 50 percent or less.[99] In Wuhan, for example, regulations called for a 50–50 division of funds between villages and townships.[100] In Shandong, provincial regulations called for the county to receive 30 percent, the township to retain 60 percent, and the village to retain 10 percent.[101] These revenue-sharing arrangements put pressure on township officials to subject fine collection to campaign methods. They denied village cadres revenues that would otherwise remain in the village, however, and reinforced their distaste for birth planning work.[102] Extracting fines was difficult and unpleasant work. Village leaders forced to turn over fines to their superiors had little incentive to accurately report local birth trends to higher authorities.[103]

The pattern of grassroots taxation gave cadres another reason to hide the true population figures and to allow unauthorized births to go unacknowledged and unregistered. New fiscal and budgeting arrangements put into

95. Yang Jing, "Urgent Efforts Should Be Taken to Rectify and Strengthen the Management of Unplanned-Birth Charges," *Renkou yanjiu* 1 (1999): 77–78, in *FBIS*, April 12, 1999.

96. Cheng Yicai, "Chaosheng zinufei guanli tanwei," 61–62.

97. Jiang Su and Yang Shounian, " 'Jizi shengyu' buzu qu" [Do not permit the pursuit of fundraising births], *Nongcun gongzuo tongxun* 4 (1988): 25.

98. Cheng Linli and Wu Yousheng, "Jiceng jihua shengyu gongzuode fancha xiaoyi yu sikao."

99. Chen, "Chaosheng zinufei," 61.

100. Interview File 902311.

101. Interview File 900722.

102. Yang, "Woguo nongcun jihua shengyu gongzuo," 61.

103. Ibid.

place after 1983 allowed villages to levy fees on peasants or extract funds from village enterprises in order to pay for collective services and projects within the village. Aside from this collective withholding (*jiti tiliu*), however, township governments were authorized to collect "overall fees" (*tongchou fei*) for townshipwide projects and public services, such as education, militia training, cadre retirement stipends, and birth planning. These revenues were controlled by the township and used to cover budgeted items. Central and local regulations limited the amount that could be levied to approximately 5 percent of annual net income, but townships were given authority to determine how this tax would be levied. Some chose to distribute the quota to villages on a per capita basis.[104] Where village industries were profitable enough to cover the *tongchou fei,* village leaders did not have to levy the tax directly on villagers—they could extract it indirectly from village enterprise profits. Where the rural industrial base was weak, however, village leaders had to levy the tax directly on peasants and turn over the income for township use. Village leaders interested in keeping the tax burden low and retaining funds in the village thus had a direct incentive to underreport the size of the population.

Confrontation

Rural violence was a persistent fact of life during the collective era, but the character of that violence began to change under the reforms. Violence during the collective era often came through corporate acts of resistance, in which grassroots cadres led or encouraged villagers to use violence against the policies or demands of higher authorities. Violence also occurred along sectarian lines, with different lineage groups, including cadres among them, fighting with one another. Individual acts of violence against local team or brigade leaders, however, were a less frequent occurrence in the strict political environment of the time.[105] When the reform process loosened the choke hold of rural cadres on peasant livelihood, however, more and more peasants began to take out their grievances on local cadres, attacking those who attempted to enforce birth planning or to collect taxes and grain quotas, or exacting revenge on cadres who had been too vigorous in carrying out these tasks. In Suining County of Jiangsu Province, for example, there were a reported 381 "incidents of revenge" between January 1987 and May

104. Interview File 900307.
105. Elizabeth J. Perry, "Rural Violence in Socialist China," *China Quarterly* 103 (September 1985): 414–40.

1988. All of these incidents involved physical attacks on cadres by angry peasants, most related to birth planning, state grain requisitions, or disputes over housing and property lines.[106]

Violence and the threat of violence against birth planning officials began to occur in the early 1980s, as pressures to limit childbirth increased dramatically, and they continued throughout the 1990s. Irate husbands attacked birth planning officials when they pressured their wives or relatives to have abortions. Others were assaulted out of anger over botched abortions, sterilizations, or IUD insertions, and the failure of local officials to provide sufficient follow-up health care.[107] The attacks were often directed against female cadres, who were on the front lines of implementation. In some cases, officials were cursed and beaten. In others, however, they were attacked by one or more family members and killed.[108]

Two cases reported in *Hubei Daily* are illustrative. In April 1982, the paper told the story of a doctor who reported a woman with a third pregnancy to the commune authorities. The doctor first urged the woman to abort, but she refused. She then sought out the woman's husband, a worker in the commune grain station, but he also refused. The doctor then reported the pregnancy to the commune birth planning officials, but they were also unable to persuade them to abort. As a punishment, they stripped the husband of his work and his status as a worker rather than a peasant. The man nursed a grudge against the doctor who had informed on them and, fortified with liquor, went to the hospital one day and began to curse and beat her. Very quickly, eight family members joined him and continued the beating, and no one intervened to stop them. On the contrary, the village party secretary was the father of the irate husband, and he cheered the family on as they beat the victim.[109] In a second case, a birth planning work team from the administrative district (*qu*, a subcounty organ) was sent to a village to mobilize women to undergo sterilization or have IUDs inserted. At the end of the day, one man who returned to discover that his wife had had

106. Of the total, 122 (32%) were related to birth planning, 115 (29%) involved state requisitions of grain and other commodities, 51 (13.4%) were related to housing disputes, and 45 (12%) were related to disputes over the state's policy of requiring cremation rather than interment. The remaining 47 incidents (12%) were not accounted for precisely. Su, "Many Causes of Strained Relations," 12.

107. As late as 1992, a woman who claimed her health had been ruined attacked and killed a birth planning official after he failed to look into her case and offer follow-up care or assistance. Interview File 920724.

108. In July of 1981, for example, a commune-level birth planning cadre was killed while carrying out her work. Shi, *Zhongguo jihua shengyu*, 222.

109. Wan Simei, "Ouda jihua shengyu gongzuo renyuan faji burong" [Beating birth planning workers in violation of law and discipline will not be tolerated], *Hubei ribao* (April 12, 1982), 2.

an IUD inserted became furious with the team and began shouting at them. Local birth planning officials interceded, trying to calm the man and persuade him of the necessity of adopting birth control. He could not be subdued, however, and began to beat members of the work team and local officials. His younger brother joined in to do further damage before they were restrained.[110] At the extremes, some aggrieved peasants resorted to arson and elaborate murder plots. One extraordinary report told of peasants adopting a "scorched earth policy" to retaliate against cadre tactics that were equally harsh, and of a plot to blow up a train in order to take revenge on birth planning officials.[111]

While some peasants resorted to violent assault, many others used tactics that were less brutal but equally effective. In a village in Yunnan province, for example, rural women caught up in a 1994 campaign that forced them into undergoing sterilizations bullied and harassed the village party secretary for his role in assisting township authorities in carrying out the campaign. The women followed him around the village, and made demands that he personally provide compensation for the permanent loss of health and vitality resulting from sterilization, and help them with daily chores they were now unable to do for themselves. The inexperienced leader, who was compared unfavorably to the leader of a neighboring village who had managed to deflect the township authorities and the campaign, and whose own wife's health was compromised when he pressed her to set an example by being the first to be sterilized, was eventually driven to attempt suicide.[112] Just as cadres sometimes seized or destroyed peasant property in order to deter or punish birth planning offenses, peasants sometimes retaliated against them in kind, destroying crops on cadres' private plots, killing their chickens or pigs, and damaging their homes and furnishings.[113] These attacks became so frequent that one county in Henan Province passed a law explicitly banning such acts of retaliation.[114] Other provinces began to follow suit, including provisions in their birth planning regulations for punish-

110. "Wang shi xiungdi shou chengfa—wuli ouda jihua shengyu ganbu" [The Wang brothers receive a penalty—unjustifiable beating of birth planning cadres], *Hubei ribao* (November 12, 1982), 2.
111. Li Yu, "Barbarous Birth Control Practices Provoking Popular Resentment," *Cheng Ming* 102 (April 1986), 73, in *JPRS*, 86055, June 16, 1986, 70–72.
112. This campaign was closely observed by Eric Mueggler, and is related in his detailed study of the village, *The Age of Wild Ghosts* (Berkeley, 2001), chapter 9. In this case, relations in the village grew so tense that township authorities eventually retreated from their campaign demands and disavowed the forceful methods they had initially urged the village party secretary to use.
113. Sichuan Provincial Service, January 15, 1983, in *JPRS* 82842, February 10, 1983, 178.
114. "Zhizhi silei pohuai jihua shengyu gongzuode xingwei," *Jiankang bao, jihua shengyu ban*, March 1, 1985.

ing those who "insult, beat up, or slander birth planning personnel and their families" (Shaanxi) or "humiliate, threaten, beat up, or retaliate against" birth planning cadres (Guizhou).[115]

Despite this more hostile and dangerous work environment, township and village cadres faced the same pressures to enforce state directives that they had during the collective era, giving them no choice but to press the peasantry for compliance. Their institutional arrangements were redesigned, their job descriptions were rewritten, and their working relationships with peasants and other cadres were made far more complex, but the expectations of their party superiors remained the same. As one cadre put it:

> [Cadres] must fulfill all tasks assigned by the state and take the peasants' feelings into consideration as well. . . . [We] have always been the scapegoats in the conflicts of interest between the two sides, and principal leading comrades at the township level have to withstand pressure from their superiors and face protests from the peasants, a very awkward situation. We never complain about the heavy work load or some minor unfair treatments that we have encountered. What we cannot tolerate is that our hard work has not been appreciated by others but brought us a nickname—"local overlords." We are disliked not only by some cadres at the higher level but also by some peasants whose vested interests have been infringed upon.[116]

Caught in this bind, there was no doubt in this cadre's mind about who had to first be accommodated when these conflicts arose:

> To complete these tasks [grain requisition, birth planning, and taxation] we usually have to force people to obey the order. In consequence, some excesses are inevitable, which may involve violations of laws and result in punishment for us. . . . Some cadres complain: it is possible that we, "in serving the party, will violate the law laid down by the party and be imprisoned by the party."[117]

The prospects for imprisonment were likely slim, but the prospects for legal action increased significantly in the 1990s, when new administrative laws were enacted that made it illegal to use coercion to implement state policies and spelled out very specifically the types of administrative actions that were prohibited.[118]

115. *Shaanxi ribao*, August 10, 1994, in *FBIS* 94–194, October 6, 1994, 52–53; *Guizhou ribao*, July 27, 1998, in *FBIS*, September 16, 1998.
116. Liu Shunguo, "The Worries of Town and Township Cadres," *Nongmin ribao*, September 20, 1988, in *FBIS*, October 5, 1988, 23.
117. Ibid.
118. One example was the law on state compensation of citizens whose rights had been violated, which went into effect on January 1, 1995. Unlawful administrative actions that entitle a citizen to compensation include: (1) unlawful detention; (2) using violence, beating someone up, or causing injury or death; and (3) illegally imposing fines, revoking licenses, or confiscating property. The full English-language text of this law may be found at the website for the

During the 1990s, peasant protests became larger, more frequent, and more frequently organized or supported by village cadres with grievances against township cadres or other officials.[119] In some cases, these protests grew into riots, most often provoked by anger over high taxes and what were seen as unreasonable and arbitrary local levies and fees. As levels of extraction escalated—much of it initiated at the provincial and county levels, but some resulting from creative grassroots fund-raising schemes— peasants complained bitterly and sometimes refused to pay. Refusal brought acts of retaliation, however, such as the confiscation of property, the revocation of land-use contracts or commercial operating permits, or even the destruction of property and physical attack.[120]

As tensions began to rise, two state initiatives designed to enhance rural stability actually gave support to aggrieved peasants and encouraged further protests. The first was the drive to promote village self-rule (*cunmin zizhi*) and village elections. This initiative, which began in the mid-1980s, focused on developing institutions of democratic self-rule at the grassroots, including open, fair, and increasingly competitive elections for village leaders; local representative congresses to supervise village elections; village compacts that outlined all laws and regulations for the village; and mechanisms for holding cadres accountable for their use of public funds.[121] The second was the effort to draw up regulations limiting the types and amounts of taxes that could be imposed on peasants, and the means by which cadres could collect those fees.[122] As these initiatives began to gain a foothold, peasants used them, and the national and local regulations and laws drafted

United Nations Economic and Social Commission for Asia and the Pacific (UNESCAP), http://www.unescap.org/pop/database/law_china.

119. On emergent patterns of protest in the 1990s, see Kevin J. O'Brien and Lianjiang Li, "The Politics of Lodging Complaints in Rural China," *China Quarterly* 143 (September 1995): 756–83; Lianjiang Li and Kevin J. O'Brien, "Villagers and Popular Resistance in Contemporary China," *Modern China* 22, no. 1 (January 1996): 28–61; and Kevin J. O'Brien, "Rightful Resistance," *World Politics* 49 (October 1996): 31–55.

120. Such tactics were said to have contributed to the peasant riots in Sichuan's Renshou County in 1993. See Jung Sheng, "Great Impact of Agricultural Issues—Tracking Incidents of Peasant Riots in Sichuan's Renshou County, parts 1 and 2," *Hsin bao*, June 10, 1993, in *FBIS*, June 11, 1993, 10–15.

121. For English-language sources discussing this reform, see note 4. In Chinese, see Zhongguo jiceng zhengquan jianshe yanjiuhui, Zhongguo jigou yu pianzhi zazhishe, eds., *Shixian yu sikao: Quanguo nongcun jiceng zhengquan jianshe lilun yantaohui wenxuan* (Luoyang, 1989).

122. Lu, "Politics of Peasant Burdens." Official documents on reducing peasant burdens include CCP Central Committee and State Council, "Urgent Circular on Earnestly Alleviating Peasant Burdens," March 19, 1993; CCP Central Committee and State Council, "Decision on Earnestly Doing a Good Job in Reducing Peasant Burdens," *Xinhua*, March 31, 1997, in *FBIS*, March 31, 1997; CCP Central Committee and State Council, "Circular on Effectively Lightening Peasant Burdens," *Xinhua*, July 27, 1998, in *FBIS*, August 6, 1998. See also "Wen Jiabao: Lightening the Peasant Burden Is an Urgent Task in Current Rural Work," *Xinhua*, September 27, 2000, in *FBIS*, September 27, 2000.

to support them, to seek redress for their grievances, and especially for their economic grievances. As Kevin O'Brien has argued, they began to use state-sanctioned values and institutions to engage in "rightful resistance" against local tyranny.[123] They began to use the state's own laws and regulations to challenge local cadres and to do so with moral authority. Villagers expressed their moral outrage by confronting village or township cadres, by appealing to higher levels of government, and by filing class action or individual lawsuits.

Many of the episodes of collective protest and violence that were reported after 1990 were triggered by economic grievances, such as excess taxation, land expropriation, and embezzlement of public funds. Others were provoked by illegal interference in village elections, and still others by local methods for enforcing birth limits. In 1997, for example, villagers in Guangdong who were angry about the imposition of stiff fines for violations of local birth planning policies staged collective protests that reportedly turned violent.[124] Rather than protest the enforcement of birth limits, they focused on the unfair economic consequences of policy violations. Other protests were organized around administrative grievances, with lawyers using China's Administrative Litigation Law (1990) and the National Population and Family Planning Law (2002) to bring lawsuits against cadres accused of abusive and illegal behavior.[125]

In 2005, for example, local activist and lawyer Chen Guangcheng was solicited by families in Linyi City, Shandong Province, to investigate the use of coercive methods to implement local policies and meet local birth planning targets. According to reports, more than 7,000 abortions and sterilizations were performed in the spring of 2005 after provincial authorities complained about poor local performance (for more details on this campaign, see chapter 8). In this case, Chen's attempts to litigate were impeded by local authorities, and he had no better luck in Beijing. After contacting foreign reporters to try to get attention for the case, Chen was detained in Beijing by Shandong authorities, beaten, and placed under house arrest.[126] Al-

123. O'Brien, "Rightful Resistance."
124. Daniel Kwan, "Caojiang Official Denies Riot over Family Planning Policy," *South China Morning Post* (September 7, 1997).
125. On collective lawsuits under the provisions of the Administration Litigation Law (ALL), see Yuen Tang, "When Peasants Sue En Masse: Large-Scale Collective ALL Suits in Rural China," *China: An International Journal* 3, no. 1 (2005): 24–49. See also Pei Minxin, "Citizens and Mandarins: Administrative Litigation in China," *China Quarterly* 152 (December 1997): 832–862; Kevin O'Brien and Li Lianjiang, "Suing the Local State: Administrative Litigation in Rural China," *China Journal* 51 (January 2004): 76–96.
126. On the Linyi campaign and Chen Guangcheng's detention, see Philip P. Pan, "Who Controls the Family: Blind Activist Leads Peasants in Legal Challenge to Abuses of China's Population-Control Policy," *Washington Post,* August 27, 2005, p. A1; also by Pan, "Rural Activist Seized in Beijing: Legal Campaign has Targeted Forced Sterilization, Abortion," *Wash-

though the prospects for successful prosecution of this case appeared poor, collective legal action that challenges the use of coercion is an important new strategy for resisting the enforcement of birth planning policy.

Accommodation

Beyond the strategies of confrontation and violence, or evasion, collusion, and cover-up was a fifth pattern of response. Caught between state demands to limit childbearing to only one or two children and cultural and social pressures to have a son, some attempted to resolve the conflict by resorting to female infanticide, infant abandonment, or, as the technology became available, sex-selective abortion. One might argue that actions such as these, which are responses to state controls, are the ultimate evidence of state domination, an indicator of defeat and subordination rather than resistance. As James Scott argues, however, material domination—in this case, control over the number of children one has—is only one form of state domination. Transformative states also seek ideological and status domination, or control over the realm of legitimate ideas and the distribution of status and prestige within society.[127] Despite the CCP's massive and prolonged effort to justify its claim to control childbearing by emphasizing the public and social costs of childrearing and insisting that population growth is an impediment to modernization, it has been unable to overcome the influence of traditional patriarchal culture, which places family loyalty and filial obligation, not socialist ethics, at the center of the childbearing calculus. To be sure, many young couples now report that they desire only one or two children, but family composition is a different matter. In the new rural world of money, markets, corruption, and clans, the weak can be bullied and preyed on by the strong. Having a son can help a family avoid the miserable fate of being among the weak. Moreover, the duty to produce a son to continue the family line remains a powerful influence.[128]

Ironically, and tragically, the state's own policy has helped to further in-

ington Post, September 7, 2005, A22; Hannah Beech, "Enemies of the State?: How Local Officials In China Launched a Brutal Campaign of Forced Sterilizations and Abortions," *Time Magazine,* September 19, 2005.

127. James C. Scott, *Domination and the Arts of Resistance* (New Haven, 1990); Joel S. Migdal, "The State in Society: An Approach to Struggles for Domination," in *State Power and Social Forces,* ed. Joel S. Migdal, Atul Kohli, and Vivienne Shue (Cambridge, 1994), 7–34.

128. In interviews with rural women in Anhui in 1998, Jie Zhenming was told that they "will do anything to have a son," because failure to do so will mean bullying, humiliation, and being unable to "raise their heads." Jie Zhenming, "Why Do People Emphasize Male Children over Female?" *Renkou yu jingji* 109 (July 25, 1998): 56–61. This urgent need to have a son does not mean that daughters are not desired. Faced with a choice, however, most choose a son first. Kay Ann Johnson, *Wanting a Daughter, Needing a Son* (St. Paul, Minn., 2004).

scribe and reproduce this traditional worldview.[129] From the beginning, there was concern that the one-child policy might lead to an imbalance in the sex ratio at birth. In the September 1980 "Open Letter" on the one-child policy, for example, several of the most common objections to a one-child policy were aired, including fears that it would lead to female infanticide and abandonment, and consequently, to an imbalance in the sex ratio. These fears were officially dismissed in the early 1980s, but they proved well founded. As discussed in chapter 6, in the early 1980s senior officials became alarmed about reports of female infanticide and female abandonment by couples desperate to have a son. The infanticide reports produced a firestorm of controversy at home and abroad, leading the regime to respond in two contradictory ways. First, it denied that there was a widespread problem—census and survey data were used to show that China's sex ratio at birth was well within what was considered to be the normal range. Though conceding that incidents of infanticide and abandonment did occur, it insisted that such cases were rare and that they occurred only in the most backward regions of the countryside, where the "feudal mentality" remained entrenched. The solution proposed was an education campaign to uproot such backward ideas, but education alone was of little use given the social and economic realities that privileged male offspring.

By 1984, as reports of female infanticide multiplied and the Women's Federation began to insist that the problem be faced and addressed, the state changed tack. Rather than address the underlying causes of gender bias, it made concessions to rural sensibilities and adjusted the one-child policy to allow single-daughter households to try again—for a son. In the countryside, the state conceded, women were socially inferior and worth less economically. Sonless couples were disadvantaged, the potential prey of stronger families and kin groups, and they were shamed by their failure to continue the male ancestral line. Single-daughter households should therefore be given special consideration, just as the parents of invalids were given special consideration. They should be allowed to try again for a son.

Although the intent of the 1984 policy change was merely to legitimize what was already the de facto rural policy in many areas, its effect was to reinforce gender prejudice and split the state's ideological hegemony into two conflicting spheres—one sphere that applied to all urban residents, state cadres, and administrative personnel and another that applied to the

129. Susan Greenhalgh and Jiali Li, "Engendering Reproductive Policy and Practice in Peasant China: For a Feminist Demography of Reproduction," *Signs: Journal of Women in Culture and Society* 20 (Spring 1995): 601–41; Ann Anagnost, "A Surfeit of Bodies: Population and the Rationality of the State in Post-Mao China," in *Conceiving the New World Order*, ed. Faye D. Ginsberg and Rayna Rapp (Berkeley, 1995), 22–41.

peasantry. Rural women were thus left in the tragic situation of being caught in the cross hairs of two mutually exclusive modes of discourse—a traditional one that idealized sons, and a state-sanctioned population discourse that idealized the one-child family. Their dilemma was complicated by the internalization of rural norms that linked their worth and value to their ability to produce a son. The state and its birth planning representatives might heap praise on a woman for having a single daughter, but in the real world of the village she could be subject to a lifetime of pity, social ridicule, and blame, much of it heaped on her by other rural women who had themselves endured such pressures. With no means of escaping this dual subjugation, many chose, or were forced by family members to choose, a strategy of accommodation that guaranteed the birth of a son.

In the early 1980s, when collective life, limited cash income, and restrictions on travel severely constrained the options of rural families, some took the desperate course of female infanticide to preserve the chance to have a son.[130] As the 1980s progressed, however, two alternative strategies of accommodation became very common. The first was infant abandonment, which increased in the late 1980s and 1990s in response to a tightening of birth control policies.[131] Civil affairs officials, who have primary responsibility for the system of social welfare institutes that care for abandoned and orphaned children, offered no reliable estimates of the size of the problem by the 1990s, though some reports suggested that as many as 160,000 were abandoned annually, the vast majority of them female.[132] As Kay Johnson has argued, however, this figure likely underestimated the size of the problem, in that many abandoned girls never enter state institutions such as those managed by the civil affairs bureaucracy.[133] Instead, birth parents arranged informal adoptions by a relative, or sought out other families in the area who had no children or a son and who would likely accept and care for a daughter.[134]

Even more disturbing was the escalating incidence of sex-selective abortion and its impact on China's sex ratio. In 1979, China produced its first

130. For an analysis of female infanticide that situates it within the larger context of a hegemonic, patriarchal state structure and discourse, see Sharon K. Hom, "Female Infanticide in China: The Human Rights Specter and Thoughts toward (An)Other View," *Columbia Human Rights Law Review* 23, no. 2 (Summer 1992): 249–314.
131. Kay Johnson, Huang Banghan, and Wang Liyao, "Infant Abandonment and Adoption in China," *Population and Development Review* 24 (September 1998): 469–510.
132. Kay Johnson, "The Politics of the Revival of Infant Abandonment in China, with Special Reference to Hunan," *Population and Development Review* 22 (March 1996): 91.
133. Ibid.
134. On adoption patterns, see Johnson, *Wanting a Daughter*. On historical patterns, see James Z. Lee and Wang Feng, *One Quarter of Humanity* (Cambridge, 2000).

ultrasound machine, designed for a variety of diagnostic purposes, including pregnancy monitoring. By 1982, mass production of ultrasound equipment had begun, and imports added to the number. Thirteen thousand ultrasound machines were in use in hospitals and clinics by 1987, or roughly six machines for each county. By the early 1990s, all county hospitals and clinics, and most township clinics and birth planning stations, had ultrasound equipment capable of fetal sex determination.[135] Henan Province, for example, spent 4 million yuan during the 1991–95 plan period to equip its more than 2,300 township technical service centers with ultrasound scanners.[136] As private clinics proliferated in the 1990s, they too were equipped with ultrasound technology, providing easy access for a fee.

Despite repeated condemnations of sex-selective abortion and attempts to outlaw the use of ultrasound technology for fetal sex identification, easy access to the technology, combined with the lure of lucrative bribes and consultation fees, made ultrasound use very popular.[137] This was especially true in newly prosperous county towns and rural townships, where prosperity and proximity made ultrasound diagnosis possible, but where modest degrees of upward mobility had done nothing to undermine the cultural prejudice and practical logic that favored male offspring. Young couples raised as peasants but now employed in township factories and living in the township seat may have been more willing than their peers a decade earlier to have only one or two children. If the first were a girl, however, it remained vital to many that the second be a boy.[138] They may have been mod-

---

135. Zeng et al., "Causes and Implications," 291; Su Ping, "Wo guo chusheng yinger xingbie wenti tanlun," *Renkou yanjiu* 1 (1993); Mu Guangzong, "Jinnian lai zhongguo chusheng xingbie bi shanggao pian gao xianxiangde lilun jieshi," *Renkou yu jingji* 88, no. 1 (1995): 48–51.

136. Henan Provincial Family Planning Commission, "Strengthen Leadership, Put an End to the Backward State in Family Planning Work," *Nongmin ribao*, March 27, 1996, 2, in *FBIS*, March 27, 1996.

137. In May 1989, the MOH issued a document banning fetal sex identification except for serious medical purposes, and in May 1993 this was reiterated in Document No. 2 of the MOH, Women's Department. In 1998, the SFPC released another, more frank document on the problem of rising sex ratios and sex-selective abortion. At the provincial level, in 1996 the Fujian People's Congress passed the first law banning fetal sex identification; it included stiff punishments for women caught aborting female fetuses on the basis of ultrasound sex identification. Shandong followed suit in 1998. All of these documents may be found on the UNESCAP website, http://www.unescap.org/pop/database/law_china, with the exception of the Fujian law. On that case, see "Fujian Bans Illegal Sex Identification of Unborn Babies," *Xinhua*, June 6, 1996, in *FBIS*, 96–111, June 6, 1996. On the popularity of ultrasound and on-the-ground views of it, see Nicholas D. Kristof, "Peasants of China Discover New Way to Weed Out Girls" *New York Times* (July 21, 1993), A1, A6.

138. For confirmation of this line of thinking among childbearing-age women and rural officials, see the important study by Chu Junhong, "Prenatal Sex Determination and Sex-Selective Abortion in Rural Central China," *Population and Development Review* (2001): 259–82.

ern in their economic preference for a small family, but when it came to desiring a son, tradition and contemporary social realities held sway. Because township and village cadres tacitly agreed with them, the couple could count on them to look the other way when they paid a fee to the medical technician to tell them the sex of the fetus. The cadres, after all, would much prefer for couples to resort to induced abortion of females to guarantee having a son than to have a second daughter and be tempted to try another pregnancy, as many two-daughter households did. If the couple kept trying for a son, the local birth plan was threatened. If the couple used available technology to guarantee the birth of a son, they were happy and the cadres' problem was solved.[139]

The impact of sex-selective abortion on China's sex ratio became increasingly clear in the 1990s. In 1981 the Chinese sex ratio at birth, 108.5 males for every 100 females, was already slightly in excess of what demographers consider a normal range for human populations—105–6 males for every 100 females.[140] Though this figure raised questions about female infanticide and "missing girls," those questions were dismissed by Chinese spokesmen, who argued that the sex ratio was well within normal bounds and in keeping with China's own population history. Over the next ten years, however, the sex ratio at birth rose dramatically, to 111 in 1985, 114 in 1989, and 117 in 2000, according to Chinese survey and census data.[141] Some of this increase was evident in first births, but sex ratios in second and higher-order births reflected a very strong male bias. In 1990, for example, the sex ratios for second and third-or-higher order births were 121 and 127 per 1,000, respectively. By 2000, they had skyrocketed to 152 and 160.[142]

Some of this gap can be accounted for by the underreporting of female births. Underreporting is suggested both by surveys of rural areas that reveal "hidden" births not reported in official statistical reports and by the lessening of the sex-ratio imbalance for school-age children. In the 1992 sample survey, the sex ratio for the age 0–4 cohort was 114. For the age 5–9 cohort, however, the ratio dropped to 108. This decline is what would be

139. Ibid. Cadres in poorer communities continued to have an incentive to collect fines for unplanned births, as noted in chapter 5. As pressures to meet birth planning targets grew more intense in the 1990s, however, the incentive structure began to shift. Failing to meet targets now meant administrative sanctions and personal fines (or withholding of bonuses).

140. Zeng Yi et al., "Causes and Implications of the Recent Increase in the Reported Sex Ratio at Birth in China," *Population and Development Review* 19 (June 1993): 283–302.

141. Ibid. See also Gu Baochang and Krishna Roy, "Sex Ratio at Birth in China, with Reference to Other Areas of East Asia: What We Know," *Asia-Pacific Population Journal* 10, no. 3 (1995): 17–42.

142. "China Sees a High Gender Ratio of Newborns," August 1, 2002, at http://www.cpirc .org.cn/enews20020514.htm. This is the website for the China Population Information Research Center.

expected if previously unreported females were registered for school and then placed on local population rolls. Such children might never have appeared in vital statistics on births and deaths, sparing local officials the consequences of exceeding their local birth targets. Once older, however, they could be registered as migrants or adoptees, and the degree of male bias in the sex ratio declined accordingly.

Chinese demographers argued in the early 1990s that such underreporting accounted for anywhere from 43 to 75 percent of the skew in the sex ratio at birth.[143] More recent studies, based on the 2000 census, suggest that about a third of the bias is due to underreporting.[144] With sex ratios rising between 1990 and 2000, however, and estimates of underreporting declining over the same period, some other factor must have contributed to the problem. By the late 1990s, Chinese scholars acknowledged publicly the impact of sex-selective abortion. Jie Zhenming, writing in one of China's premier demography journals in 1998, concluded that the main reason for skewed sex ratios in some areas of China was sex-selective abortion, and that female infanticide by drowning remained "a commonplace action" in more backward areas.[145] Similarly, a 1997 report in the popular news journal *Renmin luntan* (People's Forum) stated flatly that sex-selective abortion had become "the number-one factor in the strangulation of female fetuses and the creation of the imbalance in the male-female ratio."[146] Confirming the breadth and gravity of the problem, the State Family Planning Commission issued a new document on the subject in 1998 that acknowledged that the sex ratio at birth "in most provinces" had "exceeded the normal scope."[147]

Until the late 1990s, reports acknowledging the prominent role of sex-selective abortion in producing China's skewed sex ratios treated it as a rural phenomenon, avoiding any discussion of the increasingly urban and national character of the problem. Jie Zhenming, for example, drew on conversations with rural women in various regions to illustrate the mentality that leads to sex-selective abortion. The question the author put to them, "Why must peasants always have sons?" set the boundaries of the inquiry and prompted the respondents to contrast their situation with that of city

143. Zeng Yi et al., "Causes and Implications."

144. Yong Cai and William Lavely, "China's Missing Girls: Numerical Estimates and Effects on Population Growth," *China Review* 3, no. 2 (Fall 2003): 13–29.

145. Jie Zhenming, "Why Do People Emphasize Male Children over Female?" 56–61.

146. Wang Qiangzhuang, "China's Population: Imbalance of Gender Proportion," *Renmin luntan* [People's Forum] 11 (November 8, 1997): 50–51.

147. The text may be found on the UNESCAP website, http://www.unescap.org/pop/data base/law_china.

folk. One woman prefaced her answer with "We are not the same as in the city," and another with "The country and big cities are not the same."[148] They went on to cite the usual rural concerns of losing daughters to marriage, old-age support, and continuing the family line. In this fashion, gender bias and sex-selective abortion were associated with rural backwardness and enlightened thinking with urban modernity and its influence on the countryside. Rural women from the prosperous and highly commercialized Sunan region of Jiangsu Province, for example, were juxtaposed with those above to illustrate the impact of urbanization and economic development on women's preferences for the sex of their child.

This relentless attempt to associate sex-selective abortion with the "feudal mentality" of the countryside collapsed in the late 1990s, as new data revealed the breadth and depth of the problem. Data from the 1990 census, and from a 1995 1 percent sample survey, revealed a nationwide trend toward rising sex ratios at birth. The 1995 sample survey showed Beijing, for example, to have an overall sex ratio at birth of 122.6, and 148.8 for second- and higher-parity births. This high sex ratio at birth placed Beijing on a par with such provinces as Jiangsu (125.1), Fujian (126.2), Jiangxi (129.1), Henan (128.0), Hubei (134.6), Guangdong (125.2), and Shaanxi (125.4). Tianjin also came in high, with an overall sex ratio at birth of 110.6 and a rate of 142.9 for second and higher parity births. And while Shanghai's overall rate was within a normal range, the rate for second- and higher-parity births was an exceptionally high 175.0.[149] All of these localities, even the major metropolitan areas, include both urban and rural regions, and it may well be that people with rural residencies and origins more frequently opt for sex-selective abortion. Nevertheless, the fact that sex ratios in the very advanced and prosperous regions of Beijing and Guangdong were on a par with those of the very rural and much poorer areas of Henan and Shaanxi suggests that "rural backwardness" explains far less than is usually assumed.

A 1997 study of Beijing's sex-ratio statistics confirmed the growing trend toward skewed sex ratios in the nonrural population. The study used data from the national 1 percent sample survey of 1995 to examine in great detail Beijing's sex-ratio status. The authors found that high sex ratios occurred at all educational levels and across all occupational categories. For example, among those in the sample with one child, the sex ratio ranged from a high of 134 for those with elementary school education to 119 for

148. Jie Zhenming, "Why Do People Emphasize Male Children over Female?"

149. Gao Lin, Liu Xiaolan, and Xia Ping, "Beijing shi renkou chusheng xingbiebi fenxi," *Renkou yanjiu* 21 (September 1997): 25–33.

those with postsecondary school education, suggesting that gender bias varied incrementally across educational levels but was serious at every level. Similarly, the study's authors found that sex ratios were skewed across nearly all occupational categories but were slightly higher among workers and the unemployed than among those employed in agriculture. And perhaps most important, they found that among those with household registrations in Beijing municipality, sex ratios were seriously skewed for those with urban and rural registrations. The 1995 sex ratio at birth for rural Beijingers (the population living in rural areas surrounding the city and within its municipal boundaries) was reported to be 126.1, and the ratio for urban residents was 118.1.[150]

In light of the trends reported elsewhere in Asia in the 1980s and 1990s, these figures should come as no surprise. South Korea, Taiwan, and India all registered increases in the male-to-female sex ratio as ultrasound technology became widely available.[151] This regional pattern suggests that China's skewed sex ratios are not merely the result of the one-child policy (though they are certainly exacerbated by it), and not something that can be explained away (as the CCP has sought to do) as a product of rural backwardness. Rather, it is a cultural and structural problem that has been reinforced and made worse by the ready availability of a cheap and reliable technology.[152]

150. Ibid., 29–30. The number of births in this sample was only 1,950, a relatively small sample size from which to draw broad conclusions about sex-ratio trends. Nevertheless, what is striking is that in not one category in any of the tables do girls outnumber boys. In a small but balanced sample, one might expect odd fluctuations to occur in *both* directions, with girls occasionally outnumbering boys.

151. On skewed sex ratios elsewhere in Asia, see Chai Bin Park and Nam-Hoon Cho, "Consequences of Son Preference in a Low-Fertility Society: Imbalance of the Sex Ratio at Birth in Korea," *Population and Development Review* 21, no. 1 (March 1995): 59–84; Monica Das Gupta and P. N. Mari Bhat, "Fertility Decline and Increased Manifestation of Sex Bias in India," *Population Studies* 51 (1997): 307–15; Nicholas Eberstadt, "Asia Tomorrow, Gray and Male," *National Interest* 53 (Fall 1998): 56–65; Gu and Roy, "Sex Ratio at Birth in China, with Reference to Other Areas of East Asia." See also the excellent comparative study by Elisabeth Croll, *Endangered Daughters* (London, 2000).

152. Nicholas Eberstadt, "Mis-Planned Parenthood: The Unintended Consequences of China's One-Child Policy," *AEI Articles* (1999), online at American Enterprise Institute website (http://www.aei.org). See also Gu and Roy, "Sex Ratio at Birth in China." It should be noted that China's sex ratio imbalance has also been attributed to the prevalence of hepatitis B in the population, which tends to disproportionately suppress the birth of females. Although this factor may play some small role, it cannot account for the very rapid rise in sex ratios over the past quarter century, nor for the great regional disparities in the gravity of the problem. On this issue, see Emily Oster, "Hepatitis B and the Case of the Missing Women," Harvard University Center for International Development, Working Paper 7 (2005); and Monica das Gupta, "Explaining Asia's 'Missing Women': A New Look at the Data," *Population and Development Review* 31, no. 3 (September 2005): 529–35.

Still, the Chinese case, which set state control over childbearing against deeply imbedded cultural prejudices and childbearing preferences, remains unique. China's relentless emphasis on sheer numbers of births—on targets, quotas, and per capita accounting—combined with its conscious neglect of women's issues and its gendered politics of reproduction opened up the space within which an accommodative style of resistance could grow. Though strategies of accommodation revealed the extent of state domination and power, they also revealed vividly the extent to which the right to engineer fertility remains contested political terrain. Just as new birth control technologies and surgical advances facilitated the state's move to engineer childbearing, so too did technology become the medium through which couples struggled to engineer the sex makeup of their offspring. They may have accommodated the state's birth limitation policy, but they sought to do it on their own terms. They may have rejected the state's claim of ideological hegemony and sovereignty over the production of offspring, but they adapted its principles of social engineering to reengineer the shape of their own households.

8

Campaign Revivalism and Its Limits

By the late 1980s, the consequences of policy relaxation and grassroots resistance were becoming increasingly apparent. China's birth planning performance had begun to deteriorate, and survey data were just beginning to clarify how serious the problem was. Not only were population planning targets not being met, they were being exceeded by a wide margin. Anxieties about the disruptive effects of the reforms, and especially about grain production, were high. The leadership disagreed about how to proceed, and plans were under way to conduct a new census. Each of these elements had been in place in 1982 when the decision was made to launch the infamous sterilization campaign. In the late 1980s, they converged again, creating the same momentum for a crackdown on rural implementation. In an echo of the past, however, the crackdown soon gave way in the mid-1990s to renewed debate over the merits of a campaign approach to implementation. As in the early 1980s, scholars and population experts began to openly question the single-minded pursuit of numerical population targets at any cost, and even to challenge the cornerstone of China's population policy, the doctrine of birth planning. This time, however, they were more bold and persistent in pressing for change.

Although change came very slowly and tentatively, by the late 1990s several factors conspired to produce the beginnings of a subtle shift in theory, language, and tactics. While one still heard the argument that population control was the key to development, more voices began to turn the formula around, arguing that development was the key to achieving low fertility levels. While the language of population targets and birth quotas was still in use, one began to hear more about women's reproductive health and local enforcement flexibility. And instead of relying on the punitive approach of harsh fines and penalties, new experiments in client-centered services were undertaken.

What made these innovations possible was the weakening of four key elements that had sustained the conviction that a one-child policy was necessary. First, the obsession with grain production levels and self-sufficiency began to subside as the economy continued to grow. As fifteen years of economic reform and development transformed the character of the economy, per capita grain production figures no longer triggered the fears they had caused in the past.[1] Second, compared with their predecessors, China's post-Deng leaders were less rigid and simplistic in their view of the population problem. Though still extremely cautious with respect to formal policy change, they were more open to the increasingly sophisticated and nuanced analysis being provided by a new, highly trained cohort of demographers and policy specialists. Third, this new openness was reinforced by a shift in China's foreign policy. In the decade after 1992, China abandoned some of the defensive armor it had relied on in the 1980s, more actively participated in international organizations and institutions, and played host or sent delegations to a growing number of international conferences. Fourth, these developments coincided with a period of heightened UN focus on the interrelated problems of environmental protection, population growth, and the rights and status of women, problems that were addressed at major international conferences in Rio de Janeiro (1992), Cairo (1994), and Beijing (1995). These conferences provided a language and logic that could be used by policy reform advocates to press for change.

A New Cycle Begins

Classic studies of China's mobilization campaigns emphasize the cyclic nature of the process, and that cycle had unfolded once again in the second half of the 1980s. The mobilization for rapid and overambitious change (the promotion of a one-child policy) put pressure on party cadres at all levels to achieve and exceed the goals that had been set for the local campaign (1980–82). This pressure led to even more radicalism, as cadres (like it or not) were required to meet the inflated targets their superiors sent down to them. When they fell short of those goals (1982), their leaders responded by

---

1. The definitive statement of the regime's new view of grain production can be found in a white paper titled "The Grain Issue in China," released by the Information Office of the State Council in October 1996. Online at http://www.china.org.cn/e-white/.

pushing even harder, and the campaign reached its zenith (the sterilization campaign of 1983–84). This overreach eventually produced a backlash, as frustrated local cadres and aggrieved peasants began to complain about the campaign goals and coercive methods. Campaign overreach in birth planning coincided with leadership struggles over party rectification and the "spiritual pollution" campaign, creating the opportunity for critics of the program to press for change. The result was a gradual demobilization from the excesses of 1983, the relaxation of the one-child birth limit, and a decentralization of policy management to provincial and local governments (1984–86). As the new policy became routine and the radical phase of the campaign receded, however, policy implementers became complacent, or merely turned their attention to other matters and neglected to enforce a policy they had no enthusiasm for. Poor performance then triggered a new round of policy debate, as opponents of policy relaxation struggled once again to get the upper hand (1988–89). As their influence grew, a new mobilization got under way (1990–92), and the cycle repeated itself.

Campaigns had continued to occur in the second half of the 1980s, but they had come more and more to resemble economic production campaigns. As discussed in chapter 4, these campaigns were an institutionalized part of the planned economy and were characterized by temporary, often localized, result-oriented mobilizations that occurred at predictable intervals and for limited periods of time. By the late 1980s, the market-oriented reforms had scaled back the number and specificity of planning targets, but the activity of the political apparatus was still structured around the annual and five-year planning cycle and, in the countryside, by the rhythm of the agricultural production cycle. Party and government cadres operated on quarterly or monthly meeting schedules at which they gauged current performance levels against targets set at higher levels. That work agenda, in turn, shaped the pattern of implementation and enforcement. When performance was lax, instructions emanated from senior leaders demanding an improvement before the year's end. This would provoke a series of mobilizational meetings and propaganda activities and a mobilization drive devoted to the key problem of the moment. This process was sometimes initiated at the national level, but it could also originate at every level of local administration. Indeed, at any moment, several campaigns of varying degrees of significance could be under way within any single province, county, or township.

In the arena of birth planning, cadres were persistently urged during the 1980s to put birth planning on their regular work agenda three or four times a year, so as to monitor performance in an ongoing and routinized way and to avoid "shock attacks." Rather than reduce mobilizational impulses, however, this step merely regularized them. Local governments fell into a pattern of organizing "shock drives" several times a year. The most common pattern was to mobilize in the late winter or early spring, again in the late summer, and again in the fall, after the autumn harvest. On some occasions, these mobilizations were organized at the provincial or prefectural level, and in other cases they originated at the county or local level. In 1987, for example, Sichuan provincial authorities launched a summer "propaganda, inspection and implementation drive."[2] In Hainan, regional officials organized a springtime "shock drive." Cadres were instructed to

> summon up the greatest resolve to organize the birth planning shock drive, and achieve unified leadership, arrangements, and action. . . . It is necessary to focus on remedial measures regarding pregnancies not covered by the plan, and also do a good job in carrying out ligation surgery after the birth of a second child and inserting an intrauterine device after the birth of a first.[3]

Two weeks later, regional officials reported that between April 27 and May 9, more than 8,700 procedures, including 4,244 tubal ligations, had been performed. After criticizing areas that were still lagging behind, they called for a "new high tide" and instructed that "prior to the end of June, all cities and counties must accomplish over 50 percent of the special annual birth planning tasks set by the administrative regional authorities."[4] When Hainan officials met in February 1988 to review the previous year's work and plan for the future, their report captured precisely the effort to fuse regular work with campaign tactics:

> We must establish and put on a sound basis birth planning laws, rules and regulations, and beef up the birth planning organs and personnel. Shock birth planning drives must be regularly organized and combined in an organic way, with the emphasis on practical results.[5]

In short, shock drives did not stand in opposition to routine planning and enforcement; they were understood to be an organic part of it.

Interviews with township and village cadres confirm that this pattern was present in relatively prosperous areas and in poorer villages. In Donghu township, for example, township and village cadres reported in 1990 that birth planning "high tides" occurred regularly each year in March or April and in September or October. Village cadres placed special emphasis on the

2. Sichuan Provincial Service, July 11, 1987, in *FBIS*, July 12, 1987, Q1.
3. Hainan Provincial Service, May 1, 1987, in *FBIS*, May 4, 1987, P1.
4. Ibid.; Hainan Provincial Service, May 18, 1987, in *FBIS*, May 20, 1987, P2.
5. Hainan Island Service, February 17, 1988, in *FBIS*, February 18, 1988, 21.

autumn campaign, which focused on the fulfillment of specific sterilization quotas passed down from the district and township levels.[6] A similar pattern occurred in a more remote, predominantly agricultural township in Shandong, where campaigns occurred three times a year on a regular basis—after the fall harvest, during the Spring Festival, and again after the summer harvest. Campaigns normally originated at the prefectural level and began with the issuance of a document outlining the timing of the campaign and its specific objectives. Each campaign involved about two weeks of preparation, followed by six weeks of implementation. At the county level, township party secretaries, mayors, and birth planning cadres convened for three days to study the prefectural document and discuss the implementation process. After this meeting, township cadres called a half-day organizational meeting at the township, attended by all cadres and personnel who worked in the township government, regardless of their specific work post. Village leaders were then summoned to the township, and aggregate township targets were assigned to each village on a per capita basis. Village leaders were then given two days to determine which individuals in the village were to be targeted in the campaign in order to meet the quota. Once this preparatory work was complete, a township work team was sent into the village to mobilize individual women and transport them to the county hospital.[7]

If village cadres completed all targets before the date set for the end of the campaign, they received a bonus of 200–300 yuan. Similarly, if the township party secretary and the township mayor fulfilled the township quotas before the deadline, those two individuals split a cash bonus of 500 yuan.[8] In addition to targets for abortions, sterilizations, and IUD insertions, cadres in this township were given targets for fine collections from policy violators. The campaigns were timed for periods when the peasants were flush with cash, making it easier to collect the fines. Like other targets, county quotas for fine collection were distributed to all townships on a per capita basis, not on the basis of actual conditions. The township government, in turn, divided the quota among the villages in the same way. Those with a larger population base were responsible for larger quotas. In this township, the fine collection targets fell between 15,000 and 25,000 yuan.[9] Similarly, in 1988 Hainan officials instructed local cadres to

> regard the task of collecting fees imposed on those who have exceeded the limit to the number of births as an important task, and ensure the implemen-

6. Interview Files 901126, 901127, 901129, 901130, 901203, 901204.
7. Interview File 902207.
8. Interview File 900722.
9. Ibid.

tation of measures for sterilization through the promotion of the task of collecting fees imposed on those who have exceeded the limit to the number of births.[10]

If campaigns were occasionally timed to maximize fine collections, they were more often correlated with the rhythm of the economic planning cycle. Mobilizational pressures predictably increased near the end of the five-year-plan, when cadres began to worry about their performance in meeting five-year production targets. One example of this pattern was the campaign waged in a suburban village outside Xiamen municipality, Fujian Province, and described by Huang Shu-min in *The Spiral Road*.[11] In May 1985, the village leaders suddenly announced a strict new policy against having a second child, ordered all women of childbearing age to report for examinations to detect pregnancies, and threatened severe economic sanctions for those who failed to comply.

What happened in this village was part of a larger mobilization that began at the provincial level. Because 1985 was the final year of the sixth five year plan, extra pressure was placed on all provinces to meet the plan's targets, particularly those such as Fujian with relatively poor performance records.[12] This pressure led to the convening of a special forum on birth planning at the Third Session of the Sixth Fujian People's Congress, held in late April and early May. According to a radio report on the meeting, the delegates were told that they "must do a good job on work in May and June, a key period on which the success of the population control tasks in the whole year depends."[13] In other words, if all unauthorized pregnancies, as of May and June, could be terminated, the annual target could be met. Unauthorized pregnancies that began later in the year were next year's planning problem, not this year's, since the children would not be born until 1986. Once this provincial directive was translated into specific quotas for each county and township, it resulted in the village-level mobilization described by Huang.

A more dramatic example of this pattern came at the end of the seventh five-year plan (1986–90) and the beginning of the eighth (1991–95). Moving into 1989 and 1990, it became increasingly clear that the goals of the seventh FYP would not be met. As the extent of the performance shortfall

10. Ibid.
11. Huang Shu-min, *The Spiral Road* (Boulder, Colo., 1989), 175–85.
12. In 1984, only Xinjiang, Tibet, Guangxi, and Ningxia had higher rates of population growth than Fujian. The rate in 1984 was 13.28 per 1,000, whereas most provinces were under 11 per 1,000. Combined with a very poor record for 1981 and 1982 (15.18 and 17.55 per 1,000, respectively), Fujian was in serious jeopardy of exceeding its five-year-plan population target. *Zhongguo renkou tongji nianjian, 1985*, 618–19.
13. Fujian Provincial Service, May 3, 1985, in *FBIS*, May 9, 1985, O1.

grew clearer, momentum began to build for a return to a stricter policy and tougher enforcement measures. The result was a renewal of the national campaign and a recentralization of control of birth planning policy.

Rollback: The Critique of Policy Relaxation

The decision to relax rural childbearing limits after 1984 had been very controversial from the beginning, and the discovery of the extent to which births were being underreported galvanized the critics. The survey data from 1988 and 1989 raised doubts about China's ability to meet the targets set forth in the seventh FYP, as well as the long-range target of about 1.25 billion by the year 2000. As a result, in late 1988 the target was revised upward to 1.27 billion, but by early 1990 even this figure appeared optimistic. China's population at the end of 1989 exceeded the revised seventh FYP target figure for 1990 a year early, adding fuel to the increasingly public argument for tighter childbearing limits and more aggressive implementation (see table 10).[14]

Though some experts were resolute in arguing for a further relaxation in rural policy to allow two children per couple and reduce the incentives for fraudulent reporting, they were defeated by others who worried that this would create the misleading impression that the state was no longer serious about birth limits.[15] Joining those who had long held this hard-line view on rural implementation was a new group of pro-reform experts whose liberal views on political and economic reform were coupled with an intense authoritarianism when it came to rural procreation. The revelation in 1988 that the 1987 birthrates were much higher than originally reported, that third or additional births continued to account for as much as 17 percent of the annual total, and that urban couples were also pushing for additional births, confirmed the worst fears of these critics and led to an escalating debate between the state family planning establishment, now on the defensive, and opposition professionals, social scientists, and party officials. The latter group argued that relaxation (*fangsong*) of the one-child policy had been a

---

14. Shih Chun-yu, "NPC Deputies Say the Population Problem Is Serious," *Ta kung bao,* April 3, 1990, 2, in *FBIS,* April 9, 1990, 34.

15. Peng Peiyun, "Zai quanguo jihua shengyu weiyuanhui," 113. Wang Wei, "Zai 'qiwu' qijian," 69. Although the call for a two-child policy was rejected, its popularity among Chinese scholars was fueled by a 1985 article by John Bongaarts and Susan Greenhalgh, "An Alternative to the One-Child Policy in China," *Population and Development Review* 11, no. 4 (December 1985): 585–617. For a discussion of its influence and the diverse views held within the community of Chinese scholars, see Susan Greenhalgh, "Population Studies in China: Privileged Past, Anxious Future," *Australian Journal of Chinese Affairs* 24 (July 1990): 357–84.

TABLE 10. Seventh FYP (1986–1990) targets and actual results
(per thousand)

Year	Birthrate		
	Original targets	Revised targets[a]	Official results[b]
1986	18.8	18.4	20.77
1987	18.9	19.6	21.04
1988	19.2	19.6	20.78
1989	19.5	20.6	20.83
1990	19.8	20.7	21.06

Year	Natural rate of population growth (per thousand)		
1986	12.2	11.8	14.08 (15.57)
1987	12.2	12.8	14.39 (16.61)
1988	12.4	12.9	14.20 (15.73)
1989	12.6	13.6	14.33 (15.04)
1990	12.8	13.7	14.39

Source: Wan Qiang, "Guanyu 'qiwu' renkou jihua zhixing qingkuangde fenxi" [An analysis of the situation concerning the implementation of the Seventh Five-Year Plan population plan], *Zhongguo jihua shengyu nianjian, 1991,* 257–58; *Zhongguo renkou tongji nianjian, 1990,* 611.

[a]The revised target category refers to official revisions of the plan targets made each year on the basis of estimates of the actual performance in the preceding year.

[b]The first set of official figures were those published prior to the 1990 census. After the census was taken, the official rates for 1986–89 were revised again, showing an even greater disparity between plan targets and actual results. Those figures are given in parentheses.

mistake, and held policymakers and "personnel changes" responsible. By implication, they were calling for a reversal of the political verdict on the sterilization campaign in 1983, which had led to the downfall of SFPC chairman Qian Xinzhong, the self-criticism found in CD 7, and the policy relaxation that followed (see chapter 6). They were also joining other conservatives in holding General Secretary Zhao Ziyang responsible for this and other consequences of reform.[16]

The debate intensified in 1989, with *Jingji ribao* picking up the call for a stricter birth control policy. Two articles, on January 10 and January 24, stressed the impending population crisis. The first asked, "How many centuries must it take before people can be awakened?" The second, arguing that a "human wave is washing over China," pointed to the 1980 Marriage Law, the stimulating effect of the agricultural responsibility system on rural childbearing preferences, and the relaxation of policy after 1984 as three

16. Sharping, *Birth Control in China,* 63–73.

key "policy faults."[17] Dismissing "gloomy and feeble propaganda and education" as useless in an environment where "people no longer fear punishment," the author blasted the birth planning bureaucracy and "policymakers" for their timidity. He concluded with a call for renewed mobilization:

> As happy peace must be built on the foundation of powerful military strength, so are the people's voluntary and self-conscious actions to be formed on the basis of the legal and compulsory standard. We should justly and forcefully say that we must punish those who have turned a deaf ear to dissuasion from having additional children and that suitable coercion and control should be implemented in China's family planning. . . .
>
> Only if the country adopts effective and compulsory policies and at the same time, carries out propaganda and education, can the consciousness of the society be aroused. If we do not understand this problem and change the current situation soon, when we wake up in a number of years, we shall find that it will be too late.[18]

These open criticisms prompted a rebuttal from Peng Peiyun, Wang Wei's successor as head of the SFPC. In 1988, she and other senior officials insisted that the policy relaxation after 1984 had not been a mistake. Instead, they argued that rising birthrates were a function of an increase in the childbearing-age cohort and poor implementation of policy in some areas.[19] In taking this position, they were backed by the authority of the Standing Committee of the Politburo, which had met the previous March to discuss birth planning. The Standing Committee members reaffirmed the existing policy on birth limits, arguing that the policy of allowing single-daughter households to have a second child facilitated rural implementation, prevented female infanticide, generated a positive international reaction, and contributed to the realization of population control targets by reducing the number of third births.[20]

This reaffirmation of existing national policy implied a rollback of local policies that had allowed two children for all rural couples, and thus a tightening of enforcement, but it did not go far enough to appease the critics. Behind their anxiety was the same fundamental debate on the relationship between population growth and economic growth that had emerged in the

17. Xie Zhenjiang, "There Is No Route of Retreat," *Jingji ribao,* January 24, 1989, 3, in *FBIS,* February 15, 1989, 35–37; Liu Jingzhi, "Experts Are Not Optimistic about China's Population Situation, and Think That Interference by Officials Is an Important Reason Why Birth Rate Has Risen Again," *Guangming ribao,* March 6, 1988, 2, in *FBIS,* March 6, 1988, 14–15.
    18. Xie, "No Route of Retreat," 37.
    19. *China Daily,* April 19, 1988, 1; see also Peng, "Zai quanguo jihua shengyu weiyuanhui," 108–20.
    20. Peng, "Zai quanguo jihua," 112.

early 1980s. Since 1984, the dominant line in population policy had been to concede that population growth trends were at least partially dependent on economic growth. It was this perspective that justified a relaxation of rural birth limits; peasants in relatively poor and backward circumstances could not be expected to accept having only one child, while those in more prosperous communities could. This view had remained controversial, however, and the fresh evidence of "uncontrolled" population growth gave new impetus for a repeal of the rural two-child policy. Advocates of repeal argued that reform and economic growth alone could not be expected to resolve China's population dilemma and that population growth would directly retard the development process.[21] For these critics, declining fertility was seen as a cause, not an effect, of economic development.

The fuel for this debate came not only from population data but also from China's economic performance, particularly in grain production. Grain production had climbed steadily from 1981 to 1984, resulting in a 21 percent increase in per capita grain levels. After the record harvest of 1984, however, total grain production stagnated. Although the 1987 harvest saw some recovery, 1988 production levels declined, as did per capita production levels. Based on the official population growth statistics available at that time, per capita grain production in 1988 was less than it had been in 1983, but the population survey data from 1988 and 1989 and, subsequently the national census data from 1990 made it clear that the official figures underestimated population size by a significant margin. When per capita production figures were corrected for this undercount, the picture looked even more bleak. Even the record harvest for 1990 could not bring per capita grain production up to 1984 levels (see table 3).[22]

The Conditions for Mobilization

As the evidence about poor performance mounted in 1988 and 1989, pressures for a renewed crackdown grew more intense. There appeared to be little chance that a new campaign could do more than provide a temporary remedy, however. A campaign could succeed in reducing births during a particular year, but the underlying structural problems created by the reforms—decentralization of policy control, inadequate personnel and fund-

---

21. Zhang Kunlun, "Population Burden a Restraining Factor of Economic Structural Reform," *Zhongguo renkou bao*, February 16, 1990; Hu Angang, "Why China Lost Control of Its Population Growth in Recent Years," *Liaowang*, March 6, 1989, 22–23.

22. *Zhongguo renkou tongji nianjian*, 1990, 611; Zhonghua renmin gongheguo nongyebu jihuasi, ed., *Zhongguo nongcun jingji tongji dachuan, 1949–1986*, 148–49; *Zhongguo nongcun tongji nianjian*, 1990, 93.

ing, low incentives for aggressive enforcement combined with high personal risks, the temptations to engage in corruption and privilege short-term profit-making over long-term population control—would still be present when the campaign ended. The only way to remedy those problems was to muster the political will in Beijing to revitalize party discipline and to make cadres think twice before ignoring, neglecting, or circumventing birth planning work.

In late 1988 and the spring of 1989 nothing seemed less likely. Political discipline was poor, corruption was rife, and rural unrest was on the rise. Inflation was up, as was crime, and in the countryside clan battles and local insurrections were not unheard of. The traditional instruments of discipline—the party apparatus backed up by public security forces—were themselves increasingly weak and corrupt. With the eruption of large student-led protests in Beijing and their spread to many provincial cities, the CCP found itself weak, publicly divided, and under siege. Humiliated by the strength and temerity of the protesters and the impotence of the party, martial law was declared throughout the nation on May 20, and the PLA was mobilized to enforce it. On June 3 and 4, the army occupied Beijing by force and opened fire on protesters and bystanders, resulting in thousands of casualties. The protests were declared to have been a counterrevolutionary rebellion, and the atmosphere that descended on the country for a time in the wake of the crackdown evoked strong memories of the prereform era. Although the heated political rhetoric and the threat of a new wave of leftism gradually diminished in the early 1990s, the period between June 1989 and the end of 1990 saw an intense effort to restore party order and discipline, and to use the climate of fear and repression to reassert the primacy of the party. Fearful that the urban protests would spread catastrophically to restless and disaffected peasants (some of whom had participated in local strikes and protests in preceding years), party leaders launched a campaign to improve party-mass relations in the countryside, shore up party and mass organs, and discipline and punish those who had engaged in corrupt or abusive practices.[23]

This return to "politics in command" was a congenial climate for reasserting control over childbearing, and a series of steps were taken to strengthen the enforcement of birth limits. First, strong central control over local policy was reinstated, forcing provinces with poor performances to tighten birth limits and improve their enforcement. Though the policy al-

23. See the "Central Committee Decision on Strengthening Party-Mass Relations," March 1990. See also Frederick Crook, "Sources of Rural Instability," *China Business Review* (July–August 1990): 12–15.

lowing single-daughter households to have a second child was retained, restrictions on having a second child were strengthened overall, as provinces that had been enforcing a de facto two-child policy were forced to tighten birth limits once again. One example was Henan, where a campaign was launched in the second half of 1990 to tighten enforcement and identify and punish party members who had violated the birth limit.[24] Where a second child was permitted, the required four to five year interval between births was to be strictly enforced, and women refusing to use IUDs or undergo sterilization (the former after a first birth and the latter after a second birth) were subject to stiff monthly fines.[25] At the same time, new policies placing stricter birth limits on minority nationalities were promulgated by various regions, and new eugenics laws requiring sterilization of those with hereditary illnesses also were drafted.[26]

Second, mass propaganda was used to signal the renewed sense of urgency in birth planning. In the fall of 1989 a major propaganda campaign was launched in the countryside. As with all such campaigns, this one had two purposes—to increase education and awareness and signal the primacy of the program, and to mobilize women targeted for abortions or sterilizations. This was followed in July 1990 by a series of meetings and publicity surrounding the tenth anniversary of the "Open Letter" to party members that had formally launched the nationwide one-child campaign. In November 1990, a meeting of grassroots cadres was held to exchange work experiences and encourage continued efforts. And in 1991, meetings were held to finalize and publicize the targets for the eighth FYP and the long-term plan period of 1991–2000.[27] Although much of this activity was formal and symbolic in nature, it provided public opportunities to reward those individuals and localities that had done a good job and embarrass those that had not.

Third, concrete measures were taken to shore up the implementation system at its weakest point, the village. To ensure more sustained levels of compliance by rural cadres, the context and incentive structure had to be changed. The context for enforcement was altered by the revival of mass or-

---

24. *Zhongguo jihua shengyu nianjian, 1991*, 382–83. See also Kohn Kohut, "Henan Tightens Family Planning Laws," *South China Morning Post* (December 11, 1990), 11.

25. Kohut reports that these fines were 50 yuan per month for IUDs, and 100 yuan per month for sterilization. The high fine for failing to undergo sterilization is particularly suggestive of the new pressures being brought to bear. Ibid.

26. On eugenics regulations and policies in the 1990s, as well as in earlier periods, see Frank Dikotter, *Imperfect Conceptions* (New York, 1998). Chapter 4 covers trends in the 1980s and 1990s.

27. These activities and meetings are chronicled in Yang et al., *Zhongguo renkou yu jihua shengyu*, 216–39.

gans made up of party members, activists, and retired cadres, and the expansion of the rural cadre force. In the aftermath of June 3–4, 1989, the regime moved quickly to ensure that the urban protests would not spill over into widespread rural instability. Unlike the cities, however, in the countryside the restoration of order and stability was welcomed insofar as it meant disciplining corrupt cadres bilking collective enterprises, reducing criminal activity, making local governments pay cash—not IOUs—for peasant crops, and reducing "peasant burdens" (see chapter 7). With that in mind, the regime set about improving rural "party-mass relations" by increasing its organized presence in the village.

The revival of rural mass organs influenced birth planning work in several ways. First, village small groups (formerly production teams) that had been the lowest level of administrative power during the commune era were restored in some areas. The small groups had generally continued to exist on paper after 1984, but as their source of economic power eroded, they had ceased to play any effective administrative role. Many consisted of only a group leader who performed no ongoing collective service and drew no salary. By reviving teams and staffing them with two or three leaders who received small stipends for their work, the party could better penetrate the village organizationally and better monitor and enforce birth limits.

The emphasis on mass organs also led to a strengthening of birth planning associations and local people's militias. In 1989 and 1990, birth planning associations became more widespread, and the membership expanded rapidly. The associations, which numbered one million by 1995, became large mass organs that drew in all leading personnel, activists, party members, women's leaders, and retired cadres, effectively saturating townships and villages with a second, less formal network of policy enforcers who could be engaged in ongoing surveillance and be mobilized in force if needed. By 2002, almost 99 percent of China's villages had active associations.[28] In turn, family planning associations were supplemented by the ranks of the local people's militias, which also gained new life at this time. The people's militias were made up of select villagers led by young party members or candidate members (and usually PLA veterans) and were charged with helping to maintain local public defense and security. Militia members were especially effective in helping to mobilize the tough birth planning cases that resisted other efforts at persuasion.[29]

28. "More Than One Million Birth Control Groups Set Up," *Xinhua*, June 4, in *FBIS*, June 5, 1995, 30; "Jihua shengyu xiehuide zuzhi jianshe gongzuo" [Organizational Work of the Chinese Family Planning Association], Zhongguo jihua shengyu nianjian, 2003 (Beijing, 2003), 598–99.
29. Ibid.

Birth planning was also integrated into the village self-rule initiative. As villages drew up compacts outlining their local rules and regulations, detailing the rights and duties of leaders and villages, they included a section on birth planning that specified local rules for enforcement. In Laixi city, Shandong, for example, village regulations required new mothers to report to the township birth control station within five days of birth to adopt some form of contraceptive, and promised fines of 10 yuan per day for those who thereafter failed to report for periodic pregnancy checks. Those with unauthorized pregnancies were required to undergo early or late-term abortion (*bixu yin, liuchan*). Those who qualified to have a second child were required to first post a 1,000 yuan sterilization guaranty deposit (*jiezha xinzhi baozheng jin*) and to report for sterilization within one month after the newborn had reached one hundred days of age. Extra-plan first births resulted in a 500 yuan fine and, regardless of whether it was a girl or a boy, extra-plan second births resulted in a 5,000 yuan fine. For each additional extra-plan birth, an additional 3,000 yuan fine was imposed. The regulations went on to outline fines for early marriage (500 yuan) and for fleeing birth control cadres (20 yuan per day up to a ceiling of 10,000 yuan). Those who lied to birth control cadres in order to protect others were liable for fines of 500 yuan.[30]

In addition to strengthening grassroots work, party leadership over birth planning was also restored by re-creating the leading small group (*lingdao xiaozu*) system that had been in operation at every administrative level in the 1970s and early 1980s. The purpose of the leading groups was to oblige senior party leaders at all levels to take personal responsibility for birth planning work in their region and to make them accountable for the results.

The SFPC also lobbied successfully to expand the ranks of full-time birth planning cadres, especially at the grassroots, and to improve their training. Going into the 1990s, many provinces and localities reported increases in the number of full-time personnel that were official employees of the state. In Fujian, for example, 857 state cadres were added to prefectural and county offices in 1990. In Jiangsu, 310 were added, and Heilongjiang added 1,440. These staff increases were the result of a central-level decision in October 1990 to assign 8,000 additional personnel to the birth planning bureaucracy at the county and township levels nationwide.[31] The status was crucial, since it meant that the township collective was not responsible for the salary and benefits of these cadres. In addition, because they were often

30. The regulations of three villages under Laixi city contained exactly the same provisions. I obtained these documents during a research visit in the summer of 1992.

31. *Zhongguo jihua shengyu nianjian, 1991*, 140. The provincial figures can be found in the yearbook on pages 366, 352, and 340, respectively.

hired at the county level and dispatched to the townships, state cadres were less likely to have been born and raised in the township where they worked. Cadres paid by the collective, on the other hand, were usually local residents and vulnerable to all the temptations that arose from having close local connections. Efforts were also made to improve the salaries and benefits of birth planning workers. In Liaoning, for example, 2,000 birth planning cadres were given urban residency status in 1994, a change of status coveted in the countryside. Finally, many of these new cadres were male, reinforcing a progressive drift after the mid-1980s toward an increasingly male cadre force.[32]

Finally, efforts were also made to expand the network of comprehensive birth planning service stations that improved rural service delivery and decreased dependency on the facilities under the jurisdiction of the public health ministry. By 1995, birth planning service centers had been established in 80 percent of China's counties and 60 percent of all townships.[33] This increased the capacity of township governments to carry out abortions, IUD insertions or removals, and sterilizations locally.

Although these efforts at strengthening leadership and organization were important, the SFPC used the opportunity it had in 1990 to press hard for two other improvements. Each had been a priority in the 1980s, but efforts to achieve them had been undercut by competing reform priorities. First, the SFPC had been struggling for years to find an effective means of holding cadres fully accountable for their birth planning work. As discussed above, however, such efforts had been thwarted by the tendency to forgive cadres their shortcomings in birth planning if their economic performance was impressive, and by the opposite tendency—statistical fraud used to cover up excess births. The only way to surmount these problems was to create a climate in which party leaders, from top to bottom, were held accountable by making the fulfillment of birth planning targets a necessary condition for any and all bonuses, rewards, or recognitions. In other words, overall evaluations of cadre work had to be made contingent on birth planning performance. In the 1990s such a system was put into place. Called the "one ballot veto power" system (*yipiao foujuequan*), it made all cadre performance evaluations contingent on successfully fulfilling the annual birth planning targets. Regardless of one's economic accomplishments, no bonuses, promotions, or special citations were to be issued unless the local birth plan

32. On Liaoning, see *Liaoning ribao*, December 14, 1994, 3, in *FBIS*, December 27, 1994, 92. On the shifting gender composition of the cadre force, see Rachel Murphy, "Fertility and Distorted Sex Ratios in a Rural Chinese County: Culture, State, Policy," *Population and Development Review* 29, no. 4 (December 2003): 595–626.

33. *Xinhua*, June 4, 1995, in *FBIS*, June 5, 1995, 30.

had also been met. Accountability was to extend to senior party and government leaders at all levels, whose performance could be monitored through the mechanisms of the leading small group on birth planning for that locality.[34]

Second, the SFPC was successful in getting central-level support for an increase in funding. The bureaucracy had been plagued by a shortage of funds in the 1980s, but their pleas had been largely ignored by a regime that was making every effort to reduce budgetary expenditures and encourage bureaucracies to find ways of raising funds. Left to local governments to make up the difference, the problem got worse. The need for more funds was at odds with the desire of township and village governments to invest its scarce funds in profit-making enterprises. The result was that funding stood at only 1 yuan per capita in 1990. The SFPC called for that amount to double by 1995, and it successfully had this made explicit in a new 1991 central directive, "Stepping Up Birth Planning Work."[35]

As important as the new initiatives were for the enforcement of birth limits, it took the extraordinary political climate created by the June 3–4 crackdown to make them effective. Just as the crackdown resolved a leadership split within the party in favor of the conservatives, so it permitted hardliners on population control to press their cause and mobilize for a new campaign. Rejecting the more liberal views on the relationship between population and development that had led to a relaxation of birth limits in the mid-1980s, relentless in their strict emphasis on per capita indicators of socioeconomic progress, and obsessed with the gap between grain production and population growth, these "order and discipline" conservatives now had the momentum, just as they had in the 1982–83 sterilization campaign.

Mobilization was also aided by pressures to fulfill five-year-plan targets by the end of 1990 and by the concurrent activity under way to prepare for the July 1990 census. Already alerted to the serious problems with the statistical reporting system, central officials worried that census data would be compromised by local cadres who feared that their earlier pattern of statistical cover-up would be revealed. Their fears were validated when an army

---

34. Hubei Province formalized this evaluation system by issuing Provincial Document 7 in 1994. See Zhonggong Hubei shengwei, Hubei sheng renmin zhengfu, "Guanyu shixing jihua shengyu 'yi piao foujue quan' de jueding" [Decision on implementing the "one ballot veto system" for birth planning], in Hubei sheng jihua shengyu weiyuanhui, *Jihua shengyu zhengce fagui ziliao xuanpian, 1983–1997* (Wuhan, 1997), 596–97.

35. "Decision of CCP Central Committee and State Council on Stepping Up Family Planning Work, Strictly Controlling Population Growth," *Xinhua*, June 12, 1991, in *FBIS*, June 20, 1991, 33–36.

of party workers was mobilized for preliminary census work in late 1989 and early 1990. They discovered a 30 percent gap between household registration figures and actual population size and that the discrepancy was increasing, not decreasing.[36] As preparations for the census continued, therefore, cadres were issued a carrot-and-stick ultimatum: if the census report was accurate, there would be no recriminations, even if the figures implied previous statistical fraud; if the census report was tampered with or poorly prepared, however, the repercussions would be severe.[37]

Whether or not cadres believed that there would be no recriminations, the exhaustive census preparations paid off. Census figures for 1990 revealed that the official statistics for the 1984–89 period seriously underestimated the rates of growth and that China's population at the end of 1989 was 15.13 million larger than had been estimated by the State Statistical Bureau on the basis of annual sample surveys and 20.24 million larger than the figure implied by the household registration statistical system. Those differences translated into an annual reporting "slippage" of about 2 and 2.7 million, respectively, or approximately one-tenth of all births each year.[38] They also translated into an average rate of population growth of 15.5 per 1,000 during the five-year period, far higher than the planned target of 12.4 per 1,000.[39] Even after taking into account that portion of excess population that went unaccounted for between the 1982 census and the beginning of the seventh FYP in 1986, the performance was still poor (see table 10).[40] Provincial and local officials, especially those with the worst performance records, were put on notice. Birth planning targets would be treated in the future as "hard" targets, and failure to meet them would have serious consequences.

36. *Xinhua*, December 13, 1989, in *FBIS*, January 5, 1990, 5.

37. Beijing Domestic Service, March 21, 1990, in *FBIS*, April 17, 1990, 24–25. How cadres responded to these warnings is not entirely clear, but it is reasonable to assume that they were skeptical of Beijing's amnesty offer. If so, that skepticism was well founded. Just after the census was completed, a Liaoning provincial radio report revealed that significant statistical errors had been uncovered in some localities and that some "advanced" units did not deserve the title. See Liaoning Provincial Service, July 14, 1990, in *FBIS*, July 17, 1990, 45. Similarly, the Anhui provincial government, acting on the suggestion of the provincial people's congress, overruled a previous directive issued by the local SFPC and Census Office calling for the reduction or cancellation of penalties for cadres who confessed to underreporting. See Zeng, "Wo guo 1991–1992 nian shengyu lu shifou dada diyu tidai shuiping?" 10–11.

38. Shen Yimin, "Disici quanguo renkou pucha jige zhuyao shuzhude kekaoxing pingjia," 15–16; Qiao Shaoqun, "Gaoxiao disici quanguo renkou pucha siliao fenxi xueshu taolunhui zongshu," *Renkou yanjiu* 1 (1992): 54.

39. *Zhongguo jihua shengyu nianjian, 1991*, 258.

40. Ibid., 248.

High Tide: A Reprise

The impact of the crackdown on policy loopholes and on enforcement could be seen in the results initially reported for the eighth FYP. For the 1991–95 plan period, an extraordinary decline was reported in fertility rates and population growth. The birthrate dropped from 21.58 per 1,000 in 1989 to 17.12 per 1,000 in 1995, with most of the four point decline occurring between 1989 and 1992 (see table 10). In turn, the population growth rate, which stood at 15.04 per 1,000 in 1989, fell to an estimated 10.55 in 1995. The total fertility rate, which stood at 2.3 in 1989, was reported to have dropped to an estimated 1.85 in 1995. In stark contrast to the results for the seventh FYP, all of these figures were lower than the targets set in the eighth five-year plan. Though later adjusted upward to reflect pervasive underreporting at the local level, short-term performance was still impressive.

The martial atmosphere that dominated politics from mid-1989 until 1991, an atmosphere that glorified the role of the PLA in restoring order and stability to the country and sanctioned the use of force in service to state goals, was key to the successful performance. These political circumstances were reinforced by the troubling results of the 1990 census. As a result, cadres were signaled (as in 1982–83) that what mattered was the achievement of their targets, not how they were achieved. Evidence for the relegitimation of the use of coercion comes from several sources. First, in 1990 Peng Peiyun, head of the SFPC, told a meeting of provincial birth planning directors that it was acceptable to combine "concentrated," "stopgap" methods with regularized administrative work in areas where "the basis for work is inadequate and the tasks are heavy."[41] Though she went on to emphasize the importance of simultaneously developing the basis for ongoing, routine work, this concession signaled a continuation of official tolerance for campaign tactics, despite the SFPC's growing stake in the professionalization of its mission and methods and its evident desire to distance itself from coercive methods. The extent of the pressures on the SFPC were revealed at another meeting, where Peng noted that party and government leaders in some localities had suggested that birth planning workers be augmented and monitored by bringing in "crack troops" to assist them.[42] They also were revealed by the language of the new directive on birth planning work, which set tough new goals and signaled the victory of those voices

41. Ibid., 27.
42. Ibid., 63.

from the late 1980s who had urged no letup in population control. Insisting that the existing policies had to be implemented "without any wavering, loosening, or changes," the directive criticized and prohibited local decisions to relax birth limits.[43]

Evidence of a particularly strong campaign mobilization in the early 1990s is suggested by provincial-level data on birth control methods, which show sharp increases in numbers of tubal ligations performed between 1990 and 1993. In Shanxi, for example, the proportion of all childbearing-age women who had undergone tubal ligation jumped from 38 percent in 1990 to nearly 52 percent in 1993. Seven other provinces or autonomous regions showed similar rates of change, while one region, Guangxi, reported a much larger increase (from 12 percent in 1990 to 38 percent in 1993).[44] When these data are matched with provincial performance data for the 1986–90 period, it becomes clear that pressures to undergo sterilization grew much stronger in just those regions that had been most lax in performance during the seventh five-year plan. Fifteen of the seventeen areas registering the largest increases in sterilizations were areas that also had the highest rates of extra-plan births in 1988.

Other evidence of a new sterilization drive can be found in the official yearbook of the SFPC for 1991. Anhui, for example, was reported to have organized an autumn mobilization that contributed to an end-of-year total of more than 1.2 million sterilizations and IUD insertions. This performance exceeded by 50 percent the province's 1990 quota of 780,000 procedures in these two categories.[45] Similarly, Shaanxi reported an autumn "high tide" in 1990 that emphasized abortion and sterilization as the main focus for mobilization. The result was an all-time high in the number of birth control procedures performed. Of 1.5 million procedures performed by the year's end, nearly half were sterilizations.[46] In Jiangxi, the emphasis was placed on single- or multi-daughter households. In 1988 and 1989, a total of 57,000 women in these households had undergone sterilization. In

---

43. "Decision of CCP Central Committee and State Council on Stepping Up Family Planning Work, Strictly Controlling Population Growth," *Xinhua*, June 12, 1991, in *FBIS*, June 20, 1991, 33–36.

44. *Zhongguo jihua shengyu nianjian, 1991; Zhongguo jihua shengyu nianjian, 1992; Zhongguo jihua shengyu nianjian, 1994.*

45. *Zhongguo jihua shengyu nianjian, 1991*, 359.

46. Ibid., 434. On policy implementation in Shaanxi, see Susan Greenhalgh, "Controlling Births and Bodies in Village China," *American Ethnologist* 21 (1994): 3–30; Susan Greenhalgh, Zhu Chuzhu, and Li Nan, "Restraining Population Growth in Three Chinese Villages," *Population and Development Review* 20 (June 1994): 365–93. On Shaanxi's policy before 1990, see Susan Greenhalgh, "The Evolution of the One-Child Policy in Shaanxi," *China Quarterly* 122 (June 1990): 191–229.

just the first six months of 1990, however, another 96,000 sterilizations were performed, bringing the rate of sterilization for all such households up to nearly 44 percent. The target set by the province for the end of 1990 was the sterilization of 50 percent of the 349,000 women in households with one or more daughters.[47] In Guangxi, it was reported without comment that the 391,000 vasectomies and tubal ligations performed in 1990 represented a 140 percent increase over the preceding year.[48] In Guangdong, backward counties were mobilized in the fall of 1990 for a "concentrated shock attack" (*jizhong liliang tuchu*). As a result, the annual target for birth control procedures (including abortions and sterilizations) was exceeded. Such mobilizations continued to occur in the early 1990s. In Guizhou, for example, cadres mobilized in the spring of 1993 were instructed to "fulfill more than 50 percent of this year's ligation and vasoligation quotas before spring plowing begins."[49]

The renewed emphasis on permanent solutions to unplanned births played a significant role in the improvement in China's birth planning performance reported in the early 1990s. As in the past, this renewed mobilization produced short-term results because the full weight of the party leadership was behind it, and because the Tiananmen crackdown created a tense and militarized political climate that was conducive to enforcement. That climate did not last long, however, and as soon as it began to lift, enforcement grew more lax. The changes wrought by a decade of reform gave many grassroots cadres both the incentive and the opportunity to engage in a ritual show of compliance and report only what their superiors wanted to hear. They adapted as they had in the past when the work was hard and the campaign targets too ambitious—by lying, exaggerating, and dodging, or finding other ways to manipulate the system (see chapter 7).[50] This weak-

---

47. *Zhongguo jihua shengyu nianjian, 1991,* 434. The campaign was accompanied by serious efforts to provide generous benefits and incentives to couples to persuade them to accept sterilization. Nevertheless, by setting targets for numbers of sterilizations, the province placed pressures on local cadres to be certain that rates of acceptance matched their local quotas. These detailed targets apparently continued into the 1990s. In a report on the completion of birth planning work for 1993, for example, it was emphasized that Jiangxi's success at raising contraception and sterilization rates among married women "at a late age," and raising sterilization rates among two-daughter couples, had placed it among the highest in the country in these categories. Jiangxi People's Radio, May 23, 1993, in *FBIS,* June 2, 1993, 52.

48. *Zhongguo jihua shengyu nianjian, 1991,* 410.

49. Guizhou People's Radio Network, April 3, 1993, in *FBIS,* April 19, 1993, 59.

50. On this problem in the early 1990s, see Zeng, "Wo guo 1991–1992 nian shengyu lu," 9. Zeng reports that villagers foiled all attempts to conduct accurate surveys of village births by posting "guards and sentries" to watch the survey team and using "secret signals" and "tunnels" to coordinate their deception.

ness from below was soon complemented by a new critique from above, as population specialists questioned the merits of China's policy with new vigor and purpose.

Critiques of Population Theory and the Call for Reform

In 1989, when the Deng regime crushed the prodemocracy movement, China still inhabited a world defined by the contours of the cold war. By 1992, that world had disappeared and the CCP now faced the problem of how to adapt to a world in which state socialism had been repudiated. Responding to the new challenges, in late 1992 Deng Xiaoping broke through the political and economic stalemates that grew out of the 1989 events by fully endorsing the continuation of economic reform policies. This step paved the way for General Secretary Jiang Zemin to press an aggressive economic reform agenda, and signaled the decline of the "old Left" that had been ascendant in the 1989–92 period. In the wake of this shift in political climate, a robust and wide-ranging intellectual debate erupted, one that turned a critical eye on the reform process and its consequences.[51]

It was in this context that many of China's population specialists began again to challenge the wisdom of a campaign- and target-oriented approach to population policy, and to raise hard questions about the costs and consequences of the policy. In what began to appear as a concerted campaign of their own, they used China's population journals and other media to lay out a penetrating critique of China's administrative and punitive approach to population control. In 1992, for example, Liu Zheng, one of China's oldest and most distinguished population specialists and the longtime editor of the flagship journal *Renkou yanjiu* (Population Research), argued in that journal for the need to recast the population question from an emphasis on numbers to an emphasis on "population modernization" through investment in education, particularly female education.[52] Other critiques soon followed, focusing on the contradiction between the emergence of a market economy and the persistence of an approach to birth control geared to a planned economic system.

The critics continued to gain momentum through 1993 and 1994, and

---

51. On the politics and intellectual trends of this period, see Joseph Fewsmith, "Historical Echoes and Chinese Politics: Can China Leave the Twentieth Century Behind?" in *China Briefing 2000*, ed. Tyrene White, 11–48 (Armonk, N.Y., 2000). See also Fewsmith's *China since Tiananmen* (Cambridge, 2001).

52. Liu Zheng, "Renkou xiandaihua yu youxian fazhan jiaoyu," *Renkou yanjiu* 2 (1994): 1–10.

pro-reform arguments were increasingly prominent in China's major population journals. Two of the most revealing articles were published simultaneously in the fall of 1994. Timed to coincide with the 1994 UN International Conference on Population and Development (ICPD) held in Cairo, they set the new tone for China's top two demography journals. The first, which appeared in *Renkou yu jingji* (Population and Economics), utilized systems theory (*tizhi shuo*) to argue that birth planning would inevitably give way to "family planning" (*jiating jihua*) under conditions of a market economy.[53] The second, published in *Renkou yanjiu*, went further, laying out a sophisticated argument that constituted a fundamental challenge to China's basic strategy of birth planning. The authors, Gu Baocheng and Mu Guangzong, criticized the assumption that "fewer births is everything," arguing that it led to "short-sighted actions (such as surprise raids on big-bellied women)." Frankly acknowledging that China's fertility decline had been induced through the use of coercion, the authors insisted on the need for a broader and more complex view of population dynamics and a population policy suited to an overall strategy of "sustainable development." Writing that "the curtain is gradually closing on the era of monolithic population control," the authors went on to discuss the complexities that grew out of that approach (sex ratio imbalance and an aging population) and the necessity of shifting to a developmental approach that emphasized improvements and investments in the quality of the population.[54] In short, the authors wholly embraced the argument that development was the best route to fertility decline, rejecting the crude numerical, target-oriented approach (fewer births is everything) that was so deeply embedded in China's population control strategy.[55]

This open revolt against the theory and practice of birth planning was unprecedented, and it proved to be the leading edge of a push by professionals and demographers in China's population centers and birth planning bureaucracy to reform China's program. Like the critique of excess coercion that emerged in 1984, the timely convergence of multiple political developments, both domestic and international, helped to advance the reform agenda. Domestically, rural unrest and instability were again preoccupying the leadership. Much of that unrest was provoked by the steady growth of the local tax burden and its heavy toll on household income.[56] Not only

53. Yuan and Wu, "Lun renkou, tizhi he jiezhi shengyu," 40–43.
54. Gu Baochang and Mu Guangzong, *Renkou yanjiu* 5 (September 1994): 2–10, in *FBIS* 95–032, "A New Understanding of China's Population Problem," February 16, 1995, 28–36.
55. Ibid.; see also Yuan and Wu, "Lun renkou, tizhi he jiezhi shengyu."
56. On this issue, see Thomas P. Bernstein and Lu Xiaobo, *Taxation without Representation in Contemporary Rural China* (Cambridge, 2001).

were peasants angry about the multitude of local fees and taxes that were imposed by officials at every level (and often illegally) they were also irate about the method of extraction—the mobilization of teams of tax collectors who threatened loss of property or worse if peasants refused to pay. As these complaints were aired publicly, it became clear that the same methods were used for birth control, as well, and were deeply resented. One peasant described the process as follows:

> If peasants refused to pay [the excessive taxes], village cadres would warn us that what is used in imposing birth planning will be used to collect contributions to the retention fund, namely the method of "five procedures." The so-called "five procedures" are: Confiscating stored grain, taking away pigs, and dismantling the houses for households that have no money to contribute to the retention fund, and putting handcuffs on and putting into prison those who have an attitude problem.[57]

He went on to say that this approach was possible because the cadres hired "cannon fodder" from outside the village to do the "swearing and beating," providing housing and salaries for the recruits and their families. In this way, local cadres could sometimes avoid the direct confrontations with villagers that were a problem in the 1980s.[58]

The authenticity of this report was confirmed when the regime issued a new central document on "peasant burdens" in 1993. The document, which specified the fees and taxes that were legitimate and those that were not, set a cap on all levies at 5 percent of local average net income for the previous year, and banned certain methods of fee collection, including the "five procedures."[59] This ban angered cadres, since many of the banned levies had been imposed on townships and villages by various state bureaucracies. To collect these fees, including those for birth planning services, they had resorted to the same harsh tactics regularly used to enforce birth planning while bureaucrats and party cadres looked the other way. Now they were told that such tactics were unacceptable, leaving them vulnerable to the anger of peasants against whom they had been used. One reporter, sympathetic to cadres' frustration, revealed the extent to which birth planning relied on shock tactics and coercion:

57. Chen Wenmin, "Peasant Burdens Are an Invisible Knapsack," *Xin shiji* 50, June 10, 1993, 9–15, in *FBIS*, June 18, 1993, 15–21. This quote is taken from p. 17.
58. Ibid., 18.
59. *Jingji ribao*, May 29, 1993, in *FBIS*, June 1, 1993, 68–69; *Xinhua*, May 26, 1993, in *FBIS*, June 1, 1993, 69. Certain types of fees for birth planning services were among those outlawed.

Article 7 of the document on correcting 10 improper ways of collecting charges and irrational management methods mentioned the "use of 'small teams,' 'work teams,' and 'shock brigades,' and the use of judicial or other compulsory measures to grab grain, drag animals away, and remove furniture," which are, in fact, commonly used birth planning management methods in China's rural areas. . . . The judicial department at all levels also received instructions saying that, in principle, they may refuse to handle lawbreaking and discipline-violating cases involving birth planning work, hence grassroots cadres had acquired the imperial sword and thought they could use whatever means they deemed necessary to promote birth planning. Various kinds of birth planning "small teams," "work teams," and "shock brigades," emerged, therefore, becoming active in the rural areas; in order to pick away at the "difficult households," they sent public security officers and militiamen to grab grain, vacate houses, grab animals, and remove furniture, using extreme methods. Knowing that they would not have their legal responsibilities pursued, grassroots cadres have nothing to worry about during this sort of work and extreme behavior is unavoidable.[60]

The decision to include the "five procedures" as one of ten methods of tax collection to be banned indicates that it was a widespread phenomenon and not limited only to poorer, agricultural regions. A 1992 survey of five counties in Shandong, Jiangsu, Henan and two unspecified provinces concluded that townships employing a substantial number of staff workers to assist the local birth planning cadre (ranging from about ten to thirty) were far more likely to organize their work based on three or four "high tides" or "shock attacks" a year than were townships with few or no full-time workers.[61] Only relatively prosperous township governments would be in a position to employ and pay so many additional staffers.

Although the ban on the use of the "five procedures" was first issued in the context of tax collection, it was soon formally extended to birth control work. In 1995, the ban was codified by the SFPC in a document outlining the "seven prohibitions" (*qi bujun*) for conducting grassroots work. The prohibitions, or "disciplines," as the Chinese translation called them, forbade use of the following methods of enforcement: (1) illegally detaining, beating, or humiliating an offender or their relative; (2) destroying property, crops, or houses; (3) raising mortgages without legal authorization; (4) imposing "unreasonable" fines or confiscating goods; (5) implicating rela-

60. Jung Sheng, "Great Impact of Agricultural Issue—4 June Incident Could Be Repeated in Sichuan's Renshou County, Part II," *Hsin bao,* June 10, 1993, in *FBIS,* June 11, 1993, 12–15. This quote is taken from p. 13.
61. Mao She and Yu Jia, "Xiang (zhen) jihua shengyu ganbu peibei ying shixing xuyao yu jinggan tongyide yuanze," *Renkou yanjiu* 6 (1993): 54–55.

tives or neighbors of offenders, or retaliating against those who report
cadre misbehavior; (6) prohibiting childbirths permitted by the local plan in
order to fulfill population targets; (7) organizing pregnancy checkups for
unmarried women.[62] This ban by no means brought a speedy end to the use
of these and other coercive measures, but it did signal to local officials that
they, like other rural cadres, would need to be more careful in the conduct
of their work. Because this decision was just as controversial as the ban on
the five procedures for rural cadres, and for the same reason—a fear of failing to meet their work quotas and of peasant demands for redress of past
offenses—the SFPC specified that the directive should only be communicated orally (*koutou*) and not posted or broadcast publicly. At the same
time, the SFPC emphasized that the instructions should be communicated
to "every single birth planning worker" at every level of the bureaucracy.[63]

A second domestic factor that encouraged critics of the birth planning
program was the intellectual debate about the reform process that erupted
in the mid-1990s, a debate prompted by the social and political consequences of reform. After 1992, when Deng Xiaoping unleashed a new wave
of reform, Chinese intellectuals began to debate the merits of the reform
process. Grappling with an upsurge in private entrepreneurship, unemployment, and exceptionally rapid economic growth and urban development,
hard questions about the impact of reform began to appear in a variety of
media. China's intellectuals no longer saw leftism as the major threat, as
they had from 1989–92. Far more serious by mid-decade were the threats
posed by unbridled development, marketization, and globalization.[64] This
sustained and far-reaching debate was the ideal backdrop for raising hard
questions about the virtues and vices of China's approach to population
control. While others debated the costs and benefits of the reform process as
a whole, population specialists brooded over the *failure* to reform population policy. For reformers, rising sex ratios at birth and rapid population
aging were only the most troubling consequences of a crude program that
was out of step with China's developmental needs. What was needed now,
they believed, was a strategic plan for overall development of the population, one that focused not just on controlling numbers but also on popula-

62. See "Guojia jihua shengyu weiyuanhui guanyu yinfa zai jihua shengyu xing zheng zhifa
zhong jiande 'qige bujun' de tongzhi" and "Guanyu zai jihua shengyu xingzheng zhifa zhong
jiande 'qige bujun' de guiding," in Hubei sheng jihua shengyu weiyuanhui, *Jihua shengyu
zhengce fagui ziliao xuanpian*, 366–67. An English translation of Document 138, issued by the
SFPC Policy and Legislation Department on July 1, 1995, is available from UNESCAP, http://
www.unescap.org/pop/database/law_china.
63. Ibid.
64. Fewsmith, "Historical Echoes and Chinese Politics."

tion migration and distribution, demographic structure, the development of human resources through education and training, and sustainable development.[65]

International developments encouraged this ongoing debate and were a third factor that encouraged advocates of reform. By the mid-1990s, China had a new cohort of Western-trained demographers and family planning experts who were painfully aware of the shortcomings of the one-child policy. Sustained engagement with foreign experts, participation in international conferences and seminars, and advanced training in Western universities or United Nations Population Fund (UNFPA) training programs contributed over time to a reassessment of China's policy.[66] Debate was also encouraged by a shift in the global discourse on population growth and women's rights. When China began to implement its one-child policy in 1979, it was widely lauded by those in the international family planning community who subscribed to the dominant theory that population growth was a primary, if not *the* primary, impediment to economic growth.[67] For them, China's acceptance of this position, and its determination to place tight curbs on population growth, was so important that the very disturbing methods by which China sought to achieve its aims were often overlooked.[68] In the 1980s, this view was subjected to a liberal critique and a radical critique. Liberal critics argued that population growth was not necessarily an impediment to development. While conceding that population growth could hinder development under certain circumstances, liberals also argued that it could sometimes be an asset. This "revisionist" argument had a powerful ally in the Reagan administration (1981–88), which made it the centerpiece of its global family planning agenda.[69] At the 1984 UN Conference on Population and Development in Mexico City, however, many representatives of

65. Gu and Mu, "A New Understanding of China's Population Problem."

66. For a summary and review of UNFPA assistance in the training of Chinese demographers, see appendix 1 in Jane Menken, Ann K. Blanc, and Cynthia Lloyd, eds., *Training and Support of Developing-Country Population Scientists* (New York, 2002). Also at http://www .popcouncil.org/pdfs/trainingreport.pdf. See also Susan Greenhalgh, "Fresh Winds in Beijing: Chinese Feminists Speak Out on the One-Child Policy," *Signs* 26, no. 3 (Spring 2001): 847–86.

67. This theory is known in the literature as the "orthodox" view. For an analysis of the origins and content of "orthodoxy," see Dennis Hodgson, "Orthodoxy and Revisionism in American Demography," *Population and Development Review* 14, no. 4 (December 1988): 541–70. Simon Szreter, "The Idea of Demographic Transition and the Study of Fertility Change: A Critical Intellectual History," *Population and Development Review* 19, no. 4 (December 1993): 659–701.

68. Some who held the orthodox view were on record before 1979 in support of compulsory birth limits. See Paul Ehrlich, *The Population Bomb* (New York, 1968), and Garrett Hardin, "The Tragedy of the Commons," *Science* 162 (1968): 1243–48.

69. For statements of the liberal view, see Hodgson, "Orthodoxy and Revisionism"; Nicholas Eberstadt, "The Premises of Population Policy: A Reexamination," in *The Nine Lives of Population Control*, ed. Michael Cromartie (Washington, D.C., 1995), 17–51; and Working

developing world nations rejected this liberal view. Rapid population growth and slow development had led them to belatedly embrace much of the orthodox view. Many environmentalists shared that skepticism, provoking extensive debate at the 1992 UN Conference on the Environment, held in Rio de Janeiro. Many environmentalists continued to see population growth as one of the greatest threats to the environment, rejecting both the liberal view and the emergent and more radical feminist view.[70]

The feminist critique of population control traced its origins to the women's liberation movement. By the late 1970s, this movement had produced a critique of population control programs that objectified women by treating them as mere targets of a birth control agenda. During the 1980s and early 1990s their influence grew, and feminists came to exercise substantial influence over the agenda for the 1994 UN International Conference on Population and Development, scheduled for Cairo.[71] After years of preliminary debate and negotiation, the conference produced a consensus document that stressed a new, woman-centered approach to family planning. This new approach emphasized the organic relationship between the elevation of the status of women (especially through increased education and employment outside the home), the elimination of poverty, and declining fertility levels.

With a Chinese delegation in attendance (led by SFPC director Peng Peiyun), the Cairo delegates adopted an agenda that emphasized reproductive health and rights, and explicitly rejected the use of compulsion to achieve population goals.[72] The substance of the conference was reported in some detail in the Chinese media and in population journals, and shortly thereafter the influence of the new international language on Chinese policy

Group on Population Growth and Economic Development, National Research Council, *Population Growth and Economic Development* (Washington, D.C., 1986).

70. Dennis Hodgson and Susan Cott Watkins, "Feminists and Neo-Malthusians: Past and Present Alliances," *PDR* 23, no. 3 (September 1997): 469–523; Susan A. Cohen, "The Road from Rio to Cairo: Toward a Common Agenda," *International Family Planning Perspectives* 19, no. 2 (June 1993): 61–71. For a feminist critique of population control policies and institutions before the 1990s, see Betsy Hartmann, *Reproductive Rights and Wrongs* (New York, 1987).

71. See the International Women's Health Coalition, "Women's Voices, '94: Women's Declaration on Population Policies" (New York: International Women's Health Coalition, 1993), and also Gita Sen, Adrienne Germain, and Lincoln C. Chen, eds., *Population Policies Reconsidered* (Cambridge, 1994).

72. For an analysis of the Cairo conference, see C. Alison McIntosh and Jason L. Finkle, "The Cairo Conference on Population and Development: A New Paradigm?" *Population and Development Review* 21, no. 2 (June 1995): 223–60. For the text of the final document adopted by the delegates, see "Program of Action of the 1994 International Conference on Population and Development." Chapters 1–8 are in *Population and Development Review* 21, no. 1 (March 1995): 187–213, and Chapters 9–16 are in *Population and Development Review* 21, no. 2 (June 1995): 437–61.

became clear. In China's "Outline Plan for Family Planning Work in 1995–2000," for example, stress was placed on the impact of the socialist market economy on population control and on the necessity of linking population control to economic development. In addition, the plan placed special emphasis on the role of education and urged aggressive efforts to increase women's educational level in order to promote lower fertility. The plan also stressed the importance of adhering to the law and protecting the legitimate rights and interests of the people.[73]

Similar language appeared in the "White Paper on Family Planning" issued in August 1995, just prior to the convening in Beijing of the Fourth World Conference on Women. Anticipating the criticism it was likely to receive during the conference, however, and consistent with China's long-standing view, the white paper also contained a forceful defense of its policy. Acknowledging shortcomings in China's policy and its implementation, the document nevertheless emphasized its virtues, particularly its contribution to China's development and the achievement of the economic rights of the people. If the "reproductive freedom of couples and individuals are unduly emphasized at the expense of their responsibilities to their families, children, and societal interests," the white paper argued, everyone will suffer. China therefore was obliged to stress the duty of its citizens to adopt birth control and limit childbirth.[74]

Despite this defense, the Cairo and Beijing conferences marked a turning point. The shift of emphasis from population control to reproductive rights and the empowerment of women gave reform-minded Chinese officials more credence and provided institutional resources they could use to promote and experiment with a softer approach to enforcement. They also brought in their wake a surge in women's action to address a wide range of women's issues, including reproductive rights.[75]

The increase in international engagement that came in the wake of the Cairo and Beijing conferences was just one example of a subtle and slowly emergent change in China's foreign policy after 1992. During the Deng era, China had remained somewhat suspicious of, and aloof from, the United Nations and other international organizations, fearing that deeper engagement might circumscribe China's autonomy. After 1992, however, when

73. State Family Planning Commission, "Outline Plan for Family Planning Work in 1995–2000," *Renmin ribao*, February 24, 1995, 11, in *FBIS*, March 23, 1995, 13–19.

74. Information Office of the State Council, "White Paper: Family Planning in China" (August 1995); online at http://www.china.org.cn/e-white/.

75. On the growth and nature of women's activism, see Ellen R. Judd, *The Chinese Women's Movement between State and Market* (Stanford, 2002); Cecilia Milwertz, *Beijing Women Organizing for Change* (Copenhagen, 2003).

Deng gave his blessing to a new wave of economic reform, China's leaders and foreign policy advisers took a new tack. Facing a new, post–cold war international system dominated by the single pole of U.S. power, and with the international repercussions of the 1989 Tiananmen crackdown still fresh in their minds, they concluded that China's interests would be better served by deepening their engagement with international organizations and pursuing multilateral diplomacy.[76]

This new approach to international institutions and multilateralism in the 1990s, complemented by a major expansion of international exchanges and a new wave of economic reform and development, had a transformative impact on Chinese society over the course of the decade. In turn, these changes were reflected in, and legitimated by, a new CCP doctrine articulated by General Secretary Jiang Zemin in 2000 and 2001. In a major speech before the CCP Central Party School, Jiang laid out a framework for party leadership called the "three represents" (*sange daibiao*). The "three represents," which built on the legacy of Deng Xiaoping, emphasized the necessity of remaining current, innovative, and creative in developing China's economy and society. Rejecting dogmatic theories and rigid or old-fashioned forms of practice, and calling instead for dynamic new ideas and leadership methods appropriate to China's new conditions and needs, the "three represents" called for institutional, theoretical, and policy innovations that were responsive to China's changing realities. Jiang also emphasized the importance of learning from international experience and importing methods and practices that would best serve China's modernizing society.[77]

The new openness to innovation and international experience signaled by China's foreign policy and Jiang's leadership doctrine provided an encouraging backdrop for advocates of a new approach to birth planning. The SFPC took advantage of this political climate to encourage vigorous debate about China's changing demographic picture and its approach to population control, and to open a small wedge in the Chinese program and experiment with an alternative approach.

These developments were no doubt facilitated by a fourth and critical factor, China's economic performance. As year 2000 approached—the year that had been identified by the Deng regime as the benchmark for mea-

---

76. On China's evolving foreign policy, see Evan S. Medeiros and M. Taylor Fravel, "China's New Diplomacy," *Foreign Affairs* 82, no. 6 (November–December 2003): 22–35.

77. For analysis of the meaning and political significance of Jiang's "three represents" theory, see Joseph Fewsmith, "Rethinking the Role of the CCP: Explicating Jiang Zemin's Party Anniversary Speech," *China Leadership Monitor* 1, pt. 2 (Winter 2002), and Fewsmith, "Studying the Three Represents," *China Leadership Monitor* 8 (Fall 2003). Online at http://www.chinaleadershipmonitor.org.

suring successful modernization—it became clear that performance goals for the year 2000 had been met. China's gross domestic product (GDP) quadrupled between 1978 and 2000, and its GDP per capita was $840, exceeding the goal of $800 per capita that Deng had set in 1980. In addition, anxieties about grain production and self-sufficiency, brought on by stagnant harvests between 1990 and 1995, had been addressed. To increase self-sufficiency and production levels, a "governor's grain-bag responsibility system" was put into place in 1995. This program decentralized responsibility for grain production to the provinces, and required that they cooperate in the grain trade to even out distribution among grain-surplus and grain-deficit provinces.[78] In addition, the state began to experiment with reform of rural finance, in a bid to solve the problem of "peasant burdens," reduce their tax burden, and enhance rural stability. Although there was no sign by 2005 that this "tax-for-fee" reform had soothed rural tensions, the grain-bag policy, which also authorized new subsidies for grain production and requirements for maintaining and increasing sewn acreage, led to increases in the grain harvest in the late 1990s, and prompted reconsideration on China's overall approach to grain policy.[79] In the early 2000s, new leaders Hu Jintao and Wen Jiabao signaled their commitment to reducing urban–rural inequality and raising peasant income by increasing investment in the agricultural sector and reducing taxation.[80] At the same time, entry into the WTO and the continued diversification of China's rural economy led to a reassessment of China's traditional emphasis on national grain self-sufficiency. At long last, the state's obsession with absolute levels of grain production, and its relationship to population growth, began to wane.

Inching toward Reform in Theory and Practice

As in 1988, just prior to the Tiananmen crackdown, debate in the late 1990s focused on how best to achieve China's population goals, but now ever more urgently on what those goals should be. Growing numbers of professional demographers and family planning experts were persuaded by century's end that the cost of a numbers-oriented approach to population

78. Crook, "Grain Galore."
79. On the tax-for-fee system, see Ray Yep, "Can 'Tax-for-fee' Reform Reduce Rural Tension in China? The Process, Progress and Limitations," *China Quarterly* 177 (March 2004): 42–70.
80. See Central Document 1 (2004) and Central Document 1 (2005). For an excellent analysis of this period and the policy debate, see Edwin A. Winckler, "Chinese Reproductive Policy at the Turn of the Millennium: Dynamic Stability," *Population and Development Review* 28, no. 3 (September 2002): 379–418.

issues (i.e., setting national and local population targets and focusing obsessively on per capita indicators of development) was too high. Faced with the reality of a rapidly aging population at the top of the demographic pyramid, a bulging workforce in the middle that even the fast-growing Chinese economy could not absorb, and sex ratios at the bottom, so skewed that they posed a threat to social stability, many were persuaded that China's administrative and compulsory approach to population control had to be overhauled.[81] These arguments were offset, however, by the Chinese leaders' persistent fear that any hint of a policy relaxation would encourage a rise in fertility. To that end, the one-child policy was officially reaffirmed in 2000, and in 2001 the NPC passed a long-debated Population and Family Planning Law that upheld the existing policy and gave compliance the force of law.[82] A number of provisions included in the law, however, echoed the Cairo and Beijing conference agendas by calling for an "informed choice of safe, effective, and appropriate contraceptive methods" and prohibiting officials from infringing on "personal rights, property rights, or other legitimate rights and interests." In a related commentary, the SFPC was very blunt about the balance struck in the law, stating that despite the success of the one-child policy, the time had not yet come to relax or otherwise change the policy. Because "the distance between the current birth planning policy and the childbearing preferences of the masses" remained substantial, and because birth planning work "relied mainly on forceful [*qiang youlide*] administrative measures," and "the low birthrate remains unstable," China "does not yet possess the conditions for a relaxation (*fangsong*) of birth policy, but there is also no need to tighten it (*shouji*).[83] The commentary also reiterated the importance of adhering to the law in enforcing policy, and avoiding illegal methods and the "seven prohibitions."

Despite the reiteration of existing policy, several developments between 2000 and 2005 suggested a very slow drift in the direction of a more complex and nuanced population policy. First, by 2003 a nationwide pilot project was under way to promote a client-centered and service-oriented approach to providing family planning services. This pilot program traced its origins to 1995, when the SFPC launched a small experimental project in

81. See, for example, the report of the "Zhongguo molai renkou fazhan yu shengyu zhengce yanjiu," *Renkou yanjiu* 24, no. 3 (May 2000): 18–34.

82. For the full text of China's Population and Family Planning Law, see *Population and Development Review* 28, no. 3 (September 2002): 579–85. The reaffirmation of China's existing policy in 2000 came in the "Decision of the CPC Central Committee and the State Council on Strengthening Population and Family Planning Work and Stabilizing a Low Birthrate (2 March 2000)," *Xinhua* Domestic Service, May 7, 2000, in *FBIS*, May 7, 2000.

83. " 'Zhonghua renmin gongheguo yu jihua shengyu fa' youguan mingci jiejue," in *Zhongguo jihua shengyu nianjian, 2002*, ed. Guojia jihua shengyu weiyuanhui, 657–62.

villages scattered among six counties in eastern China. This "quality of care" project, which used incentives to encourage voluntary compliance with birth limits and emphasized routine client-oriented service rather than administrative compulsion and "shock methods," was supported by, and launched in conjunction with, UNFPA. After what the Chinese regarded as early success, the project was expanded in 1998 to include thirty-two counties in twenty-two provinces, and in 2003 it was implemented nationwide. Although residents in the project areas were still limited to two children, a constraint that made it impossible to describe the program as voluntary, birth permits and quotas were eliminated, and pressures to comply and threats of punishment were replaced by positive incentives, improved family planning service, and assistance with poverty alleviation. Couples were also given more freedom of choice as to when to give birth and what type of contraceptives to use.[84]

Second, as family planning officials were educated on the new population law and signaled to moderate their methods of enforcement, local officials who continued to rely on campaigns and "shock attacks" were occasionally subjected to public criticism or legal action when their methods were reported to higher officials. In 2001, for example, birth planning officials in southern Guangdong's Huaiji County were given a target of 20,000 abortions or sterilizations by the year's end, a campaign goal triggered by the 2000 census, which revealed their failure to meet local population control targets. After a local official complained that salaries were being docked to pay for additional ultrasound equipment, the case was brought to the attention of the SFPC. The SFPC ordered a stop to the campaign, publicly rebuked county officials,

---

84. For descriptions of this program and its results, see China Population Information and Research Centre, UNFPA China, and Division of Social Statistics, University of Southampton, *CHINA/UNFPA Reproductive Health/Family Planning End of Project—Women Survey Report: Key Findings* (2004). At China Population Information Research Centre website, http://www.cpirc.org.cn. See also Zhenming Xie, "Quality of Care in Family Planning: Programme Reform in China"; Baochang Gu and Bohua Li, "An Alternative Approach to Family Planning in China: Evidence from China/UNFPA RH/FP Project"; and Zhenzhen Zheng, Zhenming Xie, and Erli Zhang, "Toward a Client-Centered Performance Assessment: Ten Years of Evolution": all in Baochang Gu, Zhenming Xie, Zhenzhen Zheng, and Kaining Zhang, eds., *ICPD+10: In China* (Beijing, 2004). This project became the center of controversy in the United States in 2001–02 as conservatives successfully pressed the Bush administration to cut off funding for UNFPA on the grounds that the organization helped China maintain "a program of coercive abortion." This decision was made despite a State Department investigation that concluded, as did the European Union, that the UNFPA program was a positive step toward reform. For one of many media reports on this controversy, see Philip P. Pan, "China's One-Child Policy Now a Double Standard: Limits and Penalties Applied Unevenly," *Washington Post* (August 20, 2002). For the report of the State Department delegation, see "Report of the China UN Population Fund (UNFPA) Independent Assessment Team" (May 29, 2002). Online at http://www.state.gov/g/prm/rls/rpt/2002/12122.htm.

and ordered them to undergo reeducation on how to implement the policy.[85] Similarly, news in 2005 of a coercive abortion and sterilization clinic in Linyi City, Shandong Province, also brought official condemnation, this time posted prominently on their website.[86] In another case, three individuals who ran a population school in Lixin County, Anhui, were charged with imprisoning policy violators or their relatives, beating them, and demanding fines of 1,000 to 10,000 yuan to secure their release. Those responsible received lenient sentences of two or three years imprisonment each, a legal outcome that outraged victims and their families and triggered charges that the county officials had accepted bribes in exchange for light sentences.[87] Still, public reporting on cases such as these increased in the late 1990s and early 2000s, as the SFPC attempted to begin altering the culture of grassroots implementation created by thirty years of campaign-style enforcement.

A third development that encouraged the reform agenda was the alarming evidence of an advancing HIV/AIDS epidemic, followed in the winter and spring of 2003 by the outbreak of severe acute respiratory syndrome (SARS). As the AIDS epidemic escalated rapidly in parts of Asia in the 1990s, provoking aggressive (if belated) government action to slow its advance, Chinese officials remained locked in patterns of secrecy and denial, understating the severity of the problem, declining to endorse a mass education campaign, and insisting that the disease was largely limited to drug addicts and sex workers.[88] Reports of entire villages in China's heartland devastated by AIDS, the result of unsafe methods of blood collection by private entrepreneurs, changed very little, and attempts by Chinese AIDS activists to force the government to acknowledge the full scope of the problem, increase public awareness, and assist those who had contracted AIDS met with hostility. Provincial and local officials in Henan Province, where many

85. Additional evidence of just how difficult the campaign habit is to break comes from Kay Johnson, who found in 2001 that several Anhui counties, responding to the problem of rising sex ratios at birth, were cracking down on voluntary abortions, which were assumed to be for sex selection. Anyone caught aborting a second pregnancy automatically forfeited the right to eventually have an in-quota second child. Personal correspondence from Kay Johnson.

86. See Comments on the Situation of Family Planning in Linyi of Shandong Province (2005/09/08), and Dr. Yue Xuejun, NPFPC Spokesperson and Director General of the NPFPC Department of Policy and Legislation on the Preliminary Results of Investigating Family Planning Practices in Linyi City of Shandong Province (2005/09/10) at http://www.npfpc.gov.cn/en/index/htm.

87. "China's Officials Caught for Abusing 'Family Planning Rules,'" in *FBIS,* November 24, 2000, AFP–Hong Kong. According to the AFP report, the case was first reported in *China Youth Daily.*

88. For a comprehensive analysis of the epidemic in Asia, see *AIDS in Asia: Face the Facts* (2004), a report by the Monitoring of the AIDS Pandemic (MAP) Network. See http://www.mapnetwork.org/docs/MAP_AIDSinAsia2004.pdf.

of the AIDS villages were located, reacted to village protests with repression and arrests.[89]

This strategy of containment and denial was severely challenged by the outbreak of the SARS epidemic in the winter and spring of 2003. Because the deadly SARS virus appeared to have originated in South China before spreading to Southeast Asia and beyond, World Health Organization officials were eager to track its history and pathways of transmission. China's public health officials were initially reluctant to comply, and no public warnings were issued. Only after pressure mounted from abroad and domestic rumors began to stir panic did China's leaders provide accurate data on the spread of the disease in China, issue public warnings about SARS, take steps to isolate SARS patients and limit further public exposure, and cooperate more fully with international authorities in the fight to contain and treat the disease.[90] The momentum generated by the SARS outbreak helped to create a new openness on public health issues, at least temporarily. In the aftermath of the epidemic, official attitudes toward AIDS began to change and international cooperation on AIDS prevention and treatment increased.

As the SARS outbreak swept through in the spring of 2003, a bureaucratic reorganization of the State Council was implemented. The SFPC was renamed the National Population and Family Planning Commission (NPFPC), tasked with a broader range of population issues (e.g., aging, migration, employment, gender equity, education) and expected to contribute to a coordinated and coherent national program to manage their interlocking population dynamics. This organizational change was greeted with en-

89. For a complete review of the emergence and progression of China's HIV/AIDS epidemic, the government's slow response, the political struggles of infected villagers in the AIDS villages of Henan, and the detention of activist Wan Yanhai, see the "China HIV/AIDS Blood Supply Chronology," by China AIDS Survey, an online database. The chronology covers the issue from 1985 to the present, http://www.casey.org/chron/BloodSupply.htm. See also two reports by Drew Thompson, "China Faces Challenges in Effort to Contain HIV/AIDS Crisis" (May 2004) and "Anti-AIDS Effort in Central China Focuses on Former Plasma Donors" (May 2004). Online at Population Reference Bureau, http://www.prb.org. See also Oscar Grusky, Hongjie Liu, and Michael Johnston, "HIV/AIDS in China: 1990–2001," *AIDS and Behavior* 6, no. 4 (December 2002): 381–93.

90. On the SARS outbreak and its impact, see Neil J. Beck, "What Does SARS Mean for China?" *NBR Briefing: Policy Report No. 13* (National Bureau of Asian Research, May 2003), http://www.nbr.org; Bates Gill, "China and SARS: Lessons, Implications, and Future Steps," paper presented to the Congressional-Executive Commission on China (May 12, 2003), http://www.cecc.gov/pages/roundtables/051203/gill.php; "China and SARS: The Crisis and Its Effects on Politics and the Economy," a Brookings Institution panel moderated by Richard Bush, with participants Laurie Garrett, Robert A. Kapp, Michael Swaine, and Minxin Pei (July 2, 2003), http://www.brookings.org. On the broader meaning and impact of SARS, see Elizabeth M. Prescott, "SARS: A Warning," *Survival* (Autumn 2003): 207–26.

thusiasm by the SFPC, and it dovetailed nicely with their preparations for the arrival of the tenth anniversary of the 1994 International Conference on Population and Development. To commemorate the anniversary and comply with UN requests for a review of progress toward the achievement of ICPD goals, in September 2004 China hosted the International Forum on Population and Development. In preparation for that event, the NPFPC prepared a volume of papers detailing China's progress in reforming its birth planning program. In addition to reports on the new approach to birth planning in the pilot counties, the volume included papers on migration and women's empowerment; the role of NGOs in reproductive health; linkages between population control, reproductive health, and poverty alleviation; and the HIV/AIDS epidemic. In a frank and forthright manner, the distinguished authors of the reports detailed the changes implemented in these areas, acknowledging the continuing limitations of the Chinese program but also stressing the progress made toward achieving the goals of the ICPD.[91]

By 2005, the drift toward reform remained slow but perceptible. The NPFPC, with apparent backing from China's senior leaders, appeared committed to a comprehensive reform agenda and actively engaged in the range of activities—pilot projects, training conferences, research—that were required to translate this central-level agenda into local-level practice. In addition, the official language of the birth planning program had changed. As a second white paper and a new central document made clear, much of the language of Cairo had been embraced. Population control was no longer said to be the linchpin to success in China's modernization drive. Instead, emphasis was placed on the long-term stabilization of low fertility levels; on the critical role of development, poverty alleviation, and women's education and status in achieving the goal of a low fertility society; and on the importance of placing client service and quality of care at the heart of the program.[92] Language alone, of course, is insufficient evidence of a turn toward reform and does not limit the power of provincial and county officials to launch brazenly coercive campaigns in areas under their control. Once adopted, however, language can be an insidious instrument of change.

Attempts to bring about this change will confront two major challenges, however. First, because provincial, municipal, and county officials gained substantially from the decentralization of power resulting from reform, effecting change at the local level will be a monumental task. Reformers in

---

91. Baochang Gu, Zhenming Xie, Zhenzhen Zheng, and Kaining Zhang, eds., *ICPD+10: In China.*

92. The white paper, "China's Population and Development in the 21st Century," may be found at http://www.china.org.cn/e-white/.

Beijing can organize training projects for local birth planning officials and launch pilot programs in family planning, but until local party and government officials are no longer evaluated on the basis of the achievement of numerical targets and quotas, progress will be difficult. At mid-decade, as they approached the end of the tenth five-year planning cycle, many local officials were still held to that standard, as the long-standing bureaucratic practices embedded in China's local campaign culture proved hard to uproot.

The second challenge faced by pro-reform officials and experts was the uneasy compromise reached with central leaders in 2000–01, a compromise that offset approval of reform initiatives with a reaffirmation of the one-child policy, on the grounds that the low fertility levels brought about by that policy were unstable, achieved by "administrative measures" that pushed fertility levels below what could be achieved by a voluntary program. That assertion was ever more aggressively challenged after 2001, as experts openly questioned whether China's birth planning program had had any impact at all on China's fertility and called for dismantling the state's birth planning machinery.[93]

As of 2005, however, reformers had failed to persuade central leaders to formally revise or abandon the one-child policy, for fear it would trigger an increase in fertility. More fundamentally, the state was unwilling to relinquish its claim of authority over pregnancy and childbirth, or the ideological, regulatory, and legal framework that enshrined that authority. They were prepared to tolerate less dramatic steps in that direction, however, such as abolishing the requirement for an official birth certificate for the birth of a first child and, in many areas, abolishing the spacing requirement for those entitled to have a second child. And more important, the state at long last began to retreat from the claim that population control was a simple and crude mathematical equation. A quarter century after China's economic reforms began, fundamental reform of the birth planning regime was no longer out of the question.

93. See, for example, the withering critique by Liang Zhongtang, "Guanyu ershi shiji mo zhongguo dalu renkou zongliang he funu shengyu lu shuipingde yanjiu," *Shengchanli yanjiu* 5 (2003): 147–58. Liang rejects the state's fundamental claim to have a legitimate role in regulating childbirth.

9

Against the Grain: The Chinese Experience with Birth Planning

In the winter of 1995, the State Family Planning Commission published a plan outline for birth planning work for the period 1995–2000. Having recorded exceptionally low fertility and population growth rates in the early 1990s—rates that were exaggerated, it turned out, but that appeared to exceed the goals of the eighth five-year plan before schedule—China was now prepared to revise its goals for the year 2000. In 1991, the hope had been to reduce China's annual rate of population growth to under 12.5 per 1,000 by the year 2000, but that goal had been reached and breached by 1994. The new goal, therefore, was to reduce population growth to under 10 per 1,000.[1] One wonders whether the drafters realized that in articulating this goal they had come full circle, converging in 1995 on the same goal for the end of the century that Premier Zhou Enlai had set forth exactly thirty years earlier.

In retrospect, it is this moment in time forty years ago, when Zhou Enlai quite consciously began to turn the theoretical concept of birth planning into the practice of state-regulated birth limitation, that marks the crucial turning point on China's road toward the one-child campaign. By incorporating specific population goals into China's economic development plans, Zhou committed himself, and all of China, not just to the idea of subordinating childbirth to state planning but to the practice of that idea. At the time, Zhou undoubtedly presumed that comprehensive birth limits, univer-

1. State Family Planning Commission, "Outline of China's Family Planning Work (1995–2000)," *Renmin ribao*, February 24, 1995, 11, in *FBIS*, March 23, 1995, 13–19.

sally imposed, were out of the question for China's present stage of development. The best one could hope for was a campaign that encouraged a small family norm and gave interested couples the means to achieve it through the provision of birth control devices and services. Within five years, however, after the calamity of the Cultural Revolution, the unthinkable became progressively thinkable. Already committed to entering population matters into the national economic plan through the same blunt numerical formulas and goals that applied to material production, the logic of state controlled childbirth began to play itself out. What had begun as an effort to slow population growth by encouraging fewer births became a state-mandated program of birth rationing. What began as a concern to prevent population growth from undercutting economic advances became a relentlessly determined effort to force human reproduction to submit to the will of the state.

How China arrived at this juncture is a story of great irony. Above all it is the story of an idea—jihua shengyu—and how that idea came to serve a particular demographic and developmental challenge. The idea of birth planning was born out of the heady and optimistic days of socialist transformation in the 1950s, when all things seemed possible, when the quest to achieve the utopian goals seemed well within reach. And it was an idea born out of darker and well-concealed fears, fears that erupted in protest against the Malthusian pessimism of China's capitalist enemies who confidently predicted that feeding the population would be an insurmountable task. These two impulses, the one determinedly optimistic, the other broodingly realistic if not pessimistic, formed the vortex in which China struggled for a way to think and theorize about the role of population in China's development strategy.

In the 1950s, the struggle to define a socialist theory of population growth appropriate to China's conditions was intense, bitter, and increasingly dangerous. When Mao attacked birth control advocates and proclaimed the great virtue of a large population, therefore, it appeared from outside China that the optimists had won a decisive and permanent victory. As bright visions of the imagined economic future quickly gave way to the reality of widespread hunger and a limited agricultural surplus, however, it proved impossible to put the population issue to rest. Those who were determined to deny reality in the name of revolutionary socialism clashed with those who saw facing facts as the more courageous and patriotic stance.

The unlikely source of compromise in this debate turned out to be Mao Zedong. Though strongly committed to an optimistic view of China's population and its prospects for rapid socialist advance, Mao's vision of a planned socialist society was big enough to encompass the prospect of planning births according to collective need. If revolutionary socialism was about the disavowal of self in service of a collective revolutionary goal, the extension of that ethic to material needs and production was only a beginning. The true mark of a transformed society, the ultimate self-sacrifice, would be forsaking even personal childbearing preferences for the greater good of the collective. Mao understood, however, that the key to China's population future lay in the countryside and that no amount of urging could or would alter peasant childbearing preferences under the prevailing economic conditions. Only a long-term process of socialist transformation could change the peasant mentality and make birth planning a real possibility. In the meantime, the concept of birth planning could be usefully introduced as part of a comprehensive system for economic planning and socialist development, and perhaps urban residents could be encouraged to practice birth control.

If China had not been so agrarian and underdeveloped in the 1950s, if its population base had not been so large, if the necessity for rapid economic advance had not seemed so urgent, or Mao so impatient for radical political change at any price, the full implications of this theory of birth planning might never have been realized. As it was, however, the CCP became distressed very early on with per capita indicators of economic performance, which brought into question the extent and pace of China's economic advance. Grain production, above all, became an obsession, the ultimate measure of the regime's ability to keep its word to its vast peasant constituency. Despite all the cheering for gross production increases from year to year, the per capita figures told a different story. Bad harvest years were times of anxiety and even panic, as China's leaders searched for the right formula for lifting China out of poverty. Under Mao's leadership, the CCP initially resisted the idea that population growth was itself a key part of the problem. They focused instead on getting agricultural policy right so as to boost production. But as those efforts (first moderate, then more radical) proved inadequate to boost production rapidly enough, both parts of the equation—gross production and population size—were put on the table. The question became what to do to improve this ratio, and the answer, increasingly, was to focus on the denominator (population size), as well as the numerator (how much was produced).

It was in this way, and by this logic, that China tilted toward the practice of comprehensive birth planning. With each successive moment of perceived crisis in grain production—1954–55, 1960–62, 1969–70, 1974–76, the optimists, including Mao, found it harder to argue that population growth was a neutral or positive factor in China's development process. The pessimists, on the other hand, could point to the incontrovertible evidence of stagnant or declining per capita production levels. Given a political climate that set strict limits on their ability to call for agricultural reforms, they found it easier with each crisis to justify working directly to suppress population growth. And after 1956 they had the concept of birth planning to support and legitimate their position, to shield them from ideological attacks. When the regime finally resorted to specific and increasingly strict birth limits in the 1970s, therefore, it seemed only an incremental step forward on the path toward a nationwide birth control program. In reality, it was a leap forward into an uncharted territory in which the state became the arbiter of life, deciding who would be given a ration ticket (birth permit) and who would not, deciding which children would be deemed legitimate (within the plan) and which would not.

In taking this leap, the CCP made a quiet admission that Mao's great optimism about China's population had been misplaced. In this sense, the birth planning program may be said to be built on a repudiation of Mao. Without Mao's great faith in the malleability of man and the value of popular mobilization, however, birth planning on a national scale would have been inconceivable. Only the martial atmosphere of political fear and conformity created by the politics and mass campaigns of the Maoist era could galvanize a party rank and file that was deeply hostile to the idea of birth planning, and even more hostile to the notion that they should be forced to regulate the childbearing habits of their neighbors. The resistance of the population at large was a grave issue, but in the end it was only a secondary one. The single most important obstacle to be overcome in implementing a universal birth planning program was the resistance from within the party—from a predominantly male cadre force, much of it rural and poorly educated, that saw birth planning as a loathsome intrusion into one of the very few areas of life that had remained traditional and conservative, untouched by the storms of revolution.

With that in mind, it becomes easy to understand why the nationwide birth planning campaign launched in the early 1970s was so effective. Specific population targets were added to the economic plan just as China was moving beyond the most intensive, disruptive and violent phase of the Cultural Revolution. Despite the return to a partial normalization of political life after 1969, nothing was normal. Cadres at all levels were scared and watchful, and even those who had benefited from the radical politics of the period had good reason to watch their backs. This atmosphere of fear, foreboding, and intimidation was ideal for inaugurating a controversial birth planning program. It made it more likely that opposition and resistance from within the party bureaucracy would be muted and that compliance levels would be high, even if extreme methods had to be used to achieve them. At the same time, the increased autonomy and rural unrest that percolated in many areas in the 1970s made campaign mobilization an indispensable tool for successful implementation of state policies.

With the transition to the post-Mao era, however, the question became whether this extraordinary effort could or would be continued. Within China, the campaign was naturally associated by some with the radical leftist policies of the later years of the Cultural Revolution. Peasants, in particular, saw it as an abomination that had been inflicted on them by leftists, and that would be repudiated by more sensible leaders. Outside China, the extent of the 1970–77 campaign remained unclear, but the passing of the Maoist era suggested a gradual transition to a postrevolutionary phase of development in which campaign-style mobilizations would have no place. Both sets of expectations were wrong. The post-Mao era did bring about the downfall of radical leftism, and it brought to power new leaders who gravitated toward a new strategy for economic development that broke radically with the Maoist agenda. Getting rich, not waging class struggle, was the new path to glory. With an estimated two hundred million people still suffering from hunger and malnutrition after twenty-five years of CCP rule, however, and with population pressures greater than ever, there was little chance of the new regime abandoning birth planning. On the contrary, the architects of the new regime, especially Deng Xiaoping and Chen Yun, had been among the earliest and most consistent supporters of aggressive birth control. Obsessed with the idea that population growth would make it impossible to achieve the ambitious modernization goals that were expressed in simple per capita terms (i.e., a GNP per capita of $1,000, later reduced to $800, by the year 2000), pressures to limit childbearing intensified dramatically, and campaign methods were utilized in an attempt to subjugate peasant childbearing even more strictly to the dictates of the modernization plan.

If the peasantry was caught by surprise by the one-child campaign, outside observers were even more surprised. Theories of Leninist regimes predicted a transition from revolutionary to postrevolutionary politics after the passing of the revolutionary hero, a transition that implied a shift from the mobilizational politics of the period of socialist transformation to the routinization and normalization of politics as the party grew weary of the perpetual upheaval. On the surface, the rhetoric of the Deng regime seemed to point toward this transition. Yet its goals—repudiating much of the Maoist legacy, adopting far-reaching reforms, and engineering rapid socioeconomic modernization by the end of the century—were themselves sufficiently radical and ambitious that they could only be achieved through a monumental act of campaign-style mobilization. In the short run, revolutionary means would still be necessary to achieve a new set of postrevolutionary ends. The Deng regime thus began its political reign with a denunciation of political campaigns and mass movements, but that was followed by a spate of dramatic reform initiatives that demanded full mobilization of the party machine and tested its loyalties (radicalism or reform). It is true that this mobilization did not rival the grand campaigns of the Maoist era, and that rural reform was aided by popular mobilization from below, but the basic process of regime consolidation and comprehensive reform that was pushed through between 1978 and 1983 followed the classic Leninist, or "engineering," approach to social change—mobilization of the party and mass organizations to take the lead in implementation, and skillful and massive use of the propaganda apparatus to build support for the reformist line, to isolate political opponents and brand them as enemies, and to consolidate power.

Still, after 1983 the campaign momentum receded somewhat and stabilization of the new political and economic arrangements became a primary goal. To counter the people's fear that the party line could change again as rapidly as it had after Mao's death, much effort went into reinforcing the idea that the party would remain steadfast in its support for reform. Work was to be regularized, policies made predictable, and the rule of law made a reliable check on arbitrary political power. All of these changes signaled clearly the end of China's revolutionary phase. Yet campaigns did not disappear. They were employed to achieve political goals, such as party rectification (1983–86), eliminating spiritual pollution (1983), countering bourgeois liberalization (1987 and 1989), and suppressing Falun Gong practitioners (1999–2000). And they were used to achieve more concrete policy goals, such as obligatory tree planting, instituting electoral reform, reducing peasant burdens, and controlling economic crime. Rather than abandon campaign-style mobilization, it was harnessed and domesticated to serve new political purposes.

The Campaign as Political Institution

This study of China's birth planning campaign requires that we rethink the classic definition of mobilization as always entailing a process of calculated attack and disruption in pursuit of revolutionary ends. During the Maoist era, the purpose of mobilization was indeed the disruption of bourgeois social arrangements and routines in favor of new socialist arrangements. Destruction of the old often took primacy over construction of the new. In Deng Xiaoping's postrevolutionary regime, the priorities were reversed, but mobilization remained a vital tool in the regime's efforts to *reorder* the established institutions and routines of socialism. Under Deng, the party remained the instrument of mobilization and directed change, but an atmosphere of orderly determination replaced that of "crisis and attack."[2] Mobilization ceased to be synonymous with permanent revolution, but it remained an essential tool for implementing far-reaching reform while enforcing political orthodoxy. Crises of political power, like the Beijing Spring of 1989, triggered a temporary reversion to many of the revolutionary campaign methods of the past, but mobilizational methods also played important, if more subdued, roles in accomplishing ordinary policy goals on a national and local scale. It is this more ordinary face of campaign mobilization, a face that spans the Maoist and post-Mao eras, that is obscured by the emphasis on disruption and attack. From early on campaign methods of organization and implementation were applied to more routine forms of activity, such as economic production. And with that, the campaign began to have a predictable character and process. Rather than stand as the antithesis of bureaucratic process, the forms and rituals associated with mass campaigns were adapted *for* the bureaucratic process. It was this very tendency to normalize and bureaucratize that Mao battled so fiercely with his "storming" style of mobilization from below. Ironically, it may be this very persistence on Mao's part that explains the incorporation of campaign-style methods into the heart of bureaucratic practice in China. By glorifying mass mobilization and condemning bureaucratism, Mao helped create a political culture in which routine bureaucratic practice had to be coated with a mobilizational veneer. And as the bureaucracy grew larger, more powerful, and more entrenched, despite Mao's efforts, when it finally came of age in the Deng era its tendencies toward fragmentation and protracted bargaining reinforced the need for campaign rituals and protocols. Such rituals helped organize and coordinate disparate bureaucracies under the leadership of central party organs, and they helped implement policies by forcing a concentrated burst of energy toward a specific policy goal. They made social engineering across bureaucratic lines possible.

The birth planning campaign is an ideal case for illuminating this enduring role for mobilization in China. Not only does it span the Maoist and post-Mao era, allowing us to track how the campaign was waged over time, it also has several other features that make it especially useful. First, it was closely related to core issues of economic strategy, but it was not a main focal point of political struggle, like agricultural policy, for example. This meant that the birth planning campaign was bigger and more important

---

2. David Apter, *The Politics of Modernization* (Chicago, 1965), 360.

than the many smaller and more peripheral campaigns that were launched over the years, but it was also more representative, more ordinary than the campaigns that have been most closely examined in the past and that have shaped our conception of campaign politics. Second, birth planning took the form of a material production campaign, but its target was human behavior, not production quotas, and its purpose was to produce less, not more. It was a social policy, and a regulatory policy, of unprecedented magnitude, but unlike so many social policies, here it was possible to measure results with some precision. Childbirth might be planned like grain production and regulated like tattoo, but it was harder to hide babies than to cheat on state grain sales or tax receipts. Third, it was a complex campaign that involved political mobilization and technical services (providing contraceptives, carrying out birth control procedures) on an ongoing basis. This required coordination across bureaucratic systems, something the SFPC could not manage alone. Success depended on the active, ongoing support of the party leadership. Fourth, it was an indiscriminate campaign. One escaped being a target only by ageing out of the childbearing-age cohort or by undergoing sterilization. Class background and political status did not excuse anyone: cadres and peasants alike were subject to its requirements. It is true that women were the primary targets who bore the physical brunt of the campaign and that men were more often the key agents of enforcement (behind grassroots women's leaders) than they were the direct targets. But the lines between enforcers and targets were everywhere vague, since nearly all families were touched by the program eventually. And finally, it was an unpopular program, to say the least. Even cadres who began to see the economic logic of fewer births and the value of lowering fertility levels dreaded dealing with birth planning work. It was disagreeable work at best, and at worst it was rude, rough, and dangerous.

This set of characteristics produced a unique but revealing campaign process. In the early and mid-1970s, the atmosphere of political mobilization was ubiquitous, making the campaign the obvious method for inaugurating a societywide birth planning program. Because the target of the campaign was the entire childbearing-age cohort, because entrenched resistance could be expected, and because the program had to be enforced indefinitely, only a massive campaign would signal the state's resolve to subject childbearing to state planning. By the early 1980s, however, mass mobilization had lost its cachet, and "coercion and commandism" were no longer in vogue. The new language was one of patient persuasion, regularization, and fitting implementation methods to local conditions or individual needs (*yin di zhi yi, yin ren zhi yi*). Campaigns and shock attacks were out. As it turned out, however, there was no doing without them. Only a campaign atmosphere could force local governments to pursue birth planning without regard to cost, as in 1983, for example, or induce hospitals and clinics to perform abortions, sterilizations, and IUD insertions in exchange for IOUs. Between mobilizational high tides, coordination problems were epidemic, and a unit or bureau's self-interest came first. Party-led mobilization helped override these obstacles, at least for a time, and made possible policy changes that bureaucracies had resisted before the campaign.

Mobilization was also necessary for grassroots implementation. Enforcing a one-child birth limit in the countryside, or, failing that, even a two-child limit, not only cut against the grain of rural childbearing habits and preferences, it cut against the grain of the agricultural reforms, which the regime acknowledged benefited larger, labor-rich families. This contradiction put the state at odds with itself, setting the stage for a prolonged struggle over childbearing. Mobilization was essential in inducing peasant households to comply with birth limits, but even more it was the only means to compel rural cadres to undertake this work.

In pointing to the dual face of rural cadres, who are at once the local agents of the state and the objects of state power, this study echoes findings presented elsewhere in the literature on rural China that emphasize the vulnerability of the regime to this soft organizational underbelly.[3] Seeking to balance state claims against village preferences and village politics, cadres employ "strategies of survival" that frequently undercut central preferences. Here, the most pervasive strategy was to allow peasants with two or more daughters to dodge birth limits through active collusion or by simply falsifying local birth records. Historically, the regime's answer to such resistance was the mobilization campaign, but the logic and goals of the reform program suggested that campaign-style politics be set aside. In the end, the reverse proved to be true. The decentralization and diversification of power resulting from successful reform eroded both the fear of retribution and the promise of meaningful rewards necessary to maintain any degree of political control over cadres torn between obeying the state and pleasing fellow villagers. As local cadres were rewarded more for economic entrepreneurship than for enforcing unpopular central directives, as it became more important to satisfy one's regional superiors than to follow Beijing's instructions, and as a divide began to open up between an increasingly bureaucratized township government taking its cues from above and village cadres taking their cues from their neighbors, old forms of political deviance gave way to

---

3. See, for example, Siu, *Agents and Victims*; Oi, *State and Peasant*.

new ones. Under these conditions, the vital organizational role of campaign-style mobilization became clear. It was the only means, and also the most proven means, of pressing cadres into compliance with party work directives. It was the principal mechanism by which the state preserved its autonomy and organizational integrity at the grassroots. As the reforms progressed, therefore, and concerns about excessive "commandism" gave way to anxiety about "lax" enforcement of policies and "laissez-faire" attitudes among rural cadres, new mobilizations were triggered. Because the results were always partial and temporary, however, the *fang-shou* cycle of intensification followed by relaxation became a way of life.

This interpretation of the enduring role of campaigns in China—that they played a critical role in preserving organizational integrity under the extremely trying conditions of a reform process that undercut party authority and discipline—does not deny either the scholarly arguments or the empirical or historical evidence that revolutionary, Leninist regimes eventually lose their mobilizational character. Clearly they do. This study suggests, however, that mobilizational methods can survive that transition when they are integral and deeply embedded elements of the local administrative culture. They survive when state ambitions vastly exceed the regular bureaucratic resources to achieve them, and where there is a political instrument (the CCP) capable of transcending bureaucratic divisions and disciplining bureaucratic behavior. They do not retain their "mass" character; no one demands that everyone participate. They are characterized more by bureaucratic mobilization from above, focused narrowly on a target population. In the 1950s and 1960s, when China's great transformational campaigns were triggered, rescinded, and then renewed at the cue of the center, the campaign method was an administrative policy that could be employed or curtailed. Over the course of more than forty years, however, what was perfected for the grand campaigns of that era became a predictable and methodical instrument for implementing ordinary policy initiatives or improving on old ones. As it became routinized and predictable, local leaders at every level became intimately familiar with it and drew on it to implement their own local initiatives. For them, there was less choice. The method was dictated not only by politics but by the nature of the task. Birth planning required them to use every tool available to meet their targets.

With this tradition of mobilization so deeply rooted in the collective memory of the party apparatus and government bureaucracy, and so crucial to the maintenance of a disciplined party organization strewn over a vast territory and commanding a vast population, the formal repudiation of political campaigns in 1978 did little to alter the behavioral response of local cadres who had a limited repertoire of leadership methods. In the short run, lessons and rituals learned and repeated over decades ensured that party cadres remained highly sensitive to mobilizational cues from the center—so much so that they were still susceptible to the political sins of overzealousness and "commandism," even in pursuit of liberal reforms.[4] Over the longer run, and under the influence of reform, their zealousness waned and they grew more lax and poorly disciplined, even corrupt. But when the provincial party determined it was time to register illegal migrants in its jurisdiction, or the municipality decided to get tough on crime, or the county decided it was tree-planting time or time to round up tax evaders, they invariably organized a campaign. Even the drive to promote village self-rule and village elections sometimes drew on standard, top-down campaign tactics, a paradox that illustrates just how deeply such methods are imbedded in the administrative culture.[5] Mobilizational impulses were so deeply etched into bureaucratic codes and routines that local cadres could not move forward without resort to the targets and timetables that are the very essence of campaign politics.

It is a cliché to say that revolutions die, that the grand phase of revolutionary transformation and mobilization inevitably passes from the scene. Revolutions also leave imprints, however. They leave trace marks on political culture, and they leave their signature on political institutions. In China, part of that signature was an enduring propensity to rely on mobilizational patterns of administrative control long after the mobilizational era had ended. Even so, there is every reason to expect that the echoes of this institutional legacy will grow ever more faint. When mobilization is no longer needed as a means to control the countryside or as the instrument for achieving ambitious feats of social engineering or as a tool for unifying a massive and highly fractious party and administrative bureaucracy, when rules of law and professional bureaucratic cadres can achieve as much or more than periodic campaign mobilizations, or, more simply, when CCP leaders no longer feel obliged to use party mobilization as the means to achieve their goals, campaign mobilization will have served its purpose.

4. Stuart Schram, *Ideology and Policy in China since the Third Plenum, 1978–84*, Research Notes and Studies No. 6 (London: School of Oriental and African Studies, Contemporary China Institute, 1984).

5. While investigating this initiative in a Liaoning municipality in the summer of 1992, I discovered that central directives on implementing village self-rule had been translated into specific targets and directives for a local-level "operation" (*huodong*) that was carried out in 1991. Following the directive of the local party committee, the goal for 1991 was to have 50% of the villages under municipal jurisdiction meet the village self-rule standard, and by the end of 1992, 85%. To determine which villages met the standard, a detailed 100-point evaluation system was established.

State Hegemony, Elite Cohesion, and the
Limits of Resistance

In this book I began with three basic questions: How and why did the Chinese Communist regime come to impose strict birth rationing on its people? How were they able to succeed in enforcing strict birth limits? How were they able to sustain this control in the face of reforms that undercut their enforcement power at every turn? I have argued that the socialist theory of birth planning accounts for the rationing of childbearing and that the campaign has been the crucial enforcement method—crucial for overriding peasant resistance, and crucial for forcing some degree of compliance from reluctant cadres. This leads us to another important question, however. Why, despite the evidence of massive peasant resistance and the real success of that resistance as measured by the numbers of illegal or unplanned births, was the state so unmoved, so unwilling to budge on its policy, other than to grant a second child to those who first bore a girl? The substantial literature on peasant resistance provides one answer. It suggests that the Chinese experience with birth planning is a classic example of state-peasant struggle, both in terms of the pattern of resistance and the outcome. Peasants are often effective in blunting or deflecting the state's force, defending themselves on the margin as far and as long as possible by resorting to the "weapons of the weak." Strong states, however, can contain or override this resistance because the peasantry is dispersed and unorganized. Peasant action tends to be local or regional, and thus, can be ignored or crushed.[6]

In a contribution to this literature Daniel Kelliher has argued that even in the presence of a very strong state, peasants under certain conditions can have significant power in shaping state policy. Based on an analysis of peasant influence over the agricultural decollectivization process, Kelliher argues that three conditions must hold for the peasantry to exert influence over policy outcomes. First, the state must be devoted to a program of "balanced economic growth." This maximizes potential peasant leverage because of their crucial role in the agricultural sector. Second, there must be a source of cohesion to compensate for their lack of collective organization. In the case of the Chinese peasantry, the source of cohesion was the collective structure that peasants had as a common institutional framework. Because their individual and disparate actions were directed toward the common purpose of dismantling the commune system, they took on a combined significance that the state could not ignore. Even when these conditions hold, however, peasant action will only succeed if it does not threaten areas

6. Scott, *Weapons of the Weak.*

perceived as crucial to state survival. It must not trigger one of the state's "obsessions."[7]

If we apply these arguments to the case of birth planning, we are faced with a puzzle. The first two conditions, which Kelliher argues allowed scattered peasants to exert influence over agricultural policy, were of no help to peasants resisting the one-child policy. That leaves only the third condition. One might argue that population control was one of the state's obsessions and resistance to it constituted a security threat that the state was determined to thwart. But this, too, is problematic. Population control *was* an obsession but no more so than agricultural production. Population control was an obsession because the reform leaders, like Zhou Enlai before them, believed that comprehensive, all-around modernization could not be achieved on an acceptable timetable, indeed might not be achievable at all, unless population growth was strictly limited. Stagnant agricultural production, especially grain production, was equally an obsession because it was the root of China's poverty and backwardness in the eyes of the reformers. If anything was a threat to the fledgling regime's reform agenda it was the fear that they would not be able to demonstrate clearly and swiftly the effectiveness of reform in boosting agricultural production and peasant income.

If all three conditions hold for both cases, how then do we account for this outcome on population policy? The answer lies not in the countryside but in Beijing. Regarding agricultural policy, the reformers were uncertain in 1978 about exactly what they were doing and where they were going. Certainly they had a reform agenda, and they knew where to begin. But how far to go and on what timetable was undecided, just as their ability to consolidate power and defeat remaining leftists was uncertain. They therefore had to tread carefully on treacherous political terrain. Local cadres and peasants also had to tread carefully, but the mixed signals coming from Beijing, or the differing signals coming from the center, the province, and the county, opened a window of opportunity for those prepared to seize it. The party was temporarily divided and uncertain, allowing the peasantry room for maneuver. And when the peasant maneuvers began, there were reform-minded leaders who were ready to seize on them and use them for strategic political advantage as well as economic advantage.

Regarding population control, in contrast, there was no question about Beijing's intent, as the propaganda apparatus made endlessly clear in the late 1970s and early 1980s. The political consensus on strict birth control was strong, and population policy had been one of the few successes of the

7. Daniel Kelliher, *Peasant Power in China* (New Haven, 1992).

1970s. Peasants experiencing agricultural reform dared for a time to hope for a reversal in population policy, and their combined acts of resistance—up to and including the opposite but equally destructive acts of infanticide, on the one hand, and the murder of birth planning officials, on the other—provided ample justification to challenge the policy, should any central leaders have been so inclined. The difference in these cases does not lie in the nature or degree of peasant action; if anything, peasant action was far more widespread, dramatic, and protracted than in the case of decollectivization. The difference lies in the infertile ground on which these actions fell in Beijing. No one there seized on these peasant acts for their political advantage, for they were all convinced that a reversal or relaxation of population policy would work to China's extreme economic disadvantage. The debate among central leaders never ranged beyond the question of who should be allowed to have a second child: all rural couples, those whose first child was a daughter, or a much smaller percentage of single-child couples. With little hope of forming vertical alliances with sympathetic and influential leaders, peasants were left to their own creative devices in finding ways to avoid compliance.

Three moments capture well the power of elite cohesion to override opposition. The definitive test of the insensitivity of party leaders to peasant anger and opposition came with the 1983 sterilization campaign and its aftermath. The campaign was undertaken despite pervasive evidence of peasant resistance. It was prosecuted by resorting to the harshest of methods. The backlash from angry peasants and frustrated cadres was strong. Yet, as I have shown, this backlash might have been ignored had it not been for its significance for another issue of great import to the regime—the stability of rural party-mass relations. By late 1983, it was cadre resistance that was threatening the advance of the rural reforms, resistance that often involved a coercive and arbitrary work style that sought to stifle peasant innovation and crush, or at least control, peasant entrepreneurship. As the spiritual pollution campaign threatened to reinforce this anti-reform sentiment, Deng pushed the campaign to focus on the leftist errors of poor leadership, hostility to reform, and crude cadre work style that relied on commandism and coercion. The party rectification campaign emphasized similar themes. This made the widespread and excessive use of coercion in the 1983 sterilization campaign a contradiction and an embarrassment that had to be repudiated for the sake of maintaining a stable political climate in which to nurture reforms. Timing was also critical. By 1983, China's agricultural production was beginning to prosper, making the pressure to tamp down the population seem a bit less urgent. Once signaled by the center that extreme coercion was no longer acceptable, cadres down the line made the proper interpretation. A little breathing room had opened up in the implementation of the one-child policy; localities would be given more leeway in how they managed their population targets. And within tight limits, there was more room for debate over how strictly the rural one-child policy should be enforced. Nevertheless, national and local population plan targets remained exceedingly ambitious, and the goal was to offset the leeway given to one-daughter households by limiting and then eliminating third or higher order births.

Over the next several years this limited relaxation of enforcement showed up in increasing birthrates, as provincial and local leaders took advantage of the breathing room to test Beijing's limits. This led eventually to a renewed crackdown in 1990, despite the regime's anxieties once again about rural stability. What made that possible, above and beyond the revival of the mobilizational climate brought on by the events of June 1989, was the strong coalition of support for the crackdown. In 1990, as in 1980, reformers and conservatives agreed that the great tide of excess rural childbearing threatened to engulf China and cripple its march to modernization. On this, those who had denounced the June 4 crackdown and those who had applauded it were in basic accord.

The third case is the slow drift in the decade after 1995 toward a more moderate approach to population control, a trend that gained slow but steady ground. To the extent that this occurred, however, it was a response to two influential constituencies. The first was international, and included UN agencies and nongovernmental organizations that were working with China on population issues. Their ability to exert influence, however, was mediated by the role of domestic constituencies, especially those experts and officials in the SFPC and the China Family Planning Association who were gradually persuaded that the unintended consequences of China's population policy had become too severe to ignore. By the late 1990s, arguments that had first been made in the early 1980s could be backed by hard data to show that the one-child policy was producing serious demographic side effects—rapid aging (as the ratio of the elderly to the working-age population increased) and rising sex ratios at birth. This evidence, combined with the shift in international discourse from population control to reproductive health and woman-centered services, gave concerned experts and officials the leverage they needed to construct a credible and increasingly persuasive critique of the one-child policy. Notice, however, that to be persuasive they had to challenge the state on its own ground, arguing that the policy should be revised to prevent undesirable socioeconomic consequences that would threaten the national modernization project. Grassroots resistance was relevant only insofar as it contributed to the demographic outcomes that had to be addressed.

This case suggests, then, that the extent to which peasant resistance during the 1980s and 1990s was even modestly effective depended heavily on the degree of elite division or cohesion, and on decisions and developments in other policy arenas that had implications for the conduct or content of the birth planning campaign. Only when China moved into the post-Deng era, only when it was clear that China would reach and exceed its modernization goals for the year 2000, and only when China's economic transformation began to erode the fifty-year-old development imperative of taking grain as the "key link," making per capita grain statistics a far less significant measure of economic progress did the campaign begin to wane.

This conclusion is supported by consideration of another contribution to the literature on peasant resistance, one that emphasizes the impact of reform on the character of rural resistance. Writing the mid-1990s, Kevin O'Brien has argued that China's villagers have taken advantage of new rural conditions to press claims against local cadres. Charging that their rights have been violated, and justifying their actions on the basis of official state laws and regulations, villagers protest abuse or unlawful acts by local cadres and frequently succeed in their efforts. O'Brien called this pattern of popular protest "rightful resistance" but noted that the birth control policy was "of course impervious" to this approach.[8] He reiterates this view in 2004, noting that the widespread protests that were sweeping rural China had largely bypassed the issue of population control.[9] O'Brien explained the difficulty of challenging birth control by noting that two of the three conditions necessary to sustain rightful resistance were absent. Not only must resisters be able to draw on the rhetoric, values, and principles of the regime, they must also be successful in "locating and exploiting divisions among the powerful."[10]

In the case of birth planning, the dominant discourse on population control, which emphasized the necessity of personal sacrifice for the sake of the common good, left little room for maneuver. Though many peasants felt pressure to defer to the traditional discourse that expects women to produce sons, they found little space in the official discourse to justify disobedience. Paradoxically, this was true even after the state conceded the demand for a son, by allowing all single-daughter households to have a second child.

8. Kevin O'Brien, "Rightful Resistance," *World Politics* 49 (October 1996): 39.
9. Kevin O'Brien and Lianjiang Li, "Popular Contention and Its Impact in Rural China," *Comparative Political Studies* 38, no. 3 (April 2005): 235–59.
10. O'Brien, "Rightful Resistance," 33.

Two-daughter households pressed on for a son, and sympathetic cadres were often blind to their violations until forced to confront them by higher authorities. This never translated into a groundswell for further policy liberalization, however, much less a demand for the end of regulated childbirth. At best, provinces and localities formally or informally legislated a two-child policy, but there was never any question of accepting the legitimacy of a third child.

In an era when so many areas of the party's authority came into question, it seems puzzling that the challenge did not extend to childbearing. A great deal of careful research and interviewing will be necessary before we will have a satisfactory answer to this puzzle, but two factors, both of which focus on the hegemonic power of the state to shape belief systems, clearly played a large role. First, although the state never defeated the competing traditional discourse on childbearing, it did succeed in using its instruments of propaganda and indoctrination to persuade the peasantry that its policy was justifiable. That is, most accepted the state's economic analysis of the aggregate and individual costs of population growth (either local or national) and thus the reasonableness of population control efforts. Second, the absence of serious elite divisions limited villagers to protests over bias or unfairness in the enforcement of birth control rules, or about the use of illegal methods of enforcement.[11] This was the impetus for the attempt at collective action in Linyi city, Shandong Province, in 2005, when villagers hired a lawyer to initiate a class-action lawsuit charging local officials with illegally using coercive methods to force sterilizations and abortions.[12] It was also a secondary factor in many rural protests over excessive taxation. Birth planning violations led to exorbitant fines and penalties, which peasants saw as another way to extort money for illicit gain. There is another problem, however. Because protesters are likely to be policy violators, they find it hard to muster the moral authority that is so critical for successfully pressing claims to higher levels. They are thus unable to turn the "instruments of domination . . . to new purposes" or to exploit the notoriously fragmented Chinese political system.[13] They must content themselves instead with negotiations on the margins, ones that depend for their success on the help of grassroots cadres and do not question the state's self-proclaimed right to regulate childbearing.

This negotiating space at the local level was effectively exploited by mil-

11. To be sure, even such limited success could be very important in reducing the use of force or illegal, excessively punitive enforcement techniques.
12. Pan, "Who Controls the Family."
13. O'Brien, "Rightful Resistance," 33.

lions of rural childbearing-age couples during the last two decades of the twentieth century, and the early years of the twenty-first century. Beijing's success in imposing a dominant view of the population question, however, made it difficult to build momentum for a renegotiation of the policy itself. Cadres down the line may have resisted the implementation of the one-child policy, but they were convinced by, or resigned to, the state's arguments that China faced a population emergency that had to be addressed with emergency measures. They accepted the argument that population growth threatened development and that local as well as national modernization and prosperity could only be built on the back of strict population control. To be sure, Beijing never wholly succeeded in its quest for ideological hegemony, if by success one means the substitution of state ideology for the traditional rural childbearing calculus and the systematic modification of childbearing behavior in a manner consistent with state claims. But if by success we mean local cadres' reluctant acceptance of the state's claim to the right to engineer fertility, and thus, the absence of any direct challenge to that claim (just a multitude of behaviors designed to evade it), Beijing's record seems more impressive. State power may not be best served by passive or grudging compliance within the scope of its hegemonic claims, but it is served. And at the grassroots, where the porous boundaries of the state mean that cadres usually share more common ground with the villagers they rule than with the state they represent, it is service enough.

The Engineered Society

Population policies are placed on developing state agendas because elites decide to put them there. They are not initiatives that bubble up from below. What happens after they are placed on the agenda depends on two things—how central leaders define the relationship between development strategy and population issues and their perception of state capacity to shape population trends to fit that theory. Their theory about the interplay of population and economic development issues will define the goals of a population policy and determine the quantity and quality of resources that will be devoted to that goal. Their perception of the regime's capacity to mold population trends will determine the specific implementation strategy they employ.[14]

The powerful consensus on the theory of birth planning and the necessity

14. Jason L. Finkle and C. Alison McIntosh, "The New Politics of Population," *Population and Development Review* 20, supplemental issue (1994): 3–34.

of a one-child policy has changed the face of Chinese society, and it will continue to do so. The extent of this feat has sometimes been obscured by the other extraordinary changes that have transformed China in the past quarter century, but the 1970–2000 demographic transition reminds us that the era of social engineering is hardly behind us, certainly not in China.[15] In the West, we have preferred to see China's extremist policy of subjecting childbearing to direct state regulation as an aberration, the response of a Communist regime faced with economic scarcity and human abundance. As China was embarking on its population control project in the early 1970s, however, population anxieties in the West were at their peak, and many were prepared to tolerate coercive means to achieve the goal of zero population growth worldwide. Garret Hardin, for example, argued for the use of mutually agreed-upon coercion and for a lifeboat ethics that warned about the adverse effects on human populations of trying to save the "drowning."[16] Paul Ehrlich forecast the explosion of a "population bomb" so severe that coercive methods (from fines for excess children to mass sterilization efforts) were acceptable and even laudable.[17] The population control community warned that development in the Third World would be impeded by population growth and urged the aggressive implementation of family planning programs and contraceptive use even in the poorest parts of the world. Scholars in various disciplines stressed prioritizing family planning and mobilized research data to prove why it should be so.[18]

Surely it was no coincidence that China's turn to aggressive birth planning occurred in this international context, just as it was no coincidence that the new orthodoxy on the relationship between population and development, articulated so forcefully in Cairo in 1994 and Beijing in 1995, has encouraged Chinese policymakers and demographers to rethink the utility of birth planning methods and the assumptions on which the birth planning doctrine was based. This suggests that China's strategy for population control has been influenced by, and even situated within, a Western-led discourse on population control, and that China's birth planning program is less anomalous than we have assumed it to be.[19] Rather, the Chinese pro-

15. This point is made convincingly by Daniel Chirot in *Modern Tyrants* (New York, 1994). See also James C. Scott, *Seeing Like a State* (New Haven, 1998).

16. Hardin, "Tragedy of the Commons."

17. Ehrlich, *Population Bomb.*

18. On the emergence of this orthodox view, see Hodgson, "Orthodoxy and Revisionism," and Szreter, "Idea of Demographic Transition." See also Stanley P. Johnson, *World Population—Turning the Tide: Three Decades of Progress* (London: Graham and Trotman/Martinus Nijhoff, 1994).

19. Greenhalgh makes the same point in "Science, Modernity."

gram is better seen as a prime example of social engineering on a grand scale, a defining characteristic of twentieth-century politics.[20]

When the Chinese birth planning campaign is placed in this global context, as opposed to the more narrow ones of postrevolutionary socialism or comparisons between the Mao and post-Mao eras, it becomes easier to see the fundamentally mobilizational character of the campaign. Although Maoist-style mobilization had a distinctive intensity and longevity, it was a variation on a twentieth-century pattern of galvanizing large populations (through a range of methods) to achieve local goals or national ambitions that transform society in unpredictable ways and set in motion a series of unintentional consequences that can themselves provoke a new round of engineering.

The terrible price of China's attempt to engineer a fertility transition on the state's timetable has been chronicled in this study. As we reflect on that price, however, it is proper to reflect also on the dimensions of China's population dilemma today. For one can completely reject the Chinese policy—state regulation of childbirth—without denying the problem it was intended to address. Despite the unprecedented scope of China's birth planning program, and its success (to a degree) in lowering fertility, China's current situation is one to inspire awe in the most sober and dispassionate observer. Between 1980 and 2005, China's population grew by about three hundred million people. This increase exceeded the *total* population of every country in the world in 2005 except India and was roughly equivalent to the entire population of the United States.[21] In the 1990s, there were approximately twenty-one million births annually, with a net annual population increase of about fourteen million.[22] Even more astounding, rural surplus labor climbed to two hundred million by the year 2000 and the "floating population" of temporary migrants and their dependents exceeded one hundred million (a figure that exceeded the population size of all but the nine largest nations of the world). And finally, China also faced the problem of population aging. Persons aged sixty or older constituted 8.8 percent of the population in 1990 and 10 percent by the end of the century. Though this figure did not yet place China among those countries with the highest percentages of elderly population, the raw numbers were breathtaking, especially con-

20. On the quest for achieving utopian goals in the twentieth century, see James C. Scott, *Seeing Like a State* (New Haven: Yale University Press, 1998).

21. See Population Reference Bureau, *2000 World Population Data Sheet* (Washington, D.C., 2000).

22. For a comprehensive look at recent demographic trends, see Nancy E. Riley, "China's Population: New Trends and Challenges," *Population Bulletin* 9, no. 2 (June 2004).

sidering China's woefully inadequate pension, welfare, and health care systems. By the year 2003, the elderly population numbered approximately 130 million, on its way up to an estimated 230 million by 2020, and 410 million by 2050.[23]

The implications of these figures are staggering and raise fundamental questions about China's future. One of those questions is how the current or any successor regime will cope with a modernizing society of such vast proportions, particularly under the vexing conditions of the early twenty-first century (when information technology, globalization of markets, and communication flows conspire to make internal and external pressures on the regime particularly intense). If there is a population threshold beyond which no nation-state can function, China may be fast approaching it.

It is this frightening vision of the future that haunted China's leaders over the past several decades and led them to impose the most aggressive population control program ever devised. In their relentless obsession with population numbers, however (an obsession still evident in the exaggerated claim that the population policy prevented three hundred million excess births in the 1970–2000 period),[24] they lost sight of the consequences of their actions and now confront a young generation that has been irrevocably shaped by those very consequences.

As a result of the uneven implementation and enforcement of the one-child policy over the past two decades, China's urban homes, schools, and workplaces are now occupied by a youthful generation that is almost uniformly without siblings. These urban products of the one-child policy, who in their youth were dubbed by Chinese observers "little emperors" (both because of their privileged position as only children and because China's new prosperity was being showered upon them), are now heading for young adulthood in ever larger numbers. As they do, they are beginning to change the demographic and family landscape. They have no siblings, and their children, if they choose to have children, will lack the typical childhood universe of aunts, uncles, and cousins.

China's rural population, in contrast, has produced what we might call a "sibling generation"—that is, a generation coming of age marked by the

23. Hong Guodong, "Aging of Population: Trends and Countermeasures," *Beijing Review* (February 12–18, 1996): 12–14.

24. The claim that the population policy prevented three hundred million "excess" births is based on the untenable assumption that the high fertility rates of 1970 would have remained unchanged for thirty years, despite rapid socioeconomic changes. A prolific demographic literature suggests that this rapid development, combined with family planning education and the provision of free birth control products and services, would have produced a significant fertility decline even in the absence of mandated birth limits.

traditional presence of brothers and sisters. To be sure, this generation has fewer sisters and brothers on average than the one that preceded it, but the one-child policy notwithstanding, most teenagers and young adults in rural China still have at least one sibling, and about a third of them have two or more. This rural generation, then, will carry forward for Chinese society as a whole the more traditional, complex set of family bonds and relationships that result from multichild families.

What this will mean for China in the twenty-first century is impossible to say, since it is an unprecedented demographic phenomenon. Perhaps it will mean very little. China's one-child policy makes provision for couples who are both only children to have a second child. Whether many in this generation will make use of that provision is unclear, however. It is hard to predict how the one-child policy and the pervasive rhetoric about China's overpopulation will affect childbearing preferences among the young. Historically, fertility that slides to a very low level generally stays at a very low level, and so it is not clear that China's plunge to low urban fertility can readily be reversed. The sibling gap, then, a product of China's confident demographic engineering of the twentieth century, may prove resistant to retrofitting. The young childbearing-age couples of the early twenty-first century will live with the results of that engineering, and their views about it are likely to be shaped by their own experiences. Urbanites, who tend to blame overpopulation on the peasantry, already resent the "profligacy" of rural families and of the floating migrants they call "guerrilla birth corps" because of their violations of birth limits. Many peasants, by contrast, cling to a more traditional childbearing preference (the preferences for a son and for more than one child), yet they aspire to the living standards of prosperous, urban one-child families and resent their own second-class social status.

How these resentments will be expressed in years to come is unclear. What is clear, however, is that the generation now coming of age is a generation divided along a new fault line. Whatever the repercussions of such a divide, let us hope that the state will not be foolish enough to try to rectify it by further demographic engineering. That approach, born under Mao, perfected under Deng, and implemented at great human and social cost over the past thirty years, would be best left behind as a relic of the twentieth century.

References

Chinese Language References

Bai Yuwen and Cao Hui. "Shixing jihua shengyu zerenzhi shi gaohao jihua shengyu gongzuode zhongyao cuoshi" [Implementing a birth planning responsibility system is an important measure for doing a good job with birth planning work]. *Renkouxue kan* [Demography Journal] 12, special issue (September 15, 1982): 47–50.

"Beijing dierci renkou lilun taolunhui zhuanti zongshu" [A topical summary of Beijing municipality's Second Population Theory Conference]. *Renkou yu jingji* [Population and Economics] 3 (1980): 17.

Bo Yibo. "Ba shixian hongwei mubiao tong kongzhi renkou lianxichilai" [Integrate the realization of the great targets and the control of population]. *Renkouxue kan* 1 (1983): 11.

Cao Mingguo. "Luelun liangzhong shengchan" [A brief discussion of the two-fold character of production]. *Renkouxue kan* 4 (1981): 10–14.

———. "Qiantan liangzhong shengchan fazhan zhanlue" [A simple discussion of the development strategy of the two-fold character of production]. *Renkouxue kan* 3 (1984): 14–17.

Changling xian weishengju [Changling County Health Bureau]. "Baizheng guanxi, kejin zhize, jiji zuohao jihua shengyu jishu zhidao gongzuo" [Clarify relationships, fulfill duties, actively do a good job of birth planning technical guidance work]. *Renkouxue kan* 12, special issue (September 15, 1982): 53–55 and 50.

Chen Pixian. "Quan dang quan shehui yao wei funu yundong qianjin er fendou" [The whole party and society must move forward and struggle for the women's movement]. In *"Sida" yilai funu yundong wenxuan, 1979–1983*, edited by Zhonghua quanguo funu lianhehui, 182–86. Beijing: Zhongguo funu chubanshe, 1983.

Chen Yaozhong. "Wuzhi shengchan jueding renkou shengchan" [Material production determines population production]. *Renkouxue kan* 5 (1982): 18–20.

Chen Yun. "Bixu tichang jiezhi shengyu" [We must promote birth control]. In *Chen Yun wenxuan, 1956–1985* [Selected works of Chen Yun]. Beijing: Renmin chubanshe, 1986.

———. "Dongyuan chengshi renyuan xiaxiang" [Mobilize the urban population to go down to the countryside]. In *Chen Yun Wenxuan, 1956–1985*, 152–54.

Cheng Du. "Hubei sheng nongcun shengyulu diaocha" [An investigation of rural birth rates in Hubei Province]. *Renkou yanjiu* [Population Research] 5 (1982): 36–38 and 31.

———. "Nongcun renkoude zaishengchan—dui yige diaocha baogaode fenxi" [Rural population reproduction—analysis of an investigative report]. *Jingji yanjiu* [Economic Research] 6 (1982): 56.

Cheng Fenggao. "Zhongguo renkou xingbie jiegou" [Sex structure of China's population]. In *Zhongguo renkou nianjian, 1985* [Population Yearbook of China, 1985], edited by Zhongguo shehui kexueyuan renkou yanjiu zhongxin [Chinese Academy of Social Science Population Research Institute], 222–36. Beijing: Zhongguo shehui kexueyuan chubanshe, 1986.

Cheng Linli and Wu Yousheng. "Jiceng jihua shengyu gongzuode fancha xiaoyi yu sikao" [Contrasting effects of basic-level family planning work and reflections]. *Renkou yanjiu* 6 (1989): 53–54.

Cheng Yicai. "Chaosheng zinufei guanli tanwei" [Inquiry into the management of excess birth fines]. *Renkou yanjiu* 4 (1990): 61.

Cui Fengyuan. "Guanyu wo guo nongcun funu shengyu lu wenti" [On the question of our country's rural birth rate]. *Renkou yu jingji* 2 (1982): 50.

Cui Xianwu and Da Wangli. "Renkou chusheng man, lou bao wenti chanshengde yuanyin jichi fangfan" [Reasons for and guards against the appearance of the problem of evasion and leakage in reporting population and birth statistics]. *Renkou yu jihua shengyu* [Population and Birth Planning] 5 (1997): 31–34.

Deng Lichun and Ma Hong, eds. *Dangdai zhongguode weisheng shiye, xia* [Health work in contemporary China, vol. 2]. Beijing: Chinese Academy of Social Sciences Publishing House [Zhongguo shehui kexueyuan chubanshe], 1986.

Du Xin and Yu Changhong. "Zhongguo nongcunde shengyu dachao" [The great tide of rural childbearing in China]. *Liaowang choukan haiwaiban* [*Outlook*, oversees ed.] 43 (October 23, 1989): 19.

Fang Weizhong, ed. *Zhonghua renmin gongheguo jingji dashiji, 1949–1980* [Compilation of major economic events in the People's Republic of China]. Beijing: Zhongguo shehui kexue chubanshe, 1984.

Fu Zude and Chen Jiayuan. *Zhongguo renkou—Fujian fence* [China's population—Fujian]. Beijing: Zhongguo caijing jingji chubanshe, 1990.

Gao Chun. "Lun liangzhong shengchan zai shehui fazhanzhongde zuoyong" [The role of the theory of the two-fold character of production in social development]. *Renkouxue kan* 4 (1981): 15–19.

Gao Ersheng, Qian Hua, Li Rong, Yang Yiyong, and Yang Jian. "Jihua shengyu yaoju shoufei zhengcede tantao" [Inquiry into policies regarding expenses for contraceptives in birth planning]. *Renkou yanjiu* 21, no. 1 (January 1997).

Gao Lin, Liu Xiaolan, and Xia Ping. "Beijing shi renkou chusheng xingbiebi fenxi" [An analysis of the sex ratio at birth in Beijing]. *Renkou yanjiu* 21 (September 1997): 25–33.

Gu Baochang and Mu Guangzong. "A New Understanding of China's Population Problem." *Renkou yanjiu* 5 (1994): 2–10.

"Guanqie dangde shiyida jingshen, jinyibu kongzhi renkou zengzhangde xuanzhuan yao-dian" [Main propaganda points for carrying out the spirit of the Twelfth Party Congress and going a step further to control population growth]. In *"Sida" yilai funu yundong wenxuan, 1979–1983*, edited by Zhonghua quanguo funu lianhehui, 159–65. Beijing: Zhongguo funu chubanshe, 1983.

"Guanyu kaizhan quanguo jihua shengyu xuanzhuan huodongde tongzhi" [Circular on carrying out national birth planning propaganda activities]. In *"Sida" yilai funu yundong wenxuan, 1979–1983*, edited by Zhonghua quanguo funu lianhehui, 156–58. Beijing: Zhongguo funu chubanshe, 1983.

Guojia jihua shengyu weiyuanhui xuanchuan jiaoyusi, Zhonggong zhongyang dangxiao jihua shengyu weiyuanhui, ed. [State Family Planning Commission Propaganda and Education Department, Central Party School Birth Planning Committee]. *Shiyizhou sanzhong quanhui yilai jihua shengyu zhongyao wenjian xuanpian* [Selected important birth planning documents since the Third Plenum of the Eleventh Central Committee]. Beijing: Zhonggong zhongyang dangxiao chubanshe, 1989.

"Hebei sheng renmin zhengfu guanyu gaijin caizheng guanli tizhide jixiang guiding" [Some regulations of the Hebei provincial government concerning improving the financial management system]. In *Hebei jingji tongji nianjian, 1987* [Hebei economic statistical yearbook, 1987]. Beijing: Zhongguo tongji chubanshe, 1987, 488.

Henan sheng nongcun chouyang diaochadui nongjingchu [Hunan Province Rural Survey Team, Rural Economy Office]. "Yao duju chao jihua shengyude loudong" [Loopholes for extra-plan births must be stopped up]. *Nongcun gongzuo tongxun* [Rural Work Bulletin] 5 (1988): 46.

Hu Huanyong, ed. *Zhongguo renkou, Shanghai fence* [Population of China, Shanghai volume]. Beijing: Zhongguo caizheng jingji chubanshe, 1987.

Hu Zhongsheng. "Jiushijiu lie jihuawai chusheng diaocha fenxi" [An investigation of ninety-nine cases of extra-plan births]. *Xibei renkou* [Northwest Population] 3 (1987): 14.

"Huanggang xian shi zemyang zhuajin jihua shengyu gongzuode?" [How did Huanggang County grasp well its birth planning work?]. *Hubei ribao* (June 23, 1979), 3.

Hubei sheng jihua shengyu weiyuanhui. *Jihua shengyu zhengce fagui ziliao xuanpian, 1983–1997* [Selected regulations and materials on birth planning policy]. Wuhan: Hubei sheng jihua shengyu weiyuanhui, 1997.

Jiang Su and Yang Shounian. "'Jizi shengyu' buzu qu" [Do not permit the pursuit of fund-raising births]. *Nongcun gongzuo tongxun* 4 (1988), 25.

"Jianguo sanshiwunianlai renkou huodong dashiji" [A chronology of population activities in the thirty-five years since the establishment of the country]. In *Zhongguo renkou nianjian, 1985*, 1264–88.

Jin Chao. "Shixing jihua shengyu, youxiaode kongzhi renkou cengzhang" [Carry out birth planning, effectively control population increase]. *Renkou yu jingji* [Population and Economics, Jilin University] 2 (1980).

Kang Keqing. "Weihu funu ertong hefa quanyi shi fuliande guangrong zhize" [Protecting the legal rights and interests of women and infants is the glorious responsibility of the Women's Federation]. In *"Sida" yilai funu yundong wenxuan, 1979–1983*, edited by Zhonghua quanguo funu lianhehui, 337–39. Beijing: Zhongguo funu chubanshe, 1983.

Li Honggui. "Zhongguode renkou zhengce" [China's population policy]. *Zhongguo renkou nianjian, 1985*, 215–21.

Li Peng. "Zai tingchu quanguo jihua shengyu weiyuanhui zhuren huiyi huibao shide jianghua" [Talk while listening to the report of the national meeting of directors of family planning commissions]. In *Shiyizhou sanzhong quanhui yilai jihua shengyu zhongyao wenjian xuanpian*, edited by Guojia jihua shengyu weiyuanhui xuanchuan jiaoyusi, Zhonggong zhongyang dangxiao jihua shengyu weiyuanhui, 62. Beijing: Zhonggong zhongyang dangxiao chubanshe, 1989.

Li Sheng. "Jihua shengyu yu nongye xiandaihua" [Birth planning and rural modernization]. *Hubei ribao* (June 19, 1978), 3.

Liang Jimin and Peng Zhiliang. "Quanmian junquede lijie he zhixing dangde jihua shengyu fangzhen zhengce" [Understand and implement the party's family planning policies in an all-around and accurate way]. *Renkou yanjiu* 3 (1984): 11–15.

Liang Naizhong. "Nongye shengchan zerenzhi yu renkou kongzhi" [The agricultural production responsibility system and population control]. *Xibei renkou* 2 (1982): 3.

Liang Wenda. "Makesi zhuyide 'liangzhong shengchan' guan shi jihua shengyu gongzuode lilun jichu" [Marxism's concept of "two kinds of production" is the theoretical basis of birth planning work]. *Renkou yanjiu* 3 (1980).

Liang Zhongtang. "Guanyu ershi shiji mo zhongguo dalu renkou zongliang he funu shengyulu shuipingde yanjiu" [Research on population size and female fertility rates on the Chinese mainland at the end of the twentieth century]. *Shengchanli yanjiu* [Productivity Research] 5 (2005): 147–58.

Liu Haiquan. "Cong guoqing chufa, ba kongzhi renkou zengzhangde zhongdian fang zai nongcun" [Based on our country's situation, the focus of controlling population growth should be the countryside]. *Renkou yanjiu* 6 (1983): 11.

Liu Hongkang, ed. *Zhongguo renkou, Sichuan fence* [Population of China, Sichuan volume]. Beijing: Zhongguo caizheng jingji chubanshe, 1988.

Liu Shaoqi. "Tichang jieyu" [Promote birth control]. In *Zhongguo renkou nianjian, 1985* [Population Yearbook of China, 1985], edited by Zhongguo shehui kexueyuan renkou yanjiu zhongxin [Population Research Center of the Chinese Academy of Social Sciences], 4–5. Beijing: Zhongguo shehui kexueyuan chubanshe, 1985.

Liu Zheng. "Renkou xiandaihua yu youxian fazhan jiaoyu" [Population modernization and giving priority to education]. *Renkou yanjiu* 2 (1994): 1–10.

———. "Renkou zai shehui fazhanzhongde zuoyong" [The role of population in social development]. *Renkou yanjiu* 5 (1982): 6–7.

———. *Zhongguode renkou* [China's population]. Beijing: Renkou chubanshe, 1982.

Liu Zheng, Wu Cangping, and Lin Fude. "Dui kongzhi woguo renkou zengzhangde wudian jianyi" [Five suggestions on the control of our country's population growth]. *Renkou yanjiu* 3 (1980): 5.

Lu Xueyi and Zhang Houyi. "Peasant Diversification, Problems, Remedies." *Nongye jingji wenti* 1 (1990): 16–21.

Ma Qibin, Chen Wen Wu, Lin Yunhui, Cong Jin, Wang Nianyi, Jiang Tianrong, and Bu Weihua, eds. *Zhongguo gongchandang zhizheng sishinian, 1949–1989* [Forty years of rule of the Chinese Communist Party]. Beijing: Zhonggong dangshi ziliat chubanshe, 1990.

Mao Kuangsheng, ed. *Zhongguo renkou, Hunan fence* [Population of China, Hunan volume]. Beijing: Zhongguo caizheng jingji chubanshe, 1987.

Mao She and Yu Jia. "Xiang (zhen) jihua shengyu ganbu peibei ying shixing xuyao yu jinggan tongyide yuanze" [Township and town governments should follow the principle of matching needs with strong capabilities in allocating birth planning cadres]. *Renkou yanjiu* 6 (1993): 54–55.

Mu Guangsong. "Jinnian lai zhongguo chusheng xingbie bi shanggao pian gao xian-xiangde lilun jieshi" [A theoretical explanation of the elevation and deviation in recent years of the sex ratio at birth]. *Renkou yu jingji* 88, no. 1 (1995): 48–51.

Pan Zhifu, Zhang Zhendong, Chen Yongxiao, and Lu Zuo. *Zhongguo renkou—Guizhou fence* [China's population—Guizhou]. Beijing: Zhongguo caijing yu jingji chubanshe, 1988.

Panshi xian yantongshan xiang jishengban [Panshi county yantongshan township birth planning office]. "Women shi zemyang guanhao, yonghao 'sishu' fei he chaoshengfeide" [How we can manage well and use well the fees from the "four procedures" and excess births]. *Renkouxue kan* 2 (1985): 51–52 and 55.

Peng Peiyun. "Zai quanguo jihua shengyu weiyuanhui zhuren huiyi bimushide jianghua" [Speech at the close of the national meeting of directors of family planning commissions]. In *Shiyizhou sanzhong quanhui yilai jihua shengyu zhongyao wenjian xuanpian,* edited by Guojia jihua shengyu weiyuanhui xuanchuan jiaoyusi, Zhonggong zhongyang dangxiao jihua shengyu weiyuanhui, 108–20. Beijing: Zhonggong zhongyang dangxiao chubanshe, 1989.

Peng Peiyun, ed. *Zhongguo jihua shengyu quanshu* [Encyclopedia of birth planning in China]. Beijing: Zhongguo renkou chubanshe, 1996.

Peng Zhen. "Guanyu zhonghua renmin gongheguo xianfa xingai caoande baogao" [Report on the revised draft Constitution of the People's Republic of China]. In *Zhonggua renmin gongheguo xianfa, 1982* [Constitution of the People's Republic of China, 1982]. Beijing: Renmin chubanshe, 1982.

Qian Xinzhong. "Nuli kaichuang jihua shengyu xuanchuan jiaoyu gongzuo xin jumina" [Make great efforts to initiate the new phase of birth planning propaganda and education work]. *Renkouxue kan* 1 (1983): 9.

Qiao Shaoqun. "Gaoxiao disici quanguo renkou pucha siliao fenxi xueshu taolunhui zongshu" [Summary of the scholarly discussion conference of colleges and universities on the Fourth National Census]. *Renkou yanjiu* 1 (1992): 54.

"Quanguo fulian disizhou diqici changwei kuoda huiyi guanyu 'Renzhen guanqie zhongyang zhishi jingshen, jianjue weihu funu ertong hefa quanyi' de jueyi" [Decision of the National Women's Federation at the Fourth Plenum of the Seventh Enlarged Meeting of the Standing Committee on "Enthusiastically carrying out the spirit of the Central Committee directive on supporting and protecting the legal rights and interests of women and children"]. In *"Sida" yilai funu yundong wenxuan, 1979–1983,* edited by Zhonghua quanguo funu lianhehui, 340–42. Beijing: Zhongguo funu chubanshe, 1983.

"Quanguo fulian shujichu wei funu jiuye wenti gei Wan Li, Peng Chong tongzhide xin (gaoyao)" [Letter to Comrades Wan Li and Peng Chong from the Secretariat of the National Women's Federation (Summary)]. In *"Sida" yilai funu yundong wenxuan, 1979–1983,* edited by Zhonghua quanguo funu lianhehui, 86–89. Beijing: Zhongguo funu chubanshe, 1983.

"Renkou kongzhi yu renkou zhengce zhong ruogan wenti" [Some questions on population control and population policy]. In Ma Bin, *Lun zhongguo renkou wenti* [Discussion of China's population problem], 2. Beijing: Zhongguo guoji guangbo chubanshe, 1987.

Shen Yimin. "Disici quanguo renkou pucha jige zhuyao shuzhude kekaoxing pingjia" [Comments on the reliability of several important statistics in the Fourth National Census]. *Renkou yanjiu* 1 (1992): 15–16.

Shi Chengli. "Woguo jihua shengyu gongzuode fenqi" [Stages of our country's birth planning work]. *Xibei renkou* [Northwest Population] 1 (1988): 31.

————. *Zhongguo jihua shengyu huodong shi* [A history of birth planning activities in China]. Urumuchi: Xinjiang People's Publishing House, 1988.

Siping shiwei xuanchuanbu, Siping renda changwei wenjiaoban, Siping shi weishengju, Siping shi jishengban [Siping City Party Propaganda Bureau, Culture and Education Office of the Standing Committee of the Siping City People's Congress]. "Shixing liangzhong shengchan 'shuangbao' zhi, jihua shengyu gongzuo jian chengxiao" [Carrying out the "dual contract" system of two kinds of production is effective for birth planning work]. *Renkouxue kan* 4 (1983): 57–58.

Song Fulin. "Wo guo renkou lilun wenti taolun" [A general summary of questions and discussions on our country's population theory]. *Renkouxue kan* 2 (1985): 39–44.

Song Yuanzhu, Shi Yulin, and Zhang Guichao. "Funu shengyu taici zhuangquang" [Situation with women's birth order]. In *Quanguo qianfenzhiyi renkou shengyulu chouyang diaocha fenxi* [Analysis of the national one-per-thousand population fertility survey], 56. Beijing: *Renkou yu jingji* chubanshe, 1983.

Su Ping. "Wo guo chusheng yinger xingbie wenti tanlun" [Investigation into the question of our country's birth and infant sex ratio]. *Renkou yanjiu* 1 (1993): 6–13.

Sun Jingzhi. "Jiejue zhongguo renkou wentide genben tujing" [The basic way to solve China's population problem]. *Renkou yu jingji* 1 (1980): 6.

Sun Muhan. "Kai jihua shengyu gongzuo xin jumiande yijian" [Suggestions for a new breakthrough in birth planning work]. *Renkouxue kan* 1 (1983): 22.

Tang Chongtai, ed. *Zhongguo renkou—Hubei fence* [China's Population—Hubei]. Beijing: Zhongguo caijing yu jingji chubanshe, 1988.

Wan Li. "Zai quanguo nongcun gongzuo huiyishangde jianghua" [Speech at the National Rural Work Conference]. In *1984 zhongguo jingji nianjian* [Yearbook of China's Economy], 2: 44–52.

Wan Qiang. "Guanyu 'qiwu' renkou jihua zhixing qingkuangde fenxi" [An analysis of the situation concerning the implementation of the "seventh five-year-plan" population plan]. *Zhongguo jihua shengyu nianjian, 1991*, 257–58.

Wang Linchun. "Jihua shengyu tongji manbao xianxiang qianxi" [A brief analysis of the phenomenon of false reporting of birth planning statistics]. *Renkou yu jingji* 3 (1995): 25.

Wang Mingyuan, ed. *Zhongguo renkou, Hebei fence* [Population of China, Hebei volume]. Beijing: Zhongguo caizheng jingji chubanshe, 1987.

Wang Peishu. "Wanshan shengyu zhengce, kaihao 'xiao kouzi' de guanjian shi duzhu 'da kouzi' " [The key to perfecting birth policy and "opening a small hole" is stopping up the "big hole"]. *Xibei renkou* 3 (1987): 20–21.

Wang Shengbing. "Guanyu 'liangzhong shengchan' de jige lilun wenti" [Several discussion questions on the theory of "the two-fold character of production"]. *Renkouxue kan* 5 (1982).

Wang Shengduo. "Wei 'renkou jueding lun' zhengming" [A rectification of name for the "theory of population determinism"]. *Renkouxue kan* 5 (1982): 21–24.

Wang Wei. "Jihua shengyu gongzuo qingkuang" [Situation in family planning work]. In *Shiyizhou sanzhong quanhui yilai jihua shengyu zhongyao wenjian xuanpian*, edited by Guojia jihua shengyu weiyuanhui xuanchuan jiaoyusi, Zhonggong zhongyang dangxiao jihua shengyu weiyuanhui, 100. Beijing: Zhonggong zhongyang dangxiao chubanshe, 1989.

————. "Jixu tongyi zixiang, jingxin zhidao zhongyang qihao wenjiande quanmian guanqie luoshi" [Continue to unify thinking, carefully guide the complete implementation of Central Document 7]. *Renkou yu jingji* 1 (1985): 3–6 and 19.

——. "Zai 'qiwu' qijian ba jihua shengyu gongzuo zhuade geng jin geng hao" [Grasp birth planning work more firmly and better during the "seventh five-year-plan" period]. In *Shiyizhou sanzhong quanhui yilai jihua shengyu zhongyao wenjian xuanpian,* edited by Guojia jihua shengyu weiyuanhui xuanchuan jiaoyusi, Zhonggong zhongyang dangxiao jihua shengyu weiyuanhui, 68. Beijing: Zhonggong zhongyang dangxiao chubanshe, 1989.

Wang Xu et al. "Renkou wenti yao zhuajin zai zhuajin" [The population problem must be grasped more and more firmly]. *Liaowang* 28 (July 13, 1987): 14–15.

Wang Yaqin. "Nongcun shixing shengchan zerenzhi zhihou jihua shengyu gongzuo yinggai zemma ban?" [After carrying out the production responsibility system in the countryside, how should birth planning work be handled?]. *Renkouxue kan* 12, special issue (September 15, 1982): 51–52.

Wang Zhenyao. "Nongcun jiceng zhengquande zhineng fenhua taishi yu zhengce xuanzu." *Zhengzhixue yanjiu* [Political Research] 4 (1987): 29–33.

"Weishenghu guanyu rengong liuchan ji jucyu shoushude tongzhi" [Ministry of Health directive on abortion and sterilization procedures] (March 30, 1956), and "Weishengbu guanyu biyun gongzuode zhibiao" [Ministry of Health directive on contraceptive work] (August 6, 1956). *Zhongguo renkou nianjian, 1985,* 6–7.

Wen Yingqian. "Ye tan gongyoude renkou guilu" [Another discussion of the universal law of population]. *Renkouxue kan* 5 (1982): 9–13.

Wen Zhifu and Wei Cen. "Jianguo yilai funude wanhunlu he zaohunlu dongtai fenxi" [An analysis of trends in the rate of late marriage and early marriage for women since the founding of the country]. In *Quanguo qianfenzhiyi renkou shengyulu chouyang diaocha fenxi* [Analysis of the national one-per-thousand population fertility survey], 126. Beijing: *Renkou yu jingji chubanshe,* 1983.

[Working Group on Future Population Development and Fertility Policy in China, State Family Planning Commission]. "Zhongguo molai renkou fazhan yu shengyu zhengce yanjiu" [Future population development and fertility policy in China]. *Renkou yanjiu* 24, no. 3 (May 2000): 18–34.

Xi Jianwei. "Dui bianzhi 'qiwu' renkou jihuade chubu shexiang" [Initial thoughts on the formulation of the "seventh five-year-plan" population plan]. *Renkou yanjiu* 4 (1985): 3–8.

Xiao Wencheng, Li Menghua, and Wang Liying. "Wushi niandai yilai funu zonghe shengyulude bianhua" [Changes in the total fertility rate of women since the 1950s]. In *Quanguo qianfenzhiyi renkou shengyulu chouyang diaocha fenxi* [Analysis of the national one-per-thousand population fertility survey], 54. Beijing: *Renkou yu jingji chubanshe,* 1983.

Xie Lianhui. " 'Zhejiang cun' zhuke hude shengyu guan" [The views of host and guest households in "Zhejiang Village"]. *Renmin ribao,* November 30, 1988, 3.

Xin Dan and Peng Zhiliang. "Sichuan sheng peng xian shixing jieyu jishu zerenzhide jiangyan" [The experience of Peng County, Sichuan Province, in carrying out the birth control technical responsibility system]. *Renkou yanjiu* 6 (1982): 29–31.

Xing Peng. "Shifang xian 1981 nian yi wu duotai shengyu" [No multiple births in Shifang County in 1981]. *Renkou yanjiu* 6 (1982): 31.

Yang Deqing, Su Zhenyu, Liu Yuangu, eds. *Jihua shengyu xue* [Birth planning studies]. Nanjing: Jiangsu renmin chubanshe, 1984.

Yang Kuixue, Liang Jimin, and Zhang Fan, eds. *Zhongguo renkou yu jihua shengyu dashi yaolan* [Overview of main events in population and birth planning in China]. Beijing: Zhongguo renkou chubanshe, 2001.

Yang Xudong. "Woguo nongcun jihua shengyu gongzuo zhong xuyao yanjiu jiejuede jige wenti" [Several issues in need of resolution in our country's rural birth planning work]. *Renkou yanjiu* 6 (1989): 62–64.

"Yao juyi fangzhi xifang sichan jieji renkou lilun dui womende yinxiang" [We must pay attention to and guard against the influence of Western bourgeois population theory on us]. *Jiankang bao, jihua shengyu ban* [Health News, birth planning ed.], November 1, 1983.

Yao Minhua and Li Shenye. "Renkou yu fazhan" [Population and development]. *Zhongguo renkou bao* [China Population News] (February 16, 1990): 3.

Yu Gang. "1997 nian woguo renkou jixu pingwen cengzhang" [Our country's population continued to steadily increase in 1997]. In *1998 Zhongguo renkou tongji nianjian* [China Population Statistical Yearbook], 439. Beijing: Guojia tongji chubanshe, 1999.

Yuan Huarong and Wu Yuping. "Lun renkou, tizhi he jiezhi shengyu" [On population, systems, and birth control]. *Renkou yu jingji* 5 (1994): 40–43.

Zeng Yi. "Wo guo 1991–1992 nian shengyu lu shifou da da diyu daiti shuiping?" [Has our country's 1991–1992 fertility rate dropped far below replacement level?]. *Renkou yanjiu* 19, no. 3 (1995): 7–14.

Zhang Guangzhao and Yang Zhiheng. "Zai lun liangzhong shengchan tong shi lishi fazhanzhongde juedingxing yinsu" [Another opinion that the two forms of production are the determining factors in historical development]. *Xibei renkou* 3 (1982): 23–29.

Zhang Guangzu. "Liangzhong shengchan yu 'wanquan jingji xunhuan'" [The two-fold character of production and the "complete economic cycle"]. *Renkouxue kan* 5 (1982): 14–17.

Zhang Huaiyu. "Lun renkou yu jingji jianji dangqian nongcun renkou kongzhi wenti" [A discussion of population and economics concurrently as the current problem of rural population control]. *Jingji yanjiu* 12 (1981): 37.

Zhang Huaiyu and Dong Shigui. "Shixing nongye shengchan zerenzhi dui kongzhi nongcun renkou tichude xin keti" [New problems in the control of population in the rural areas brought about by the implementation of agricultural production responsibility systems]. *Renkou yanjiu* 1 (1982): 31–34.

Zhang Li. "Liangzhong shengchan lilunde taolun zongshu" [Summary discussion of the theory of the two-fold character of production]. *Renkou yanjiu* 5 (1982): 2–5.

Zhang Wen and Xin Hai. "Nongye baochan daozu hou jihua shengyu gongzuo ruhe kaizhan" [How to undertake birth planning work after implementation of group quotas in agricultural production]. In *Zhongguo renkou kexue lunji* [Symposium of Chinese Population Science], edited by Beijing jingji xueyuan renkou jingji yanjiusuo [Population and economics research group, Beijing Academy of Economics], 189. Beijing: Zhongguo xueshu chubanshe, 1981.

Zhang Xinxia. "Dusheng zinu hu ye you tiaojian fufuqilai" [Single-child households also have the conditions for becoming rich]. *Renkou yanjiu* 5 (1982): 32–33 and 43.

Zhang Yongchen and Cao Jingchun. "Shengchan zerenzhi yu kongzhi nongcun renkou zengzhang [The production responsibility system and the control of rural population increase]. *Renkou yu jingji* 1 (1982): 13.

Zhen Huaixin. "Qiongkun shanqu jihua shengyu ruhe zuochu digu" [How to get through the deep valley of birth planning work in poor mountain districts]. *Zhongguo renkou bao* (February 16, 1990): 3.

Zheng Yuling, Gao Benghua, Cheng Fenghou, and Yang Guangrui. *Zhongguo renkou—Anhui fence* [China's population—Anhui]. Beijing: Zhongguo caijing jingji chubanshe, 1987.

"Zhizhi silei pohuai jihua shengyu gongzuode xingwei" [Stop four kinds of behavior that wreck birth planning work]. *Jiankang bao, jihua shengyu ban* [Health News, birth planning ed.], March 1, 1985.

Zhonggong guojia jihua shengyu weiyuanhui dangzu, "Guanyu jihua shengyu gongzuo qingkuangde huibao" [Report on the situation in birth planning work], in *Jihua shengyu zhongyao wenjian*.

Zhonggong hebei shengwei yanjiushi nongcunchu [Hebei Province CCP Committee Research Institute, Rural Office]. "Fangshou rang xiang zhengfu dang jiali cai" [Let go and allow township governments to set up their own finances]. *Nongcun gongzuo tongxun* 6 (1986): 32–33.

"Zhonggong zhongyang guanyu nongcun renmin gongshe fenpei wentide zhishi" [Central Committee directive on the question of distribution in rural people's communes]. *Zhonggong yanjiu* [Studies in Chinese Communism] 6, no. 9 (September 1972): 98–104.

"Zhonggong zhongyang, guowuyuan guanyu 1984 nian nongcun gongzuode tongzhi" [Central Committee and State Council directive on 1984 rural work]. In *Xiangcun gongzuo shouce* [Handbook on township and village work], 353–65. Beijing: Nongcun maiwu chubanshe, 1990.

"Zhonggong zhongyang, guowuyuan guanyu jinyibu huoyue nongcun jingjide shixiang zhengce" [Central Committee, State Council directive on ten policies to further enliven the rural economy]. *Xinhua yuebao* [New China Weekly] 3 (1985): 52–55.

"Zhonggong zhongyang, guowuyuan guanyu jinyibu zuohao jihua shengyu gongzuode zhishi" [Central Committee and State Council directive on further improving birth planning work]. In *Shiyizhou sanzhong quanhui yilai jihua shengyu zhongyao wenjian xuanpian*, edited by Guojia jihua shengyu weiyuanhui xuanchuan jiaoyusi, Zhonggong zhongyang dangxiao jihua shengyu weiyuanhui, 8–14. Beijing: Zhonggong zhongyang dangxiao chubanshe, 1989.

"Zhonggong zhongyang pizhuan 'guanyu liu wu qijian jihua shengyu gongzuo qingkuang he qi wu qijian gongzuo yijiande baogao' de tongzhi" [CCP Central Committee directive approving the "Report on the conditions of birth planning work during the sixth Five-Year-Plan period and recommendations on work during the seventh Five-Year Plan"]. In *Shiyi zhou sanzhong quanhui yilai jihua shengyu zhongyao wenjian xuanbian* [Selection of important documents on birth planning since the Third Plenum of the Eleventh CCP Central Committee], 27–35. Beijing: Zhongyang dangxiao chubanshe, 1989.

Zhongguo jiceng zhengquan jianshe yanjiuhui, Zhongguo jigou yu pianzhi zazhishe [Research Committee on the Construction of Grassroots Political Power in China], eds. *Shixian yu sikao: Quanguo nongcun jiceng zhengquan jianshe lilun yantaohui wenxuan* [Achievements and reflections: Selections from the National Theory and Discussion Conference on the Construction of Rural Basic-Level Governance]. Luoyang: Liaoning daxue chubanshe, 1989.

Zhongguo jihua shengyu nianjian, 1991 [China Family Planning Yearbook]. Beijing: Kexue puji chubanshe, 1992.

Zhongguo jihua shengyu nianjian, 2002. [China Family Planning Yearbook]. Beijing: Kexue puji chubanshe, 2003.

Zhongguo jihua shengyu nianjian, 2003. [China Family Planning Yearbook]. Beijing: Kexue puji chubanshe, 2004.

Zhongguo nongye nianjian, 1985 [Agricultural Yearbook of China, 1985]. Beijing: Nongye chubanshe, 1986.

Zhongguo nongye nianjian, 1986 [Agricultural Yearbook of China]. Beijing: Nongye chubanshe, 1987.

Zhongguo renkou—Anhui [China's Population—Anhui]. Beijing: Zhongguo caizheng jingji chubanshe, 1987.

Zhongguo renkou—Fujian [China's Population—Fujian]. Beijing: Zhongguo caizheng jingji chubanshe, 1988.

Zhongguo renkou—Guangdong [China's Population—Guangdong]. Beijing: Zhongguo caizheng jingji chubanshe, 1988.

Zhongguo renkou—Guizhou [China's Population—Guizhou]. Beijing: Zhongguo caizheng jingji chubanshe, 1988.

Zhongguo renkou—Hubei [China's Population—Hubei]. Beijing: Zhongguo caizheng jingji chubanshe, 1988.

Zhongguo renkou—Liaoning [China's Population—Liaoning]. Beijing: Zhongguo caizheng jingji chubanshe, 1988.

Zhongguo renkou—Qinghai [China's Population—Qinghai]. Beijing: Zhongguo caizheng jingji chubanshe, 1988.

Zhongguo renkou—Shanxi [China's Population—Shanxi]. Beijing: Zhongguo caizheng jingji chubanshe, 1988.

Zhongguo renkou yu jihua shengyu nianjian, 2004. [China Population and Family Planning Yearbook]. Beijing: Kexue puji chubanshe, 2005.

"Zhongguo renminde jihua shengyu gongzuo burong waiqu" [Misrepresentation of China's birth planning work will not be tolerated]. In *Jiankang bao, jihua shengyu ban* [Health News, birth planning ed.], May 3, 1983.

Zhongguo tongji nianjian, 1990 [China Statistical Yearbook]. Beijing: Guojia tongji chubanshe, 1991.

Zhongguo tongji nianjian, 2003 [China Statistical Yearbook]. Beijing: Guojia tongji chubanshe, 2004.

Zhonghua quanguo funu lianhehui [All-China Women's Federation], ed. *"Sida" yilai funu yundong wenxuan, 1979–1983* [Selected articles on the women's movement since the Fourth National People's Congress]. Beijing: Zhongguo funu chubanshe, 1983.

"Zhonghua renmin gongheguo hukou dengji tiaolie" [Regulations on household registration of the People's Republic of China]. *Zhongguo renkou nianjian, 1985,* 83–84.

" 'Zhonghua renmin gongheguo yu jihua shengyu fa' youguan mingci jiejue" [An explanation of relevant terms in the "Population and Family Planning Law of the People's Republic of China"]. In Guojia jihua shengyu weiyuanhui, *Zhongguo jihua shengyu nianjian, 2002,* 657–62. Beijing: Kexue puji chubanshe, 2002.

Zhou Enlai. "Guanyu fazhan guomin jingjide disange wunian jihuade jianshede baogao" [Report on the second five-year construction plan for the development of the national economy]. September 27, 1956. In *Zhongguo renkou nianjian, 1985,* 9.

——. "Jingji jianshede jige fangzhenxing wenti" [Several policy questions related to economic construction]. In *Zhou Enlai xuanji, xia* [Selected works of Zhou Enlai, vol. 2]. Beijing: Renmin chubanshe, 1984, 229–38.

Zhu Chuzhu, Liang Jizhong, Zhang Yuanguang, Hou Fuxiang, and Liang Qianzhong. *Zhongguo renkou—Shanxi fence* [China's population—Shanxi]. Beijing: Zhongguo caijing jingji chubanshe, 1988.

Zhu Mian. "Nongye shengchan zerenzhi yu nongcunde jihua shengyu gongzuo" [The rural production responsibility system and rural birth planning work]. *Renkou yanjiu* 5 (1982): 27.

Zhu Yuncheng, ed. *Zhongguo renkou, Guangdong fence* [Population of China, Guangdong volume]. Beijing: Zhongguo caizheng jingji chubanshe, 1988.

Zong Xin and Bai Jian. "Shilun nongcun shengchan zerenzhi yu jihua shengyu" [An exploratory discussion of the agricultural production responsibility system and birth planning]. *Renkouxue kan* 1 (1982): 10.

English Language References

Aird, John S. "Population Policy and Demographic Prospects in the People's Republic of China." In *People's Republic of China: An Economic Assessment*, edited by the Joint Economic Committee, Congress of the United States. Washington, D.C.: U.S. Government Printing Office, 1972, 220–331.

Anagnost, Ann. "A Surfeit of Bodies: Population and the Rationality of the State in Post-Mao China." In *Conceiving the New World Order: The Global Politics of Reproduction,* edited by Faye D. Ginsberg and Rayna Rapp, 22–41. Berkeley: University of California Press, 1995.

Apter, David. *The Politics of Modernization.* Chicago: University of Chicago Press, 1965.

Arnold, Fred, and Liu Zhaoxiang. "Sex Preference, Fertility, and Family Planning in China." *Population and Development Review* 12, no. 2 (June 1986): 221–46.

Ash, Robert F. "The Evolution of Agricultural Policy." *China Quarterly* 116 (December 1988): 529–55.

Ashton, Basil, Kenneth Hill, Alan Piazza, and Robin Zeitz. "Famine in China, 1958–61." *Population and Development Review* 10, no. 4 (December 1984): 613–45.

Bachman, David. *Bureaucracy, Economy and Leadership in China: The Institutional Origins of the Great Leap Forward.* Cambridge: Cambridge University Press, 1991.

Banister, Judith. *China's Changing Population.* Stanford: Stanford University Press, 1987.

——. "Population Changes and the Economy." In *China's Economic Dilemmas in the 1990s: The Problems of Reforms, Modernization and Interdependence*, vol. 1, edited by Joint Economic Committee, U.S. Congress. Washington, D.C.: U.S. Government Printing Office, 1991.

——. "Shortage of Girls in China Today." *Journal of Population Research* 21, no. 1 (May 2004): 19–45.

Barlow, Tani E., with Gary J. Bjorge, eds. *I Myself Am a Woman: Selected Writings of Ding Ling.* Boston: Beacon Press, 1989.

Barnett, A. Doak. *Cadres, Bureaucracy, and Political Power in Communist China.* New York: Columbia University Press, 1967.

Baum, Richard. "The Road to Tiananmen: Chinese Politics in the 1980s." In *The Politics of China, 1949–1989*, edited by Roderick MacFarquhar, 351–60. Cambridge: Cambridge University Press, 1993.

Baum, Richard, and Frederick Teiwes. *Ssu-Ch'ing: The Socialist Education Movement of 1962–1966.* Berkeley: University of California, Center for Chinese Studies, 1968.

Beck, Neil J. "What Does SARS Mean for China?" *NBR Briefing: Policy Report No. 13* (National Bureau of Asian Research). May 2003; http://www.nbr.org.

Becker, Jasper. *Hungry Ghosts: Mao's Secret Famine.* New York: Henry Holt, 1996.

Beech, Hannah. "Enemies of the State?: How Local Officials in China Launched a Brutal Campaign of Forced Sterilizations and Abortions." *Time Magazine*, September 19, 2005.

Bennett, Gordon A. *Yundong: Mass Campaigns in Chinese Communist Leadership.* Berkeley: University of California, Center for Chinese Studies, 1976.

Bernstein, Thomas P. "Cadre and Peasant Behavior under Conditions of Insecurity and Deprivation: The Grain Supply Crisis of the Spring of 1955." In *Chinese Communist Politics in Action,* edited by A. Doak Barnett, 365–99. Seattle: University of Washington Press, 1969.

———. "The Limits of Rural Political Reform." In *Chinese Politics from Mao to Deng,* edited by Victor C. Falkenheim and Ilpyong J. Kim, 299–330. New York: Paragon House, 1989.

———. "Reforming China's Agriculture." Paper prepared for the conference, "To Reform the Chinese Political Order," Harwichport, MA (June 18–23), 1984.

———. *Up to the Mountains and Down to the Villages: The Transfer of Youth from Urban to Rural China.* New Haven: Yale University Press, 1977.

Bernstein, Thomas P., and Lu Xiaobo. "Taxation without Representation: Peasants, the Central, and the Local States in Reform China." *China Quarterly* 163 (September 2000): 742–63.

———. *Taxation without Representation in Contemporary Rural China.* Cambridge: Cambridge University Press, 2001.

Bongaarts, John, and Susan Greenhalgh. "An Alternative to the One-Child Policy in China." *Population and Development Review* 11, no. 4 (December 1985): 585–617.

Burns, John P. "Local Cadre Accommodation to the 'Responsibility System' in Rural China." *Pacific Affairs* 58, no. 4 (Winter 1985–86): 614–19.

Butler, Steven Bailey. "Conflict and Decision-Making in China's Rural Administration, 1969–1976." PhD diss., Columbia University, 1980.

Cai, Yong, and William Lavely. "China's Missing Girls: Numerical Estimates and Effects on Population Growth." *China Quarterly* 3, no. 2 (Fall 2003): 13–29.

Cell, Charles P. *Revolution at Work: Mobilization Campaigns in China.* New York: Academic Press, 1977.

Chan, Anita, Richard Madsen, and Jonathan Unger. *Chen Village: The Recent History of a Peasant Community in Mao's China.* Berkeley: University of California Press, 1984.

Chen, Pi-Chau. *Population and Health Policy in the People's Republic of China.* Washington, D.C.: Smithsonian Institution, 1976.

China AIDS Survey. "China HIV/AIDS Blood Supply Chronology." China AIDS Survey website, http://www.casey.org/chron/BloodSupply.htm.

"China and SARS: The Crisis and Its Effects on Politics and the Economy." Brookings Institution panel, moderated by Richard Brooks, with participants Laurie Garrett, Robert A. Kapp, Michael Swaine, and Minxin Pei. July 2, 2003. Transcript at http://www.brookings.org.

China Population Information and Research Centre, UNFPA China, and Division of Social Statistics, University of Southampton. *CHINA/UNFPA Reproductive Health/Family Planning End of Project—Women Survey Report: Key Findings.* 2004. China Population Information Research Centre website, http://www.cpirc.org.cn.

Chirot, Daniel. *Modern Tyrants: The Power and Prevalence of Evil in Our Age.* New York: Free Press, 1994.

Chu Junhong. "Prenatal Sex Determination and Sex-Selective Abortion in Rural Central China." *Population and Development Review* 27, no. 2 (2001): 259–81.

Clarke, Christopher M. "Changing the Context for Policy Implementation: Organizational and Personnel Reform in Post-Mao China." *Policy Implementation in Post-Mao*

China, edited by David M. Lampton, 25–47. Berkeley: University of California Press, 1987.

Cohen, Susan A. "The Road from Rio to Cairo: Toward a Common Agenda." *International Family Planning Perspectives* 19, no. 2 (June 1993): 61–71.

Croll, Elisabeth. *Chinese Women since Mao.* London: Zed Books, 1983.

———. *Endangered Daughters: Discrimination and Development in Asia.* London: Routledge, 2000.

———. "The Single-Child Family in Beijing: A First-hand Report." In *China's One-Child Family Policy,* edited by Elisabeth Croll, Delia Davin, and Penny Kane, 190–232. New York: St. Martin's, 1985.

Crook, Frederick, "Sources of Rural Instability." *China Business Review* (July–August 1990): 12–15.

———. "The Reform of the Commune System and the Rise of the Township-Collective-Household System." In *China's Economy Looks toward the Year 2000,* vol. 1, *The Four Modernizations,* edited by U.S. Congress, Joint Economic Committee, 354–75. Washington, D.C.: Government Printing Office, 1986.

Dali Yang, *Calamity and Reform in China: State, Rural Society, and Institutional Change Since the Great Leap Famine.* Stanford: Stanford University Press, 1996.

Das Gupta, Monica. "Explaining Asia's 'Missing Women': A New Look at the Data." *Population and Development Review* 31, no. 3 (September 2005): 529–35.

Das Gupta, Monica, and P. N. Mari Bhat. "Fertility Decline and Increased Manifestation of Sex Bias in India." *Population Studies* 51 (1997): 307–15.

Dikotter, Frank. *Imperfect Conceptions: Medical Knowledge, Birth Defects, and Eugenics in China.* New York: Columbia University Press, 1998.

Dittmer, Lowell. *China's Continuous Revolution: The Post-Liberation Epoch, 1949–1981.* Berkeley: University of California Press, 1987.

Donnithorne, Audrey. *China's Economic System.* London: C. Hurst, 1981.

Duara, Prasenjit. *Culture, Power, and the State: Rural North China, 1900–1942.* Stanford: Stanford University Press, 1988.

———. "State Involution: A Study of Local Finances in North China, 1911–1935." *Comparative Studies in Society and History* 29, no. 1 (January 1987): 132–61.

Eberstadt, Nicholas. "Asia Tomorrow, Gray and Male." *National Interest* 53 (Fall 1998): 56–65.

———. "Mis-Planned Parenthood: The Unintended Consequences of China's One-Child Policy." *AEI Articles* (1999). Online at American Enterprise Institute website, http://www.aei.org.

———. "The Premises of Population Policy: A Reexamination." In *The Nine Lives of Population Control,* edited by Michael Cromartie, 17–51. Washington, D.C.: Ethics and Public Policy Center; Grand Rapids, Mich.: William B. Eerdmans, 1995.

Ehrlich, Paul. *The Population Bomb.* New York: Ballantine, 1968.

Engels, Friedrich. *The Origin of the Family, Private Property, and the State* (1884), 1972.

Feeney, Griffith, and Wang Feng. "Parity Progression and Birth Intervals in China: The Influence of Policy in Hastening Fertility Decline." *Population and Development Review* 19, no. 1 (March 1993): 61–101.

Fewsmith, Joseph. *China since Tiananmen.* Cambridge: Cambridge University Press, 2001.

———. "Historical Echoes and Chinese Politics: Can China Leave the Twentieth Century Behind?" In *China Briefing 2000,* edited by Tyrene White, 11–48. Armonk, N.Y.: M. E. Sharpe, 2000.

——. "Rethinking the Role of the CCP: Explicating Jiang Zemin's Party Anniversary Speech." *China Leadership Monitor* 1, pt. 2 (Winter 2002). Online at http://www.chinaleadershipmonitor.org.

——. "Studying the Three Represents." *China Leadership Monitor* 8 (Fall 2003). Online at http://www.chinaleadershipmonitor.org.

Freedman, Ronald, Xiao Zhenyu, Li Bohua, and William Lavely. "Local Area Variatins in Reproductive Behavior in the People's Republic of China, 1973–1982." *Population Studies* 42, no. 1 (1988): 39–57.

Friedman, Edward, Paul G. Pickowicz, and Mark Selden, with Kay Johnson. *Chinese Village, Socialist State*. New Haven: Yale University Press, 1991.

Fu Zude, and Chen Jiayuan. *Zhongguo renkou—Fujian fence* [China's population—Fujian]. Beijing: Zhongguo caijing jingji chubanshe, 1990.

Gill, Bates. "China and SARS: Lessons, Implications, and Future Steps." Paper presented at roundtable of the Congressional-Executive Commission on China, May 12, 2003, http://www.cecc.gov/pages/roundtables/051203/gill.php.

Gilmartin, Christina Kelley. *Engendering the Chinese Revolution: Radical Women, Communist Politics, and Mass Movements in the 1920s*. Berkeley: University of California Press, 1995.

Greenhalgh, Susan. "Controlling Births and Bodies in Village China." *American Ethnologist* 21 (1994): 3–30.

——. "The Evolution of the One-Child Policy in Shaanxi." *China Quarterly* 122 (June 1990): 191–229.

——. "Fresh Winds in Beijing: Chinese Feminists Speak Out on the One-Child Policy." *Signs: Journal of Women in Culture and Society* 26, no. 3 (Spring 2001): 847–86.

——. "Population Studies in China: Privileged Past, Anxious Future." *Australian Journal of Chinese Affairs* 24 (July 1990): 357–84.

——. "Science, Modernity, and the Making of China's One-Child Policy." *Population and Development Review* 29 (June 2003): 163–96.

Greenhalgh, Susan, and Edwin Winckler, *Governing China's Population: From Leninist to Neoliberal Biopolitics*. Stanford: Stanford University Press, 2005.

Greenhalgh, Susan, and Jiali Li. "Engendering Reproductive Policy and Practice in Peasant China: For a Feminist Demography of Reproduction." *Signs: Journal of Women in Culture and Society* 20 (Spring 1995): 601–41.

Greenhalgh, Susan, Zhu Chuzhu, and Li Nan. "Restraining Population Growth in Three Chinese Villages." *Population and Development Review* 20 (June 1994): 365–93.

Gu Baochang and Krishna Roy. "Sex Ratio at Birth in China, with Reference to Other Areas of East Asia: What We Know." *Asia-Pacific Population Journal* 10, no. 3 (1995): 17–42.

Gu Baochang, Zhenming Xie, Zhenzhen Zheng, and Kaining Zhang, eds. *ICPD+10: In China* Beijing: Prepared for the International Forum on Population and Development, Wuhan, China, September 2004.

Hardee, Karen, Zhenming Xie, and Baochang Gu. "Family Planning and Women's Lives in Rural China." *International Family Planning Perspectives* 30, no. 2 (June 2004): 68–76.

Hardin, Garrett. "The Tragedy of the Commons." *Science* 162 (1968): 1243–48.

Harding, Harry. *Organizing China: The Problem of Bureaucracy, 1949–1976*. Stanford: Stanford University Press, 1981.

Hartford, Kathleen. "Socialist Agriculture Is Dead; Long Live Socialist Agriculture! Organizational Transformations in Rural China." In *The Political Economy of Reform in*

Post-Mao China, edited by Elizabeth J. Perry and Christine Wong, 31–62. Cambridge: Harvard University, Council on East Asian Studies, 1985.

Hartmann, Betsy. *Reproductive Rights and Wrongs: The Global Politics of Population Control and Contraceptive Choice.* New York: Harper and Row, 1987.

Hilts, Philip J. "Chinese Statistics Indicate Killing of Baby Girls Persists." *New York Times,* July 11, 1984, A14.

Hirschman, Albert O. *Exit, Voice, and Loyalty: Responses to the Decline in Firms, Organizations, and States.* Cambridge: Harvard University Press, 1970.

Hodgson, Dennis. "Orthodoxy and Revisionism in American Demography." *Population and Development Review* 14, no. 4 (December 1988): 541–70.

Hodgson, Dennis, and Susan Cott Watkins. "Feminists and Neo-Malthusians: Past and Present Alliances." *Population and Development Review* 27, no. 3 (September 1997): 469–523.

Hom, Sharon K. "Female Infanticide in China: The Human Rights Specter and Thoughts toward (An)Other View." *Columbia Human Rights Law Review* 23, no. 2 (Summer 1992): 249–314.

Hong Guodong. "Aging of Population: Trends and Countermeasures." *Beijing Review* (February 12–18, 1996): 12–14.

Hong Ying. "Women in China Making Headway to Full Equality." *China Daily* (March 6, 1982), 5.

Hu Angang. "Why China Lost Control of Its Population Growth in Recent Years." *Liaowang* (March 6, 1989): 22–23.

Hu Yaobang. "Create a New Situation in All Fields of Socialist Modernization." *Beijing Review* 37 (September 13, 1982): 11–40.

Huang Shu-min. *The Spiral Road: Change in a Chinese Communist Village through the Eyes of a Communist Party Leader.* (Boulder, Colo.: Westview, 1989).

Information Office of the State Council. "White Paper: Family Planning in China." August 1995. Online at http://www.china.org.cn/e-white/.

International Women's Health Coalition. "Women's Voices, '94: Women's Declaration on Population Policies." New York: International Women's Health Coalition, 1993.

Jacobs, J. Bruce. "Political and Economic Organizational Changes and Continuities in Six Rural Chinese Localities." *Australian Journal of Chinese Affairs* 14 (1986): 105–30.

Johnson, Kay. "The Politics of the Revival of Infant Abandonment in China, with Special Reference to Hunan." *Population and Development Review* 22 (March 1996): 77–98.

Johnson, Kay Ann. *Wanting a Daughter, Needing a Son: Abandonment, Adoption, and Orphanage Care in China.* St. Paul, Minn.: Yeung and Yeung, 2004.

Johnson, Kay Ann. *Women, the Family, and Peasant Revolution in China.* Chicago: University of Chicago Press, 1983.

Johnson, Kay, Huang Banghan, and Wang Liyao. "Infant Abandonment and Adoption in China." *Population and Development Review* 24 (September 1998): 469–510.

Joseph, William A., Christine P. W. Wong, and David Zweig, eds. *New Perspectives on the Cultural Revolution.* Cambridge: Harvard University, Council on East Asian Studies, 1991.

Judd, Ellen R. *The Chinese Women's Movement between State and Market.* Stanford: Stanford University Press, 2002.

Kane, Penny. *Famine in China, 1959–61: Demographic and Social Implications.* Basingstoke, Eng.: Macmillan, 1988.

——. "The Single-Child Family Policy in the Cities." In *China's One-Child Family Policy,* edited by Elisabeth Croll, Delia Davin, and Penny Kane, 83–113.

Kelliher, Daniel. *Peasant Power in China: The Era of Rural Reform, 1979–1989.* New Haven: Yale University Press, 1992.

Kohut, Kohn. "Henan Tightens Family Planning Laws." *South China Morning Post* (December 11, 1990), 11.

Kornai, Janos. *Contradictions and Dilemmas: Studies on the Socialist Economy and Society.* Cambridge: MIT Press, 1986.

Kristof, Nicholas D. "Peasants of China Discover New Way to Weed Out Girls." *New York Times,* July 21, 1993, A1, 6.

Kwan, Daniel. "Dozen Held over One-Child Policy Protest." *South China Morning Post* (September 9, 1997), 9.

——. "Guangdong Promotes 'Flexible' One-Child Policy, Sparking Protests." *South China Morning Post* (September 8, 1997), 8.

——. "Riot Erupts over One-Child Rule." *South China Morning Post* (September 8, 1997), 1.

Lampton, David M. *The Politics of Medicine in China: The Policy Process, 1949–1977.* Boulder, Colo.: Westview, 1977.

Lardy, Nicholas R. *Agriculture in China's Economic Development.* Cambridge: Cambridge University Press, 1983.

Lee, James Z., and Wang Feng. *One Quarter of Humanity: Malthusian Mythology and Chinese Realities, 1700–2000.* Cambridge: Harvard University Press, 1999.

Li Jianguo, and Zhang Xiaoying. "Infanticide in China." *New York Times,* April 11, 1983, A25.

Li Lianjiang. "Political Trust in Rural China." *Modern China* 30, no. 2 (April 2004): 228–58.

Li Lianjiang, and Kevin J. O'Brien. "The Struggle over Village Elections." In *The Paradox of China's Post-Mao Reforms,* edited by Merle Goldman and Roderick MacFarquhar, 129–44. Cambridge: Harvard University Press, 1999.

——. "Villagers and Popular Resistance in Contemporary China." *Modern China* 22, no. 1 (January 1996): 28–61.

Li, Lillian. "Life and Death in a Chinese Famine: Infanticide as a Demographic Consequence of the 1935 Yellow River Flood." *Comparative Studies in Society and History* 33, no. 3 (July 1991): 466–510.

Lieberthal, Kenneth G. *Governing China: From Revolution to Reform.* New York: W. W. Norton, 1995.

Lieberthal, Kenneth G., and David M. Lampton, eds. *Bureaucracy, Politics, and Decision-Making in Post-Mao China.* Berkeley: University of California Press, 1992.

Liu Suinian and Wu Qungan, eds. *China's Socialist Economy: An Outline History, 1949–1984.* Beijing: Beijing Review, 1986.

Liu Zheng, Song Jian, et al. *China's Population: Problems and Prospects.* Beijing: New World Press, 1981.

Lu Xiaobo. "The Politics of the Peasant Burden in Reform China." *Journal of Peasant Studies* 24, no. 4 (October 1997): 113–18.

MacFarquhar, Roderick. *The Coming of the Cataclysm, 1961–1966.* New York: Columbia University Press, 1997.

MacFarquhar, Roderick, Timothy Cheek, and Eugene Wu, eds. *The Secret Speeches of Chairman Mao: From the Hundred Flowers to the Great Leap Forward.* Cambridge: Harvard University, Council on East Asian Studies, 1989.

Mao Tse-tung. "The Bankruptcy of the Idealist Conception of History." In *Selected Works of Mao Tse-tung,* vol. 4, 451–59. Beijing: Foreign Languages Press, 1961.

McCormick, Barrett. *Political Reform in Post-Mao China: Democracy and Bureaucracy in a Leninist State.* Berkeley: University of California Press, 1990.

McIntosh, C. Alison, and Jason L. Finkle. "The Cairo Conference on Population and Development: A New Paradigm?" *Population and Development Review* 21, no. 2 (June 1995): 223–60.

Medeiros, Evan S., and M. Taylor Fravel. "China's New Diplomacy." *Foreign Affairs* 82, no. 6 (November–December 2003), 22–35.

Menken, Jane Ann K, Blanc, and Cynthia Lloyd, eds. *Training and Support of Developing-Country Population Scientists: A Panel Report.* New York: The Population Council, 2002.

Migdal, Joel S. "The State in Society: An Approach to Struggles for Domination." In *State Power and Social Forces: Domination and Transformation in the Third World,* edited by Joel S. Migdal, Atul Kohli, and Vivienne Shue, 7–34. Cambridge: Cambridge University Press, 1994.

——. *State in Society: Studying How States and Societies Transform and Constitute One Another.* Cambridge: Cambridge University Press, 2001.

Milwertz, Cecilia. *Accepting Population Control: Urban Chinese Women and the One-Child Policy.* Richmond: Surrey, 1997.

——. *Beijing Women Organizing for Change: A New Wave of the Chinese Women's Movement.* Copenhagen: Nordic Institute of Asian Studies, 2003.

Minxin, Pei. "Citizens and Mandarins: Administrative Litigation in China." *China Quarterly* 152 (December 1997): 832–62.

Monitoring of the AIDS Pandemic (MAP) Network. *AIDS in Asia: Face the Facts.* Washington, D.C: MAP, 2004.

Mosher, Steven W. *Broken Earth: The Rural Chinese.* New York: Free Press, 1983.

Mueggler, Eric. *The Age of Wild Ghosts.* Berkeley: University of California Press, 2001.

Muramatsu, Minoru. "Japan." In *Family Planning and Population Programs: A Review of World Developments,* edited by Bernard Berelson, Richmond K. Anderson, Oscar Harkavy, John Maier, W. Parker Mauldin, and Sheldon J. Segal, 7–20. Chicago: University of Chicago Press, 1967.

Murphy, Rachel. "Fertility and Distorted Sex Ratios in a Rural Chinese County: Culture, State, Policy." *Population and Development Review* 29, no. 4 (December 2003): 595–626.

Naughton, Barry. "Industrial Policy during the Cultural Revolution: Military Preparation, Decentralization, and Leaps Forward." In *New Perspectives on the Cultural Revolution,* edited by Joseph, Wong, and Zweig, 153–82. Cambridge: Harvard University, Council on East Asian Studies, 1991.

Nee, Victor. "Peasant Entrepreneurship and the Politics of Regulation in China." In *Remaking the Economic Institutions of Socialism: China and Eastern Europe,* edited by Victor Nee and David Stark. Stanford: Stanford University Press, 1989.

Nie, Yilin, and Robert J. Wyman. "The One-Child Policy in Shanghai: Acceptance and Internalization." *Population and Development Review* 31 (June 2005): 313–36.

Nordlinger, Eric. "Taking the State Seriously." In *Understanding Political Development,* edited by Myron Weiner and Samuel P. Huntington, 353–90. Boston: Little, Brown, 1987.

Norgren, Tiana. *Abortion before Birth Control.* Princeton: Princeton University Press, 2001.

O'Brien, Kevin J. "Implementing Political Reform in China's Villages." *Australian Journal of Chinese Affairs* 32 (July 1994): 33–59.

——. "Rightful Resistance." *World Politics* 49 (October 1996): 31–55.

O'Brien, Kevin J., and Lianjiang Li. "Accommodating Democracy in a One-Party State: Introducing Village Elections in China." *China Quarterly* 162 (June 2000): 490–512.

——. "The Politics of Lodging Complaints in Rural China." *China Quarterly* 143 (September 1995): 756–83.

——. "Popular Contention and its Impact in Rural China." *Comparative Political Studies* 38, no. 3 (April 2005): 235–59.

——. "Suing the Local State: Administrative Litigation in Rural China." *China Journal* 51 (January 2004): 76–96.

Oi, Jean C. "Commercializing China's Rural Cadres." *Problems of Communism* (September–October 1986): 1–15.

——. *Rural China Takes Off: Institutional Foundations of Economic Reform.* Berkeley: University of California Press, 1999.

——. *State and Peasant in Contemporary China: The Political Economy of Village Government.* Berkeley: University of California Press, 1989.

Orleans, Leo A. *Every Fifth Child: The Population of China.* London: Eyre Methuen, 1972.

Oster, Emily. "Hepatitis B and the Case of the Missing Women." Harvard University Center for International Development, Working Paper 7, 2005.

Pan, Philip P. "Who Controls the Family? Blind Activist Leads Peasants in Legal Challenge to Abuses of China's Population-Growth Policy." *Washington Post,* August 27, 2005, A1.

——. "Rural Activist Seized in Beijing: Legal Campaign Has Targeted Forced Sterilization, Abortion." *Washington Post,* September 7, 2005, A22.

——. "Detained Chinese Activist Put Under House Arrest." *Washington Post,* September 10, 2005, A20.

Parish, William L., and Martin King Whyte. *Village and Family in Contemporary China.* Chicago: University of Chicago Press, 1978.

Park, Chai Bin, and Nam-Hoon Cho. "Consequences of Son Preference in a Low-Fertility Society: Imbalance of the Sex Ratio at Birth in Korea." *Population and Development Review* 21, no. 1 (March 1995): 59–84.

Peng, Xizhe. "Demographic Consequences of the Great Leap Forward in China's Provinces." *Population and Development Review* 13 (1987): 639–70.

Perry, Elizabeth J. "Rural Violence in Socialist China." *China Quarterly* 103 (September 1985): 414–40.

——. "Trends in the Study of Chinese Politics: State-Society Relations." *China Quarterly* 139 (September 1994): 704–13.

Perry, Elizabeth, and Mark Selden, eds. *Chinese Society: Change, Conflict and Resistance,* second edition. New York: Routledge, 2003.

"Population and Family Planning Law of the People's Republic of China." *Population and Development Review* 28, no. 3 (September 2002): 579–85.

Population Reference Bureau. *2000 World Population Data Sheet.* Washington, D.C.: Population Reference Bureau, 2000.

Prescott, Elizabeth M. "SARS: A Warning." *Survival* (Autumn 2003): 207–26.

"Program of Action of the 1994 International Conference on Population and Development." Chapters 1–8, *Population and Development Review* 21, no. 1 (March 1995): 187–213; chapters 9–26, *Population and Development Review* 21, no. 2 (June 1995): 437–61.

"Regulations on the Work in the Rural People's Communes (Revised Draft). *Issues and Studies* 15, no. 10 (October 1979): 93–111; 15, no. 12 (December 1979): 106–15.

Riskin, Carl. *China's Political Economy: The Quest for Development since 1949.* Oxford: Oxford University Press, 1987.

Schram, Stuart. "Economics in Command? Ideology and Policy since the Third Plenum, 1978–84," *China Quarterly* 99 (September 1984): 437–61.

Schram, Stuart. *Ideology and Policy in China since the Third Plenum, 1978–84,* Research Notes and Studies No. 6. London: University of London, School of Oriental and African Studies, Contemporary China Institute, 1984.

Scott, James C. *Domination and the Arts of Resistance: Hidden Transcripts.* New Haven: Yale University Press, 1990.

———. *Seeing Like a State: How Certain Schemes to Improve the Human Condition Have Failed.* New Haven: Yale University Press, 1998.

———. *Weapons of the Weak: Everyday Forms of Peasant Resistance.* New Haven: Yale University Press, 1985.

Sen, Gita, Adrienne Germain, and Lincoln C. Chen, eds., *Population Policies Reconsidered: Health, Empowerment, and Rights.* Cambridge: Harvard University Press, 1994.

Sharping, Thomas. *Birth Control in China, 1949–1999: Population Policy and Demographic Development.* Richmond: Curzon, 1999.

Shi, Tianjian. "Village Committee Elections in China: Institutionalist Tactics for Democracy." *World Politics* 51, no. 3 (1999): 385–412.

Short, Susan E., Ma Linmao, and Yu Wentao. "Birth Planning and Sterilization in China." *Population Studies* 54, no. 3 (November 2000): 279–91.

Shue, Vivienne. "The Fate of the Commune." *Modern China* 10, no. 3 (July 1984): 259–83.

———. *Peasant China in Transition: The Dynamics of Development toward Socialism, 1949–1956.* Berkeley: University of California Press, 1980.

———. *The Reach of the State: Sketches of the Chinese Body Politic.* Stanford: Stanford University Press, 1988.

Siu, Helen F. *Agents and Victims in South China: Accomplices in Rural Revolution.* New Haven: Yale University Press, 1989.

Smil, Vaclav. "China's Great Famine: Forty Years Later." *British Medical Journal* 319 (December 18, 1999): 1619–21.

Solinger, Dorothy. "China's Floating Population." In *Paradox of China's Post-Mao Reforms,* edited by Merle Goldman and Roderick MacFarquhar, 220–40. Cambridge: Harvard University Press, 1999.

———. *Contesting Citizenship in Urban China: Peasant Migrants, the State, and the Logic of the Market.* Berkeley: University of California Press, 1999.

Szreter, Simon. "The Idea of Demographic Transition and the Study of Fertility Change: A Critical Intellectual History." *Population and Development Review* 19, no. 4 (December 1993): 659–701.

Tang, Yuen Yuen. "When Peasants Sue *En Mass:* Large-Scale Collective ALL Suits in Rural China." *China: An International Journal* 3, no. 1 (2005): 24–49.

Tian, H. Yuan. *China's Population Struggle: Demographic Decisions of the People's Republic of China, 1949–1969*. Columbus: Ohio State University Press, 1973.

———. *China's Strategic Demographic Initiative*. New York: Praeger, 1991.

Tong, James. "Fiscal Reform, Elite Turnover and Central-Provincial Relations in Post-Mao China." *Australian Journal of Chinese Affairs* 22 (July 1989): 1–28.

Unger, Jonathan. "The Decollectivization of the Chinese Countryside: A Survey of Twenty-Eight Villages." *Pacific Affairs* 58 (Winter 1985–86): 585–606.

United States Department of State. *The China White Paper, August 1949*. Reissue. Stanford: Stanford University Press, 1967.

Vogel, Ezra F. *Canton under Communism: Programs and Politics in a Provincial Capital, 1949–1968*. Cambridge: Harvard University Press, 1969.

Walker, Kenneth R. *Agricultural Development in China, 1949–1989: The Collected Papers of Kenneth R. Walker, 1931–1989*. Collected and edited by Robert F. Ash. Oxford: Oxford University Press, 1998.

Wan Li. "Developing Rural Commodity Production." *Beijing Review* 27, no. 9 (February 27, 1984).

Wang Zhenyao. "Village Committees: The Basis for China's Democratization." In *Cooperative and Collective in China's Rural Development*, edited by Eduard B. Vermeer, Frank N. Pieke, and Woei Lien Chong, 239–55. Armonk, N.Y.: M. E. Sharpe, 1998.

Wasserstrom, Jeffrey. "Resistance to the One-Child Family." *Modern China* 10 (July 1984): 345–74.

Weisskopf, Michael. "China's Birth Control Policy Drives Some to Kill Baby Girls." *Washington Post* (January 8, 1985), A1.

White, Lynn T., III. *Policies of Chaos: The Organizational Causes of Violence in the Cultural Revolution*. Princeton: Princeton University Press, 1989.

White, Tyrene. "Below Bureaucracy: The Burden of Being a Village under the Local State." Paper presented at the annual meeting of the Association for Asian Studies, Chicago, April 5–8, 1990.

———. "Political Reform and Rural Government." In *China on the Eve of Tiananmen*, edited by Deborah Davis and Ezra Vogel, 38–60. Cambridge: Harvard University, Council on East Asian Studies, 1989.

———. "Reforming the Countryside: Rebuilding Grassroots Institutions." *Current History* 91, no. 566 (September 1992): 73–77.

———. "Village Elections: Democracy from the Bottom Up?" *Current History* 97, no. 620 (September 1998): 263–67.

———, ed. "Family Planning in China." Special Issue of *Chinese Sociology and Anthropology* 24, no. 3 (Spring 1992).

Winckler, Edwin A. "Chinese Reproductive Policy at the Turn of the Millennium: Dynamic Stability." *Population and Development Review* 28, no. 3 (September 2002): 379–418.

Wolf, Margery. *Revolution Postponed: Women in Contemporary China*. Stanford: Stanford University Press, 1985.

Wong, Christine, Christopher Heady, and Wing T. Woo. *Fiscal Management and Economic Reform in the People's Republic of China*. Hong Kong: Asian Development Bank; New York: Oxford University Press, 1995.

Working Group on Population Growth and Economic Development, National Research Council. *Population Growth and Economic Development: Policy Questions*. Washington, D.C.: National Research Council, 1986.

Wu Naitao. "Rural Women and the New Economic Policies." *Beijing Review* 10 (March 7, 1983): 19.

Yan, Yunxiang. *Private Life under Socialism: Love, Intimacy, and Family Change in a Chinese Village, 1949–1999*. Stanford: Stanford University Press, 2003.

Yep, Ray. "Can 'Tax-for-Fee' Reform Reduce Rural Tension in China? The Process, Progress and Limitations." *China Quarterly* 177 (March 2004): 42–70.

Yu Youhai. "U.S. $1,000 by the Year 2000." *Beijing Review* 43 (October 27, 1980): 16–18.

Zeng Yi. "Family Planning Program 'Tightening Up'?" *Population and Development Review* 2 (June 1989): 333–37.

Zeng Yi, Tu Ping, Gu Baochang, Xu Yi, Li Bohua, and Li Yongping. "Causes and Implications of the Recent Increase in the Reported Sex Ratio at Birth in China." *Population and Development Review* 19 (June 1993): 283–302.

Zhao Ziyang. "Advance along the Road of Socialism with Chinese Characteristics." *Beijing Review* (November 9–15, 1987).

———. "Report on the Sixth Five-Year Plan." *Beijing Review* 51 (December 20, 1982).

Zweig, David. *Agrarian Radicalism in China, 1968–1981*. Cambridge: Harvard University Press, 1989.

———. "Context and Content in Policy Implementation: Household Contracts and Decollectivization, 1977–1983." In *Policy Implementation in Post-Mao China*, edited by David M. Lampton. Berkeley: University of California Press, 1987.

Zweig, David, Kathy Hartford, James Feinerman, and Deng Jianxu. "Law, Contracts, and Economic Modernization: Lessons from the Recent Chinese Rural Reforms." *Stanford Journal of International Law* 23, no. 2 (1987): 319–64.

Index

Page numbers with a *t* indicate tables; those with an *n* indicate footnotes.